Medicare

A Wiley Brand

Medicare

5th Edition

by Patricia Barry
Medicare Expert

Medicare For Dummies®, 5th Edition

Published by: **John Wiley & Sons, Inc.**, 111 River Street, Hoboken, NJ 07030-5774, www.wiley.com

For general information on our other products and services, please contact our Customer Care Department within the U.S. at 877-762-2974, outside the U.S. at 317-572-3993, or fax 317-572-4002. For technical support, please visit https://hub.wiley.com/community/support/dummies.

Wiley publishes in a variety of print and electronic formats and by print-on-demand. Some material included with standard print versions of this book may not be included in e-books or in print-on-demand. If this book refers to media such as a CD or DVD that is not included in the version you purchased, you may download this material at http://booksupport.wiley.com. For more information about Wiley products, visit www.wiley.com.

Library of Congress Control Number: 2024942275

ISBN 978-1-394-26796-5 (pbk); ISBN 978-1-394-26798-9 (ebk); ISBN 978-1-394-26797-2 (ebk)

Contents at a Glance

Table of Contents

Introduction

For most people, turning 65 or otherwise becoming eligible for Medicare feels like stepping into alien territory without a map. The signposts you think should be there often aren't immediately visible. When you ask for directions, you can't always be sure you're being pointed down the right path.

Medicare For Dummies, 5th Edition, is the map you need. It gives accurate, practical information about Medicare in plain language. It shows you how to skirt pitfalls and avoid wrong turns that can cost you dearly. The goal of this book is to help you make informed, confident decisions that take you where you want to be. How can I promise that? Because this book is, in essence, the result of thousands of questions I've received over the years from people just like you.

I know from many of those questions that people eligible for Medicare often receive incorrect information from sources — such as government officials — they should be able to trust. That's why these pages provide you with information that's firmly based in law but sometimes also identify certain specific regulations (by name, number, and website) that you can use if you need to prove to an official the legal authority for a particular point about eligibility, enrollment, late penalties, and so on.

Confusion about Medicare is almost inevitable for two main reasons. Medicare regulations apply to different people in different ways, according to their specific circumstances, so the decisions you need to make may be unlike the next person's. Also, the array of choices can be bewildering if you don't know how to sift through them to get to the one that's right for you.

So think of your Medicare card as your passport into the terrain of guaranteed healthcare, where you're welcome regardless of income or pre-existing medical conditions, but you still have to find your way around. And consider this book the road map that helps you navigate the highways and some of the more obscure byways of that system and keeps you on track.

About This Book

This fifth edition of *Medicare For Dummies* provides information that was accurate at press time. While federal policymakers often propose radical changes to the major programs described in this book — the Affordable Care Act (Obamacare), Medicaid, and Medicare itself — at the time of this writing, none of these proposals have passed into law. And in the case of Medicare, any major change to the program wouldn't take place for several years and wouldn't affect people older than 55 at the time it goes into effect.

Therefore, in the chapters that follow, you find out what you need to know to get through the Medicare maze right now and get the most out of your coverage. You find answers to some questions that are barely addressed — and sometimes not touched upon at all — in official consumer publications about the program. You discover where to turn for additional help, if you need it. And, as in any *For Dummies* book, you can easily locate and understand the specific information you're looking for because of the reader-friendly organization and straightforward language.

As you may expect from a program run partly by a federal bureaucracy and partly by private insurance plans, you're going to meet some unavoidable jargon in this book. These terms are worth getting to know because notices you get from the government or the plans — or any to-and-fros you have with either — will be easier to understand. So you'll see the following conventions:

- New terms in Medicare-speak are explained the first time they appear in the text. They're also defined in the glossary in Appendix B.

- When you see the word *Medicare* used on its own, it usually means the whole Medicare program (as in "When you join Medicare . . ."). Sometimes it means the federal agency that runs Medicare (as in "Medicare may send you a notice . . ."). The agency's official name, the Centers for Medicare & Medicaid Services (CMS), appears as the source of information in some tables.

- The basic Medicare program (Part A plus Part B) is referred to as "original Medicare." The private plans that comprise the alternative Part C program are called "Medicare Advantage plans" or "Medicare health plans."

- *Part D* and *Medicare drug coverage* are used interchangeably to discuss the Medicare prescription drug program. The plans that provide this coverage are referred to as "Part D plans" or "Medicare drug plans."

Feel free to skip anything marked with the Technical Stuff icon as well as the sidebars — those chunks of text that appear in shaded boxes. They're not necessary to understanding how to find your way through Medicare. Still, you may find them interesting. Ever wonder how on earth Congress dreamed up some of the more oddball bits of this program? You can find the answers in sidebars scattered throughout this book.

Within this book, you may note that some web addresses break across two lines of text. If you're reading this book in print and want to visit one of these web pages, simply key in the address exactly as it's noted in the text, as though the line break doesn't exist. If you're reading this text as an e-book, you've got it easy — just click the address to be taken directly to the page.

Foolish Assumptions

This book assumes that you don't have any working knowledge of Medicare — really, none at all! But even if you do, you can still find practical insights and useful tips to help you navigate the system more quickly, easily, and confidently. If you recognize yourself in any of the following scenarios, you can find help in these pages:

>> Your 65th birthday is on the horizon or coming up fast, and you realize you know nothing about Medicare or how to get it.

>> You're younger than 65 but will soon qualify for Medicare as a result of disability and need to know how it works for you.

>> You intend to continue working beyond 65 in a job that provides health insurance, and you aren't sure whether you should join Medicare.

>> You have good retiree health benefits from a former employer and wonder how they fit in with Medicare or whether you even need it.

>> You live outside the United States and want to know about Medicare enrollment and coverage rules — whether you're an American abroad or an immigrant.

>> You're already enrolled in Medicare but can use some help to troubleshoot problems, find a better deal, or reduce your expenses.

>> You need a crash course on Medicare issues because you're helping a parent, relative, or friend navigate the system.

>> In your job or volunteer time working with seniors or people with disabilities, you could use a plain-language reference to Medicare.

Another point: This book assumes no political standpoints. Medicare has always been a controversial hot potato, gingerly tossed between those who think of it as a social safety net that should be extended to everyone and those who see it as an expensive luxury that is a growing drain on the economy. If you hold strong opinions, fine; that's your privilege. But in these pages, the only "us versus them" undertone is a bias toward consumers (us) rather than politicians, government bureaucracies, and insurance companies (them). The aim of this book is to help you understand and deal with the system as it is now. If you want it changed — or don't want it changed — please tell your members of Congress!

Icons Used in This Book

Icons are those cute drawings you see in the page margins now and again. Here's what they mean.

REMEMBER

This icon signals important information. If you take anything away from this book, it should be information highlighted with this icon.

TIP

This icon draws your attention to on-target advice and practical insights that will save you time, effort, and maybe even money.

WARNING

This icon raises a red flag to alert you to a Medicare rule or potential pitfall that may trip you up if you remain blithely unaware of it.

TECHNICAL STUFF

This icon points out information that's interesting but not crucial to understanding the ins and outs of Medicare.

Beyond the Book

In addition to the material in the print or e-book you're reading right now, this product also comes with some access-anywhere goodies on the web. For important Medicare dos and don'ts, pointers on enrolling in Medicare at the right time, and key sources of Medicare help, go to www.dummies.com and type "Medicare For Dummies Cheat Sheet" in the Search box.

Where to Go from Here

Nobody expects you to read this book cover to cover. It's not a thriller or a bodice-ripper! But it does act as a plain-language reference to a program that millions of people use but few understand. So you can jump in anywhere to the bit you need, at whatever point you happen to be when grappling with Medicare. For example:

>> Want to know how Medicare works? Start with Part 1 to see what Medicare covers, how much it costs, and how you can lower expenses.

>> Don't know when you should sign up or how to go about it? Chapters 6 and 7 show you the way, according to your circumstances.

>> Need to make a choice among Medicare's many options and private plans? Find out how to do so in Chapters 9, 10, 11, and 12.

>> Want to get the best out of your Medicare coverage and avoid pitfalls? You'll find lots of pointers in Part 4.

1

Getting Started with Medicare

Discover the basics of Medicare with a quick primer on how it's divided into four separate programs: Part A (hospital stays), Part B (doctors' and outpatient services), Part C (Medicare's private health plans), and Part D (prescription drug coverage).

Find out which services Medicare helps pay for, which services it doesn't cover at all, and which ones come with certain coverage limits.

Recognize what you're likely to pay toward your costs in Medicare — the basic premiums, deductibles, and co-payments, plus the premium surcharges you may have to pay if your income is over a certain level.

Get the scoop on ways to reduce your out-of-pocket expenses in Medicare, including special help if your income is under a certain level.

Chapter **1**

The Nuts and Bolts of Medicare: What It Is and How It Works

edicare is a federal government insurance system that helps 66 million seniors and people with disabilities pay for their healthcare. It's the only truly national healthcare program in the United States — meaning that it's available regardless of your income, the state of your health, or where you live nationwide — and it has been enduringly popular since it began in 1966.

Yet Medicare works like no other insurance you may have known in the past. To avoid total confusion, you're wise to gain at least a broad understanding of how the program is put together and how its rules may affect you personally.

This chapter provides an overview of the program: addressing common concerns about how Medicare is different from other types of health insurance; describing the four parts of Medicare coverage (A, B, C, and D); and providing a checklist for the decisions that you have to make in choosing among the coverage options that Medicare offers.

This stuff is basic information aimed primarily at people who are new to the program. (You can find more details of benefits and costs in later chapters.) But if you're an old hand looking for specifics in navigating Medicare more easily, feel free to skip these pages and plunge into Part 3 or 4.

Addressing Some Upfront Questions

When the prospect of becoming a Medicare beneficiary looms on the horizon, you suddenly become aware — if you're like most people — of how little you know about the program. And even if you think you know, can you be sure that the information you have is accurate? Based on questions I've received, I can tell you that a lot of perceptions about Medicare are way off base; quite often, they're gleaned from the internet or even mass emails that are deliberately designed to spread misleading information and scare seniors.

If you've had health insurance in the past, especially from an employer, you may be nervous about how Medicare coverage compares with it. So before I examine how Medicare actually works later in this chapter, I want to tackle some of the concerns people frequently raise about the program:

>> **As a government-run system, will Medicare give me inferior care?** No (or at least, not inherently). The federal government runs and regulates Medicare and also largely pays for the medical services you use. Even so, those actual services are almost wholly private. The doctors you go to are *not* government employees; the hospitals and laboratories that provide services to you are *not* government-owned. Instead, they're free to enter or not enter into contracts with Medicare as they choose. Those who accept you as a Medicare patient are the same kind of independent, private practitioners that you would've seen for diagnosis and treatment before coming into Medicare.

>> **Will Medicare allow me fewer choices than I have now?** No. In fact, the reverse may be true. If you've had health insurance from a private employer, for example, you probably had only two or three plans to choose from each year. In contrast, Medicare offers a choice between the original program (in which you can go to any doctor or other provider in the United States that accepts Medicare patients) and a variety of private Medicare Advantage health plans, which are likely similar to health plans you may have known in the past. Depending on where you live, you may be overwhelmed by the number of options; in some areas, the average beneficiary may be able to choose from as many as 43 Medicare Advantage plans. Also, there are an average of 21 Part D plans available in each state that offer Medicare prescription drug coverage. (I explain Medicare Advantage and Part D plans, and how they differ from the original program, in the next section.)

>> **Will my health issues and pre-existing medical conditions work against me?**
Current and past health problems don't bar anybody from Medicare coverage
or cause anybody to pay higher premiums or co-pays than somebody who is in
perfect health. That kind of discrimination, which has been common in the past in
private health insurance, has never existed in Medicare. (For the record: A history
of smoking, alcohol use, or obesity doesn't increase rates either.)

>> **Will Medicare be less expensive than the insurance I have now?** Medicare
isn't free. Just like other insurance, it requires monthly premiums, deductibles,
and co-pays that you're responsible for paying unless you qualify for a
low-income program or have extra insurance that covers these costs (see
Chapter 4 for details). However, you need to consider the alternatives.
Without Medicare, most older and disabled people wouldn't be able to
find affordable insurance on the open market.

Compared to most employer insurance (which as a whole covers younger
and healthier people), Medicare is reasonably priced. In 2024, Medicare
Part B premiums cost $174.70 per month per person, whereas, according
to the Kaiser Family Foundation's 2023 survey of employer health benefits,
workers' monthly contributions to employer insurance averaged $117 for a
single person and $548 for a family of two or more. Still, this isn't an apples-
to-apples comparison; many employees pay more than these averages
for health benefits, and Medicare beneficiaries usually pay extra for drug
coverage, while those with higher incomes pay higher Part B premiums than
the standard premiums. Medicare Part A, which covers hospital and nursing
care, is free for most people who paid (or have spouses who paid) Medicare
taxes long enough while they were working — generally at least 10 years. If
you don't qualify for premium-free Part A, you might be able to purchase it.

>> **Will I pay a large deductible before getting Medicare coverage?** Medicare
does have some deductibles, but they're relatively small compared with the
ones many people pay in high-deductible health plans that are sponsored
by employers or bought through the 2010 Patient Protection and Affordable
Care Act (commonly known as the Affordable Care Act or Obamacare) or on
the open insurance market. (I examine deductibles, along with co-pays and
other Medicare costs, in detail in Chapter 3.)

>> **Will my out-of-pocket expenses be capped in Medicare?** Not necessarily.
Original Medicare sets no limit on the costs you pay out-of-pocket during a
year, although you may buy Medigap insurance to cover those costs (see
Chapter 4). But all Medicare Advantage plans are required by law to set caps
on these expenses (up to $8,850 per year in 2024). In the Part D program,
after you've spent a certain amount out-of-pocket on your prescription drugs
in a year, you qualify for catastrophic coverage that greatly lowers your costs
for the remainder of the calendar year. Beginning in 2025, people with Part D
will have annual out-of-pocket drug costs capped at $2,000.

>> **Do I have to sign up for Medicare again every year?** No; your coverage just rolls over from year to year unless you decide to change it. But you do have the opportunity to change your coverage if you want to during the open enrollment period that runs from October 15 to December 7 each year. During this time, you can switch from original Medicare to a Medicare Advantage plan (or vice versa), from one Medicare Advantage plan to another, or from one Part D prescription drug plan to another, as explained in Chapter 15.

>> **Will Medicare cover my younger spouse or other dependents?** No. Family coverage doesn't exist in Medicare — not for spouses, dependent children, or other family members. Each person must wait until age 65 to join the program unless they qualify through disability at a younger age, as explained in Chapter 5. Also, if you and your spouse are both in Medicare, each of you must pay premiums separately and in full unless you receive government assistance to help pay for them. Medicare doesn't give price breaks for married couples, even in its private Medicare Advantage health plans and Part D drug plans.

>> **Will Medicare coverage be cut off when I grow old?** No! Medicare coverage is based on medical necessity, not age. So if you need a hip replacement when you're in your 90s or even over 100, Medicare picks up most of the cost in the usual way.

REMEMBER

The idea of Medicare rationing care and denying coverage for people over a certain age has been spread through mass emails designed to discredit the Affordable Care Act. In fact, the act doesn't cut Medicare benefits or allow rationing, and no Medicare regulation limits care for people based on their age.

Coming to Terms with the ABCs (and D) of Medicare

Do you really need to know the details of what Parts A, B, C, and D stand for? Doesn't Medicare just pay its share of your bills and that's it? Well, not entirely. Medicare's architecture is more than a tad weird, but each of its building blocks determines the coverage you get and what you pay.

Besides that, however, is the simple fact that making sense of the information in the rest of this book is difficult unless you understand what Parts A, B, C, and D actually mean. The following sections break down the basics.

Part A

Medicare Part A is usually described as *hospital insurance* — a term originally coined to distinguish it from medical insurance (Part B). But the phrase is misleading. "Hospital insurance" sounds as though Part A covers your entire bill if you're admitted to a hospital, but it doesn't work that way. The services you receive from doctors, surgeons, or anesthetists while you're in the hospital are billed separately and are covered under Part B. And you don't even have to be hospitalized to get services under Part A, because some are provided in settings outside the hospital or even in your own home.

REMEMBER

A more accurate way to think of Part A is as coverage primarily for *nursing care.* It helps pay for the following:

>> The services of professional nurses when you're admitted to a hospital or a skilled nursing facility (such as a nursing home or rehab center) for short-term stays or when you qualify for home health services or hospice care in your own home

>> A semiprivate room in the hospital or nursing facility

>> All meals provided directly by the hospital or nursing facility

>> Other services provided directly by the hospital or nursing facility, including lab tests, prescription drugs, medical appliances and supplies, and rehabilitation therapy

>> All services provided by a home health agency if you qualify for continuing care at home, as explained in Chapter 2

>> All services provided by a hospice program if you choose to stop treatment for a terminal illness, as explained in Chapter 2

The vast majority of people in Medicare are eligible for Part A services without paying any premiums for it. That's because Part A is essentially paid for in advance by the Medicare payroll taxes that you or your spouse contributed from every paycheck while working. I explain the details of how that setup works — and your options if you don't qualify for premium-free Part A — in Chapter 5.

But of course Part A services themselves aren't free. You still pay deductibles and co-payments for specific services. I itemize these costs in Chapter 3 and explain how you may be able to lower them in Chapter 4. I also provide more detailed information on certain Part A coverage issues in Chapters 2 and 14.

Part B

Many people in Medicare never need to go into the hospital, but almost everybody sees a doctor or needs diagnostic screenings and lab tests sooner or later. That's where Part B — known as *medical insurance* — comes in. The wide range of services it covers includes the following:

>> Approved medical and surgical services from any doctor who accepts Medicare patients, whether those services are provided in a doctor's office, in a hospital, in a long-term-care facility, or at home

>> Diagnostic and lab tests done outside hospitals and nursing facilities

>> Preventive services such as flu shots, mammograms, screenings for depression and diabetes, and so on, many of which are free

>> Some medical equipment and supplies (for example, wheelchairs, walkers, oxygen, diabetic supplies, and units of blood)

>> Some outpatient hospital treatment received in an emergency room, clinic, or ambulatory surgical unit

>> Some inpatient care in cases where patients are placed under observation in the hospital instead of being formally admitted

>> Inpatient prescription drugs given in a hospital or doctor's office, usually by injection (such as chemotherapy drugs for cancer)

>> Some coverage for physical, occupational, and speech therapies

>> Outpatient mental health care

>> Second opinions for non-emergency surgery in some circumstances

>> Approved home health services not covered by Part A

>> Ambulance or air rescue service in circumstances where any other kind of transportation would endanger the patient's health

>> Free counseling to help curb obesity, smoking, or alcohol abuse

You must pay a monthly premium to receive Part B services unless your income is low enough to qualify you for assistance from your state. Most people pay the standard Part B premium, which is determined each year by a formula set by law ($174.70 in 2024). If your income is over a certain level, however, you're required to pay more.

You also pay a share of the cost of most Part B services. In original Medicare, this amount is almost always 20 percent of the Medicare-approved cost. Medicare Advantage health plans charge different amounts — usually flat dollar co-pays for each service. I go into detail about the out-of-pocket costs for Part B in Chapter 3, and I explain ways to lower them in Chapter 4.

Part C

In the previous two sections, I describe coverage provided by Part A and Part B, which together form what is known as *traditional* or *original Medicare* — so named because that was the extent of the program's coverage when it began back in 1966. It's also called *fee-for-service Medicare* because each provider — whether it's a doctor, hospital, laboratory, medical equipment supplier, or whatever — is paid a fee for each service.

But these days Medicare also offers an alternative to the original program: a range of health plans that mainly provide managed care through health maintenance organizations (HMOs) or preferred provider organizations (PPOs). These plans are run by private insurance companies, which decide each year whether to stay in the program. Medicare pays each plan a fixed fee for everyone who joins that plan, regardless of how much or little healthcare a person actually uses. This health plan program is called *Medicare Advantage* or Medicare Part C.

REMEMBER

Medicare Advantage plans must, by law, cover exactly the same services under Part A and Part B as original Medicare does. (So if you need a knee replacement, for example, the procedure is covered — regardless of whether you're enrolled in a Medicare Advantage plan or in the original program.) But the plans may also offer extra benefits that original Medicare doesn't cover — such as routine vision, hearing, and dental care. Most plans include Part D prescription drug coverage as part of their benefits package.

Still, being enrolled in one of these plans is a very different experience from using the original Medicare program. Your out-of-pocket costs are different, and so are your choices of doctors and other providers. I discuss the differences between original Medicare and Medicare Advantage plans in Chapter 9. I describe the different types of plans, and how to compare them properly to find the one that best meets your needs, in Chapter 11.

Part D

Part D is insurance for outpatient prescription drugs — meaning medications you take yourself instead of having them administered in a hospital or doctor's office. Medicare's drug benefit was only added to the program in 2006, a full 40 years after Medicare began. Since then, it has saved huge amounts of money for millions of people and allowed many to get the meds they need for the first time.

Still, I can't gloss over the fact that Part D is a complicated benefit that takes a lot of getting used to. Here are just some of the peculiar ways it differs from other drug coverage you may have used in the past:

>> Coverage goes through four distinct phases during a calendar year, and in each phase the same drug can cost a different amount.

>> To get coverage, you must select just one private plan that provides Part D drugs out of many plans that are available to you.

>> Different plans cover different sets of drugs, and no plan covers all drugs.

>> Plans set their own co-pays for each drug, and these amounts can vary enormously, even for the same drug.

>> Plans may require you or your doctor to ask permission before they cover certain drugs or to try a less-expensive version before they cover the one you were prescribed.

>> Plans are allowed to change their costs and benefits or to withdraw from Medicare entirely each calendar year.

If this all sounds mystifying, you're probably wondering how on earth anyone can possibly navigate Part D to find good drug coverage. But yes, it's possible! In Chapter 10, I describe a strategy for effectively comparing plans and finding the one that best meets your needs, and Chapter 12 lets you know who can help you do it. I also discuss what Part D covers (Chapter 2), the costs you can expect (Chapters 3 and 4), and how to troubleshoot any problems that show up (Chapters 13 and 14).

Recognizing That You Have Choices and Must Make Timely Decisions

Despite assertions to the contrary, Medicare is *not* a one-size-fits-all system. It comes with many options, which require you to make decisions within certain time frames. Here's a quick checklist for getting it right:

>> **Enroll at the right time, according to your circumstances.** If you misunderstand or ignore the rules, you face permanent financial penalties and may go without coverage for several months. I explain those potential traps and how to avoid them in Chapter 6.

>> **Research your options.** You need to understand the differences between being in the original Medicare program and enrolling in a private Medicare Advantage health plan. See Chapter 9 for details.

>> **Determine how to make smart choices if you opt for original Medicare.** That means deciding whether you need to add Part D prescription drug coverage and, if so, how to choose the drug plan that works best for you. It also means deciding whether you want to purchase Medigap supplemental insurance and, if so, understanding when you should buy it to ensure you receive all-important federal guarantees and protections. I discuss these choices in Chapter 10.

>> **Figure out how to make smart choices if you opt for a Medicare Advantage plan.** That means comparing plans according to your needs and preferences and understanding your options if you change your mind and want to return to original Medicare. See Chapter 11 for more info.

>> **Get help making your choices if you need to.** I explain how to get personal help from legitimate, informed sources (and avoid scamsters and frauds) in Chapter 12.

>> **Understand your right to change your coverage every year and at other times in certain circumstances.** I describe the purpose of various enrollment periods, their deadlines, and the process of switching to another plan or type of coverage in Chapter 15.

Chapter **2**

Spelling Out What Medicare Covers (A Lot, but Not Everything)

M edicare is huge — a program of Titanic proportions. It covers so many medical services that just to list them all would fill this entire book. And describing each service or item in detail — in terms of the coverage requirements or limitations that apply in different circumstances — would take several books. So I need to use a big brush here.

In this chapter, I broadly paint in the categories of care that Medicare pays for under Part A, Part B, and Part D so that you get a good idea of its scope. (The Medicare Advantage program, also known as Part C, gets its own explanation in Chapters 1, 9, and 11.) I also explain some types of care that you may expect to be covered by Medicare but that actually aren't. And finally, I show that a few services come with limitations on coverage, meaning that Medicare helps pay for them only up to a certain point in a particular period of time.

I'm not skimping on giving more-detailed information that you need to know in order to deal with certain aspects of Medicare. Some coverage issues are very straightforward — basically, you just show your Medicare card (or Medicare Advantage plan card or Part D drug plan card, as appropriate) to get a covered service for the required co-pay or, in some cases, for free. But other issues are more complex and may pose pitfalls that can trip you up if you're not expecting them. I zoom in on those issues in Chapter 14, where I share the inside scoop on some of the finer points of Medicare coverage that are good to know about in advance, so you don't have to find out the hard way.

Understanding What Part A and Part B Cover

Part A and Part B form the core of Medicare. They provide the coverage that you have if you enroll in the *traditional* or *original Medicare* program that has been around since 1966, although many more services have been added since then. Parts A and B are also the basis of your coverage if you're in a Medicare Advantage health plan, because all those plans must by law cover the same services as the traditional program, although the plans can provide extra benefits if they want to. (I go into detail about the differences between original Medicare and Medicare Advantage plans in Chapter 9.)

These two parts of Medicare cover entirely different services, as I explain in Chapter 1. But sometimes Parts A and B work in tandem. For example, if you need to go into the hospital, in most cases, Part A covers the cost of your room, meals, and nursing care after you've met the deductible. But Part B covers the cost of your medical treatment — services provided by surgeons, other doctors, and anesthetists. This division of coverage also applies to staying in a skilled nursing facility for continuing care after leaving the hospital, using home health services, and receiving hospice care.

In the following sections, I describe broad categories of services that Parts A and B pay for.

Necessary medical care

In essence, Medicare covers services that are reasonable or necessary to save life and maintain or improve health. That includes really big-ticket items — such as transplants of the heart and other organs, delicate surgery to repair severe injuries, cancer treatments, and many others — that cost Medicare tens of thousands, and in some cases hundreds of thousands, of dollars. The program also, of course, covers more-routine and less-expensive services, from allergy shots to X-rays.

No doubt about it: Medicare can split hairs. It may cover a service in some circumstances but not others. One glaring example of this discrepancy is that Medicare covers power-operated vehicles, such as scooters and manual wheelchairs (as opposed to the conventional type) only if you need one to get around inside your home but not if you need one just to be mobile outdoors. In 2018, Medicare began requiring prior authorization for the coverage of certain types of power wheelchairs (46 in all) before Medicare will cover the cost. Medicare may also cover a treatment in some parts of the country but not everywhere. (I go into the difference between *national coverage determinations,* which cover people in need of them throughout the country, and other coverage determinations that are made regionally, in Chapter 14.) But on the whole, Medicare pays for a vast range of medical services that people need.

REMEMBER

I've heard from people who've used a lot of services, or a few really expensive ones, and are scared to death that their Medicare coverage is going to "run out." This isn't something to worry about. In general, no limit caps the amount of coverage you can get from Medicare for necessary services — except for a few specific situations that I explore later in this chapter.

Preventive care

Being able to treat a medical problem is good, but dodging it altogether is better! These days, that seems an obvious truth. Yet Medicare has only fairly recently expanded coverage for services that help prevent or stave off some of the diseases that make people very ill and — not coincidentally — cost Medicare mountains of money. Even better: Many of these preventive tests, screenings, and counseling sessions now come free (no co-pays or deductibles) thanks to the 2010 Affordable Care Act.

REMEMBER

But to get these services for free, you need to see doctors who accept *assignment* — meaning that they have agreed to accept the Medicare-approved amount as full payment for any service provided to a Medicare patient. (I go into detail about what Medicare doctors can charge in Chapter 13.) Otherwise, you have to pony up a co-pay or, in some circumstances, even the full cost.

Now take a look at Table 2-1, which shows the range of preventive tests, screenings, and counseling sessions that Medicare covers under Part B and whether they cost you anything. It's a pretty impressive list!

TABLE 2-1   ## Preventive Care Services Medicare Covers

Service	Frequency Covered	Cost to You
"Welcome to Medicare" checkup	Once only, during first 12 months in Part B.	Free, but any other tests the doctor refers you for may require a co-pay.
Wellness checkup	Once every 12 months, after you've had Part B for one year.	Free as long as you ask for a wellness visit and not a "physical."
Abdominal aortic aneurysm screening	One-time ultrasound for people at risk.	Free.
Alcohol misuse screening and counseling	One screening and up to four counseling sessions a year.	Free.
Bone mass measurements	Once every 24 months if you're at risk for broken bones; more if medically necessary.	Free.
Breast cancer screening (mammograms)	Once a year for women age 40 or older.	Free.
Cardiovascular disease (behavioral therapy)	Once a year.	Free.
Cardiovascular disease screening	Once every five years.	Free for the tests, but a co-pay is usually required for the doctor visit.
Cervical/vaginal cancer screening	Once every 24 months, or every 12 months if you're at high risk.	Free.
Colorectal cancer screening — barium enema (when used instead of flexible sigmoidoscopy or colonoscopy)	Once every 48 months, or every 24 months if at high risk.	A co-pay is required.
Colorectal cancer screening — colonoscopy	Once every 120 months, or every 24 months if at high risk.	Free for the test, but a co-pay is required if a polyp is found and removed during the test.
Colorectal cancer screening — fecal occult blood test	Once every 12 months if you're 45 or older.	Free.
Colorectal cancer screening — flexible sigmoidoscopy	Once every 48 months if you're 45 or older.	Free.
Colorectal cancer screening — blood-based biomarker test and multi-target stool DNA test	Once every three years.	Free.
COVID-19 vaccines	As needed to complete vaccine series and any additional boosters.	Free.

Service	Frequency Covered	Cost to You
Depression screening	Once a year in a primary-care setting.	Free screening, but a co-pay is required for doctor visit and follow-up care.
Diabetes prevention	Once per lifetime for those with pre-diabetes; 6-month weekly core sessions with six monthly follow-ups.	Free.
Diabetes training	Training on how to self-manage diabetes — up to 12 hours in the first year and up to two hours every year after that.	A co-pay is required, and your Part B deductible applies.
Diabetes screening	Up to two screenings a year if you're at risk of developing diabetes.	Free.
Flu shots	Once a year in flu season.	Free.
Glaucoma (eye disease) tests	Once every 12 months if you're at high risk.	A co-pay is required, and your Part B deductible applies.
Hepatitis B shots	One series (2–4 doses) for those at medium or high risk.	
Hepatitis B virus (HPV) infection screening	Annually only for those considered at risk who don't get a Hepatitis B vaccination.	Free.
Hepatitis C screening test	One-time screening; yearly screening for people at high risk or those born between 1945 and 1965.	Free.
HIV screenings	Once every 12 months or up to three times during pregnancy.	Free.
Lung cancer screening	Once a year for people age 55–77, who are current or former smokers averaging one pack a day for 30 years, but without symptoms of lung disease.	Free.
Obesity screening and counseling	Behavioral counseling sessions if your body mass index (BMI) is 30 or higher.	Free.
Pneumococcal shot	After age 65, up to three doses.	Free.
Prostate cancer digital rectal exam	Once every 12 months for men over 50.	A co-pay is required, and the Part B deductible applies.
Prostate cancer PSA test	Once every 12 months for men over 50.	Free.

(continued)

TABLE 2-1 *(continued)*

Service	Frequency Covered	Cost to You
Sexually transmitted infections screenings and counseling	Tests once every 12 months or more often if pregnant. Up to two counseling sessions with a primary-care provider.	Free if tests are ordered by a doctor and performed in a Medicare-approved laboratory.
Smoking and tobacco use cessation counseling	Up to eight sessions in any 12-month period.	Free.
X-rays, MRIs, CT scans, EKGs, and so on	As ordered for diagnosis by a doctor.	A co-pay is required, and your Part B deductible applies.

Source: *Centers for Medicare & Medicaid Services(CMS)/Public Domain*

Note: *Services labeled "free" (meaning no co-pay or deductible required) assume that you go to a doctor who accepts Medicare's payment in full.*

Specialized care in certain circumstances

Medicare Part A is usually associated with care within the hospital, of course. But it also covers certain specialized services outside the hospital, most of which focus on nursing. Part B, too, covers some types of specialized care, such as physical therapy. The following sections provide a quick overview.

Care in a skilled nursing facility

Say you've been in the hospital and are being discharged but still need more-specialized nursing care than you can receive at home — physical therapy to help you walk again after a hip replacement, speech therapy after a stroke, a continuing need for intravenous fluids, or wound care. Medicare covers this type of ongoing care under Part A, usually at what's called a *skilled nursing facility* — most often a nursing home — under certain conditions.

The most important condition for Medicare coverage of care in a skilled nursing facility is that you must have been in the hospital as a formally admitted patient for at least three days. (This three-day rule conceals a hidden pitfall — situations where the hospital places you under "observation" — that you really need to know about; see Chapter 14.) A doctor must order the services that you need from professionals such as registered nurses and qualified physical therapists and speech or hearing pathologists. And the skilled nursing facility you go to must be one that Medicare has approved.

Original Medicare covers stays in a skilled nursing facility for up to 100 days in a benefit period. The first 20 days cost you nothing; from day 21 through day 100, you pay a daily co-pay, which goes up slightly every year (in 2024, $200 a day). Some Medigap supplemental insurance policies cover these co-pays 100 percent.

(Head to Chapter 4 for details about Medigap insurance.) If you're enrolled in a Medicare Advantage health plan, look at your coverage documents or call your plan to find out what it charges for stays in skilled nursing facilities.

TIP

For more information, check out the official publication "Medicare Coverage of Skilled Nursing Facility Care" at www.medicare.gov/Pubs/pdf/10153-Medicare-Skilled-Nursing-Facility-Care.pdf.

Home healthcare services

These services provide some of the same types of care that you may get in a skilled nursing facility but bring them to you in your own home. They include

>> **Skilled nursing care** provided on a part-time basis (no more than eight hours a day over a period of 21 days or less) and including services such as injections, feeding through a tube, and changing catheters and wound dressings.

>> **Physical, speech, and occupational therapy** from professional therapists to help you walk again, overcome problems in talking, or regain the ability to perform everyday tasks, such as feeding and dressing yourself — whichever your medical condition requires.

>> **Help from home health aides** in personal activities such as going to the bathroom, bathing, dressing, or preparing a light meal if these are necessary in relation to your illness or injury. (But if this personal care is the only kind of care you need, you don't qualify for home health coverage.)

>> **Medical supplies** such as catheters and wound dressings.

>> **Medical social services** such as counseling for social or emotional concerns related to your illness or injury and help finding community resources if you need it.

Medicare covers all these services in full by paying a home health agency a single payment to provide for 60 days of care at a time. Home healthcare is a valuable benefit, but the rules for qualifying are pretty strict. To get Medicare coverage, you must meet all these conditions:

>> You must be *homebound* — that is, unable to leave home without considerable effort, unaided, or at all.

>> A doctor must certify that you need one or more of the professional services in the preceding list (skilled nursing, physical or occupational therapy, or speech pathology).

>> You must be under a plan of care established and regularly reviewed by a doctor.

>> The home health agency caring for you must be approved by Medicare.

If you qualify, the agency must provide all the services specified in the doctor's plan of care for you. But if you need (or ask for) an item or service that Medicare doesn't cover, the agency must tell you so in advance and explain what it would cost you. If you need medical equipment, such as a wheelchair or a walker, while receiving home healthcare, you may get it through the agency, but you pay the normal 20 percent co-pay (as explained later in this chapter) unless you have Medigap insurance that covers that cost.

TIP

For more details on the home health benefit and how to choose and evaluate a home health agency, see the official publication "Medicare and Home Health Care" at www.medicare.gov/Pubs/pdf/10969–Medicare–and–Home–Health–Care.pdf.

Hospice care

There may come a time when a treatment intended to cure a serious illness stops working effectively or is more than the patient can bear. *Hospice care* offers an alternative in the last days or months of life. It focuses not on trying to cure the disease but on providing as much comfort as possible — medical, social, emotional, and spiritual — during the time left.

Medicare began covering hospice care in 1983, and it's one of the most generous benefits that the program provides — at little cost to terminally ill patients or their caregivers. Patients who choose hospice care are offered a full range of medical and support services, most often in their own homes. It also allows them to be cared for temporarily in an inpatient facility, such as a hospital or nursing home, if their regular caregivers need a break.

To qualify for the hospice benefit, you must meet all these conditions:

>> You must choose to receive hospice care and give up treatments intended to cure your terminal illness.

>> Your doctor and the medical director of a hospice program must certify that you probably have less than six months to live.

>> You must enroll in a hospice program that Medicare has approved.

>> You must have Medicare Part A hospital insurance.

If you qualify, Medicare pays in full — 100 percent — for a wide range of services, including

>> Medical and nursing care, plus round-the-clock on-call support

>> Medical equipment and supplies

>> Homemaker and home healthcare services

>> Physical therapy

>> Social worker services and dietary counseling

>> Support for your caregiver

>> Grief and loss counseling for you and your family

Your share of the cost is limited to a maximum of $5 per prescription for drugs used to control the symptoms and pain of your terminal illness, and 5 percent of the cost of respite care if you're taken into a nursing home to give your caregiver a break. However, if you have Medigap supplemental insurance, both these costs are fully covered, as Chapter 4 explains. (Costs related to any medical conditions other than your terminal illness are covered by Medicare Part B or Part D in the usual way.)

REMEMBER

You're free to stop hospice care any time you want to — and also to resume it again if that's your wish. Coverage continues for as long as your doctor and a hospice doctor continue to certify that you're terminally ill, even if you live longer than six months. If your health improves and the doctors decide you no longer need hospice care, the benefit ends — though you still have the right to appeal. If your health deteriorates again, the benefit can resume.

TIP

For more details, see the official publication "Medicare Hospice Benefits" at www.medicare.gov/Pubs/pdf/02154-Medicare-Hospice-Benefits.pdf.

Palliative care

Palliative care seeks to relieve the symptoms of pain and suffering associated with an illness that may not be terminal but is serious enough to be considered life-threatening. It focuses on improving the quality of life for patients and their caregivers. How is palliative care different from hospice? Well, palliative care does not require patients to give up attempts to cure their illness, and it can be administered at any time, without regard to how long they're expected to live.

Medicare doesn't recognize palliative care as a separate benefit. But Medicare may cover its components in other ways under Part B — for example, through the home healthcare service described earlier in this chapter or through hospital outpatient departments. If you want to find out more about palliative care or where you can get it in your area, discuss local options with your doctor. The Center to Advance Palliative Care offers an online directory of hospitals that provide palliative care at getpalliativecare.org/providers/.

End-of-life care counseling

While nobody wants to be morbid, people are increasingly seeing the sense of drawing up plans for care at the end of their lives — to ensure that their own wishes are respected at that time, even if they've reached a point of illness where they're unable to say what they want. Discussing with a doctor how to make those plans is known as end-of-life counseling, or advance care planning.

The counseling session may include information on making an advance care directive — a legal document in which you specify whether or not you want to continue treatment or be revived if close to death — and on giving someone (a family member, friend, or legal advisor) legal power of attorney to make medical decisions for you if you are incapacitated. It may also provide information about hospice and palliative care (which I cover earlier in this chapter).

Medicare has provided coverage for such discussions since the beginning of 2016 as a benefit you can choose to receive. As it's voluntary, nobody can require you to take it, and if you are offered it but don't want it, you're free to decline, without forfeiting the right to take part sometime in the future. You can decide if and when the time is right to receive counseling: while you're still well, with no health issues; when you become ill; or while you're receiving hospice or palliative care.

Under this benefit, Medicare pays your doctor (or another authorized medical professional, such as a nurse practitioner) for a first counseling session of up to 30 minutes, and for further 30-minute sessions if you need them. There is no limit on the number of sessions, and they can take place in a variety of settings — doctors' offices, hospitals, and nursing facilities, for example. If the counseling takes place during an annual wellness visit (which I describe in the earlier section on preventive care), the counseling is free, provided that the doctor accepts assignment. If you schedule a separate session outside the wellness visit, you pay the usual Part B co-pay and the Part B deductible is applied, unless you have supplemental insurance that covers these expenses.

Pregnancy and childbirth

Medicare does indeed cover pregnancy and childbirth. Are you astonished? That's probably because you see Medicare as a program only for people way past child-bearing age. But of course Medicare is also for much younger people who qualify through disability, and some of them become pregnant.

The relevant regulation in the Medicare Benefit Policy Manual explains the scope of coverage: "Skilled medical management is appropriate throughout the events of pregnancy, beginning with the diagnosis of the condition, continuing through delivery, and ending after the necessary postnatal care." Medicare also helps cover the cost of treatment for miscarriages and for abortions in circumstances where pregnancy is the result of incest or rape or would threaten your life if you went to term. It doesn't cover elective abortion if you choose to terminate your pregnancy.

To receive hospital services, you need Part A hospital insurance. For doctors' services and outpatient procedures (such as lab tests), you need Part B coverage. If you're enrolled in Medicaid because your income is low, that program may pay some or all of your out-of-pocket Medicare costs, depending on your state's eligibility rules. Medicaid may also pay for your infant's medical care. But after the birth, Medicare doesn't cover services for your baby at all.

Medical supplies and equipment

What if you need a wheelchair, an artificial limb, an oxygen tank, or other items that help you function but really qualify as things rather than services or treatments? Medicare has a suitably bureaucratic name for these things — *durable medical equipment* — and its meaning is precise. *Durable* means long-lasting, and Medicare covers only items that will stick around awhile. With only a few exceptions, it doesn't cover disposable items that you use once or twice and then throw away.

To get Medicare coverage for durable medical equipment, it must be

>> Medically necessary for you, not just convenient

>> Prescribed by a doctor or another primary-care professional

>> Not easily used by anyone who isn't ill or injured

>> Reusable and likely to last for three years or more

>> Appropriate for use within the home

>> Provided by suppliers that Medicare has approved

Durable equipment is covered under Medicare Part B and includes walkers and crutches; scooters and manual and powered wheelchairs; commode chairs; hospital beds; respiratory assistance devices; pacemakers; artificial limbs and eyes (prosthetics); limb, neck, and back braces (orthotics); and many other items. Medicare also covers some supplies, such as diabetic test strips and lancets, but otherwise does not generally cover disposable items, such as diapers.

REMEMBER

For some items — such as oxygen equipment or seat lifts that help incapacitated people get into or out of a chair — Medicare requires a doctor to fill out and sign a Certificate of Medical Necessity; without it, Medicare will deny coverage. In fact, to combat fraud and manage resources, Medicare is very picky about the evidence it requires for coverage — but your doctor and the supplier (not you) are responsible for providing this proof.

Medical equipment is most often rented, but some items may be purchased. In either case, Medicare Part B pays 80 percent, and you pay the remaining 20 percent (unless you have Medigap insurance that covers your share). That's the breakdown in original Medicare if you use a supplier that accepts the Medicare-approved amount as full payment. Otherwise, you pay whatever the supplier asks. If you're in a Medicare Advantage plan, coverage is the same, but you may have different co-pays; check with your plan for details.

TIP

For more information, and to find out how to select an approved supplier, see the official publication "Medicare Coverage of Durable Medical Equipment and Other Devices" at www.medicare.gov/media/publication/11045-medicare-coverage-of-dme-and-other-devices.pdf.

Knowing What Part D Covers

Part D, Medicare's program for covering prescription drugs, is a complicated benefit that resembles no other type of drug coverage ever devised. That's why understanding how it works before plunging in is really important. This section focuses on the peculiarities of Part D coverage — how it can fluctuate during the year, how different plans have their own lists of drugs they cover, and which drugs are excluded from Part D and which must be covered.

Making sense of drug coverage that can vary throughout the year

REMEMBER

It sounds crazy, but you may find yourself paying different amounts for the same medicines at different times of the year. That's because Part D drug coverage is generally divided into four phases over the course of a calendar year. Whether you encounter only one phase or two, three, or all four depends mainly on the cost of the prescription drugs you take during the year — unless you qualify for Extra Help (see Chapter 4). Here's the breakdown:

>> **Phase 1, the annual deductible:** If your Part D drug plan has a deductible, you must pay full price for your drugs until the cost reaches a limit set by law ($545 in 2024) and drug coverage actually begins. Many plans don't charge deductibles or

charge less than the limit. But if your plan has a deductible, this period begins on January 1 or whenever you start using your Medicare drug coverage.

>> **Phase 2, the initial coverage period:** This stage begins when you've met any plan deductible. Otherwise, it begins on January 1 or whenever you start using Medicare drug coverage. You then pay the co-payments required by your plan for each prescription, and the plan pays the rest. This period ends when the total cost of your drugs — what you've paid plus what your plan has paid — reaches a certain dollar limit set in law ($5,030 in 2024).

>> **Phase 3, the coverage gap:** This gap — often called the *doughnut hole* — begins when you hit the limit of initial coverage and ends if and when the amount you've spent out-of-pocket on drugs from the beginning of the year hits another dollar limit set in law ($8,000 in 2024).

In the coverage gap, instead of paying a co-pay, you pay 25 percent of the cost of brand-name and generic drugs, plus 25 percent of the drug dispensing fee (which usually is only $2–$3). For brand-name drugs, what you pay and what the manufacturer pays (95 percent of the cost of the drug) will count toward your out-of-pocket spending. For generic drugs, only what you pay for your drugs will count. (I explain the gap in more detail in Chapter 14.)

REMEMBER

Starting in 2025, the doughnut hole will officially close due to the Inflation Reduction Act, which imposed a maximum out-of-pocket spending cap of $2,000 for all Medicare Part D beneficiaries. By eliminating the coverage gap, it's estimated $7.4 billion in reduced spending on out-of-pocket drug costs will occur.

>> **Phase 4, catastrophic coverage:** Once you hit the out-of-pocket spending limit ($8,000 in 2024), you enter the catastrophic coverage phase. In this phase, you pay nothing for your Part D covered drugs for the rest of the year. Catastrophic coverage ends on December 31. The next day, January 1, you return to Phase 1 (or Phase 2 if your plan has no deductible), and the whole cycle starts over again.

Figure 2-1 is a quick way of looking at the same cycle of coverage.

Figure 2-2 shows this information in a different way. Here, you can see examples of brand-name drugs costing (for the sake of simplicity) $100, $200, or $300 per one-month prescription — and what you'd pay for them in each phase of coverage. These examples assume co-pays during the initial coverage period of $45 for each prescription, although co-pays vary widely among Part D plans.

Phase of Coverage	What It Means in Each Calendar Year	2024 Limits	2025 Limits
1. Annual deductible (if you plan has one)	You pay 100% of your drug costs before coverage begins, until you reach your plan's deductible, which must fall under the maximum limit set by law.	$545	The Inflation Reduction Act of 2022 caps out-of-pocket costs for beneficiaries at $2,000 a year beginning in 2025.
2. Initial coverage	You pay a co-pay for each prescription, and your plan pays the rest until these total drug costs reach the limit.	$5,030	
3. Coverage gap (doughnut hole)	Your plan provides no coverage, but you receive discounts from the drug makers and the government until your out-of-pocket spending in the year (including most discounts) reaches the limit.	$8,000	
4. Catastrophic coverage	You pay nothing until the end of the calendar year.		

FIGURE 2-1: Phases of Part D drug coverage and dollar limits.

© John Wiley & Sons, Inc.

Phase of Coverage	What You Pay for a Drug Whose Full One-Month Cost is $100	What You Pay for a Drug Whose Full One-Month Cost is $200	What You Pay for a Drug Whose Full One-Month Cost is $300
1. Annual deductible (if your plan has one)	$100	$200	$300
2. Initial coverage (with a co-pay of $45)	$45	$45	$45
3. Doughnut hole (you pay 25% for brand-name drugs in 2024)	$25	$50	$75
4. Catastrophic coverage (you pay nothing in 2024)	$0	$0	$0

FIGURE 2-2: Examples of costs through four phases of coverage.

© John Wiley & Sons, Inc.

Finding out about formularies

REMEMBER

Formulary is jargon that becomes familiar when you're in Part D because it directly affects what you pay. A *formulary* is simply the list of drugs that each Part D plan decides to cover. (No national formulary exists.) Here's why it's important that *your* drugs are included on *your* plan's formulary:

>> **You usually have to pay the whole tab for drugs that aren't covered.** Your plan pays its share of the cost during the initial and catastrophic coverage phases (Phases 2 and 4). But for any drug the plan doesn't cover, you pay full price in all phases of coverage unless you win an exception from the plan. (I explain coverage exceptions in Chapter 14.) The difference in your out-of-pocket expenses between a covered and uncovered drug can be hundreds of dollars a month.

>> **You don't get doughnut-hole credit for uncovered drugs.** If you fall into the doughnut hole (Phase 3), the cost of any drugs not covered by your plan doesn't count toward the out-of-pocket limit that gets you out of the gap and triggers the no-cost catastrophic coverage.

>> **You're more likely to properly fill and take your medicines.** You need the meds you're prescribed for the sake of your health. If you get coverage for them and don't have to pay full price, you're much more likely to fill all your prescriptions and not skip doses.

No Part D plan covers all prescription drugs, and the number covered varies greatly among plans. So the goal is to choose a plan that covers all, or at least most, of the specific drugs you take. I describe a strategy for doing so in Chapter 10.

In the following sections, I note the drugs that Part D has to cover and the ones that it doesn't pay for.

Laying out the drugs Part D plans must cover

Although Medicare law doesn't require Part D plans to cover every drug, it does require each plan to cover at least two drugs in each class of medications. A *class* means all the similar drugs that are used to treat the same medical condition. Many plans cover more than two in each class. But every plan must cover "all or substantially all" drugs in each of the following six classes:

>> Anticancer drugs (used to halt or slow the growth of cancers), unless covered under Part B

>> Anticonvulsants (used mainly to prevent epileptic seizures)

>> Antidepressants (used to counteract depression and anxiety disorders)

>> Antipsychotics (used to treat mental illnesses such as schizophrenia, mania, bipolar disorder, and other delusional conditions)

>> HIV/AIDS drugs (used to block or slow HIV infection and treat symptoms and side effects)

>> Immunosuppressants (used to prevent rejection of transplanted organs and tissues and treat immune system disorders and some inflammatory diseases)

Medicare requires every Part D plan to cover pretty much all drugs in these categories because of the clinical problems that can occur when patients abruptly stop taking such medications or switch to others.

Recognizing the drugs Medicare doesn't pay for

WARNING

By law, Medicare doesn't pay for certain kinds of drugs. Part D plans aren't prohibited from covering them; Medicare just doesn't reimburse their cost. So although a few plans may cover some of these drugs, most plans don't cover any. The types of excluded drugs are:

>> Medicines sold over the counter (not needing a doctor's prescription)

>> Drugs used for anorexia, weight loss, or weight gain

>> Drugs used for cosmetic reasons and hair growth

>> Drugs used to promote fertility

>> Drugs used to treat sexual or erectile dysfunction

>> Medicines used to treat cough or cold symptoms

>> Prescription vitamins and mineral products

Sometimes Medicare will pay for medications in these categories if they're used for a "medically acceptable" purpose — for example, cough medicines when prescribed by a doctor to alleviate medical conditions such as asthma, drugs for impotency when prescribed to treat different medical conditions that affect veins and arteries, or antismoking drugs if prescribed by a doctor rather than bought over the counter.

Until 2013, Medicare also excluded barbiturates (used for anxiety and seizures) and benzodiazepines (used for anxiety and sleeping problems) because these drugs are often abused. But the ban has now been lifted wholly on both types of drugs, allowing Part D plans to cover them for any medically accepted indication.

Determining when drugs are covered by Part A, Part B, or Part D

REMEMBER

As confusing as it sounds, some medications may be covered not only under Medicare Part D but also under Part A or Part B. Sometimes an identical drug may be covered by all three but charged under one or another according to different circumstances. That's because certain drugs were covered under A or B before D came into existence, and that practice continued. Here's the general rule of thumb:

- **Part A** covers drugs administered when you're a patient in the hospital or a skilled nursing facility.

- **Part B** covers drugs administered in a doctor's office (such as injected chemotherapy drugs), hospital outpatient departments, and in some circumstances, by a hospice or home healthcare professional.

- **Part D** covers outpatient drugs that you administer to yourself, a caregiver administers to you at your home, or you receive if you live in a nursing home. (These drugs are usually pills but also include self-injected insulin for diabetes, for example.)

These general rules are more complicated in some situations. For example, if your organ transplant was covered by Medicare, the immunosuppressant drugs you need afterward are covered by Part B. But if your transplant surgery wasn't covered by Medicare (perhaps because you had it before joining the program), the drugs are covered under Part D.

WARNING

Part D doesn't pay for drugs covered by Parts A or B. So if any of your meds are in question, your Part D plan may require information from you and your doctor — usually concerning any related medical treatment, such as surgery — before covering them. For this reason, Part D plans often place a *prior authorization restriction* on such drugs to determine whether Part A, B, or D should cover them. Your doctor may be able to settle this matter over the phone or may help you file a speedy exception request, as Chapter 14 explains. Either way, your doctor needs to explain why a prior authorization shouldn't apply in this case.

The Gaps: Discovering What Medicare Doesn't Cover

Although Medicare covers a multitude of medical services, it also has some yawning gaps. Some may surprise you, so the following sections address the broad areas that Medicare doesn't normally cover, together with some tips for alternative ways of filling in the gaps. Being aware of them from the start is better than being disappointed if Medicare denies coverage after the fact.

Routine hearing, vision, dental, and foot care

The older you get, the more you're likely to need professional attention for your ears, eyes, teeth, and feet. But Medicare doesn't cover routine services to take care of these parts. *Routine* is the key word here. Medicare pays to treat problems it considers medically necessary (including cataract surgery, jaw restoration after injury, and treatment for diseases of the ear) but not the kind of care you may need on a regular basis, such as the following:

>> Ear exams, hearing aids, or having hearing aids fitted

>> Vision tests, eyeglasses, or contact lenses

>> Oral exams, teeth cleaning, extractions, or dentures

>> Toenail clipping or the removal of corns and calluses

TIP

However, routine services for ears, eyes, and teeth may be covered if you're enrolled in a Medicare Advantage plan that provides them as extra benefits. Some plans offer them as separate benefit packages for an additional premium. Not all plans offer coverage for this routine care, but those that do are identified in the plan finder program on Medicare's website (www.medicare.gov/find-a-plan/questions/home.aspx). See Chapter 11 for info on using the plan finder to compare details of Medicare Advantage plans.

Of course, as always in Medicare, some exceptions exist. You can get coverage for foot care in certain circumstances — for example, if you have foot problems caused by conditions such as diabetes, cancer, multiple sclerosis, chronic kidney disease, malnutrition, or inflammation of the veins related to blood clots — especially if the act of toenail clipping would be hazardous to your health unless done by a professional. But the bottom line is that to get Medicare coverage for foot care, you need your doctor or podiatrist to provide evidence that said care is medically necessary.

Home safety items

Medicare spends billions of dollars a year on treating the results of falls, and older Americans are five times more likely to end up in the hospital for falls than for any other injuries. So you'd think that Medicare would try to save at least some of those billions by covering safety items that help prevent people from falling. But no, it doesn't.

To be sure, Medicare covers a few items it deems medically reasonable if prescribed by a doctor — for example, seat lifts that help incapacitated people sit down or get up from a chair, or trapeze bars that help people sit up or alter positions when confined to bed. But Medicare doesn't pay for equipment it considers items of convenience rather than of medical necessity. A long list of noncovered items includes stair lifts or elevators, bathtub lifts or seats, grab bars, room heaters, air conditioners, humidifiers, posture chairs, massage devices, physical fitness equipment, and medical emergency alert systems.

TIP

But you may be able to get help in other ways:

>> Medicare Advantage plans may offer supplemental benefits such as equipment to improve indoor air quality and to prevent falls. Check with the individual plans to find out more and to determine whether you qualify to receive these as a plan member.

>> If you're a veteran with disabilities, be aware that the Department of Veterans Affairs has little-known programs that provide cash grants to help eligible vets make safety improvements in their homes. Call the VA benefits hotline at 877-827-1000, or go to www.benefits.va.gov/homeloans/adaptedhousing.asp.

>> If your income is limited, contact the nonprofit organization Rebuilding Together, which provides volunteers to make housing repairs and install safety equipment free of charge. Call 800-473-4229 or go to rebuilding together.org for local information.

>> If you file itemized tax returns, you may be able to deduct the costs of home improvements for medical reasons, as I indicate in Chapter 4.

Nursing home care

Many people are surprised, and often alarmed, to discover that Medicare doesn't cover long-term care in nursing homes. I'm not talking here about short-term stays in a skilled nursing facility (most of which are nursing homes) after leaving the hospital; Medicare does cover those stays in specific circumstances. (I describe this kind of skilled nursing care earlier in this chapter and explain the ins and outs of qualifying for it in Chapter 14.)

But what if you become too sick or incapacitated to live at home and need the constant long-term care that a nursing home provides? Medicare will continue to cover your medical needs, but it won't pay for what it calls *custodial care,* which refers to help with the activities of daily life such as using the bathroom, dressing, and so on. Nor will Medicare pay for your room and meals in a nursing home. These same rules apply to assisted living facilities.

Most people living in nursing homes pay for their custodial care out-of-pocket — with the help of long-term-care insurance, if they've purchased it — until their resources run dry. At that point, they usually become eligible for Medicaid, the state-run healthcare system for people with very limited incomes and resources, which does pay the custodial care bills of people who qualify. (Because of the similarity in names, many people confuse Medicare and Medicaid, especially when it comes to thinking about long-term care.)

Eligibility rules for Medicaid vary from state to state. (And the name of the program is different in some states — for example, MediCal in California, MassHealth in Massachusetts, and TennCare in Tennessee.) To find out how the rules apply to you or a family member, you may need to consult an informed counselor or a qualified elder care attorney.

TIP

For contact information of people who can help, check out the official document "Your Guide to Choosing a Nursing Home or Other Long-Term Services and Supports" at www.medicare.gov/Pubs/pdf/02174-Nursing-Home-Other-Long-Term-Services.pdf. You can also visit www.medicare.gov/nursinghomecompare/search.html.

Medical services abroad

Medicare doesn't pay for medical services outside of the United States and its territories except in these extremely rare circumstances:

>> You're traveling between Alaska and another state and have a medical emergency that means you must be treated in Canada.

>> A medical emergency occurs while you're in the United States or its territories, but the nearest hospital is in a foreign country — for example, across the border in Canada or Mexico.

>> You live within the United States or its territories and need hospital care (regardless of whether it's an emergency), but your nearest hospital is in a foreign country.

Some Medigap supplemental insurance policies (those labeled C, D, F, G, M, or N) cover emergency or urgently needed treatment abroad. (I explain Medigap insurance in Chapter 4.) In this situation, you pay a deductible and 20 percent of the cost of the medical services you use up to a lifetime maximum of $50,000. Some Medicare Advantage plans also cover emergencies abroad, and so do some employer benefits and TRICARE military benefits. But otherwise, you need to buy travel insurance that includes medical emergencies when planning journeys abroad.

TIP

What if you live abroad? Medical treatment in other countries is almost always less expensive than in the United States, so paying out-of-pocket may not bankrupt you. And in some circumstances, you may be taken care of by the national health program of the country you're living in. But buying health insurance on the open market may be difficult or very expensive. One option is to join a nonprofit organization called the Association of Americans Resident Overseas (www.aaro.org), which has long lobbied Congress to make Medicare available abroad. AARO offers its members access to a variety of private health insurance plans that can be used in many countries. (You may be able to enroll in Medicare while living abroad, however; turn to Chapter 6 for important information about this kind of enrollment.)

Services that may be nice but aren't necessary

You probably aren't surprised to know that you can't get a face-lift or a tummy tuck at taxpayers' expense. Surgery solely for cosmetic purposes is one of the absolute no-no's of Medicare coverage. (Medicare does cover bariatric surgery to reduce the size of the stomach in very obese people, but this procedure is to lessen their risk of serious health disorders and not to improve their looks.)

Acupuncture and other alternative medical practices are barred under original Medicare. Physical fitness classes and gym memberships are also excluded. But some of these services (notably gym memberships) are covered as extras in some Medicare Advantage plans.

Even something as relatively mainstream as chiropractic care may be excluded from Medicare coverage in many circumstances. *Chiropractors* help lessen the pain of spine and joint problems, most often by the manipulation of bones. Medicare covers manipulative treatment from a licensed chiropractic physician when you're injured or in pain because of a problem with the spine, provided that the treatment is clearly improving your condition. But Medicare doesn't pay for the manipulation of other joints (such as shoulders and knees) or for other types of chiropractic care such as massage or traction. And it doesn't pay for maintenance care to keep you stable if you aren't demonstrably improving.

Finally, in the hospital, Medicare doesn't cover a private room (unless sharing one would be medically inadvisable), private nursing, or conveniences like a telephone or television if these items are billed separately.

Distinguishing When Coverage Comes with Limits

If you've had a hip replacement but fall again and need another, Medicare isn't going to turn around and deny you coverage for the second one. If you're fighting your third bout of pneumonia, Medicare isn't going to shut you out of the hospital because of the first two episodes. If you're in your 90s and have heart failure or cancer, Medicare isn't going to refuse you treatment because you're too old. For all the loose and cruelly inaccurate talk about "death panels" and "rationing" that still circulates in mass emails meant to exploit older people's fears of being denied coverage, Medicare simply doesn't — and can't, by law — ration care like that. "Medical necessity" is what usually counts.

At the same time, Medicare has always placed limits on certain areas of coverage — and although Washington policymakers may regard these caps as reasonable attempts to rein in runaway costs and guard against fraud, the limits can adversely affect some patients. So on the basis that forewarned is forearmed, the following sections provide an overview of the four main areas where coverage comes with limits: stays in the hospital, stays in a skilled nursing facility, mental health benefits, and therapy services.

Limits on hospital stays

Most people these days don't spend more than a few days in the hospital, and the fear of catching a really bad hospital infection — known as a leading cause of death — is enough to make anyone want out of there as soon as possible. So the chances that you'll exhaust Medicare coverage during a hospital stay are remote. Still, in case you get sick enough to need a long spell in the hospital, the following sections clue you in to how the limits work.

If you're enrolled in original Medicare

If you need to stay for a long period in the hospital for one spell of illness that's known as a *benefit period,* Medicare will cover 100 percent of your nursing and living costs for the first 60 days after you've met a deductible. For days 61 to 90, you're required to pay a daily co-pay. (I explain these costs in Chapter 3, and I go into detail about benefit periods in Chapter 14.)

No limit caps the number of benefit periods you can have, provided that 60 days have elapsed between each one. But if you still need to be in the hospital longer than 90 days in any one benefit period, you must either pay the full cost yourself or draw on up to 60 more days for which you pay hefty daily co-pays. These 60 days are called *lifetime reserve days.* You can use as many as you want or save some in case you need them in the future. But as the phrase implies, when you've used them, they're gone for good.

However, all Medigap supplemental insurance policies (explained in Chapter 4) extend Part A hospital coverage for up to an additional 365 days in your lifetime after Medicare benefits are exhausted. And most Medigap policies pay for the Part A hospital deductible, too. If you're enrolled in Medicaid (state medical assistance), this program usually covers the co-pays for lifetime reserve days.

If you're enrolled in a Medicare Advantage health plan

Medicare Advantage plans usually have a simpler system for charging for hospital stays. Often, they charge a daily co-pay for the first several days and nothing for the remaining days. Most plans set no limits on the number of days they cover, so you don't need to draw on lifetime reserve days. But some plans do set limits, although sometimes they charge no co-pays for the lifetime reserve days. Comparing the differences between Medicare Advantage plans and original Medicare when it comes to hospital stays is an important topic that I discuss in Chapters 9 and 11.

Limits on skilled nursing facility stays

If you need continuing skilled nursing care after you've been in the hospital and meet certain conditions (as explained earlier in this chapter and in Chapter 14), Medicare covers a stay in a skilled nursing facility — but it comes with limits. Beyond 100 days in each benefit period, you'll pay the full cost unless you have additional insurance. Some or all of these costs may be covered if you have additional insurance coverage through Medicaid, employer health benefits, long-term-care insurance, or Medigap supplemental insurance. Check your policy to find out. Most Medicare Advantage plans also limit coverage to 100 days in a benefit period.

Limits on mental health benefits

Like many other insurance plans, Medicare treats care for mental health disorders differently from other health problems. This kind of discrimination is less common than it used to be in Medicare, but some limits are still placed on mental health benefits, as described in the following sections.

Outpatient psychiatric services

For outpatient psychiatric care, you pay the standard 20 percent co-pay and Medicare pays the rest, as long as you see a participating provider. If you have Medigap insurance, these co-pays are covered. If you're in a Medicare Advantage plan, you pay what your plan requires.

Psychiatric care in a hospital

Medicare patients are limited to 190 days over their lifetime for receiving inpatient treatment in psychiatric hospitals — those that specialize in mental health conditions. Yet Medicare places no such limit on care in general hospitals. So any days you spend in a non-psychiatric hospital — even if you're being treated for a mental health condition — don't count toward the 190-day lifetime limit.

REMEMBER

Whether you receive mental health care in a psychiatric or a general hospital, the Part A hospital deductible and co-pays are the same as those for other medical conditions. These costs are explained in Chapter 3.

In some circumstances, Medicare covers *partial hospitalization,* which means receiving treatment at a hospital's outpatient department or clinic or at a community mental health center during the day, but not spending the night there. Your costs for this type of service vary according to the treatment provided, but under Medicare rules it can't be more than 40 percent of the Medicare-approved amount.

TIP

For more details, see the publication "Medicare & Your Mental Health Benefits" at `www.medicare.gov/Pubs/pdf/10184-Medicare-and-Your-Mental-Health-Benefits.pdf`.

Mental health benefits in Medicare Advantage plans

Because mental health benefits may vary among Medicare Advantage plans, look at the evidence of coverage documents for your plan. But most plans stick to the same limit of 190 lifetime days for inpatient care in a psychiatric hospital.

Limits on therapy services

Medicare Part B covers physical therapy (PT), speech-language pathology (SLP), and occupational therapy (OT). Previously, Medicare limited the amount of coverage you could get for therapy services in any given year as an outpatient or in a hospital outpatient department or emergency room, known as the therapy cap; however, in 2019, Medicare removed the cap, covering outpatient therapy at 80 percent of the Medicare-approved amount. When you receive services from a participating provider, you pay a 20 percent co-pay after you meet your Part B deductible, which in 2024 is $240.

These dollar limits are the total cost of the services received in a year — including what Medicare pays (80 percent of the Medicare-approved amount) and what you pay (20 percent). Medicare may continue to cover these services beyond the annual limits if you have a condition that requires ongoing therapy, such as extensive rehabilitation for stroke or heart disease. To get this exception, therapists must justify the need when they bill Medicare. If the total cost reaches $3,000 in a year, Medicare automatically reviews your case.

TIP

For specific information, see the publication "Medicare Coverage of Therapy Services" at es.medicare.gov/publications/10988–medicare–coverage–therapy–services.pdf.

Chapter **3**

Understanding What You Pay Toward Your Costs in Medicare

What will Medicare cost you, and how much will it save you? That's the killer question for people just coming into the program. In a way, the answer really depends on where you started out. Did you have low-cost insurance from an employer when you were working? Then Medicare may seem expensive in comparison. Were you paying through the nose for an individual policy that didn't actually provide much coverage? Or perhaps you just couldn't find insurance that you could afford? In those cases, Medicare probably seems like the promised land.

This point bears repeating: Medicare isn't free. Some people do think that the Medicare payroll taxes they pay while working will net them totally free healthcare after they hit 65. Sorry, not so. In fact, on average, Medicare is said to cover only about half of beneficiaries' total healthcare costs if they have no extra insurance.

In this chapter, I explain the way in which all the various costs of Medicare — premiums, deductibles, and co-payments — may hit your pocket in each of the parts of Medicare. I also go into detail about the higher-income premiums for Part B and Part D because you need to know whether they affect you and, if so, by how much. (However, you may be able to lower some of those costs, a topic I delve into in Chapter 4.) Finally, I explain why some people may pay different premiums than others in certain years and the instances when you need to pay Medicare taxes while receiving Medicare benefits.

Boning Up on Premiums, Deductibles, and Co-payments

REMEMBER

What Medicare pays toward your medical care is *coverage.* What you contribute out of your own pocket can be several kinds of expenses: premiums, deductibles, and co-payments. If you've had U.S.-style health insurance before, you know exactly what these terms mean. If not, here's a quick primer:

>> **Premium:** A *premium* is an amount you pay each month to receive coverage. In other words, it's your entrance ticket to the program.

>> **Deductible:** A *deductible* is an amount you pay before coverage kicks in. You can think of it as a kind of down payment before Medicare starts picking up the tab.

>> **Co-payment:** This amount is what you pay as your share of the cost of each service you receive. Strictly speaking, *co-pays* are fixed dollar amounts (such as $20), whereas *coinsurance* is the correct term when your share is a percentage of the cost (such as 20 percent). But because *coinsurance* is too wonky for words, I use *co-pays* in these pages.

If you had insurance in the past, you probably paid a single premium for all your healthcare and a single deductible for the whole year (maybe a hefty one if you were in a high-deductible plan), with co-pays for each service. But Medicare, of course, is divided into four parts, each with its own costs and charges. The following sections explain each set of costs under Part A, Part B, Part D, and Medicare Advantage (Part C) plans. Finally, Figure 3-1 shows the costs for Parts A, B, and D at a glance. *Note:* The costs in the chart are for people enrolled in original Medicare plus stand-alone Part D drug plans. Medicare Advantage plan costs are different and vary among plans.

	Part A	Part B	Part D
Premiums	None if you or your spouse has earned 40 or more work credits through paying payroll taxes at work. $278 a month if you or your spouse has 30-39 credits. $505 a month if you or your spouse has 0-29 credits.	For most people: $174.70 a month depending on circumstances. If you're liable for higher-income surcharges, you pay premiums between $244.60 and $594 a month, depending on income level.	Premiums vary among Part D plans, from $0 to $200 a month, with most in the $35 range. If you're liable for higher-income premiums, you will pay an additional surcharge between $12.90 and $81 a month, depending on income level.
Deductible	$1,632 for each hospital benefit period.	Annual deductible: $240	Annual deductible: $0 to $545 depending on the plan.
Co-payments	<u>Hospital stays:</u> **Days 1-60:** No co-pays after deductible is met. **Days 61-90:** $408 a day in each benefit period. **Days 91-150:** $816 a day for each lifetime reserve day. <u>Skilled nursing facility:</u> **Days 1-20:** No co-pays. **Days 21-100:** $204 a day in each benefit period. **After 100 days:** You pay all costs.	None for most preventive services. 20 percent of the Medicare-approved cost for other services, unless you have other insurance that covers those costs.	Co-pays depend on what your plan charges for each drug and which phase of coverage you're in at any given point in the year.

FIGURE 3-1:
2024 premiums, deductibles, and co-payments at a glance.

© *John Wiley & Sons, Inc.*

Part A costs

Part A covers nursing care, room, and meals in a hospital or *skilled nursing facility* (such as a rehab center or a nursing home); home health services; and hospice care. The following sections describe the possible out-of-pocket costs that you may pay for those services. *Note:* The costs in the following sections apply if you're enrolled in the original Medicare program. They'll likely be different if you're in a Medicare Advantage health plan such as an HMO or a PPO — see the later section "Medicare Advantage costs."

Premiums

You don't pay premiums for Part A coverage if you or your spouse paid enough in Medicare payroll taxes to earn at least 40 *credits* (sometimes called *quarters*) while working. If you don't have enough credits through your own or your spouse's work record, you can buy Part A services by paying premiums for them: in 2024, $278 a month if you have 30 to 39 credits and $505 if you have fewer than 30 credits. These amounts tend to go up or down a little each year. (I explain work credits in more detail in Chapter 5.)

Deductible

Part A doesn't have an annual deductible but rather applies a deductible to each *hospital benefit period.* This unit of time begins when you're first admitted to a hospital and ends only when you've been out of the hospital for 60 days. Huh? Yes, this timeline is a weird concept that I explain thoroughly in Chapter 14. All you need to know here is that the deductible for each hospital benefit period is $1,632 in 2024 (it goes up a little each year) and that after you've met it, Medicare picks up the whole tab for up to 60 days.

Co-payments (hospital and skilled nursing facility)

If you stay in the hospital for more than 60 days in any one benefit period, you're charged a daily co-pay for each day from the 61st to the 90th. In 2024, the co-pay is $408 a day, but this amount increases a little each year. If you still need to remain in the hospital after 90 days, you can choose to draw on some of your *lifetime reserve days.* These days require a hefty co-pay — $816 a day in 2024 — and they're limited to 60 days for the rest of your life. After these reserve days are exhausted, you must pay full costs.

If you're admitted to a skilled nursing facility (SNF) after being in the hospital for the required 3 days, Medicare picks up the whole SNF tab for the first 20 days, and you pay nothing. After that, you pay a daily co-pay ($204 in 2024) for the next 80 days. If you need to be in the facility longer than 100 days in any one benefit period, you're responsible for the full cost.

You can't use your lifetime reserve days to extend coverage in an SNF.

Co-payments (home healthcare and hospice care)

If you qualify for home health services (see Chapter 2), Medicare pays a home health agency for your care; you pay nothing. If you need or want a service that isn't covered under the agency contract, you have to pay for it yourself — either in full or as a regular 20 percent Part B co-pay (see the later section "Part B costs").

If you receive hospice services from a Medicare-approved agency (see Chapter 2), you pay almost nothing for this care. Two exceptions exist:

>> If you need prescription drugs to control the symptoms, such as pain, of your terminal illness, you pay up to $5 per prescription.

>> If you need to enter a nursing home for a short time so that your caregiver can catch a break, you're expected to contribute 5 percent of the cost.

Out-of-pocket limits

Medicare places no annual upper limit on your expenses in Part A. But if you have a Medigap policy (which I describe in Chapter 4) or other supplemental insurance, it may cover Part A's hospital deductible and co-pays.

Part B costs

Part B covers doctors' services (in their offices, in hospitals or other facilities, or at your home), outpatient care such as lab tests and screenings, and some medical equipment and supplies. *Note:* The Part B costs described in the following sections apply if you're enrolled in original Medicare. If you're in a Medicare Advantage plan, see the later section "Medicare Advantage costs."

Premiums

All people enrolled in Part B must pay a monthly premium to receive services (unless they're eligible for state assistance, as explained in Chapter 4). In late fall, the federal government announces the Part B premium amount for the following year. In 2024, the standard premium is $174.70 a month. Note that qualifying word: *standard.* If your income is over a certain level, you pay more. Also, if there is no Social Security cost-of-living adjustment (COLA) in any given year, or only a very small one, you may pay different premiums from some other people. I explain the higher-income surcharge, and the impact of zero or small COLAs in some years later in this chapter.

Deductible and co-payments

In 2024, the annual Part B deductible was $240. The amount usually goes up a little each year and is announced at the same time as the Part B premium. Typically, Medicare pays 80 percent and you pay 20 percent of the Medicare-approved cost of Part B services. Note that you may be charged more than 20 percent if you go to a provider who doesn't accept the Medicare-approved cost as full payment, as I explain in Chapter 13.

Out-of-pocket limits

In original Medicare, Part B has no upper limit on out-of-pocket expenses. But if you have Medigap supplemental insurance (described in Chapter 4), it covers your Part B co-pays in full or in part, depending on the policy you buy.

Part D costs

Part D covers outpatient prescription drugs — the kind that are prescribed by a doctor and used by you at home. You can receive this coverage by enrolling in a stand-alone Part D drug plan (if you have original Medicare for your medical benefits) or in a Medicare Advantage plan that combines medical and Part D drug coverage in its benefit package.

Premiums

All stand-alone Part D plans charge monthly premiums. The amounts vary among plans, ranging from $1 to a high of $108 a month in 2024, with most charging around $34.50 a month. Most Medicare Advantage plans combine both health and drug services under one premium, but some charge no premiums at all. Both types of plans can change their premiums every calendar year.

Deductible

You can't be charged more than a certain amount in any one year for the annual Part D deductible, whether you're enrolled in a stand-alone plan or a Medicare Advantage plan. In 2024, the maximum deductible was $545. But many plans charge lower amounts or, in some cases, nothing at all.

Co-payments

Two factors determine your Part D co-pays:

>> **The amount your plan charges for each specific drug you take:** Flat dollar co-pays stay the same all year, but those that are percentages of the cost of the drug can fluctuate throughout the year as the full price goes up or down. (I explain how plans determine co-pays in Chapter 14.)

>> **Which phase of coverage applies to you in Part D's annual cycle:** Are you in the deductible, initial coverage, doughnut hole, or catastrophic coverage phase when you fill prescriptions at different times of the year? (I explain the four phases of Part D coverage in Chapter 2.)

Part D plans can change the co-pays they charge for each drug every calendar year. And co-pays vary widely among different plans, even for the same drug. Both of these issues are good reasons to carefully compare plans each year to ensure you get the best deal. I explain how to do so in Chapter 15.

Out-of-pocket limits

Part D doesn't place a flat cap on your drug expenses in any one year, but you do get some relief if your costs rise over a certain level during the year. When that happens, *catastrophic coverage* kicks in, meaning that you do not pay anything for your drugs until the end of the calendar year. However, to qualify for catastrophic coverage, you must spend quite a bit out-of-pocket, as I explain in Chapter 2.

Medicare Advantage costs

Under the *Medicare Advantage program*, you can choose to receive your Medicare benefits through a private health plan, such as an HMO or a PPO, as an alternative to original Medicare. If you enroll in a Medicare Advantage plan, you must accept its terms, conditions, and specific costs.

Premiums

Most plans require a monthly premium, always in addition to the one you pay to the government for Part B services. The average number of Medicare Advantage plan choices increased from some 33 plans in 2019 to 43 plans in 2024. Plan premiums range from zero to more than $100 a month. Yes, that's right, from zero — $0 a month. Low premiums don't mean that these plans are inferior; usually it's because they're offered in dense urban areas where competition is fierce and they want your business. In 2024, the average monthly Medicare Advantage plan premium was $18.50.

Deductible

Most Medicare Advantage plans don't charge annual deductibles of their own for medical services, apart from the standard Part B deductible. However, some do. These amounts vary by plan and can change each year. Plans that include prescription drug coverage in their package of benefits may charge an annual Part D drug deductible up to a certain limit ($545 in 2024), but some charge less and some charge none. Most Medicare Advantage plans don't charge a deductible for hospital stays.

Co-payments

In Medicare Advantage plans, co-pays are very different from those in traditional Medicare:

>> You may pay a flat dollar co-pay for each medical service rather than a percentage of the cost. For example, a plan may charge $25 to see a primary-care doctor and $35 to see a specialist instead of charging original Medicare's 20 percent. However, co-pays based on percentages are becoming more common in Medicare Advantage plans.

>> Co-pays vary enormously from plan to plan and, within a plan, can change from year to year, but the amount you're charged in January for any specific service can't be increased for the rest of the year.

>> Some types of plans, especially PPOs, charge higher co-pays if you go to doctors and other providers outside of their contracted networks.

>> Most plans don't charge a fixed deductible for a hospital stay as original Medicare does but instead charge daily co-pays that vary greatly from plan to plan. This arrangement may or may not work out less expensively than a fixed deductible, as I discuss in Chapter 11.

>> Plans that offer routine vision, hearing, and/or dental care as extra benefits either charge co-pays for these services or offer them as optional packages that you can get only by paying a separate premium.

>> Medicare Advantage plans can't charge you more than original Medicare for some services, such as chemotherapy treatment for cancer, dialysis for kidney failure, and medical equipment.

Out-of-pocket limits

REMEMBER

Medicare Advantage plans, unlike original Medicare, are required to set annual limits on the expenses (deductibles and co-pays) for covered services that people enrolled pay each year. Limits can depend on the type of plan and whether the cost is in network or out of network. Contact your plan for details.

Paying Higher-Income Premiums

For most of its history, Medicare had no means-testing; everybody paid the same premium for its services. Even today, nobody is denied Medicare coverage on the basis of being wealthy. But since 2007, as a result of the 2003 Medicare

Modernization Act, people with incomes over a certain level have been required to pay higher premiums for Part B. And under the 2010 Affordable Care Act, those same people must pay more for Part D, too.

Looked at another way, it means that people who pay these higher premiums are receiving a smaller subsidy from the federal government for their healthcare. The feds provide a hefty chunk of money toward Part B and Part D services out of general revenues (that is, taxpayer dollars) — about 75 percent of the actual costs — while beneficiaries as a whole contribute about 25 percent through premiums. So the rationale for the higher-income surcharge was based on fairness; surely wealthier people can and should pay more than 25 percent of the cost of their Medicare.

Most people, of course, don't pay the higher premiums. Nonetheless, the income cutoffs aren't so high that they affect only millionaires. So you need to know whether you're likely to be asked to pay the surcharge — and what you can do about it if you are and think it's unwarranted. The following sections examine those issues in detail.

Understanding who's liable for the surcharges

You're required to pay higher premiums for Part B and Part D services if your modified adjusted gross income (MAGI), as shown on your latest federal tax return, is greater than $103,000 (if you're a single person) or $206,000 (if you're married, living together, and filing joint returns).

That statement, in a nutshell, is an accurate answer to the question of liability. But to understand whether the surcharge may affect you, you have to examine the wording more closely:

>> First, consider the phrase *as shown on your latest federal tax return.* The last tax return you filed showed the income you received in the previous year. So that year's income is what counts in determining whether you pay the surcharge next year. That's right: The surcharge for any one year is calculated on the income you received two years earlier. For example, whether you pay surcharges on your 2024 premiums is calculated on income you had in 2022, as declared on the tax returns you filed in 2023.

>> Now, look at that phrase *modified adjusted gross income* (MAGI) — IRS jargon that only an accountant could love. What on earth does it mean? What it doesn't mean is your total income. Your total (*gross*) income is all the money

you receive from any source. Your *adjusted gross income* (AGI) is the amount on which you can be taxed after allowed deductions are taken out. *MAGI* is the amount left after certain deductions that were excluded from the AGI, such as tax-exempt interest and student loan deductions, are added back in. It's a complicated calculation, but the real point here is that in many cases the MAGI is much less than full income.

TIP

Obviously, some people's incomes change a lot in two years — especially those who have retired or lost their jobs during that period. If you're in that situation or a few other specific circumstances, you aren't liable for the surcharge and can take action to avoid paying it. I explain this process in the later section "Getting the surcharges waived."

In the following sections, I dig deeper into some situations that may affect whether you pay higher premiums.

Determining when you may be liable, even if your income isn't high

Several factors can push some people up above the surcharge threshold even if their regular incomes are quite modest, including the following:

>> A one-year increase in income from the sale of property, such as a house, even if it's your main residence

>> A one-year increase in income from cashing in part or all of a tax-deferred asset such as an individual retirement account (IRA) or from selling some stocks and shares

>> A one-year increase in income from a windfall, such as an inheritance

REMEMBER

Be aware that such boosts to your income in just one year can land you with a premium surcharge. However, it will not be permanent. The following year, your premiums will be based on your regular income.

Here are some examples illustrating how surcharge liability can change:

>> In 2020, a few years after Bob and Julia retired, they sold their family home and downsized to an apartment. On the joint tax return they filed in April 2021, they declared the money earned from the house sale in 2020. This amount was enough to raise their MAGI above the threshold for a married couple. So in 2022, they had to pay a surcharge on their Part B and Part D premiums, even though their income was now much lower than it had been two years earlier. In 2024 — based on the 2023 tax returns that reflected their

regular income for 2022 — they no longer had to pay a surcharge and returned to paying standard premiums.

>> When Jim retired, he put some savings into a tax-free IRA. In 2022, on reaching age 70.5, he was then required by law to draw money out of the account. This withdrawal counted as taxable income on the tax return he filed in 2023. It pushed his MAGI over the threshold for a single person, so he paid surcharges on Part B and Part D premiums in 2024.

Recognizing that you may be liable for a Part D surcharge, even without a Part D plan

I've heard from people who are utterly outraged to be hit with the higher-income Part D surcharge when, they point out, they don't even get their prescription drug coverage from Medicare! Instead, their meds are covered under retiree benefits provided by former employers. When I checked with Medicare, I found (to my surprise) that yes, it's true: Some people in retiree plans can be required to pay the Part D surcharge. So what's going on here?

"A lot of people think they have [purely] retiree drug coverage, but the employer actually contracts with a Part D plan to provide it," Medicare officials say. This setup means that people aren't always aware that they're receiving Medicare drug coverage for which the Part D surcharge applies.

Here's how to tell whether you have to pay the Part D surcharge:

>> If you're enrolled in a regular Part D drug plan or a Medicare Advantage health plan that includes drug coverage — in other words, a plan that you've chosen and paid for yourself and that has nothing to do with retiree benefits — the issue is quite clear. If your income makes you liable for the surcharge, you pay that amount on top of your plan's premium.

>> If your former employer's retiree healthcare plan receives a retiree drug subsidy from the government, you aren't liable for the surcharge.

>> If your former employer's retiree health plan contracts with Medicare to provide Part D coverage — either through a Part D drug plan or through a healthcare plan that includes Part D coverage — you're liable for the surcharge if your income is above the specified level.

TIP

If you have drug coverage through a retiree plan, how do you know whether you're liable for the surcharge? The plan may inform you, or the first clue may come when the Social Security Administration sends a letter that says so. In that case, call your retiree plan to check it out — and also ask whether you or your former employer will pay the surcharge.

If the retiree plan pays your Part D premiums (as some plans do), the employer may choose to pay any surcharges as well but isn't obliged to. But be aware that even if your former employer springs for the surcharge, you're still legally responsible for ensuring that it's paid each month.

Figuring out what the surcharges cost you

If you're liable for the surcharge, what you pay in higher premiums is calculated on a sliding scale according to your MAGI. Keep in mind that most people pay roughly 25 percent of Medicare costs through the standard premiums. Those paying surcharges, depending on their MAGI, pay premiums at four different levels, which are equivalent to 35, 50, 65, or 80 percent of Part B and Part D costs. To see how this breakdown works, look at Table 3-1, which shows the different surcharge amounts required in 2024 for Part B and Part D premiums based on your 2022 MAGI as filed on your 2023 tax returns.

TABLE 3-1   **2024 Higher-Income Part B and Part D Premiums**

Your 2022 MAGI (per 2023 Returns)	Your Part B Monthly Premium in 2024	Your Part D Monthly Premium in 2024
Single person: $103,000 or less Married couple filing jointly: $206,000 or less	Standard 2024 premium: $174.70	Your regular Part D plan premium
Single person: $103,000 to $129,000 Married couple filing jointly: $206,000 to $258,000	$244.60	Your Part D plan premium plus $12.90
Single person: $129,000 to $161,000 Married couple filing jointly: $258,000 to $322,000	$349.40	Your Part D plan premium plus $33.30
Single person: $161,000 to $193,000 Married couple filing jointly: $322,000 to $386,000	$454.20	Your Part D plan premium plus $53.80
Single person: $193,000 to $500,000 Married couple filing jointly: $386,000 to $750,000	$559.00	Your Part D plan premium plus $74.20
Single person: $500,000 or above Married couple filing jointly: $750,000 or above	$594.00	Your Part D plan premium plus $81.00

Source: Centers for Medicare & Medicaid Services(CMS)/Public Domain

One other calculation isn't shown in Table 3-1. It relates to married couples filing separate tax returns. In that case, each spouse pays a surcharge based on their individual MAGI in one of two levels: from $103,000 to $397,000 and $397,000 and above.

TECHNICAL STUFF

The dollar amounts of the surcharges change slightly each year because they're based on percentages of the total costs of Part B and Part D in the previous year, and these costs, of course, may fluctuate from year to year. But the *thresholds* — the MAGI amounts that take you to a higher level of premium — were frozen through 2019 and were adjusted in 2020 and thereafter each year for inflation.

Getting the surcharges waived

A lot can happen in the two years that pass between the year in which your income is assessed and the year in which surcharges are applied. For example, in the former (I'll call it year A), you may be working and pulling in high earnings, while in the latter (year B) you're retired with a greatly reduced income. In year A you're married; in year B you're widowed or divorced. In year A you're doing okay with your stocks and shares; by year B, the market has crashed and you've lost your shirt.

In any of these cases, can you have the surcharges waived? The following sections explain events that qualify as life changes and other instances in which you may be able to secure a waiver from Social Security. (The Social Security Administration, *not* Medicare, assesses higher-income surcharges.)

Knowing what qualifies as a life-changing event

In certain specific circumstances when your income has recently gone down, you may be able to avoid paying a higher-income premium surcharge. The Social Security Administration calls the following circumstances *life-changing events:*

>> You marry, divorce, have your marriage annulled, or are widowed.

>> You or your spouse stops work — for example, you retire or lose your job.

>> You or your spouse works fewer hours.

>> You or your spouse loses income because your former employer's pension plan ends or is altered.

>> You or your spouse receive a settlement as a result of your current or former employer's closure, bankruptcy, or reorganization — so in this case, the increased income doesn't count toward a premium surcharge.

>> You or your spouse loses income-producing property (such as a house you rent out, farmland and crops, or animals you'd otherwise have sold) due to a disaster or other event beyond your control.

If any of these events has happened to you, resulting in reduced income, and you're already paying the premium surcharge or have been told that you must pay it soon, contact Social Security (at 800-772-1213 or TTY 800-325-0778) immediately and ask for a *new initial determination,* which is the phrase Social Security uses in this situation. Social Security decides whether you need to pay the surcharge without your having to go through a formal appeal.

If you request a new initial determination, you need to provide proof of the life-changing event on which it's based, such as a death certificate or a letter from your former employer confirming that you're no longer in your job. You also need to show a more recent tax return with evidence of reduced MAGI — or, if you haven't yet filed a tax return for the current year, you must give Social Security an estimate of your reduced earnings and then provide a signed copy of the return after you've filed it with the IRS.

Social Security officials told me that a new determination request is usually processed on the day it's received if it's supported by proper documentation. Otherwise, the request will be delayed or denied for want of evidence. If Social Security agrees that one of the life-changing events on the list applies to you, it will revise its records and the premium surcharges will be waived or reduced. This adjustment may take a while, but any overpayments you've already made will be refunded. If your request is denied or you disagree with the new determination, you have the right to file an appeal by calling Social Security at 800-772-1213.

Check out some example scenarios:

>> Kate had a well-paying job with health benefits and worked until she turned 68 in the fall of 2022. On retirement, she was dismayed to find that her Medicare Part B and D premiums included hefty high-income surcharges. The amounts had been based on her latest tax return, filed early in 2023, which reflected the large salary she had earned in 2022. But in retirement, her income had fallen sharply. However, retirement counts as a life-changing event, so Kate was able to apply to Social Security for a reassessment. Her premiums were reduced to the standard amounts, and Social Security refunded the excess payments she'd made.

>> Jose and Maria didn't grumble too much about paying the higher-income surcharges because, though well into his 70s, Jose was still earning good money as a self-employed consultant. That ended abruptly with his sudden death from a heart attack. Without his earnings, Maria's income more than halved. Acting on a friend's advice, she asked Social Security to reduce her Medicare premiums to the standard rate. Because Jose's death counted as a life-changing event, Maria's request was granted.

Verifying whether other situations qualify for a waiver

What if your income went down for other reasons? For example, what if you lost investment income after being wiped out in a stock market crash? Social Security doesn't count this occurrence as a life-changing event, even if it seems like one to you, so you can't apply for a new determination. All you can do is file an amended tax return to the IRS and then, if that is accepted, submit it to Social Security as proof that your MAGI is now much lower.

One other situation is worth mentioning. If your income is reduced by fraud or other criminal activity — such as being duped in a Ponzi scheme — Social Security will consider a request to waive a premium surcharge. But you have to provide proof that fraud or a crime has been committed and show that the perpetrator has been convicted for it.

Finally, what if you simply can't afford to pay the surcharge because of lost income but don't qualify for a life-changing event waiver? In most cases, you just have to suck it up and pay the higher premium until your next tax return shows your true income. Still, Social Security says it will consider waiving the surcharge "if payment of the premiums would create severe financial hardship." If that's the case, call Social Security and request a waiver.

Paying Different Premiums than Other People in Certain Years

It has happened rarely — most recently in 2021 — but there are certain years when some Medicare beneficiaries pay one Part B premium and others pay much more. I'm not talking here about the higher-income premium described in the previous section. This is a different scenario, the direct result of Social Security not providing a cost-of-living adjustment (COLA) — that is, an increase — or only a very tiny one, during some years.

Under the law, people who receive Social Security benefits are protected from having those payments cut due to increased Part B premiums. So if there is no or a very low Social Security COLA in a given year but the Part B premium is increased in that year, those people are "held harmless" — meaning that the increase is waived and they do not have to pay higher premiums than they did the previous year, which sounds only fair.

However, under another long-established law, Part B premiums must be set to cover about 25 percent of expected costs in the program for the coming year. When costs rise, premiums go up. But if the people who are held harmless cannot contribute to that increase, who pays? The answer is this: everybody else in Medicare. They include

>> **Those who do not receive Social Security or Railroad Retirement benefits:** These include people who have not yet applied for benefits; former federal, state, or local government workers who have their own pension systems; and people under age 65 whose disability benefits have been discontinued because they returned to work, but still qualify for Medicare.

>> **Those who are new to Medicare, even if they do receive Social Security benefits:** You must have received benefits in November and December and had Medicare premiums deducted from them (in advance) for the months of December and January to be held harmless during the rest of the year.

>> **All those who pay the higher income-related premiums, regardless of whether they receive Social Security payments:** Refer to the earlier section "Paying Higher-Income Premiums" for more info on whom this applies to.

>> **Lower-income beneficiaries who receive Medicaid or whose Part B premiums are paid by their state:** But in this case, it is the state that pays the increased premium, not the beneficiary.

This is where the Medicare Hold Harmless provision comes in. The provision ensures that people who receive Social Security won't see significant reductions in their monthly payments when Medicare Part B premiums outpace the cost-of-living adjustment (COLA) each year.

TECHNICAL
STUFF

The Social Security COLA is always pegged to the Consumer Price Index (CPI), a measure that shows overall inflation in consumer prices. The CPI in 2024 was 3.9 percent, significantly lower than 6.3 percent for the prior year. However, the CPI does not include healthcare costs, which are a big slice of everyday expenses for Americans, especially those in the Medicare age bracket.

Paying Medicare Taxes While Receiving Medicare Benefits

I've been asked this question quite frequently: "I'm over 65 and still working, but I'm enrolled in Medicare. Should my employer still be deducting Medicare payroll taxes from my earnings?"

REMEMBER

Yes, indeed. The law requires you to pay Medicare taxes on all your earnings for as long as you continue to work — regardless of whether you're already receiving Medicare benefits.

I've also been asked the exact reverse of the preceding question: "I'm 60, and my employer recently quit taking Medicare and Social Security out of my wages. Should this be happening?"

WARNING

No, *absolutely not!* Failing to pay these taxes can jeopardize your benefits in later years. But it's not an uncommon situation. "Sometimes employers stop withholding tax from employees' wages under the mistaken notion that they can choose to treat employees as independent contractors," IRS officials told me. "Employee misclassification is a serious problem that can result in penalties against the business." Yet misclassification can make a big difference to your income. If you're an employee, your employer must by law pay half of your Medicare and Social Security payroll taxes. If you're an independent contractor, your share is much more.

TIP

The IRS says that if you're an employee who believes you're being incorrectly treated as an independent contractor, you should file Form SS-8, Determination of Worker Status for Purpose of Federal Employment Taxes and Income Tax Withholding. An employer can also file this form to clarify how a worker should be classified. Form SS-8 is available online at www.irs.gov/pub/irs-pdf/fss8.pdf.

Chapter **4**

Reducing Your Out-of-Pocket Expenses in Medicare

Yes, Medicare comes with a lot of out-of-pocket costs: premiums, deductibles, and co-pays, not to mention those services you pay for because Medicare just doesn't cover them. If you're lucky, you may have retiree benefits from a former employer that help reduce them. (I cover how other insurance fits in with Medicare in Chapter 8.) But otherwise, perhaps you're gulping a bit and wondering whether you can find any respite out there. Help does exist, though it takes several different forms that don't apply to everybody:

» **Medigap insurance:** If you can afford it, you can buy Medigap supplemental insurance to lower your costs — which essentially means paying extra (through Medigap premiums) to pay less (in deductibles and co-pays that original Medicare charges). Topsy-turvy as it sounds, you can actually save quite a lot of money this way. About one in five people in Medicare purchases these policies.

>> **Medicare Advantage:** An alternative is to join a Medicare Advantage plan, which may be another way to reduce costs. These plans are discussed in detail in Chapters 9 and 11, so I don't include them here.

>> **State and federal help:** If your income is very limited, you may qualify for different kinds of assistance from your state to help pay Medicare costs. And a limited income may also get you through the door of the federal program called Extra Help, which provides Part D prescription drug coverage at a much lower cost than you'd otherwise pay for it.

This chapter looks in detail at Medigap, state and federal options, and other ways of cutting down on expenses, with tips on how to put them into practice.

Purchasing Medigap Insurance

Medicare supplemental insurance — also known as *Medigap* — isn't a government program. It's private supplemental insurance you can choose to buy separately to reduce your costs in original Medicare. If you don't have supplemental coverage from elsewhere (such as retiree benefits) and can afford the extra premiums, Medigap is worth considering. It pays many of the co-pays and deductibles you'd otherwise pay out of your own pocket, plus some extra coverage, depending on the specific policy you buy.

REMEMBER

This section considers the ins and outs of Medigap policies and how to compare them. In Chapter 10, I discuss how to choose the one that best suits your needs and when to buy it (even if you're under 65). But first, here are some important facts to know upfront about Medigap:

>> You must be enrolled in both Medicare Part A and Part B.

>> You can use Medigap insurance only if you're enrolled in original Medicare. It doesn't work with a Medicare Advantage plan.

>> You must pay a monthly premium in addition to your Part B premium.

>> Medigap provides no coverage for prescription drug costs unless you still have an old policy that you bought before 2006.

>> If you're 65 and older, you get important consumer protections under federal law — but only if you buy a policy at the right time. During specific time frames, an insurance company can't deny you coverage or charge higher premiums for current or past health problems.

>> If you're under 65, you don't get these federal protections, but some states have laws that give similar rights to their residents.

TIP

For more detailed information on buying Medigap insurance, see the official publication "Choosing a Medigap Policy" at www.medicare.gov/publications/02110-medigap-guide-health-insurance.pdf.

Examining Medigap policies

Note: I'm assuming here that you're 65 or older. If you're younger — and therefore come under different rules — skip this section and use the information I give in Chapter 10.

The ten Medigap policies currently available are each labeled with a letter of the alphabet: A, B, C, D, F, G, K, L, M, and N. (The missing letters in this sequence — E, H, I, and J — belong to older policies that are no longer sold.) Each lettered policy offers a different set of benefits that is standardized by federal law. This uniformity means that each policy with the same letter must have exactly the same benefits, even though the premiums charged by different insurance companies vary a good bit. So it pays to shop around.

REMEMBER

Beginning in 2020, Medigap plans sold to new Medicare beneficiaries were no longer allowed to cover the Part B deductible. Because of this, Plans C and F are no longer available to people who are new to Medicare. If you previously held these plans, you may keep them, and if you were eligible but not enrolled in Medicare before January 2020, you may buy one of these plans. Plans C and F are the only standardized plans currently available for sale that cover the Part B deductible.

Take a look at Figure 4-1, which broadly shows which policies cover which benefits and to what extent. A percentage shows a policy that pays only half or three-fourths of a benefit's cost; you pay the rest.

Figure 4-1 shows only the bare bones of Medigap coverage. The fine print, for example, shows that

>> The emergency care abroad benefit has limits not shown here. The six policies that cover this benefit charge a deductible of $250, a 20 percent co-pay, and a lifetime limit of $50,000.

>> The Part B excess charges benefit, available only in policies F and G, covers your expenses in situations where a doctor or other provider charges more than the Medicare-approved cost. This practice is called *balance billing,* and you can find details about it in Chapter 13. Note again that supplemental F policies are no longer available to people who are new to Medicare.

Covered Benefits	A	B	C	D	F	G	K	L	M	N
Part A hospital co-pays plus 365 extra days	Yes	Yes	Yes	Yes	Yes	Yes	Yes	Yes	Yes	Yes
Part A hospital deductible	No	Yes	Yes	Yes	Yes	Yes	50%	75%	50%	Yes
Part B co-pays	Yes	Yes	Yes	Yes	Yes	Yes	50%	75%	Yes	Yes
Part B deductible	No	No	Yes	No	Yes	No	No	No	No	No
Part B excess charges	No	No	No	No	Yes	Yes	No	No	No	No
Skilled nursing facility co-pays	No	No	Yes	Yes	Yes	Yes	50%	75%	Yes	Yes
Hospice care co-pays	Yes	Yes	Yes	Yes	Yes	Yes	50%	75%	Yes	Yes
First 3 pints of blood	Yes	Yes	Yes	Yes	Yes	Yes	50%	75%	Yes	Yes
Emergency care abroad (to plan limits)	No	No	Yes	Yes	Yes	Yes	No	No	Yes	Yes

FIGURE 4-1: Benefits covered in Medigap policies.

© John Wiley & Sons, Inc.

>> Although policy N covers most of Part B's 20 percent co-pays, it does require small co-pays of its own in a couple of situations: up to a $20 co-pay for some office visits and up to a $50 co-pay for emergency room visits that don't end in admission to the hospital.

>> Two policies, K and L, pay only half or three-fourths of the costs for most services but pay 100 percent for the rest of the year if your out-of-pocket costs go over certain annual limits.

>> An alternative high-deductible version of policy F and G is available in some states, with a lower premium but a hefty annual deductible ($2,800 in 2024) before the policy pays anything. This amount can change each year. (The standard F policy has no deductible.)

>> Some policies have another version labeled "SELECT." These options typically charge lower premiums than other policies, but they cover your bills only when you go to providers in their networks, except in an emergency.

>> Policies C and F cover the annual Part B deductible ($240 in 2024), but as mentioned earlier, this benefit was eliminated on policies sold from 2020 onward.

So if you're thinking of buying Medigap, you need to look at the details of each policy so that you can compare the policies properly. You can do this very easily on Medicare's website by following these steps:

1. Go to www.medicare.gov/medigap-supplemental-insurance-plans/.

2. Enter your zip code and click "Start."

    You'll see a list of all the Medigap policies.

3. Click on "Plan Details."

    To see which insurance companies sell any plan, click the "View Policies" link. To find out the exact premium you would be charged, you need to contact the companies by phone or through their websites, using the contact information provided on the results page.

This online process is very straightforward. But if you prefer, you can call the Medicare help line at 800-633-4227 (TTY 877-486-2048) and ask a customer representative to mail you the details of Medigap policies and/or insurers in your area. Or you can get personal help from a counselor at your State Health Insurance Assistance Program (SHIP). For SHIP phone numbers, head to Appendix A.

If you live in Massachusetts, Minnesota, or Wisconsin

Massachusetts, Minnesota, and Wisconsin passed laws that established standardized Medigap policies earlier than federal law did, so these programs were allowed to continue.

Most Medigap benefits in these states are very similar to those in the national policies, with some differences. For example, Wisconsin's basic set of benefits adds 175 more days of inpatient mental health coverage than Medicare provides and 40 more home health visits. Minnesota adds a benefit for physical therapy. But you don't get as many policies to choose from as you would elsewhere in the country.

If you live in one of these states, entering your zip code into the Medigap plan finder program on Medicare's website, as explained in the preceding section, shows you the choice of policies available to you and the exact benefits provided in those policies.

If you live in a state where "innovative" Medigap policies are sold

In recent years, some states have approved Medigap policies that are called "innovative" because they are new and offer more benefits than the standardized ones described earlier.

These new-style policies vary a lot from state to state and from company to company. The extra benefits they offer may include coverage for routine dental, vision, and/or hearing care; annual physical exams; a nurse's advice phone line; fitness programs; extended coverage for skilled nursing facilities; and more. In most states, policies provide only one or two of these benefits.

The extra coverage builds on existing standardized policies. For example, an "innovative policy" includes all the benefits of the regular policy (as shown in Figure 4-1), plus whatever extras a state allows and an insurance company chooses to provide. Also, you can't be charged higher premiums than the company charges for the regular lettered policy in your area.

For information on these policies, contact your state department of insurance. (For contact info, go to www.naic.org/state_web_map.htm and select your state.)

If you have a Medigap policy that's no longer sold

Medigap insurance has changed over the years, most often in giving more protections to consumers. More than 20 years ago, federal law simplified the range of available policies, limiting them to ten standardized sets of benefits (except in the three states noted earlier in this chapter), which made it far easier to choose among them. Some policies — E, H, I, and J — have been discontinued, which means they can no longer be sold to new customers but can still be used by policyholders who choose to keep them.

If you still have one of these policies, their original benefits are unchanged for you. But you may find your premiums going up. This increase happens because each year the pool of people who have the same policy becomes smaller. Those folks get older and their health problems increase, driving up costs for the insurance company, which in turn charges you more.

Policies H, I, and J used to be popular but expensive policies because they included some coverage for prescription drugs at a time when this coverage didn't exist in Medicare. But these policies haven't been sold to new customers since 2006, when Medicare prescription drug coverage (Part D) began. At that time, people with these policies were offered the option of dropping the drug portion of the policies or changing to a Medigap policy that didn't cover medications — and, in each case, signing up for Part D drug coverage instead — or keeping those policies intact.

Similarly, if you enrolled in policy C or F before 2020 (because those plans covered the Part B deductible), you may be able to switch to another policy. But be aware that in most states you may have to go through medical underwriting — under which the insurance company can charge you higher premiums based on your current health status and pre-existing medical conditions. A few states, however, allow residents to switch policies at certain times without medical underwriting. (For more details on switching policies, see Chapter 15.)

WARNING

The snag is that the drug coverage under policies H, I, and J isn't *creditable*, meaning that Medicare doesn't consider it as good as Part D coverage. So if you kept one of these policies all this time and now choose to switch to Part D, you pay permanent late penalties in the form of higher Part D plan premiums. The penalty amounts are calculated on how many months have elapsed since May 2006 — the deadline for Part D enrollment among people already receiving Medicare at that time.

For example, Alice had a Medigap J policy, which covered 50 percent of the cost of her drugs up to an annual dollar limit, and she kept it after the Part D drug benefit began in 2006. By late 2016, this policy had become expensive, and she considered switching to a Part D plan for her drugs. But because she had gone 127 months without creditable coverage (June 2006 through December 2016), she faced late penalties of about $43 a month permanently added to her Part D plan's premiums.

Choosing and buying a Medigap policy

In Chapter 10, I focus on points you need to consider when making Medigap choices. I explain how to buy a Medigap policy at the right time — when you have consumer protections under federal law, if you're 65 or older — and why the timing really matters in terms of how much Medigap will cost you. I also explain in that chapter that federal protections do not apply if you're under 65, although, depending on where you live, your state may provide similar or other protections.

Qualifying for Help from Your State

What if you find it difficult to afford the most basic costs of Medicare, let alone extras like Medigap (described earlier in this chapter)? You may qualify for at least one form of assistance from your state, as millions of others have done. Certainly, you should consider applying — especially if you've reached the point of wondering whether to stop paying your premiums. You need to look at all the possibilities for keeping your coverage.

Many people who may qualify for state programs don't actually apply, probably for a variety of reasons. But a major reason must be that many don't realize the programs exist or don't know how to apply. This section describes the assistance that's out there. If you're hurting financially, the following options are worth checking out:

- >> **Medicaid:** *Medicaid* is a state-run program that supplements your Medicare coverage significantly and provides you with virtually free healthcare if you qualify.

- >> **Medicaid medical spend-down programs:** If you don't qualify for Medicaid outright, you may become eligible for it temporarily in some circumstances under spend-down programs.

- >> **Medicare Savings Programs:** If you're not eligible for Medicaid, you may qualify to at least have your Medicare premiums paid for through one of the Medicare Savings Programs (MSPs).

- >> **A PACE plan:** *Programs of All-Inclusive Care for the Elderly* (PACE) are an especially valuable service for people with low incomes and poor health, but they aren't available everywhere.

- >> **State Pharmacy Assistance Programs:** These programs (abbreviated SPAPs) help people afford prescription drugs.

Medicaid

Medicaid is the national safety net of healthcare, paying the medical costs of people in certain groups (including seniors and people with disabilities) who have very limited incomes. Some 80 million people are enrolled in Medicaid; more than one in five are Medicare beneficiaries who receive both benefits. In the official jargon, these folks are known as *dual eligibles* because they're eligible for both Medicare and Medicaid services.

If you qualify for full Medicaid benefits, you should pay little or nothing for medical care, because Medicaid

- >> Pays your out-of-pocket expenses in Medicare.

- >> Provides more coverage than Medicare does for some services, such as extended stays in skilled nursing facilities.

- >> Pays for certain items that Medicare doesn't cover, such as eyeglasses and hearing aids.

- >> Pays for long-term care in a nursing home, which Medicare doesn't cover.

- >> Qualifies you automatically for free or low-cost prescription drug coverage through Part D's Extra Help program. (I discuss Extra Help later in this chapter.)

REMEMBER

Medicaid is administered by each state, which shares costs with the federal government. (In some states, it goes by a different name — for example, MaineCare in Maine, MassHealth in Massachusetts, and Green Mountain Care in Vermont.) Of course, this setup means that each state has different rules for eligibility. But in general, you need to show all the following to qualify:

>> Your monthly income is under a level set by your state.

>> Your savings and other resources are under a certain value.

>> You live in the state.

>> You're a U.S. citizen or legal resident (green-card holder).

Note that if you are married and living with your spouse, your eligibility for Medicaid is assessed on your joint income. If you are living in somebody else's home (such as with a family member), you may still count as a "household of one" and be assessed on your own income — but only if you aren't married or claimed as a dependent on the tax returns of the householder(s). If they do claim you as a dependent, their income as well as yours is counted, so you probably won't qualify for Medicaid.

Is there red tape? Yes; moving through the eligibility process may take a while. Can you get Medicaid one year and lose it the next? That's possible in some circumstances. Can finding doctors who take Medicaid be harder than finding those who accept other insurance? It happens. The Commonwealth Fund found in 2023 that since the end of the COVID-19 public health emergency, nearly 3.8 million Medicaid beneficiaries lost their health coverage, many because of administrative barriers.

To find out whether you're eligible for Medicaid, contact your local Medicaid office — call Medicare at 800-633-4227 (TTY 877-486-2048) for its phone number — or go to www.medicaid.gov/about-us/beneficiary-resources/index.html, a website that provides information about each state Medicaid program.

If you qualify for Medicaid as well as Medicare, it's worth knowing that some Medicare Advantage plans — known as Special Needs Plans (SNPs) — specifically cater to dual eligibles. SNPs each serve a particular group of people: those with chronic health conditions, like diabetes or heart disease; those in long-term care; and those who are dually eligible for Medicare and Medicaid. The latter plans focus on coordinating Medicare and Medicaid services to help beneficiaries get the most out of both types of benefits. However, these SNPs aren't available everywhere. For more info, turn to Chapter 9.

Medicaid medical spend-down programs

Some states have a system that allows people whose income is above the state limit for Medicaid to become eligible for it when their out-of-pocket medical expenses reach a certain level in a calendar year. This option is called a *medical spend-down* or *medically needy program.*

The states that run these programs have a variety of rules for eligibility, although it's usually granted for only a limited period — for example, six months at a time — after which you may have to start the process all over again. This yo-yo effect happens because when receiving Medicaid, your own medical expenses naturally go down — to a point where you lose eligibility and have to run up more medical bills to qualify again.

Still, if you have Medicaid through one of these programs, most of your out-of-pocket Medicare costs are covered, at least for chunks of time. You also automatically qualify for Extra Help — low-cost Medicare drug coverage that I explain later in this chapter. And after you're in the Extra Help program, you continue to receive its benefits until at least the end of the calendar year, even if your Medicaid coverage runs out earlier.

To find out whether your state has a medical spend-down program, contact your local Medicaid office — call Medicare at 800-633-4227 (TTY 877-486-2048) for its phone number.

Medicare Savings Programs

To be eligible for a Medicare Savings Program (MSP), your income and savings must be below certain limits, which vary according to the state you live in. However, the limits are generally higher than those required to qualify for Medicaid, and some states don't take savings into account at all. So it's well worth applying.

MSPs come in four varieties, each with a different income limit — and each with a name of jumbled letters that only bureaucrats could devise. Here's what each means:

>> **Qualified Medicare Beneficiary (QMB, or "quimby"):** Pays your Part B premiums — and also Part A premiums if you have to pay these — and other Medicare costs such as deductibles and co-pays

>> **Specified Low Income Medicare Beneficiary (SLMB, or "slimby"):** Pays only Part B premiums

>> **Qualifying Individual (QI):** Pays only Part B premiums, with a slightly higher income and resource limit than SLMB

>> **Qualified Disabled and Working Individuals (QDWI):** Pays only Part A premiums for low-income people who have Medicare through disability but are no longer entitled to free Part A coverage because they've returned to work

Qualifying for a Medicare Savings Program — even if it pays only the Part B premium — has another huge advantage: You're automatically entitled to full Extra Help under the Part D prescription drug program, which means very low costs. (I explain the Extra Help program later in this chapter.) Another benefit of qualifying for an MSP is that if you're required to pay a late penalty because you delayed enrolling in Part B beyond your deadline, the state will pay your Part B premium and the penalty will be waived.

To find out whether you're eligible for an MSP, contact your State Health Insurance Assistance Program (SHIP) (see Appendix A). Or reach out to your local Medicaid office — call Medicare at 800-633-4227 (TTY 877-486-2048) for its phone number.

PACE plans

Programs of All-Inclusive Care for the Elderly (PACE) integrate Medicare and Medicaid services and provide valuable benefits at low cost for people who qualify. But they're not available everywhere. In 2024, PACE had more than 70,000 people enrolled in 155 programs nationwide in 32 states and the District of Columbia.

PACE plans help people who'd otherwise need nursing home care to continue to live in their own homes or with their families in the community for as long as possible. They provide comprehensive medical and social services — including home care, day care, physical therapy, dentistry, meals, social work counseling, transportation, and many other services. They also provide hospital and nursing home care if you need it.

You can't choose your own doctors in a PACE plan. Instead, you're assigned a primary-care physician who is one of a team of healthcare professionals working with you and your family to help maintain your overall health. The team also provides support for your caregivers. PACE services include drug coverage, so you don't have to join a separate Part D prescription drug plan.

REMEMBER

You can join a PACE plan if the following are true:

>> You're 55 or older.

>> You're certified by your state as being eligible for a nursing home level of care after an assessment by the PACE plan's care team.

>> A program serves the area where you live and is accepting new enrollees.

>> You're enrolled in Medicare, Medicaid, or both.

>> You're able to live safely in the community with the help of PACE.

PACE charges no deductibles or co-payments for any service, care, or prescription drug approved by your care team. Other costs depend on your situation:

>> If you qualify for Medicaid, you pay a small monthly payment — and nothing for long-term care if you need it. The PACE plan determines the amount of the payment.

>> If you don't qualify for Medicaid, you pay a monthly premium to cover the long-term-care part of the PACE benefit and also a monthly premium for Medicare Part D drugs, in each case paying what the plan requires.

REMEMBER

If you qualify for an available PACE, you can join it at any time. If you're enrolled in Medicare, you get a special enrollment period to leave original Medicare or a Medicare Advantage private health plan to join the program. (You can't be in either of these programs at the same time as being enrolled in a PACE.) Also, you can leave a PACE any time you want to switch to original Medicare or to a Medicare Advantage plan.

To find out whether a PACE exists in your area, call Medicare at 800-633-4227 (TTY 877-486-2048), or go to www.npaonline.org/find-a-pace-program and enter your zip code or state. If a program is available and you're interested in joining it, contact the plan to arrange a home visit with you or your caregiver or a visit to the PACE center. The plan will schedule a meeting between you and its care team for a medical and social assessment that determines your eligibility for the program. For more on how PACE plans work, go to the National PACE Association's website at https://www.npaonline.org/.

State Pharmacy Assistance Programs

Forty-three states, the District of Columbia, Puerto Rico, and the U.S. Virgin Islands have State Pharmacy (or Pharmaceutical) Assistance Programs (SPAPs). All help people pay for prescription drugs if their incomes are limited but too high to qualify for Medicaid. Some SPAPs have income limits above the maximums set by Medicare Part D's Extra Help program (which I explain in the following section) and/or no *asset tests* (meaning that your savings and other resources may not be counted).

Benefits vary a great deal among these programs. Some provide a range of services that wrap around Extra Help and assist many Part D enrollees who don't qualify for Extra Help. Some help patients with a particular medical condition (such as cancer) or offer discount cards to use at pharmacies.

To see whether your state has an SPAP and, if so, details on how to qualify and apply, go to www.medicare.gov/pharmaceutical-assistance-program/state-programs.aspx. You also can call Medicare at 800-633-4227 (TTY 877-486-2048) and ask for a brochure to be mailed to you.

Examining Whether Extra Help Can Lower Your Drug Costs

Filling prescriptions may be your biggest medical expense if you take a lot of drugs or a few hugely expensive ones. The Part D prescription drug program (introduced in Chapters 1 and 2) helps up to a point, but its premiums, deductibles, and co-pays — not to mention the higher costs of the doughnut hole, if you fall into it — add up to outlays of cash that many people just can't afford. (As I explain in Chapters 2 and 14, the *doughnut hole* generally requires you to pay more out-of-pocket for your prescriptions after the total cost of your drugs exceeds a certain dollar amount and before you reach catastrophic coverage.)

That's where *Extra Help* comes in. This special program within Part D provides low-cost drug coverage — and even does away with the doughnut hole altogether! — for people with incomes and savings under a certain level.

Millions of people in Medicare have been able to save many hundreds or even thousands of dollars per year on their drug bills because of the Extra Help program. Even more crucially, Extra Help has allowed many folks who didn't previously have any drug coverage to fill all the prescriptions they need for the first time. This benefit is truly valuable.

REMEMBER

In this section, I explain the mechanics of Extra Help — how it works and how you can apply for it. But first, here's a list of the main points you need to know about the program:

>> If you were receiving Medicaid before joining Medicare, you'll now get your drug coverage from Part D's Extra Help program and not from Medicaid — even if you continue to qualify for Medicaid.

>> If you have full Medicaid coverage or Supplemental Security Income (SSI — a federal financial assistance program run by Social Security), if your state pays your Medicare premiums, or if you qualify for a Medicaid medical spend-down

program, you qualify automatically for *Extra Help* (lowest-cost drug coverage). Medicare will send you a letter (in a purple envelope) confirming that you don't need to apply. Otherwise, you do need to apply.

>> Extra Help is easier to apply for than many assistance programs, but you have to provide details of your income and assets or resources (which mainly means your savings).

>> Everybody, whether qualifying for full or partial assistance, gets full drug coverage throughout the year. Nobody receiving Extra Help has to face the dreaded doughnut hole.

>> Anybody with Extra Help can switch to a different Part D drug plan throughout the year — no waiting until open enrollment rolls around.

>> Getting Extra Help doesn't affect your eligibility for SSI or assistance that pays the costs of heating or cooling your home. Food stamps and subsidized housing may be reduced, but the money Extra Help saves should outweigh what you lose.

>> Be aware that qualifying for Extra Help, even automatically, is only one step in the process. You still have to enroll in a Part D drug plan to get your prescriptions covered. You can sign up with a plan of your own choosing — but if you don't, Medicare will pick one and enroll you in it, even though that plan may not be ideal for you. (For details on choosing a plan, see the later section "Choosing a drug plan with Extra Help" and Chapters 10, 11, and 12.)

Qualifying for Extra Help

Extra Help has five levels of eligibility. The first three levels take only your income into account. But all three depend on your having already qualified for other assistance programs, which is why you automatically qualify for Extra Help, too. In that case, you receive a letter from Medicare confirming it. But at levels four and five, you must apply by filling out a form that asks questions about your income and assets — mainly savings. After reviewing your application, the Social Security Administration will send a letter saying whether you can receive Extra Help.

The following shows how you qualify for Extra Help and what you'd pay for drug coverage at each level in 2024:

>> **Level one: You have full Medicaid benefits and live in an institution, such as a nursing home.** You qualify for Extra Help automatically, paying no premium or deductible and nothing for your medications.

>> **Level two: You have full Medicaid coverage and you have home- and community-based services.** You qualify for Extra Help automatically, paying no premium or deductible and nothing for your medications.

>> **Level three: You have full Medicaid benefits and yearly income no higher than $22,590 ($30,660 for couples).** You qualify for Extra Help automatically. You pay no premium or annual deductible. You pay $4.50 for *generic* drugs (copies of brand-name drugs) or $11.20 for brand-name drugs per prescription.

>> **Level four: You have full Medicaid benefits and your income is above $22,590 ($30,660 for couples); or you receive SSI; or your state pays your Medicare premiums.** You qualify for Extra Help automatically. You pay no premium or annual deductible. You pay co-pays of $4.50 for generics or $11.20 for brand-name per prescription.

>> **Level five: Your income is no higher than $22,590 ($30,660 for couples) and your savings are under $17,220 ($34,360 for couples).** You qualify for Extra Help but must apply for it. You pay no premium or annual deductible. You pay $4.50 (generics) or $11.20 (brand names) per prescription.

The dollar amounts shown here apply to income and asset limits in 2024. The amounts go up a little each year. The dollar amounts for co-pays also go up slightly each year. You can find out the amounts for later years by calling Social Security (800-772-1213 or TTY 800-325-0778) or by looking at Section 3 of the booklet "Your Guide to Medicare Drug Coverage" at `www.medicare.gov/ publications/11109-Medicare-Drug-Coverage-Guide.pdf`.

TIP

So are you looking at those income limits and figuring that yours just misses the boat? Here's some important advice: Apply anyway! The limits are higher in some circumstances than those shown in the preceding list — for example, if you have some earnings from work that aren't counted, or live in Alaska or Hawaii, or have dependent relatives living with you.

Applying for Extra Help

Perhaps your income and resources are limited but you're not enrolled in one of the programs that qualify you for Extra Help automatically. In this case, you need to apply for Extra Help. You can apply at any time — when you first join Medicare, when you experience some change in your life that lowers your income, or if you're already enrolled in Part D and have only just realized that Extra Help exists.

Applying involves filling out a form and sending it to the Social Security Administration (not Medicare), which then decides whether you qualify. The following sections provide answers to questions people often ask about this process.

How can I obtain the form?

Use one of the following methods to get the application form:

>> **Online:** You can fill out and file the form online on the Social Security site at secure.ssa.gov/i1020/start. You can use this site to apply directly online, but only in English. You can print this form to fill out as a practice run before you make the proper online application, but you can't mail in that hard copy in lieu of applying online. Full instructions are also on this site.

>> **By phone:** Call Social Security toll-free at 800-772-1213 (TTY 800-325-0778) and ask to have the form (in English or in Spanish) sent to you.

>> **In person:** You can get a form (and help filling it out if you need it) at your local Social Security office or State Health Insurance Assistance Program (SHIP) office. To call your SHIP, flip to the contact info in Appendix A.

What if English isn't my first language?

The application can be filled out only in English or Spanish, but detailed instructions are available in 13 languages besides English: American Sign Language, Arabic, Chinese, Farsi, French, Greek, Italian, Korean, Polish, Portuguese, Russian, Spanish, and Vietnamese. You can find these directions online at www.socialsecurity.gov/multilanguage. Click on the name of the language you speak and then choose the Extra Help information. You can also get help from your SHIP by requesting to speak to a counselor who speaks your own first language, as explained in Appendix A.

What counts as income?

You should include on the form any of these that apply to you:

>> Pre-tax wages or earnings from self-employment

>> Social Security or railroad retirement benefits before deductions

>> Veterans' benefits

>> Pensions and annuities

>> Workers' compensation

>> Alimony

>> Net income from rental property

You can leave out

>> Cash or credit from a loan or a reverse mortgage

>> Federal income tax refunds and earned income tax credit payments

>> Victims' compensation

>> Education grants and scholarships

>> Help from food stamps, a housing agency, an energy assistance program, or a public relocation program

>> Help from anyone who contributes toward your food, mortgage, rent, heating fuel, gas, electricity, water, and property taxes

>> Help paying for medical treatment and drugs

>> Disaster assistance

What counts as assets?

Assets, also called *resources*, are the value of certain things you own, mainly savings. You should include any of these that you have:

>> Bank accounts, including checking, savings, and certificates of deposit

>> Proceeds of a loan if saved beyond the month they're received

>> Cash kept at home or anywhere else

>> Individual retirement accounts (IRAs) and 401(k)s

>> Stocks and bonds

>> Mutual funds

>> Real estate (other than your primary home)

You can leave out

>> Your primary home and the land it stands on

>> Your vehicle(s)

>> Personal possessions, including jewelry and furnishings

>> Property you need for self-support, such as land used to grow your own food

>> Burial plots

>> Life insurance policies

REMEMBER

Social Security rules for Extra Help don't prevent you from spending down or giving away some of your savings to reduce them below the asset limit. Only what you have during the month you apply is counted. However, keep in mind that gifts or spending down may affect your eligibility for other assistance programs — especially Medicaid, which has strict rules about this subject — if you find you need them within a few years.

What counts as "single" and "married" for income purposes?

Income levels are for either single people or married couples "who are living together," regardless of whether they are opposite-sex or same-sex spouses. If you're married and living with your spouse, you can both apply on the same form. If only one of you is applying, you still have to provide info on your spouse's income and assets. You count as single if you're married but living apart; your spouse is living permanently in a nursing home or another type of long-term care; or you have a domestic partner. However, if you're in a common-law marriage, check with Social Security because being recognized as single or married may depend on the laws of your state.

What if I'm supporting other family members?

If any relatives — related to you by blood, marriage, or adoption — live with you and depend on you (or your spouse) for at least half of their support, be sure to answer the question on family size. Every extra person raises the income limits and increases your chances of qualifying for Extra Help.

Who can help me apply?

TIP

Many circumstances — like being sick or recently widowed, to name just two — may make you feel that dealing with this application on your own is beyond you at this time. In that case, don't hesitate to get help. Many people can lend you a hand in applying:

>> **Someone you know:** Anybody can help you fill out the application or even apply on your behalf — a family member, a friend, a legal representative, a social worker, or anyone you choose to act for you.

>> **Free, expert personal help:** Counselors at your SHIP are trained to help people sort through their Part D options, including helping them apply for Extra Help. For the number of your SHIP, see Appendix A.

>> **Social Security:** If you need help on how to answer specific questions, call Social Security at 800-772-1213 (TTY 800-325-0778) or visit your local Social Security office.

>> **Community groups:** You may be a member of a house of worship, senior center, or other community group that can assist you in filling out the form. If English isn't your first language, an organization or group for people of your own nationality may be especially helpful in this regard. (Head to Appendix A for non-English sources of help.)

How do I complete the application process?

You sign the form, which means that you're legally declaring that all the information you've provided is true to the best of your knowledge. If you're married and living together, your spouse must also sign it, even if they aren't applying for Extra Help. If someone else signs for you, that person should fill out the section of the form that asks for their name, address, and personal or professional relationship to you. Then you can submit the form by

>> **Using the printed application form:** Just put it in the pre-addressed envelope and mail it in. If the envelope is missing or lost, send the form to the Social Security Administration, Wilkes-Barre Data Operation Center, P.O. Box 1020, Wilkes-Barre, PA 18767.

>> **Applying to Social Security online:** The online instructions on the Social Security website (at secure.ssa.gov/i1020/start) tell you exactly what to do. You must answer all the questions before signing the form electronically and submitting it.

What happens after I apply?

So you've sent in your application and crossed your fingers, waiting for a decision. What's next?

>> **Social Security sends you a notice saying it has received your application and is processing it.** If you don't get this notice within a couple of weeks of applying, call Social Security at 800-772-1213 (TTY 800-325-0778) to check what's going on.

>> **You may hear from Social Security by phone or mail if it has additional questions.** The agency will contact you if your application is incomplete or if some of your financial information doesn't match other government records.

>> **You may receive a *pre-decisional notice* saying your application is likely to be turned down.** This document specifies what information on your application will cause you to be denied Extra Help — for example, that your income or assets are above the limits. If that information is wrong, this notice gives you the opportunity to correct it. You must do so within ten days of the date

of the notice by calling or visiting your local Social Security office at the number or address given on the notice.

>> **Social Security decides whether you're eligible for Extra Help.** You should hear within 60 days of Social Security's receiving your application — maybe sooner. You'll receive either a "Notice of Award" saying that you qualify for either full or partial Extra Help or a "Notice of Denial" saying that you don't qualify. The denial notice contains full instructions on how to appeal the decision if you don't agree with it.

What if Social Security turns me down?

You can always appeal Social Security's decision if you don't agree with it. You must appeal within 60 days of receiving a decision, in one of two ways:

>> **Request a telephone hearing.** Call your local Social Security office or the national number (800-772-1213 or TTY 800-325-0778) and ask to be sent an appeal request form. Fill it out and mail it in. You'll receive a letter confirming the date of your hearing and the number to call. (You can ask for a conference call if you want someone else on the phone to help you.) The letter also explains how to send in any documents that support your case.

>> **Ask for a case review.** A *case review* means a Social Security agent reviews your application and any additional information you've sent in, but you can't present your case in person.

After Social Security has reviewed your appeal, you receive a letter notifying you of the decision. If you win, you receive Extra Help backdated to the first day of the month in which you originally applied for the benefit. If you lose but still disagree with the decision, you can file a further appeal in a federal court (as explained in Chapter 16) within 60 days of receiving the letter.

If you're denied Extra Help this time, don't let it put you off reapplying, especially if your income or assets weren't far over the limits. Keep in mind that the limits rise slightly each year, and even a small dip in your own finances may allow you to qualify through a new application.

If I qualify, how long does my Extra Help last?

In most cases, you continue to receive Extra Help until the end of the year, regardless of whether your financial circumstances have changed during the previous 12 months. But continuing to get Extra Help next year, starting January 1, depends on whether you've become financially better off this year. You can lose Extra Help (or receive a reduced benefit) next year if

>> Your income rises above the limits for Extra Help

>> The value of your savings and other countable assets rises above the asset limits for Extra Help

>> You cease to qualify for one of the programs that makes you automatically eligible for Extra Help — Medicaid, SSI, having your premiums paid by your state, or being in a Medicaid spend-down program

Also, if any of the following marital events occur during the year, you're expected to report them immediately so your eligibility for Extra Help can be reviewed:

>> Your spouse dies.

>> You and the spouse you've been living with start living apart, divorce, or have your marriage annulled.

>> You and your spouse start living together again after being apart.

>> You get married.

If any of these events happens to you, call Social Security (800-772-1213 or TTY 800-325-0778) to report it. You're asked to complete a redetermination form on the phone, at your local Social Security office, or by mail. If you do so within 90 days of filing the report, Social Security decides whether to end your Extra Help or leave it unchanged. Any change takes place the month following the month in which you filed the report. But if you don't complete the required form within 90 days, your Extra Help is terminated.

How do I know whether my Extra Help will continue?

What will happen next year, and how you find out, depends on how you qualified for Extra Help in the first place, as follows:

>> **If you qualified for Extra Help automatically:** If nothing has changed, you don't need to do anything. You'll continue to get Extra Help. But if you no longer get help from Medicaid or SSI or have your premiums paid by your state, Medicare will send you a notice on gray paper saying that you no longer automatically qualify for Extra Help but can still apply for it.

>> **If you qualified for Extra Help through a Medicaid medical spend-down program:** If your medical expenses this year have been high enough to keep you on Medicaid at the end of the year, you'll still get Extra Help next year. But if those expenses are no longer high enough to qualify you for Medicaid, you'll probably get a letter saying that your Extra Help benefits stop as of January 1.

The timing can make a difference here. If your name is still in the system in July, when Medicare compiles its list of people automatically eligible for Extra Help next year, you continue to receive benefits for all next year.

>> **If you qualified for Extra Help by applying:** In August or September, you may get a letter from Social Security asking whether your financial circumstances have changed. If so, you must fill out the form and return it within 30 days. If you don't return it, your Extra Help ends on December 31. Social Security reviews your information and lets you know whether you still qualify for Extra Help next year and, if so, whether your benefits will change. For example, if your income has gone down, you may get lower co-pays next year — or, if it has risen above a certain level, you may get partial rather than full Extra Help. Any changes begin on January 1.

Choosing a drug plan with Extra Help

Qualifying and applying for Extra Help is just one step in the process. You still have to be in a Medicare Part D drug plan to get coverage for your drugs. Just like anybody else, you have the right to enroll in a Medicare drug plan of your own choosing. And you should do so by comparing plans carefully according to the drugs you take. (I explain the details of how to make this comparison in Chapters 10 and 11.) But you need to be aware of two rules that are specific to Extra Help enrollment, so that they don't catch you off guard.

Understanding the automatic enrollment system

If you qualify for Extra Help automatically and don't immediately sign up with a plan on your own, Medicare enrolls you in one to make sure you continue to get your medications, especially if you're being moved from Medicaid to Medicare for your drug coverage.

WARNING

However, Medicare enrolls Extra Help people in plans at random. This system is the computerized version of taking your name out of a hat and matching it to the name of a plan taken out of another hat. In other words, Medicare makes no effort to put you into a plan that suits your needs or even to ensure that the plan you're assigned to covers your drugs. So you may find yourself in a plan that's not ideal for you unless you take action and choose a plan for yourself. Having Extra Help allows you to switch to another plan whenever you want to.

If Medicare automatically signs you up with a plan (a process officially called *facilitated enrollment*), it informs you in a notice printed on green paper. The notice contains the name and contact information for the plan, plus a list of other plans in your area that you can enroll in if you want to.

Clarifying zero premiums

Earlier in this chapter, I say that with full Extra Help, you don't have to pay a premium for your coverage. However, that statement comes with a catch: The premium is waived only if you join a drug plan that charges regular premiums below a certain dollar amount.

Under Medicare rules, you don't pay a premium if you're in a plan with a premium that's below the average of all plan premiums in your region in any given year. But if you join a more expensive plan, you have to pay the difference between the average premium and the full premium. For example, if the average monthly premium in your region is $30, and the premium in the plan you join is $37, you pay $7 each month for your drug coverage.

This regional average (which bureaucrats call the *benchmark*) changes every year. That's why each fall Medicare sends letters to some Extra Help beneficiaries, warning them that if they stay in their current plan for the following year, they'll no longer be able to claim zero premiums. Or, in some cases, the letter says they've been switched *(reassigned)* to another plan that has zero premiums. Therefore, be sure to read any notices printed on blue paper that come from Medicare or your plan during the fall, so you're not caught in January having to pay a premium you didn't expect.

TIP

How do you know which plans in your area give you a zero premium and which don't in any given year? These plans and their phone numbers are included in the blue notice Medicare sends you. But to be certain of what you'd pay for each of your drugs, according to your Extra Help co-pays, you have three options:

>> **Use Medicare's online plan finder program.** I describe how this program works generally in Chapters 10 and 11. But here's how to find details that are specific to Extra Help:

1. **Go to** www.medicare.gov, **and click on "Find health & drug plans."**

   Here, you're prompted to either log in, create an account, or continue without logging in. Then you have to answer a quick question about the type of 2024 Medicare coverage you want; select "Drug plan (Part D)." You're prompted to enter your zip code and confirm your county.

2. **You see a screen that asks a question.**

   Here you're asked: "Do you get help with your costs from one of these programs?" Options include Medicaid, SSI, MSP, Extra Help from Social Security, "I'm not sure," or "I don't get help from any of these programs." Because this section is about Extra Help, choose "Extra Help from Social Security."

3. **Enter your search preferences.**

First you're asked, "Do you want to see your drug costs when you compare plans?" Click yes or no. You're then asked, "How do you normally fill your prescriptions?" Select "Retail pharmacy," "Mail order pharmacy," or "Both." Click "Next."

Here you begin adding your prescription drugs. Enter information about your first drug and click "Add Drug." If a generic version is available, a window appears that describes your drug and the lower-cost generic version's name, as well as asks you whether you would like to add the generic to the list. Either click "Add Generic" or "Add brand instead."

You then need to identify your dosage, quantity, and frequency. Then click on "Add to My Drug List." Continue to add your drug information until you're finished and click "Done Adding Drugs."

Next, a list of pharmacies appears. Select three pharmacies from which to compare drug prices and click "Done." You can also select "Mail-order Pharmacy" from the top of the list if you prefer to order your prescriptions by mail.

4. **As of 2024, plans are sorted by "lowest drug + premium cost" to show plans with the lowest estimated total cost for your drugs and plan premiums first.**

You can change the sort order at any time.

The plan finder shows your costs under each plan in your area. If you see "$0.00" for the premium, it means this plan is below the regional average and you pay nothing. If you see a dollar amount, that amount is what you need to pay — the difference between the regional average and the full premium, as explained earlier in this section.

Note: You must be logged in with an account to see the co-pays reflect the amount you pay with Extra Help. If you use only the general plan search without logging in, you will see the co-pays for a member without Extra Help. But if you see a $0.00 co-pay, it means that the plan regularly charges nothing for this drug, so you wouldn't pay anything either.

» **Call Medicare's help line (800-633-4227 or TTY 877-486-2048).** Tell the customer service representative that you qualify for Extra Help and want to compare Part D plans in your area. Give the rep a list of the drugs you take (name, dosage, and how often you take them), and ask for a search of the plan finder. You can ask to have the results mailed to you.

» **Call your State Health Insurance Assistance Program (SHIP).** Talk with a SHIP counselor who can give you free personal help in choosing a Part D drug plan that meets your needs according to your level of Extra Help benefits. Find the number of your SHIP in Appendix A.

Considering Other Ways to Cut Costs

Medigap supplemental insurance, Medicaid programs, and Extra Help can save a lot of out-of-pocket expenses in Medicare. But not everybody qualifies for Medicaid and Extra Help, and not everybody can afford Medigap or wants to be in a Medicare Advantage plan. The following sections show you some of the other options available.

Taking income tax deductions for Medicare costs

This strategy is a possibility that many people never consider, but it's legitimate: You can deduct the costs of healthcare (including those incurred in Medicare) from federal income tax as an authorized medical expense if you file an itemized Schedule A (Form 1040) tax return.

Of course, you have to meet IRS rules. And the important one is that you can deduct only those expenses that exceed 7.5 percent of your adjusted gross income (AGI). (*AGI* is the amount of income on which you can be taxed after certain allowed deductions have been taken out.) So it's a tax break that generally favors people with high healthcare costs and limited incomes over people who are in good health and well off.

Here's an example: Say your AGI is $30,000. Of that, 7.5 percent is $2,250. If your total allowable medical expenses for the year are, oh, $4,000, you can deduct $1,750 ($4,000 minus $2,250). Here's a different example: Say your AGI is $60,000 and your total allowable medical expenses are $3,000. Because the $3,000 is only 5 percent of your AGI, you can't deduct any of it.

TIP

The list of allowable medical expenses, as defined by the IRS, is surprisingly long. It even covers some you wouldn't expect — such as the cost of traveling to get medical care and the cost of altering your home or installing special equipment for medical reasons. For a complete list, see IRS Publication 502, "Medical and Dental Expenses," at www.irs.gov/publications/p502/index.html and search for the keywords "what medical expenses are includible." You can also find Chapter 4 of Publication 554, "Tax Guide for Seniors," through a search at www.irs.gov/publications/p554/ch04.html.

As a Medicare beneficiary, the specific items you can count include the following:

>> Premiums for Part A (if applicable), Part B, Part D drug plans, Medicare Advantage plans, Medigap insurance, and in some circumstances, long-term-care insurance

>> Out-of-pocket deductibles and co-payments for Medicare services

>> Amounts you pay out-of-pocket for prescription drugs, including those in the Part D doughnut hole and those your plan doesn't cover

>> Amounts you pay for services that Medicare doesn't cover, such as hearing aids, eyeglasses, dental treatment, nursing home care, and so on

>> Wages or the costs of private nursing care, in your own home or another care facility

>> Cost of altering your home for medical reasons or installing safety equipment

Costs you can't count include

>> Premiums for employer-sponsored group health insurance that are paid out of pre-tax dollars

>> Payments for services made by an insurer or any other source

>> Expenses that have been paid out of a health savings account or an Archer medical savings account

>> Late penalties added to Part B or Part D premiums

>> Surgery or other treatments for cosmetic reasons

>> Expenses for your general health — even if recommended by a doctor — such as health club dues, costs of activities like swimming, and costs of hiring household help

>> Non-prescription medications, vitamins, and supplements

>> Medications brought or ordered from outside of the United States

Lowering drug costs without Extra Help

In many cases — though not all, admittedly — you can reduce the costs of prescription drugs without assistance from Extra Help or your state. In the following sections, I highlight practical ways to save money (that may also serve to stretch your Part D drug coverage so that it lasts longer), starting with one that may surprise you.

Taking a hard look at your meds

Think about all the medications you take. Do you really need them all? It's a question well worth asking because many people are being overprescribed without realizing it. In a health system where you can see many different doctors with little or no coordination among them, taking more meds than you need is quite easy. Your primary-care physician may prescribe two or three drugs, and various specialists may prescribe more.

REMEMBER

This drug review isn't just a matter of cost. Some drug combinations can work against each other in complex and subtle ways that harm your health. Sometimes you may develop new symptoms that are actually side effects of one of the drugs you're already taking. But without realizing that, you go back to your primary-care doctor, who often, yes, prescribes more pills.

REMEMBER

Don't think I'm suggesting that you stop any drugs or lose faith in your doctor. Far from it. But make sure that all your meds are necessary and safe when used together. If some aren't, cutting back can save you money *and* protect your health.

Put all the meds you're taking — not just prescription drugs but also over-the-counter medicines, vitamins, herbal remedies, and supplements — into a bag, take it to your doctor or a pharmacist, and ask for a review. Ask specifically about each med: Do I still need it? Is it safe to take with others I'm taking? Is it appropriate for people my age? Keeping a list of your drugs and their dosages in your wallet is also a good idea so you can show it to any doctor who prescribes a new medicine for you. (If you're in a Part D plan, you may qualify for a free benefit called Medication Therapy Management that essentially does all this and maybe more. Flip to Chapter 14 for details.)

Switching to less-expensive drugs

One way to lower expenses dramatically is to switch to less-expensive drugs that work equally well for your medical conditions, if you have that option. The newest brand-name drugs — often the ones that doctors like to prescribe — are almost always the most expensive. Sometimes hugely expensive. But a fancy new drug may have an alternative version that's just as good but much less pricey: either a generic or an *older brand-name* (a drug that may be less convenient than a new one — for example, it may require you to take two or three pills per day rather than one — but still does exactly the same job medically).

Changing to a lower-cost drug means that you stretch your Part D coverage in two ways:

» It reduces the total cost of your drugs in the initial coverage period so that you stave off the doughnut hole or avoid it altogether.

» Part D plans usually charge much lower co-pays for generics — in some cases nothing at all — and for older drugs. So if you have this option, it's a win-win.

Ask your doctor whether a generic or older drug would work just as well for you as the brand-name one you're taking.

Switching to a less-expensive Part D drug plan

The vast majority of people in Part D could save a lot of money if they'd choose another drug plan, studies show. That's mainly because co-pays vary enormously among different plans, even for the same drug. Carefully compare the plans available to you according to the specific drugs you take, *every year,* as explained in Chapter 15.

Using mail order or preferred pharmacies

Many Part D plans offer the option of purchasing 90-day supplies of drugs through their mail-order service, often with reduced co-pays. Be careful, though: In some cases, your drugs may be slightly more expensive when bought in this way, so check with the plan first according to the specific drugs you take.

Your Part D plan may offer reduced co-pays if you buy your drugs at a "preferred" pharmacy instead of a standard or regular pharmacy in its network. For example, a plan's co-pay for a drug may be $45 at a standard pharmacy, but $35 at a preferred pharmacy with which the plan has a special arrangement. Not all plans provide this option. If yours does, you can ask the plan for a list of preferred pharmacies in your area or use the plan finder on Medicare's website, as explained in Chapter 10.

Note: This information on mail-order service or preferred pharmacies applies equally to stand-alone Part D plans and to Medicare Advantage plans that include Part D prescription drug coverage in their benefit packages.

Finding free or low-cost prescription drugs

Sometimes, even with Part D coverage, some prescribed drugs are just not affordable, especially if you go into the coverage gap. Even if you're not yet in the gap, you may not be able to afford the co-pays — usually a percentage of the price — that plans charge for the most expensive drugs, such as those used for organ transplants and some cancers. What then? Unfortunately, I can't give you a good answer. But the following possibilities are worth checking out:

>> **Supplies from the manufacturers:** Some drug manufacturers' patient assistance programs offer free or reduced-cost supplies of their brand-name products to people in Part D in some circumstances (such as being in the coverage gap). For details, go to medicineassistancetool.org/.

>> **Certified charities and patient organizations:** You may be able to get help from one of these sources, which usually specialize in one specific medical condition. To find out, go to www.benefitscheckup.org.

WARNING

>> **Low-cost drugs from abroad:** If you obtain drugs from abroad by mail order, you must be careful. The internet is Wild West territory, full of scams for the unwary. So you need to pick a licensed pharmacy with a reputation for good, ethical service. One safeguard is to use pharmacies that are prescreened by bona fide organizations (such as www.pharmacychecker.com) or that earn professional accreditation (such as those listed on www.cipa.com).

>> **Free samples from your doctor:** Most doctors receive drug samples from the manufacturers to pass on to patients, so don't be shy about asking.

>> **Pharmacy discounts:** Many pharmacies sell selected drugs at very low cost — often $4 per prescription. Drug manufacturers also offer similar prices with discount cards used through pharmacies. Most of these services can't be used if you're in a government program, such as Part D. But pharmacies do often offer other discounts — inside and outside Part D plans — that may be worth using.

2

The Hows and Whens of Medicare

Find out how you qualify for Medicare; the rules on eligibility provide more possibilities than you may think.

Discover when to enroll in Medicare. Determine the right time to sign up according to your own circumstances, and see how missing your enrollment deadline can cost you permanent late penalties and delays in coverage.

Get a handle on the actual mechanics of enrollment, which depend on your situation, such as whether you'll be enrolled automatically or need to apply, whether you live in the United States or abroad, whether you can delay enrollment without risking late penalties, and when your coverage will begin.

Understand how Medicare fits in with other health insurance you may have, including coverage from a current or former employer, the Federal Employees Health Benefits Program, the Veterans Affairs health program, the military's TRICARE programs, the Indian Health Service, the federal Black Lung Program, the Workers' Compensation program, and no-fault and liability insurance.

Chapter **5**

Qualifying for Medicare

Q ualifying for Medicare and being eligible for Medicare essentially mean the same thing: You've passed a legal hurdle that allows you to receive Medicare benefits. Don't worry; you don't have to take a test to qualify for Medicare. You don't have to go before a judge or take part in some formal cere-mony. But you do have to meet certain conditions required by law.

Very broadly, you must meet one of two conditions:

» You've reached your 65th birthday (or will reach it very soon) or are older than 65.

» You're under 65 but have a disability that is officially recognized and meets the requirements for Medicare coverage.

Within these two categories are several other conditions that may or may not affect you, depending on your specific circumstances. All are explained in detail in this chapter. You also find out about the options for healthcare if you don't imme-diately qualify for Medicare at 65, are a few years short of 65, or are stuck in that two-year limbo in which most people who are under 65 and disabled must wait for Medicare coverage.

Note: If you know for a fact that you qualify for Medicare or soon will, you may want to skip this chapter and go straight to the ins and outs of signing up, which are explained in Chapter 6. But if you're the least unsure about your eligibility, this chapter is required reading because your chances of qualifying for at least some Medicare benefits may be a lot higher than you think.

Hitting the Milestone of Age 65

This birthday is a big milestone. Maybe it feels more like a quantum leap than a puny mile. (Where did all the time go, anyway?) But whatever else it may mean for the generation of baby boomers whose mantra was once "Don't trust anyone over 30," turning 65 comes with a valuable birthday present. For most people, it's their passport to guaranteed health coverage under Medicare.

Still, nobody qualifies for Medicare just by reaching 65. You also have to meet certain other conditions, according to your circumstances, which are explained in the following sections. Some misconceptions about Medicare qualification are also clarified.

Debunking some qualification myths

REMEMBER

Let's be very clear about what "qualifying for Medicare" actually means. Many people think that if they haven't paid into the system by paying enough payroll taxes while working, they're not eligible for any Medicare benefits. But that's not true. Those payroll taxes cover only Part A premiums; in other words, they allow you to get Part A services without paying monthly premiums for them. But even if you're not entitled to premium-free Part A, you can still get Part B and Part D services by paying premiums for them just like everybody else. (See Chapter 1 for descriptions of Parts A, B, and D.)

And even if you haven't worked long enough to get premium-free Part A, you may be able to qualify on the work record of your spouse (current, divorced, or deceased). Otherwise, you may have the option to receive Part A benefits by paying monthly premiums for them.

REMEMBER

Let's also be clear about a few other points that often confuse people:

>> The law doesn't force you to take Medicare Part B (which requires monthly premiums) at 65 or any other age. If you want to sidestep it completely, that's up to you. (However, if you change your mind later on, after your enrollment deadline has passed, you'll face costly consequences such as late penalties.)

>> You can enroll in Medicare at age 65 or later even if you haven't begun receiving Social Security or railroad retirement benefits.

>> You can delay enrolling in Part B beyond age 65 — without incurring late penalties — for as long as you're covered by health insurance provided by an employer for whom you or your spouse is actively working, provided that the employer has 20 or more employees.

These points are really enrollment issues, which are explained in detail in Chapter 6. But I feel it's necessary to emphasize them here too because so much guidance written about Medicare eligibility gives the impression that all people are obliged to sign up as soon as they hit 65, which isn't necessarily so. That said, the following sections focus on qualifying for Medicare at age 65 even if you don't enroll at that time.

Meeting the requirements for Parts A, B, and D

As you may expect, the different parts of Medicare come with different rules for eligibility, as well as for coverage and costs. The following sections include checklists of the conditions you need to meet to qualify for *Part A* (hospital insurance), *Part B* (medical insurance), and *Part D* (prescription drug coverage) at age 65. (Find more detail on qualifying for Part A, either on your own work record or someone else's, later in this chapter.)

Even if you don't qualify for premium-free Part A, you may still be eligible for Part B and Part D coverage at age 65; therefore, if you don't sign up for them at the right time, you may set yourself up for permanent late penalties, as explained in Chapter 6.

Part A

You qualify to receive Part A benefits (without paying premiums for them) at age 65 or older if you're a U.S. citizen or permanent legal resident (green-card holder) and at least one of the following is also true:

>> You've earned 40 credits through paying payroll taxes at work, which makes you eligible for Social Security or railroad retirement benefits — flip to the later section "Qualifying for Part A on your own work record" for details on work record requirements — even if you're not yet receiving retirement benefits.

>> You qualify on the work record of your current spouse (or, in some circumstances, your divorced or deceased spouse), as explained in the later section "Being eligible for Part A on someone else's work record."

You qualify to receive Part A benefits *without* 40 work credits at age 65 or older if you're a U.S. citizen or legal resident who has lived in the United States for at least five years before applying for Medicare, you enroll in Part A and Part B (see the next section), and one of the following applies to you:

>> You have 0 to 29 work credits and pay the full Part A premium ($505 a month in 2024).

>> You or your spouse has 30 to 39 work credits, and you pay the partial Part A premium ($278 a month in 2024).

Part B

You can receive Part B benefits at age 65 or older if you're a U.S. citizen or a legal resident (green-card holder) who has lived in the United States for at least five years, you're enrolled in Part B, and one of the following is true:

>> You pay a monthly premium — either the standard Part B premium ($174.70 a month in 2024) or more if your income is high enough to require a surcharge (as explained in Chapter 3).

>> Your Part B premium is paid by your state (as explained in Chapter 4).

Part D

You can receive Part D benefits at age 65 or older if you're enrolled in Part A or Part B, or both; you enroll in a stand-alone Part D drug plan or a Medicare Advantage plan that provides Medicare prescription drug coverage; and one of the following applies to you:

>> You pay the monthly premium that your plan requires.

>> Your Part D plan premium is paid by the Extra Help program or a State Pharmacy Assistance Program (as explained in Chapter 4).

Qualifying for Part A on your own work record

You need to earn 40 work credits — sometimes called *quarters of coverage* — before becoming eligible for premium-free Part A benefits at age 65 or over or to qualify for Social Security retirement benefits. Here's how credits are calculated:

>> Work credits are calculated on income that you work for and that's taxable — that is, earnings on which you pay Social Security and Medicare payroll taxes. This category includes wages from an employer and earnings from self-employed work. It doesn't include income from pensions or from interest or dividends on investments and savings.

>> You must earn a certain amount of money to get one work credit; the amount tends to go up a little each year. In 2024, the amount was $1,730.

>> You can earn a maximum of only four work credits in any one year. In 2024, this limit would amount to earnings of $6,920. When in the year you earn your credits doesn't matter. You may have to work all year to earn four credits, or you may earn all four much earlier in the year, even within the first three months.

>> However, regardless of when in the year you earn four credits, Social Security won't credit the fourth one until the first day of the last quarter of the year, October 1. So, for example, if you earn your 40th credit in June, you must wait until October 1 to become fully insured and eligible to receive Part A benefits without paying monthly premiums for them.

>> Racking up 40 credits usually takes at least ten years of work, but these years need not be consecutive. You earn credits whenever you work and pay payroll taxes, even if you have long breaks between spells of work.

Not everyone works in jobs that require paying Social Security taxes. For example, federal workers have their own retirement system and don't have to contribute to Social Security. However, since 1983, all federal workers have been required to pay Medicare payroll taxes, which entitles them to Part A benefits without paying premiums but not to Social Security retirement benefits.

Different rules relating to work credits may apply in certain circumstances. Contact Social Security to discuss your credits if you're

>> Self-employed and earning less than $400 a year

>> Employed by a local or state government that opted not to participate in Social Security

>> In the military (you may get additional credits in some situations)

>> Performing domestic work or farm work

>> Working for a church or church organization that doesn't pay Social Security taxes

TIP

Social Security keeps a record of your earnings and work credits, compiled from employers' reports and tax records. It sends out statements telling people age 60 or older how near they are to being "fully insured" — meaning entitled to Medicare and retirement benefits. You can also go to www.ssa.gov/myaccount to create an online account to access these statements. For more information, call Social Security at 800-772-1213 (TTY 800-325-0778) or read its consumer guide "How You Earn Credits" at www.ssa.gov/pubs/EN-05-10072.pdf.

Being eligible for Part A on someone else's work record

If you haven't worked long enough to get Part A benefits without paying premiums, you may qualify on the work record of your current or former spouse. But the rules vary according to different circumstances.

Your current/former spouse has enough credits

If your current or former spouse has earned 40 work credits, you can qualify for premium-free Part A on their work record under these circumstances:

>> **Current spouse:** You've been married to your current spouse for at least one year, you're age 65 or older, and your spouse is at least 62.

>> **Divorced spouse:** You were married to your divorced spouse for at least ten years before the divorce became final, you haven't remarried, you're age 65 or older, and your ex is at least 62. (Whether your ex has remarried doesn't matter.)

>> **Late spouse:** You had been married to your deceased spouse for at least nine months immediately they died, you're 65 or older, and you didn't remarry before age 60 (or 50 if you're entitled to disability benefits).

>> **Divorced late spouse:** You were married for at least ten years before the divorce became final, you didn't remarry before age 60 (or 50 if you're entitled to disability benefits), and you're 65 or older.

Neither you nor your spouse has 40 work credits

If your current or former spouse has fewer than 30 credits, they aren't any use to you (for Medicare purposes, that is) because you still have to pay full premiums to get Part A benefits. But if they have 30 to 39 credits, you're entitled to pay reduced Part A premiums on their work record even if you have no credits at all — as long as you also meet the conditions described in the previous section. This arrangement makes a big difference financially. In 2024, the full Part A premium is $505 a month, whereas the reduced premium is $278 a month. Of course, if your current or ex-spouse continues working until they have earned 40 credits, you then qualify for Part A benefits on their work record without having to pay premiums.

REMEMBER

You can't add your work credits to those of your spouse to qualify for premium-free Part A. For example, if you have 20 credits and your spouse has 31, you meet only the conditions to pay a reduced Part A premium based on your spouse's 31 credits. You can't use the 51 credits you have between you.

You're the foreign spouse of a U.S. citizen or legal resident

Normally, non-citizens who haven't worked in the United States need to become permanent legal residents (green-card holders) and live in the United States continuously for at least five years in order to qualify for Medicare benefits. But if you're 65 or older and are a green-card holder who's been married to a U.S. citizen or a legal resident for at least one year — and your spouse is age 62 or older and has earned 40 work credits — you're entitled to full Medicare benefits (including premium-free Part A) on their work record without being required to live in this country for five years. In case you need to argue this point, you can find the official regulation in section GN 00303.800 — "Eligibility Under the HI/SMI Program for Uninsured Individuals" — of the Program Operations Manual System (POMS) at secure.ssa.gov/poms.nsf/lnx/0200303800.

You're in a same-sex marriage

Couples in same-sex marriages have the same rights to all federal benefits as those in opposite-sex marriages, thanks to a June 2015 U.S. Supreme Court decision that ruled people throughout the nation have a constitutional right to same-sex marriage. This ruling means, among many other things, that one same-sex spouse can qualify for full Medicare benefits, without paying premiums for Part A, on the work record of the other spouse, if all the conditions described in the preceding sections are met.

You are unmarried but live in a domestic partnership

You usually can't qualify for premium-free Part A benefits on the work record of a domestic partner to whom you aren't formally married — regardless of whether your partner is the same sex as you or the opposite sex, or whether you've been covered by health insurance from their employer.

One exception to this rule is if you're in a relationship that is formally recognized as a common-law marriage by the laws of your state. (For info on these laws, see Unmarried Equality's fact sheet at www.unmarried.org/common-law-marriage-fact-sheet.)

REMEMBER

If you're in any kind of domestic partnership and you're covered by a health plan from your partner's employer, you need to know the rules about signing up for Medicare Part B, which is explained in Chapter 6.

Qualifying for Medicare under Age 65 on the Basis of Disability

People with disabilities have historically had a hard time finding affordable health insurance because of their medical problems. But Medicare helps by covering three categories of disabled people — those who

>> Have received Social Security disability payments for at least two years

>> Have permanent kidney failure (ESRD)

>> Have Lou Gehrig's disease (amyotrophic lateral sclerosis, or ALS)

The following sections explain how you get to qualify for Medicare if you fall into any of these categories.

Receiving disability payments

TIP

If you have any illness, injury, or disability that prevents you from earning more than a certain amount of money each month and this medical condition is expected to last for at least one year, you may be eligible for Social Security Disability Insurance (SSDI). For information on eligibility and how to apply, call Social Security at 800-772-1213 or the TTY number 800-325-0778, or go to ssa.gov/pubs/EN-05-10029.pdf.

After Social Security has reviewed your application, it will let you know whether you qualify for SSDI. If you do, you'll receive monthly cash payments, starting five months after the date that Social Security determines your disability began. And eventually, you'll also qualify for Medicare benefits that are exactly the same as those for people who are 65 or older. The catch, though, is that the law generally requires you to wait 24 months before your Medicare coverage kicks in.

The following sections answer some common questions about Medicare for folks who receive disability payments.

How does the 24-month waiting period work?

Most often, Medicare coverage begins on the first day of the 25th month that you receive SSDI payments. That 25th month counts as the fourth month of your seven-month initial enrollment period (which is explained in Chapter 6). However, you don't need to actively apply for Medicare. When you receive SSDI, Social Security automatically enrolls you in Part A and Part B and mails your Medicare card to you two or three months before your coverage becomes effective. (If you want to opt out of Part B, you can do so, but you should also be aware of possible pitfalls, as discussed in Chapter 6.)

However, in some cases the waiting period may be shorter than two years. For example, if you apply for SSDI and get turned down, you can file an appeal against the decision. If you win the appeal, Social Security's approval of your application is backdated to the first month in which you should have been entitled to receive SSDI. So the 24-month waiting period for Medicare begins on that date — which may be many months or even years earlier — and not on the date when you actually begin receiving SSDI payments. (For more information on this situation, see Chapter 7.)

Note: The 24 months of waiting for Medicare don't have to be consecutive. For example, if you got SSDI for a few months and then lost eligibility but qualified again at some later date (even years later), all the months you received SSDI collectively count toward the 24-month waiting period.

REMEMBER

If you haven't received your Medicare card by, say, your 23rd month of receiving SSDI, call Social Security at 800-772-1213 or the TTY number 800-325-0778 to see whether a problem has occurred.

How long does Medicare coverage last?

If you qualify for Medicare through disability, your Medicare benefits continue for as long as you receive SSDI payments and maybe longer. If you lose SSDI because you return to work, your Medicare benefits will continue for an additional eight and a half years under some circumstances and up to a certain level of income. If your employer offers health benefits, you must accept them, and then Medicare becomes available to you as secondary insurance. (But if the employer's health insurance includes having a health savings account, you probably won't be able to use it for reasons addressed in Chapter 6.)

Beyond the eight and a half years, if you still have disabilities and are working, your Medicare benefits can continue, but you need to pay a monthly premium for Part A services as well as for Part B (unless you qualify for help from your state through a Medicare Savings Program, as explained in Chapter 4).

TIP

If you're still receiving Medicare when you reach 65, your coverage will continue seamlessly, but you'll then be entitled to it on the basis of age and not disability. During this transition, you don't have to do anything. But you do get another seven-month initial enrollment period (starting three months before you turn 65) in which you can

>> Get a better deal on Medigap supplemental insurance (see Chapter 4), which may have been unaffordable or denied to you under age 65

>> Change your Medicare coverage choices if you want to (see Chapter 15)

>> Stop paying for any late enrollment penalties that you incurred earlier (see Chapter 6)

Does railroad retirement disability work in the same way?

If you have disabilities and are insured under the railroad retirement system rather than Social Security, the rules are a little different depending on the classification of your disability:

>> **Total:** If you have *total disability* (you're unable to work at any job), you qualify for Medicare coverage after you've been receiving disability payments for 24 months.

>> **Occupational:** If you have *occupational disability* (you can't do your regular railroad job but may be able to work at something else), you don't qualify for early Medicare benefits under age 65. However, if at some stage you're granted a *disability freeze* because you develop a severe medical condition that prevents you from performing any work or because you're 55 or older and blind, you'll become eligible for Medicare 29 weeks after the freeze period begins.

TIP

For more information, contact the Railroad Retirement Board toll free at 877-772-5772 (or the TTY number 312-751-4701), or visit its website at rrb.gov/.

Suffering from permanent kidney failure (ESRD)

Permanent kidney failure is a chronic medical condition that is known as *end-stage renal disease* (ESRD) in Medicare. It means that your kidneys have stopped working properly and you need either regular dialysis to keep them functioning or a kidney transplant. In this situation, you face no waiting period for Medicare but still have to meet certain conditions. You must either

>> Be fully insured — that is, have earned 40 work credits from your own work record to qualify for Social Security or railroad retirement benefits or worked as a government employee who qualified for Medicare through payroll taxes, as explained in the earlier section "Qualifying for Part A on your own work record"; or

>> Qualify as the spouse or dependent child of a person who is fully insured

The rules for when Medicare coverage starts depend on what kind of care you need (dialysis or transplant) and whether you also have coverage under an employer plan. If you receive Medicare on the basis of having ESRD only, the coverage continues until 12 months after you stop dialysis or 36 months after you've had a kidney transplant and no longer need dialysis. But if you need to resume dialysis or you have another transplant, Medicare coverage begins again without any waiting period.

TIP

Because these rules are quite complicated and depend on your condition, call Social Security at 800-772-1213 (TTY 800-325-0778) to find out how they apply to you. You may also want to check out the official publication "Medicare Coverage of Kidney Dialysis and Kidney Transplant Services" at www.medicare.gov/Pubs/pdf/10128-Medicare-Coverage-ESRD.pdf.

Living with Lou Gehrig's disease (ALS)

Amyotrophic lateral sclerosis (ALS) is commonly known as *Lou Gehrig's disease* after the great New York Yankees baseball star who died from it in 1941. ALS is a wasting disease that attacks the nerve cells of the brain and spinal cord, eventually shutting down the muscles' ability to move. In 2001, Congress passed legislation waiving the 24-month Medicare waiting period for people diagnosed with ALS.

To qualify for Medicare if you have ALS, you must be approved for Social Security or railroad retirement disability benefits in the usual way. Medicare coverage begins on the first day of the month when your disability benefit payments begin.

Falling through the Cracks: Healthcare Options if You Can't Get Medicare Yet

Inevitably, in a system that is as patchworked together as American healthcare, some people slip through the net. For example, consider the following situations:

>> You're under 65 and have qualified for disability payments, but you must wait up to two years for Medicare coverage.

>> You're 65 or older, but you're a legal immigrant who hasn't yet lived in the United States for the five years required to qualify for Medicare.

>> You have only a few years to go before getting Medicare, but you've lost (or never had) a job with health benefits and you're in poor health.

>> You've had health insurance from your spouse's employment, but they're older than you and are now retiring, losing employer benefits for both of you. Your spouse can join Medicare, but what about you?

In any of these situations, you'll be anxious to know how you can get healthcare while waiting for Medicare. The following sections deal with possibilities to check out and consider — though keep in mind that not all of them are available to everybody.

Nice work if you can get it: Landing a job with benefits

A job that comes with health benefits is always the best option if you or your spouse can get access to one. By law, employers that provide health insurance (and have 20 or more employees) must offer the same benefits, including spousal coverage, to all employees regardless of age, health status, or pre-existing medical conditions.

What if you have no employer insurance of your own, you're younger than your spouse, and they're contemplating retirement? Some employers continue to insure a younger spouse after the employee has retired until the younger spouse also reaches Medicare age or to provide retiree benefits that cover both of them. But very often the younger spouse is just left out in the cold. If you're in this situation, the best solution is for your spouse to continue working until you become eligible for Medicare if at all possible. If it isn't, read on.

Paying for COBRA temporary insurance

The COBRA law (short for the Consolidated Omnibus Budget Reconciliation Act of 1986) allows most people who've left or lost a job to continue health coverage through their former employer for up to 18 months by paying the full premiums (the employer's share as well as their own), which can be expensive. If eligible, spouses and dependent children can receive this coverage even if the departing employees don't take it themselves.

If you take COBRA and then become eligible for Medicare, your COBRA benefits cease. But your spouse may then become eligible for COBRA coverage for a longer period — up to 36 months. Some state laws also allow COBRA coverage for extended periods. If you're already enrolled in Medicare before becoming eligible for COBRA, you can use both. But be aware that COBRA is secondary coverage, so if you don't sign up for Medicare when you're eligible, COBRA won't cover your bills.

TIP

You must apply for COBRA within a certain time frame of leaving your job, so pay attention to deadlines. For more information, refer to the Department of Labor's guidance at www.dol.gov/sites/dolgov/files/ebsa/about-ebsa/our-activities/resource-center/faqs/cobra-continuation-health-coverage-consumer.pdf.

Purchasing individual insurance through the online Marketplace

The Affordable Care Act of 2010, often known as ACA or Obamacare, allows people who are uninsured to buy private health insurance through federal- or state-run insurance exchanges known collectively as the "Marketplace." The huge change that this law brought about is that, since the start of 2014, people have been able to buy "individual" (non-employer) health insurance regardless of their health status or pre-existing medical conditions. Many millions of previously uninsured (or even uninsurable) people have now bought this coverage.

The information that follows here is current unless the ACA is repealed.

If you don't have health insurance from an employer or the government (such as Medicare and Medicaid), you can use the one-stop online Marketplace to comparison-shop and choose from a menu of different healthcare plans. These plans must all offer comprehensive care that includes at least the essential items and services specified by law — including doctors' services, hospital care, prescription drugs, screenings, tests, vaccinations, and mental health services.

Insurance companies selling plans through the Marketplace can charge older folks more than younger ones — and they can also add surcharges of up to 50 percent on the premiums of smokers — but they can't deny or limit coverage or charge higher premiums based on past or present health conditions. Nor can they place annual or lifetime dollar limits on coverage.

The law provides subsidies or tax credits for individuals and families whose incomes are under a certain level to buy policies at lower cost. (In June 2015, the U.S. Supreme Court confirmed that subsidies are available to all eligible people nationwide, even in states that haven't established their own marketplaces.) The law also makes Medicaid (the state-run healthcare safety net) available to many more people of all ages, giving them virtually free healthcare. However, under a 2013 ruling, the Supreme Court allowed individual states to decide whether to expand Medicaid for their residents, and many states chose not to do so.

Can you have Marketplace insurance rather than — or as well as — Medicare? In most cases, no. It's illegal for insurers to sell plans to people who have Medicare, and even if you could buy one, you wouldn't qualify for subsidies. However, you may be able to buy a Marketplace plan rather than Medicare if you'd have to pay premiums for Part A. (For more information on the rules, go to www.healthcare.gov/medicare/medicare-and-the-marketplace.) Be careful, though: If you don't sign up for Medicare Parts A and B when you should, you'll still be liable for late penalties, as explained in Chapter 6.

Open enrollment for Marketplace insurance runs from November 1 to January 15. If you select a plan before December 15, your coverage will start January 1; if you enroll later, coverage will begin February 1.

But you can get a special enrollment period (SEP) to sign up with a plan at other times of the year in certain circumstances — for example, losing other insurance, getting married or divorced, adding a child to the family, gaining citizenship, entering the United States as a lawful resident, being released from prison, or moving out of your plan's service area. The SEP generally lasts for up to 60 days after these events.

To find details of plans available to you, how much you'd pay in premiums (after any subsidies have been deducted), and how to enroll in a plan, go to www.healthcare.gov. If you need personal help in navigating this site to choose a plan, click the "Find Local Help" button on the home page, or go to localhelp.healthcare.gov. (If your state runs its own marketplace, you'll be directed to its website.)

There is no federal tax penalty for forgoing health insurance coverage under the ACA, although a few states do impose penalties. You don't need to buy extra health insurance, and therefore can't be penalized, if you have employer coverage, Medicaid, or Medicare Part A, which all count as comparable coverage. Having only Part B, however, does not count and makes you liable for tax penalties.

Buying health insurance outside of the Obamacare Marketplace

It's worth considering the possibilities of buying individual health insurance on the open market. This is how many people without employer insurance bought coverage before 2014, when the main provisions of the Affordable Care Act kicked in.

In those pre-ACA days, most people older than 50 had a hard time buying health insurance, or at least found it very expensive. That's because, before the ACA, insurance companies could legally deny coverage or require higher premiums on the basis of current or pre-existing medical conditions.

One previous law, though, gave limited protections to some people buying individual insurance policies for themselves or their families. This law, which still exists, is HIPAA (the Health Insurance Portability and Accountability Act of 1996). It says that if you've had group or COBRA insurance for at least 18 months, you have the right to buy insurance that doesn't exclude or limit coverage for preexisting medical conditions. Even so, it may still be expensive, with none of the ACA's government subsidies that help reduce premiums. For details, check out the Department of Labor's guidance on HIPAA, at www.dol.gov/agencies/ebsa/laws-and-regulations/laws/hipaa.

TIP

To find contact information for companies that sell individual health insurance policies in your area, call your state department of insurance. Go to content.naic.org/state-insurance-departments and click on your state.

Getting healthcare without insurance

TIP

If you can't buy insurance you can afford and don't qualify for assistance, you may still be able to get medical care from community clinics that provide care for uninsured people for free, at low cost, or according to your ability to pay. To find contact information for any clinics available in your area, go to the U.S. Health Resources and Services Administration directory at findahealthcenter.hrsa.gov. Or go to www.needymeds.org and click on "Healthcare Savings" and then on "Find Free/Low-Cost/Sliding Scale Clinics."

IN THIS CHAPTER

» **Signing up for Medicare during your initial enrollment period**

» **Qualifying for a special enrollment period**

» **Knowing when to enroll in other special circumstances**

» **Figuring out your Part D enrollment options**

» **Facing the music for not enrolling at the proper time**

Chapter **6**

Enrolling in Medicare at the Right Time for You

When you're about to dive into Medicare, the most important item on your to-do list is to make sure you enroll at the right time for you. Why is this timing such a big deal? Because if you get it wrong, the mistake may cost you a lot of money — not just in the short term but for all future years. Not something you want to risk, right?

This chapter provides absolutely critical information on the best time to sign up for Medicare services according to your individual circumstances. Don't be clueless about this stuff! Nobody's going to send your Medicare ID card tucked inside a 65th birthday bouquet or send a welcoming little letter informing you that it's time to sign up for Medicare, with kindly advice on how to go about it. (Okay, you'll get both letter and card if you already receive Social Security or railroad retirement benefits, but many people aren't yet collecting these at age 65.) No, you're expected to find out on your own, and sadly, most of the folks you'd normally turn to for advice (including family, friends, the HR department at work, and even some government officials, sorry to say) may well give inaccurate pointers that send you blindly in the wrong direction. This chapter helps you cut through all that.

REMEMBER

The information here is all about timing — when the appropriate time for you to enroll is — and not about the mechanics of how to sign up, which are explained in Chapter 7.

At a Glance: Surveying Situations That Affect Enrollment Timing

The timing of Medicare enrollment is critical. There's really a world of difference between enrolling in Medicare when you're retired and enrolling when you continue to work beyond age 65; between becoming eligible for Medicare because you've reached 65 and becoming eligible because you have disabilities; between living in the United States and living abroad; between being married and being in another kind of domestic relationship; and so on. Whichever situation you're in, it comes with certain rules that you need to be aware of before signing up.

Take a look at Table 6-1, which identifies 12 separate situations that affect the timing of Part B enrollment alone. (Part B is the tricky one to pay attention to if you want to avoid hefty late penalties down the road.) Find your situation to see when you should sign up if you want to avoid penalties. You can use this table to see at a glance whether you should sign up for Part B during your initial enrollment period (IEP) at age 65 or whether you can wait until a later date and qualify for a special enrollment period (SEP).

REMEMBER

Table 6-1 applies only to people who qualify for Medicare at age 65 or older — including non-U.S. legal residents (green-card holders) who have lived in the United States for at least five years or have been married to a U.S. citizen or legal resident for at least one year. It doesn't apply to those who qualify for Medicare at younger ages through disabilities.

The rest of this chapter explains the rules for these situations in more detail and considers Part D enrollment, which has different rules and conditions. Finally, you'll find out about the consequences of not enrolling by the time your personal deadline has come and gone. To understand just what's at stake, you may want to flip to that section and read it first.

TABLE 6-1   Situations That Affect Part B Enrollment Deadlines

Your Situation	Should You Sign Up during Your IEP at 65?	Can You Delay Part B at 65 and Sign Up during an SEP?
1. You have no other health insurance.	Yes.	No.
2. You still work and have group health insurance from a current employer.	Only if the employer has fewer than 20 employees and Medicare is primary (pays before other insurance), or if you want to drop this insurance.	Yes — any time while you still work for this employer or within eight months of retirement.
3. You have group health insurance from your spouse's current employer.	Only if the employer has fewer than 20 employees and Medicare is primary, or if you want to drop this insurance.	Yes — any time while your spouse still works for this employer or within eight months of retirement.
4. You have individual (non-employer) insurance that you pay for yourself.	Yes.	No.
5. You're covered by COBRA insurance.	Yes.	No.
6. You're covered by retiree health benefits from your or your spouse's ex-employer.	Yes.	No.
7. You're in a nonmarital relationship with someone of the same or opposite sex and are covered by their employer insurance.	Yes, unless your relationship is considered a common-law marriage under the laws of your state.	No, unless your relationship is considered a common-law marriage under the laws of your state.
8. You have veterans' health benefits from the VA system.	Yes, unless you also fall into situation 2 or 3.	No, unless you also fall into situation 2 or 3.
9. You live outside the United States, where you can't use Medicare services.	Yes, if you're not working. But if you don't qualify for premium-free Part A, you must delay enrollment until you return to the United States.	Yes, if you work and have employer insurance or access to the host country's national healthcare system.
10. You're in prison, where you can't use Medicare services.	Yes.	Yes, if released from incarceration after January 1, 2023.
11. You don't qualify for premium-free Part A benefits.	Yes, unless you fall into situation 2 or 3.	No, unless you fall into situation 2 or 3.
12. The employment that provides your health insurance ends before the end of your IEP.	Yes.	No.

Understanding Your Initial Enrollment Period

The *initial enrollment period* (IEP) is the earliest time that you're entitled to sign up for Medicare. Typically, it occurs around the time you reach 65. But of course, it would happen at an earlier age if you qualify for Medicare because of disability.

As I discuss in detail in Chapter 7, the Social Security Administration automatically enrolls you in Medicare Parts A and B if you're already receiving Social Security (or Railroad Retirement Board) disability or retirement payments by the time your IEP rolls around. But if you're not yet getting these benefits, you need to apply for Medicare.

This section explains when your IEP begins and ends and considers the circumstances in which you should use your IEP to actively enroll in Parts A and B — first if you're doing so around age 65, and then if you're qualifying for Medicare because of disabilities.

Note: Later in this chapter, you'll read about the special enrollment period that allows you to delay Part B without penalty beyond the end of your IEP if you have health insurance from your or your spouse's current work. If this is your situation, you may want to head straight to the section "Delaying Part B if You'll Qualify for a Special Enrollment Period Later."

Using your IEP at age 65

This initial enrollment period lasts for seven months — usually beginning three months before the month of your 65th birthday and ending three months after that month. For example, if your birthday is in July, your IEP begins April 1 and ends October 31. However, if your birthday happens to fall on the first day of the month, your whole IEP occurs one month earlier. For example, if you turn 65 on July 1, your IEP begins March 1 and ends September 30.

REMEMBER

To avoid late penalties, you should use your IEP to sign up for Medicare Part A and Part B in the following circumstances:

>> You have no other health insurance.

>> You have individual (non-employer) insurance that you pay for yourself.

>> You have other health insurance from your or your spouse's current job but want to drop it as soon as possible to rely on Medicare, perhaps because the employer insurance costs too much or has inadequate benefits.

- » You have only retiree benefits or COBRA extension coverage from a former employer or union. These don't count as current employer coverage.

- » You aren't covered by health insurance from your or your spouse's current active employment, even though you're continuing to work.

- » You're covered by health insurance from your (or your spouse's) job, but the employer has fewer than 20 employees and requires you to enroll in Medicare.

- » You're covered by health insurance from your or your spouse's current active employment, but this is due to end before your IEP expires.

- » You're eligible for health benefits under the military's TRICARE For Life (TFL) retiree program, which requires you to take Medicare Part B as a condition for continuing to receive TFL coverage.

- » You're a veteran and have health benefits from Veterans Affairs, which doesn't require you to sign up for Medicare Part B. But if you don't enroll during your IEP (or SEP, if applicable) and you decide in future years that you want Part B, you risk late penalties.

- » You're a federal retiree and have health insurance under the Federal Employees Health Benefits (FEHB) Program, which doesn't require you to enroll in Part B. But if you don't take Part B during your IEP (or SEP, if applicable) and decide in the future that you want it, you risk late penalties.

- » You're not entitled to premium-free Part A benefits (which I explain in Chapter 5), but you're eligible to buy Part A services by paying premiums and/or you're eligible for Part B coverage.

Note: Other specific, more-complicated situations in which you may be uncertain whether you need to sign up for Medicare during your IEP are discussed later in this chapter. These include not being a U.S. citizen, living abroad or in prison, being in a same-sex marriage, and being in a nonmarried relationship with a partner of the same or opposite sex.

Taking advantage of your IEP when you have disabilities

When you qualify for Medicare on the basis of disability, you don't usually need to concern yourself about deadlines for signing up. Enrollment happens automatically, and Social Security mails your Medicare card to you in good time before your eligibility starts. It sends a letter with the card, explaining that you've been enrolled in Part A and Part B. This letter also explains that you can decline Part B if you want to — and, if you do, provides instructions on how to go about it.

Technically, there is an IEP. It also lasts seven months. But in this case, the fourth month — when your Medicare benefits become effective — is typically the month in which you receive your 25th disability payment. For example, the 25th check is due in April, so your IEP begins January 1 and ends July 31.

REMEMBER

You need to be very careful about declining Part B. In fact, the issue of opting out of Part A and/or Part B is so important — and comes with some serious pitfalls that you must be aware of — that a whole section is devoted to it in Chapter 7. Also in Chapter 7, we look at a scenario in which Social Security awards disability benefits only after people have won them on appeal and then offers them backdated Medicare coverage.

Delaying Part B if You'll Qualify for a Special Enrollment Period Later

More and more people are working beyond age 65. Questions that now come up frequently are "What do I do about Medicare if I continue to work beyond 65?"; "I still have health insurance from my spouse's job, so do I need Medicare?"; and "I work and pay for my employer's health benefits, but won't I be penalized if I don't sign up for Medicare now that I'm 65?"

REMEMBER

Let's dispel this confusion straightaway. In a nutshell: For as long as you're covered beyond age 65 by group health insurance provided by an employer for whom you or your spouse still actively works — and that employer has 20 or more employees — you can delay Part B enrollment until this employment or the health coverage ends (whichever comes first). At that point, you're entitled to a special enrollment period to sign up for Part B immediately and without penalty. (That's the rule for people 65 and older. If you have Medicare due to disability, it's a little different, as explained in the previous section.)

This section looks more closely at this nutshell statement in terms of the conditions for being able to delay Part B and how you can use the special enrollment period to eventually sign up for Part B. Whether you need to delay Part A is also considered, and a special warning is noted for folks who have a health savings account at work.

REMEMBER

Even if you can delay Part B in favor of employer insurance, note that you're free to choose whether you want to continue with the employer insurance and postpone Medicare, whether you want to drop the employer benefits and rely totally on Medicare, or whether you want to have both. It's entirely up to you.

Another super-important point: If you continue working beyond age 65 for an employer with 20 or more workers, the law requires the employer to offer you exactly the same health benefits that are offered to younger workers in the same company or organization. This law also gives the same protection to spouses age 65 or older who are covered by the employer plan. These rights are explained in more detail in Chapter 8.

WARNING

One other situation also requires a special explanation. If you retire or otherwise stop work *before* your IEP ends — even on its very last day — you aren't entitled to an SEP but must enroll in Medicare during your IEP to avoid late penalties. (Under Social Security rules, an IEP always trumps an SEP if they overlap.) For example, say you turn 65 in April, so that your IEP runs from January 1 to July 31. But you plan to retire at the end of June, so you need to sign up in June to ensure that Medicare coverage begins on July 1.

Being able to delay Part B without penalty

Why delay Part B? When you're covered by health insurance at work (whether from your own or your spouse's employer) as well as Medicare, that insurance is automatically primary to Medicare unless the employer has fewer than 20 workers. *Primary* means the employer plan pays your medical bills first; Medicare kicks in only in the event that your plan doesn't cover a service or item that Medicare covers. (Make no mistake: Medicare doesn't cover any out-of-pocket costs, such as deductibles and co-payments, that the employer insurance requires.) So unless your employer plan provides lousy coverage — and of course that can certainly happen — you probably wouldn't use Medicare at all. So why would you want to pay monthly premiums for it?

That's really what this special enrollment period is all about. It allows you to postpone Part B — and the monthly premiums it requires — if you want to, without risking late penalties. But only in certain circumstances. Therefore, this section takes apart that earlier nutshell statement so that you can be sure whether these circumstances apply to you.

"For whom you or your spouse still actively work"

This part is the key phrase. It doesn't matter whether you or your spouse is working full time or part time for the company or organization that provides you with health insurance. But you or your spouse must be in what government officials call "current employment" for you to be able to delay Part B enrollment and become entitled to a special enrollment period later on.

The Social Security Administration (which handles Medicare enrollment and imposes Part B late penalties) is very strict about this rule, so let me be very clear: *Current employment* doesn't include any time when the only health insurance you receive from an employer comes in the form of retiree or COBRA coverage — because, by definition, you're not actively working when receiving these benefits. Also, it means that you must be working for the same employer that provides this health insurance. If you still work beyond 65 and have health benefits — but these benefits come from an employer you or your spouse no longer work for — you aren't entitled to delay Part B without penalty.

"That employer has 20 or more employees"

Small employers' workforces are often much more fluid than larger ones. Especially in seasonal jobs, workers come and go, so companies may have more than 20 employees at some times of the year and fewer at other times. Also, some small employers band together with others to buy health insurance in groups, with the result that, collectively, the pool of workers eligible for health benefits is a lot greater than 20.

Broadly, employers meet the "20 or more" rule for Part B purposes if they have at least 20 full-time, part-time, or leased workers on the payroll for 20 or more weeks in the current or preceding year. These workers don't all have to be enrolled in the employer's health plan; the total number of workers employed is what counts. Employers also meet the rule if they participate in some kinds of multi-employer health insurance programs.

Even if you work for an employer with fewer than 20 employees, the law still allows you to delay Part B and get an SEP when you retire. However, be warned: Small employer plans are usually secondary to Medicare, and in that case, they won't pay for any services that Medicare covers. In this situation, if you don't sign up for Part B during your IEP, it's the same as having no insurance at all. So if you have health coverage from a small employer, be sure to find out in advance whether Medicare will become your primary coverage when you turn 65.

Still, one obscure rule is worth knowing: If you fail to sign up during your IEP and then realize that your employer plan isn't paying because it's become secondary to Medicare, you're entitled to an immediate SEP to sign up for Parts A and B without penalty at any time while you're still working. Your coverage begins on the first day of the month after you enroll.

Definitions can be quite complex and depend on the situation. So if you work for a small employer but aren't sure whether the size of your company or organization meets the "20 or more" rule, consult your employer. Failing that, you can also call Medicare's Benefits Coordination & Recovery Center at 855-798-2627 (TTY 855-797-2627).

"Until this employment or the health coverage ends (whichever comes first)"

This wording underscores the rule about needing to actively work for the employer that provides health insurance as a condition for delaying Part B. After the employment ends — even if the coverage continues — you need to enroll in Part B to avoid penalties.

WARNING

Many people think of "employer coverage" as any type of health benefits that come directly or indirectly from their jobs. After all, retiree and COBRA benefits are usually provided by the same insurance company that covers an employee while working: same name, same card, and (at least in the case of COBRA) exactly the same coverage. But when it comes to delaying Part B, neither type of benefit counts as employer coverage. Too many people fall into this trap, often with serious consequences, as explained in detail in the later section "Missing your deadline for Part B."

REMEMBER

In some circumstances, employer coverage comes to an end before the employment actually ends. So keep in mind that the Part B late penalty clock starts ticking when the job ends or when the insurance is terminated — whichever happens first.

Knowing what to do about Part A if you delay Part B

Most people who delay Part B nonetheless sign up for Part A during their initial enrollment periods at age 65. In most cases, doing so has no downside because Part A requires no premiums if you or your spouse has contributed enough payroll taxes at work, as Chapter 5 explains.

In most circumstances, you don't risk late penalties if you delay Part A enrollment beyond age 65. (For exceptions, flip to information on Part A in the later section "Passing your deadline for Part A.") But the advantage of signing up for Part A during your initial enrollment period is in making sure that a Social Security official enters into your record the fact that you're delaying Part B on the basis of current employment — just in case any argument about it arises later on. Also, if you need to be in the hospital, Part A may provide additional coverage to your employer plan.

TIP

One situation, however, comes with a very good reason for delaying Part A as well as Part B until you stop work: Your employer health insurance takes the form of a high-deductible plan paired with a health savings account. This situation will be discussed in detail in the next section.

Heeding a special warning if you have a health savings account at work

The decision to delay Part B isn't normally affected by what kind of health coverage you have at work. But if your employer insurance combines a high-deductible health plan with a health savings account (HSA), you need to sit up and pay attention. That's because, under IRS rules, you can't continue to contribute to an HSA if you're enrolled in any part of Medicare.

This rule may sound screwy. But under the law, you don't pay tax on earnings you put into an HSA, and you can't qualify for that benefit if you have other health insurance, including Medicare. (If you want to see the rule in black and white, go to IRS publication 969, "Health Savings Accounts and Other Tax-Favored Health Plans," at www.irs.gov/publications/p969/index.html and click on "Qualifying for an HSA contribution.")

This IRS regulation affects anybody who wants to work beyond age 65 and whose employer offers only the kind of health insurance that includes a health savings account. It's a situation that affects more and more people because HSAs have become popular with employers in recent years. Yet Medicare and Social Security hardly ever mention this important rule in their enrollment info for consumers.

Here's what it means:

>> **If you're an employee with an HSA at work:** You can't continue to contribute any money to it in any month that you're enrolled in Medicare. You can draw on any funds left in the account to pay for approved medical purposes, but you can't add any new funds to it.

>> **If you're covered by your spouse's HSA at work and you're enrolled in Medicare:** You aren't affected by the rule because you aren't the contributing employee. You can continue to use funds in the account.

Being *enrolled in Medicare* means Part A as well as Part B and Part D under this rule. So if you want to contribute to an HSA at work after age 65, you're better off not signing up for Part A during your initial enrollment period. It won't cost you anything, because you're legally entitled to delay Part A (as well as Part B) until you stop work, without risking any late penalties.

REMEMBER

Note also that when you have an HSA, you're better off not signing up for Part D either. For as long as you delay enrolling in both Parts A and B, you aren't eligible for Part D and therefore can't receive any late penalties if you postpone Part D enrollment until you stop work — even if the prescription drug coverage provided by your employer plan isn't *creditable* (a concept explained later in this chapter).

If you're already receiving any kind of Social Security benefits (retirement, disability, or spousal) when you become eligible for Medicare, you'll be automatically enrolled in Medicare Parts A and B. (Similarly, if you start drawing benefits after age 65 and aren't already signed up for Medicare, Social Security automatically enrolls you.) And although you're given the option to opt out of Part B, you can't opt out of Part A if you receive Social Security benefits.

These are your options if you have an HSA and are eligible for Medicare, according to different circumstances:

>> **You haven't yet applied for Medicare or drawn Social Security retirement benefits.** You can continue to contribute to your HSA after age 65 and postpone applying for Social Security and Medicare Parts A and B until you stop working. You won't be penalized for this delay.

>> **You're enrolled in Part A but haven't applied for Social Security retirement benefits.** You can withdraw your application for Part A. (To do so, contact Social Security at 800-772-1213 or at the TTY number 800-325-0778.) You face no penalties or repercussions, and you're free to reapply for Part A when you stop working.

>> **You've already applied for or are receiving Social Security retirement benefits.** If you're 65 or older when you apply for Social Security retirement benefits, you will be automatically enrolled in Medicare Part A. Therefore, you can't continue to contribute to your HSA. The only way you can opt out of Part A is to pay back to the government any money you already received in Social Security payments, plus anything Medicare has spent on your medical claims. You must repay these amounts before your application to drop out of Part A can be processed. If you take this action, you're no longer entitled to Social Security or Medicare, but you can reapply for both at any time in the future, such as when you end or lose your HSA coverage.

>> **You're receiving Social Security disability benefits but can return to work.** If you're under 65 and receiving Social Security disability benefits but are able to return to work, your Medicare entitlement may continue for another eight and a half years, even though your disability payments have stopped. (This topic is explained in more detail in Chapter 5.) So if your employer's health insurance includes an HSA, you won't be able to take it because you have Medicare. Again, the only way you can opt out of Medicare is to repay Social Security for all the disability payments you've received and repay Medicare for any medical services you've used. For most disabled people in this situation, that amount may add up to hundreds of thousands of dollars, and opting out of Medicare is therefore not a viable option.

If you have an HSA at work and have delayed Parts A and B enrollment until you retire, be sure to stop contributing to the HSA several months before you start drawing Social Security benefits. (That's because Social Security will backdate your enrollment in Part A by up to six months, depending on how long it's been since you turned 65.) Otherwise, the IRS will tax you for those months when you had an HSA and were enrolled retroactively in Medicare.

Using the special enrollment period

So if you've delayed Part B enrollment beyond age 65 because of current employment (either your own or your spouse's), how does the special enrollment period work?

In essence, this SEP comprises two quite different time periods. You can actually use it

>> At any time while you or your spouse is still working — between the end of your initial enrollment period at age 65 and the time when you or your spouse stops work or loses your employer coverage

>> For up to eight months after this employment or coverage has ended

In other words, your absolute deadline for enrolling in Part B without penalty in this situation is the end of that eighth month. For example, say you're 69 years old and retired but are covered under your spouse's health insurance at work. Your spouse's last day of work is March 15. Your special enrollment period begins on the first day of the following month, April 1, and ends eight months later on November 30.

Whenever you choose to sign up for Part B — whether you're still covered by employer health benefits or are in that eight-month grace period — your Part B coverage begins on the first day of the month after you enroll. Of course, you can time your enrollment so that Part B kicks in as soon as the employer insurance ends to ensure you have no gap in coverage. If you enroll in Part B before your employment ends, or during the month after it ends, the law allows you to specify a beginning date for coverage up to three months in advance.

At the same time, you can sign up for Part A (if you haven't already done so), for Part D prescription drug coverage (as explained in Chapter 10), or for a Medicare Advantage health plan (see Chapter 11), according to your preferences. (You don't have to wait for any other enrollment period.) If you choose to buy Medigap supplemental insurance, you get full federal protections when you purchase a policy within six months of enrolling in Part B, as explained in Chapter 4. Here are some examples of how this SEP works in different situations:

>> Dan is 85 years old, but he's only just beginning to think about signing up for Medicare Part B. That's because his wife, Lily, is 15 years younger than he is, and he's been covered on her health insurance from work since he turned 65. Now Lily is about to retire at age 70, and both of them will be applying for Part B together, using their SEP. To avoid any break in coverage, they'll both enroll during Lily's last month at work and start receiving Medicare benefits on the first day of the following month.

>> Eduardo continued to work after age 65, and his employer's health benefits covered both him and his 66-year-old wife, Rosa. But these benefits came with a hefty monthly premium and a high annual deductible, and after a few years they decided that Medicare would be more affordable. The couple was free to sign up for Medicare at any time while covered under the employer plan. So when the company's open enrollment came around, they opted out of that plan and its coverage terminated at the end of the year. They enrolled in Medicare in December and their new coverage began January 1.

>> Margaret was 68 when her job was downsized. Her hours were reduced from full time to part time, and consequently she lost her company health benefits. But the SEP enabled her to enroll in Medicare before those benefits came to an end on May 31, so her Medicare coverage began June 1.

Enrolling in Other Specific Situations

Some situations just don't fit neatly into the regular enrollment processes. And if you're in one of those circumstances, you need to know the specific rules that apply to them. So this section explains the ins and outs of enrolling in Medicare Part A and/or Part B if you're a legal resident but not a U.S. citizen, you're living outside of the United States, you're in a nontraditional marriage or domestic partnership, or you're in prison.

Note: This doesn't explain whether you qualify for Medicare in these circumstances — that's covered in Chapter 5. This section looks only at the best time to enroll in order to avoid late penalties if you're in one of these situations.

You're a legal permanent resident

The general rule is that at age 65 or older, you must have established legal residency (gotten a green card) and have lived continuously in the United States for at least five years before becoming eligible for Medicare benefits. But some people get their green cards only after living in the United States for more than five years, and some (for example, those who win U.S. immigration "lotteries" in their own countries) get a green card even before moving to the United States.

So the Social Security Administration's rule is that you become eligible for Medicare as soon as both conditions (green card and five-year residency) have been met. That point in time becomes the middle (fourth) month of your seven-month initial enrollment period (IEP).

For example, Katerina had lived in the United States for just four years when she was granted her green card in October 2022, but she needed another year of residency before becoming eligible for Medicare in October 2023. So her IEP for Medicare enrollment began July 1, 2023, and ended January 31, 2024.

Note that as a legal resident, your enrollment may be affected by different rules. For example, if you've paid U.S. payroll taxes long enough to have earned 40 work credits, you qualify for full Medicare benefits in your own right with no waiting period. If you're married to a U.S. citizen or another legal resident, the five-year residency requirement may not apply, as I explain in Chapter 5. Also, if you're covered by an employer health plan from your or your spouse's current work, you're entitled to delay Part B, provided you meet the conditions explained in the earlier section "Being able to delay Part B without penalty."

TIP

Because specific circumstances for non-citizens can vary greatly, calling the Social Security Administration at 800-772-1213 (TTY 800-325-0778) to find out exactly when you can enroll in Medicare is a wise idea.

You live outside the United States

Foreign residency can be a tricky situation when it comes to enrolling in Medicare. You can't use any Medicare services outside the United States, yet in most situations you're faced with a deeply unfair Catch-22. When your 65th birthday is coming up and you live abroad without working, you can do either of the following:

>> Sign up for Part B during your initial enrollment period and pay monthly premiums for services that you can't use.

>> Face late penalties if you return to the United States and sign up for Medicare at some stage in the future.

Some choice! This rule — which dates back to 1966 — doesn't make any kind of sense in the modern, mobile world. Many older Americans now live abroad, often to be near their kids and grandkids, to have a late fling with new adventures, or just to enjoy a bit of the dolce vita in exotic lands. But you're likely to be stuck with this dilemma if you live abroad and you're not working.

However, the following sections go into three important exceptions to this general rule, when you can delay enrollment without penalty until your return to the United States: if you're actively working overseas and meet certain conditions, if you don't qualify for Part A benefits without paying premiums for them, and if you need to sign up for Part D prescription drug coverage when you return to the United States.

Working overseas

Until somewhat recently, the preceding rule applied even to most people who worked abroad beyond age 65. Exceptions were made only for some volunteers serving overseas and for workers whose foreign employers provided them with American-style group health insurance — a type of coverage that barely exists outside the United States. Medicare rules now allow special Part B enrollment periods for people who had worked abroad but received medical care from their host country's publicly available national health system.

REMEMBER

Therefore, Medicare officials say you can now delay Part B at age 65 or over without penalty while abroad and get a special enrollment period when you stop working or return to the United States (whichever comes first) in the following circumstances:

>> You work for an employer (U.S. or foreign) that provides you with private group health insurance.

>> You work for an employer without special health benefits, but you're covered under the national health system of the country where you live.

>> You're self-employed and covered under the national health system of the country where you live.

>> You're the spouse of anybody in the three preceding categories and have the same coverage.

>> You're volunteering abroad and have health coverage from an approved sponsoring organization (for example, the Peace Corps).

This special enrollment comes with rules similar to the regular SEP described earlier in this chapter. Like that rule, it lasts for up to eight months after employment ends. So if you stop working but don't return to the United States within that time frame, you still confront the dilemma that nonworking people abroad face — either sign up for Part B and pay premiums or face late penalties on your return to the United States. And note that if you fail to enroll in Part B during the eight-month SEP, any late penalties are based on the date you finished work, not the end of the SEP.

For example, Frank worked for a French company in Paris for five years and retired at age 68. He and his wife, Pamela, enjoyed life there so much that they decided to stay on for a couple of years, returning to the United States when he was 70 and she was 69. Throughout their time in Paris, they received medical care from the French national health system. When they returned home and enrolled in Part B, the three years when Frank worked after 65 were exempt from late penalties. But they were assessed penalties based on the two years that had elapsed since his retirement — penalties they could've avoided entirely if they'd signed up for Part B within eight months of his retiring.

When you eventually enroll in Part B, you need to satisfy Social Security officials that you were indeed working abroad and covered by health insurance provided by your employer, your volunteer sponsoring organization, or the national health system of your host country. This requirement means producing documents such as employer contracts, tax records, and maybe health records showing that a third party contributed to your medical bills. If you were working for an employer but covered by a national health system, getting a letter from the employer explaining this situation is helpful.

Not qualifying for premium-free Part A

Some people don't qualify for Part A benefits without paying monthly premiums for them, because they or their spouses haven't contributed enough in payroll taxes at work. (Flip to Chapter 5 for details.) In this situation, you can receive Part A benefits if you pay monthly premiums for them — but under the rules, you cannot sign up for Part A or Part B outside the United States. Therefore, in this specific circumstance, you can delay Medicare enrollment until your return, without being subject to late penalties. (For more details, see Chapter 7.)

Signing up for Part D drug coverage

For people who live abroad, the rules for Part D enrollment are utterly different from those for Part B. You don't need to enroll while living overseas because, officials say, you can't use Part D services outside the United States. (Hello? Isn't that the case with Part B services as well? Oh, well . . .) Instead, you can wait until you return to the United States. You'll then get a special enrollment period of up to two months, starting with the date of your return, to sign up with a Part D drug plan without incurring late penalties. (For more detailed information, see the later section "Deciding Whether and When to Sign Up for Part D Drug Coverage." For info on choosing plans that offer Part D drug coverage, see Chapters 10 and 11.)

Note: If you're looking to enroll in Part A or Part B when you're outside the United States, you need to know how to go about it, depending on your circumstances. These enrollment processes are discussed in Chapter 7.

You're in a domestic partnership

This section considers the scenario in which you are living together as an unmarried couple in a domestic partnership. In many situations such as these, one partner gets health insurance under the other partner's employer benefits. So this question arises: If you're the covered partner (as opposed to the partner whose employer provides the benefits), can you delay Part B enrollment if your other half is still working?

Domestic partnership is an arrangement in which you're living as a couple with a person of the same or opposite sex but are not formally married. In general, you're not permitted to delay Part B in this situation without incurring late penalties on the basis of receiving health coverage from your partner's employer plan. But some exceptions do exist:

>> Medicare allows you to delay Part B after age 65 and have a special enrollment period to sign up without penalty when your partner stops work or loses employer health benefits, as long as you live together in one of the states that accept common-law marriages and your domestic partnership meets the legal definition of common-law marriage where you live. (For info on these laws, see Unmarried Equality's fact sheet at www.unmarried.org/common-law-marriage-fact-sheet.)

>> You're allowed the same exception if all the following are true:

- You're under age 65 and have Medicare because of disability.

- Your partner's employer has 100 or more employees. (Note that Medicare requires the employer to have at least 100 employees if you are disabled and covered by a family member's insurance. When you are 65 and covered by your spouse's employer-based insurance, the employer needs to have only 20 employees to qualify for the exception.)

- You're accepted on your partner's employer insurance as a "family member" — even if you aren't legally married to the employee and regardless of whether they are the same or opposite sex to you.

>> You're also allowed the same exception if all the following are true:

- You're 65 or older, or you're younger but have Medicare due to disability.

- Your initial enrollment period began in December 2004 or earlier.

- You declined Part B during that IEP or voluntarily opted out of Part B coverage that you'd had before December 2004.

You're incarcerated

If you turn 65 when living in prison or any other type of correctional institution, you have two options:

>> Enroll in Part B during your initial enrollment period and pay monthly premiums, even though you can't use Medicare services while incarcerated.

>> Use the 12-month special enrollment period to sign up for original Medicare when you are released.

Similarly, if you're imprisoned after age 65 and already enrolled in Medicare, you're expected to continue paying the premiums to avoid penalties when you come out.

WARNING

Of course, if you have no income — and imprisonment makes you ineligible for Social Security payments — how can you pay Part B premiums while serving time? But the law ignores this practical predicament. So unless someone else can continue to pay your premiums for the duration, you'll most likely get penalties in the future. However, if you continue to be covered by insurance from your spouse's active employment (as explained earlier in this chapter), you may be able to avoid penalties.

Part D drug coverage has different rules. You can't use this coverage while you're in prison, but you're entitled to a special enrollment period after your release to enroll in a Part D drug plan without penalty, as explained in the next section.

Deciding Whether and When to Sign Up for Part D Drug Coverage

Part D coverage for prescription drugs comes with its own set of rules on enrollment. But these rules are more flexible and allow more choices to fit your situation. So if you get drug insurance from another source (for example, a current or former employer), you may not need to sign up for Part D at all.

This section explains what alternative creditable drug coverage from other sources means — which types of coverage meet that definition and which don't. Whether you need Part D if you don't have other coverage but don't actually take any medications is also discussed. And finally, the best times to sign up for Part D to avoid penalties, according to your own circumstances are listed.

Assessing drug coverage you have from elsewhere

You don't need Part D if you already have creditable drug coverage from another source. *Creditable* means something that can be credited or counted. So under Medicare rules, your drug coverage is creditable if its value is at least as good as Part D's — specifically, if whoever sponsors it pays at least as much money overall for everybody in the plan as Medicare would. You can't determine this accountancy measure on your own, so the following sections provide the rules of thumb on which kind of coverage is, may be, or definitely isn't creditable.

REMEMBER

In general, having creditable coverage means you don't need to enroll in Part D and would be able to switch to a Part D drug plan without penalty if you lost this coverage sometime in the future. But you may want to consider signing up with Part D anyway if it would benefit you significantly — for example, if you're eligible for the Extra Help program, which provides low-cost drug coverage to people with incomes under a certain level. (For details, head to Chapter 4.)

WARNING

However, don't even think of dropping your drug insurance from other sources without being sure of the consequences. In some cases, dropping drug coverage may mean losing your medical benefits, too. Contact your health plan for information before taking any action.

Coverage that's creditable

REMEMBER

You can assume your coverage is creditable — allowing you to stay out of Part D without risking late penalties — if you have it from any of the following:

>> The Federal Employees Health Benefits (FEHB) Program for federal workers or retirees (and their covered spouses)

>> The TRICARE or TRICARE For Life (TFL) program for active or retired military personnel (and their covered spouses)

>> The Veterans Administration (VA) health program for veterans

>> Federal health programs for Native Americans, such as the Indian Health Service

>> State Pharmacy Assistance Programs (SPAPs) if qualified under Medicare rules; I introduce these programs in Chapter 4

Note: If your current drug coverage comes from Medicaid, you'll be automatically transferred to Part D when you become eligible for Medicare, as explained in Chapter 4. So although Medicaid provides coverage that's at least as good as Part D, creditability isn't an issue.

Coverage that you need to check out

Some types of drug coverage may or may not be creditable. So you need to find out — by looking at your plan's enrollment materials or by contacting its administrators, who are legally required to provide this information — if your coverage comes from any of the following:

>> A current or former employer or union

>> COBRA temporary insurance

>> Individual (non-employer or non-union) insurance that you pay for yourself, including drug coverage purchased under the Affordable Care Act ("Obamacare")

REMEMBER

An important point to remember is that if you aren't enrolled in Part A or Part B, you're not eligible for Part D, and therefore you can't incur late penalties — even if your drug coverage at work isn't creditable. This scenario could happen if you continue to work after age 65 and postpone both Part A and Part B enrollment because you have a health savings account (HSA) at work — a situation discussed earlier in this chapter.

Coverage that isn't creditable

WARNING

If you get drug coverage under a Medigap supplemental insurance policy, you have an older type of policy (labeled H, I, or J) that dates from before 2006. You're free to keep this policy if you choose, but be aware that the drug coverage it provides isn't creditable. So if you switch to Part D now or in the future, you'll face late penalties. And the longer you continue to keep this type of policy, the more expensive it will become; because it's no longer sold, over time the pool of people who have it will dwindle — and the higher the penalties will grow. (Chapter 4 has more info on Medigap.)

Coverage that isn't coverage

I bring this category up because people sometimes think they have coverage when they really don't. The term *coverage* means insurance for which you (or maybe a third party, such as an employer or the government) pay premiums to reduce your drug costs in the future as well as now. So the following don't count as creditable coverage for Part D purposes:

>> Pharmacy discount programs

>> State drug discount programs

>> Drug manufacturers' assistance programs

>> Patient assistance programs or charities

>> Medical/health cost-sharing plans (these are typically faith-based programs where members pool money to help pay for health expenses)

>> Low-cost drugs from Canada, Mexico, or other foreign countries

>> Low-cost drugs from medical clinics

>> Free samples from doctors

Debating whether you need Part D if you don't take medications

People new to Medicare very often have asked, "Why should I pay good money for Part D when I don't use any prescription drugs?" It's a perfectly fair question. But the standard answer is "Because you don't have a crystal ball." No one does. In other words, you can't peer into the future and know for a fact that you won't fall victim to some unforeseen illness or injury that takes expensive drugs to treat — next month, next year, or a decade down the road. And that's true even if you lead the healthiest of lifestyles. The strictest regimens of salads and workouts can't guarantee immunity from genetic disease or the results of a serious car crash.

The point is that Part D is insurance, just like homeowners insurance and auto insurance. You pay premiums to protect yourself from the high costs of fire and accidents, even if you never expect to make a claim. Part D plays a similar role: It's there if and when you need it. The difference is that, as you get older, your chances of needing prescription drugs are far higher than your chances of totaling your car.

TIP

Nonetheless, when you don't take any medications, or take only a few occasional ones, those monthly premiums can seem a waste of money. So you may want to consider a compromise: Pick the Part D plan with the lowest premium in your area. That way, you get coverage, but at the least cost.

Figuring the best time to enroll in Part D

The "best" time always depends on your circumstances. Check out your own situation on the following list to see how to avoid late penalties by choosing the most appropriate timing for Part D enrollment:

>> **You don't have creditable drug coverage.** You need to sign up with a Part D drug plan during your seven-month initial enrollment period around age 65. In this case, the deadline is the last day of your IEP. (IEPs are discussed earlier

in this chapter.) The exception is if you have health insurance from a current employer beyond 65 and delay Part A and Part B enrollment. In this situation, you can also delay signing up for Part D until the job ends, even if the drug coverage you receive at work isn't creditable, without risking late penalties.

>> **You have creditable drug coverage.** You don't need to enroll in a Part D drug plan. But if you lose this coverage in the future, you'll be entitled to a special enrollment period of two months to enroll in a drug plan and avoid late penalties. (Note that if you delayed Part B because of having health insurance from your or your spouse's current employment, your SEP for enrolling in a Part D drug plan is much shorter — by six months — than the SEP for enrolling in Part B. SEPs are discussed in detail earlier in this chapter.)

>> **You're living in a place where you can't use Part D benefits — either outside the United States or in prison.** You also get a special enrollment period on your return to this country or on your release. But the length of this SEP depends on your situation:

  - If you turned 65 during this period of absence, the month of your return or release counts as the fourth month of your seven-month IEP. So your deadline is the last day of the third month after the month you returned or were released.

  - If you turned 65 before you left the United States or went to prison, you get an SEP of two months after your return or release to enroll (or re-enroll) in a Part D drug plan without penalty.

>> **You have Medicare under age 65 because of disability.** The rules according to any of the situations in this section also apply to you.

>> **You sign up for Medicare in a general enrollment period (January 1 to March 31) because you missed your original sign-up deadline.** You're entitled to an SEP to sign up with a Part D plan to get drug coverage without waiting for open enrollment at the end of the year. This SEP runs from April 1 to June 30, and coverage begins July 1.

WARNING

The law says that if you have Medicare Part A and/or Part B, and you go for more than 63 days without Part D or other creditable coverage, you get permanent late penalties. So 63 days is often given as the length of the special enrollment period you can use to avoid a penalty. But that isn't precisely accurate. Rather, you must be actually receiving Part D coverage within 63 days to avoid a penalty.

Say you lose your creditable coverage on March 31. Counting 63 days from that date brings you to June 2. If you leave it to the last minute and sign up with a Part D plan on June 1 or 2, you're still within the 63-day time frame. But you won't avoid a late penalty because, under Part D rules, your drug coverage actually begins on the first day of the month *after* you enroll — in this example, July 1.

You're then penalized for one month without coverage. So think of the special enrollment period as being limited to two months rather than 63 days — as noted earlier in this section — and you'll be okay.

Understanding the Consequences of Not Signing Up at the Right Time

Nobody can force you to sign up for Medicare and pay premiums if you don't want to. But if you think you'll need Medicare at some stage in the future, you should be aware of the consequences of late enrollment.

This section focuses on what happens if you miss your personal deadlines for Part B (in which enrolling late has the costliest repercussions), Part A, and Part D. Each — of course! — has different rules.

REMEMBER

However, you won't have to pay late penalties in these circumstances:

>> **Part A or B:** If you qualify for Medicaid or a Medicare Savings Program.

>> **Part D:** If you qualify for Extra Help or are not enrolled in Part A and Part B.

>> **Part A, B, or D:** If you pay penalties for any of these when receiving Medicare under age 65, the penalties will stop as soon as you reach 65 and become eligible for Medicare through age rather than disability.

For info on Medicare Savings Programs and Extra Help, flip to Chapter 4.

PENALTIES ON BENEFITS? WHAT WERE THEY THINKING?

Signing up later than your personal deadline can result in having to pay higher premiums for Part B and Part D for all future years and to wait months for coverage to begin. The reason is that Medicare wants to persuade you to sign up as soon as possible, and financial penalties or delays in coverage are the big sticks it uses to convince you. That rationale is rooted in basic insurance principles, which require a large pool of enrollees to spread the financial load. If all users were able to delay enrollment until they needed Medicare, the program would either cease to function or become so expensive that few people could afford it.

(continued)

(continued)

However, it seems patently unfair that late penalties can cause lifelong financial consequences for many people who never realized they were breaking any rules. Very often, they are folks who have other health coverage — for example, retiree benefits or COBRA — and who argue reasonably that by delaying Part B enrollment, they've saved Medicare money. In 2020, roughly 776,000 beneficiaries were paying Part B late penalties.

In 2020, Congress passed the Beneficiary Enrollment Notification and Eligibility Simplification Act (known as the BENES Act) to help simplify Medicare enrollment. In 2023, bipartisan lawmakers proposed the BENES Act 2.0, which would provide additional advance notice to those approaching Medicare eligibility about enrollment rules and penalties.

Missing your deadline for Part B

REMEMBER

Depending on your situation — which you can quickly identify in Table 6-1 earlier in this chapter — your personal deadline for Part B enrollment is one of the following:

>> The end of your seven-month IEP around the time you turn 65

>> The end of the eight-month SEP that you're entitled to if you were able to delay Part B beyond age 65 because you had health insurance from your (or your spouse's) current job

For example, say your 65th birthday falls in October. That month is the fourth month of your seven-month IEP, so the last day of your IEP is January 31. Or say that you continue working beyond 65 in a job with health benefits, and retire a few years later at the end of March. In this case, the last day of your eight-month SEP would be November 30.

Whichever final date applies to you is your deadline. Beyond it, you can certainly still enroll in Part B, but you then face two consequences:

>> You can sign up only during the *general enrollment period* (GEP), which runs from January 1 to March 31 each year; your coverage begins the month following enrollment.

>> You may be hit with late penalties that are added to your monthly Part B premiums for all future years.

WARNING

For some people, there's a third consequence: If you retire and continue to receive health benefits from your former employer, Medicare often becomes your primary coverage, meaning that it pays your medical bills first. So if you don't sign up for Medicare as soon as you can, your retiree plan may refuse to pay for medical services you've received, leaving you to foot the entire expense yourself. This situation doesn't always happen, but if you have a retiree health plan you need to find out — in advance! — exactly how it fits in with Medicare, as explained in more detail in Chapter 8.

The following sections delve into the details of the first two consequences.

Going without health coverage

For many people, the first of these consequences is the worst because it can mean going for months without health coverage. Here's a real-life example:

> When Bill and Barbara showed up at their local Social Security office to sign up for Medicare, they were confident they were doing things right. After Bill retired from his job, the couple had been covered by COBRA, which extended his employer insurance for 18 months. Now those benefits were ending, and Bill and Barbara needed Medicare. But they didn't know — and nobody had told them — that COBRA doesn't count as employer insurance for Part B enrollment purposes, so they should've signed up when he retired. Bill and Barbara had to wait until the following general enrollment period (January – March) to sign up for Medicare, with coverage beginning the month after they signed up. Because their COBRA benefits had run out at the end of May, they had to wait until February, or eight months, for Medicare to kick in — a long time when they couldn't get other insurance and were terrified of becoming seriously sick or injured.

Other circumstances — especially receiving retiree health benefits from a former employer — can land you in a similar scary situation if you don't know the rules or if you ignore them.

Paying more for Part B services than you need to

The worst thing about being hit with Part B late penalties after age 65 is that they're permanent — you continue paying them as extras added to every monthly premium for as long as you continue in the program. So you'll always pay more (perhaps a lot more) for exactly the same coverage than if you hadn't missed your deadline. (If you get the penalties when you're under 65, the penalties continue only until you're 65; at that point, when you become entitled to Medicare based on age rather than disability, they cease.)

In a nutshell, here's how the Part B penalty is calculated: It amounts to an extra 10 percent for every full 12-month period during which you could have signed up for Part B but didn't (and didn't qualify for a special enrollment period).

But these words need parsing if you're to understand exactly when the Part B penalty clock may start ticking in your own case:

>> If you should've signed up at age 65 but missed the deadline, it's straightforward: Your liability for penalties begins on the day after your seven-month IEP ends.

>> If you should've signed up during the eight-month SEP that followed your or your spouse's retirement from work and you missed that deadline, the Part B penalty clock is reset to the time of the retirement or when your group health coverage ended (whichever is earlier) and starts ticking then — not when your SEP expired.

And that's not all. Here are some other things about Part B penalties that you should be aware of:

>> **Meaning of *full 12-month period*:** In the definition of how the Part B penalty is calculated, this wording — "You pay an extra 10 percent for every full 12-month period" — is very precise and may even work to your advantage. It means that if the length of time between those two crucial dates — your enrollment deadline and the end of the GEP when you eventually sign up — falls short of 12 months (even by a day or two), the 10 percent penalty isn't applied.

>> **Penalty increase over time:** Not only are Part B late penalties permanent, but the amounts you pay are also likely to increase a little every year. That's because the penalty is always calculated as a percentage of the Part B premiums for any given year. For example, a person who received a 50 percent penalty on the $144.60 Part B premium in 2020 paid a total of $2,602.80 — $1,735.20 in standard premiums plus $867.60 in Part B penalties. In 2024, when the standard premium is $174.70, that same person paid a total of $3,144.60 — $2,096.40 in premiums plus $1,048.20 in penalties.

>> **Penalties for people with higher incomes:** Late penalties are applied only to the standard Part B premium, not to the additional surcharges that people with higher incomes pay. (These surcharges are explained in Chapter 3.)

>> **When late penalties may be waived:** If your Part B premiums are paid by your state under Medicaid or one of the Medicare Savings Programs (see Chapter 4 for details), you don't have to pay late penalties. Also, if you incur late penalties when you have Medicare through disability, these will stop when you reach 65, as noted earlier in this section.

All these rules are enough to make anyone's eyes glaze over. But these examples may make them clearer:

>> Melinda missed signing up at the end of her IEP in May but enrolled the following February during a GEP. Because fewer than 12 months had elapsed

between May 31 and March 11 (the day her GEP enrollment coverage started), she didn't have to pay a late penalty.

>> George worked in a job with health insurance until age 69, and although he was entitled to an eight-month SEP on retirement to sign up for Part B, he chose not to because as a veteran he had VA health benefits. But later he decided he needed Medicare coverage as well. When he signed up in January, almost four years (46 months) had gone by between the end of the month when he retired and when he received coverage during the GEP. The three full years counted toward the penalty, but the remaining 10 months didn't. So George paid an extra 30 percent (but not the 40 percent he expected) for his Part B coverage.

>> Clint and Maria didn't see the point of paying for Part B after he retired at 65 because they got good retiree health benefits from his former employer. But ten years later, the premiums for this insurance had risen so high that the couple could no longer afford them. Medicare was their only alternative, but by then they each had to pay 100 percent more for their coverage (a 10 percent penalty for each of the ten years of delay) — double what they'd have paid if they'd enrolled when he retired.

Passing your deadline for Part A

Here's the good news: If you or your spouse paid enough payroll taxes while working (as explained in Chapter 5), you automatically qualify for Medicare Part A services when you turn 65 and don't need to pay premiums for them. And in that case, you *can't* be charged any Part A late penalty — even if you don't formally enroll during your IEP or SEP.

WARNING

However, you can be hit with late penalties if you could've gotten Part A services by paying monthly premiums for them but failed to enroll as soon as you were eligible. This trap is one that quite a lot of people fall into, mainly because they don't realize they can buy into Part A if they haven't managed to acquire enough work credits.

You're eligible for Part A benefits by paying monthly premiums if you're at least 65 and you're one of the following:

>> A United States citizen

>> A legal resident (green-card holder) who has lived in the United States for at least five years

In this situation, you're liable for Part A late penalties if you don't sign up before your personal enrollment deadline. That may be during your IEP. However, if you're covered by health insurance from your own or your spouse's current employer beyond age 65, you can delay enrolling in both Part A and Part B until this employment ends — by which time you may be entitled to an SEP to sign up for both without penalty.

Part A premiums are pretty expensive, and penalties make this coverage even more costly. However, the Part A penalty is calculated differently from the Part B penalty and isn't as harsh. It adds 10 percent to the premium, but that percentage isn't multiplied by the number of years you've delayed enrollment. Also, Part A penalties don't go on forever in the way Part B penalties do. You have to pay the Part A penalties for only double the length of time that you delayed signing up. So if the delay was two full years, you'd pay an extra 10 percent each month for four years; if you delayed five years, you'd pay the same penalties for ten years, and so on.

The actual penalty amounts are calculated according to whether you're required to pay the full Part A premium (based on having fewer than 30 work credits) or the reduced premium (30 to 39 work credits):

>> **Full premium:** In 2024, the full Part A premium is $505 a month, of which 10 percent is $50.50. So premium plus penalty in 2024 is $555.50 a month. If you'd delayed enrollment for two full years, you'd pay a penalty for four years but no longer. In each of these years, the penalty is 10 percent of the full Part A premium required for that year.

>> **Reduced premium (30 to 39 work credits):** In 2024, the reduced Part A premium is $278 a month, of which 10 percent is $27.80. So premium plus penalty in 2024 is $305.80 a month. If you'd delayed enrollment for three years, your penalty would continue for six years. In each of these years, the penalty is 10 percent of the reduced Part A premium required for that year.

For example, Craig assumed he didn't qualify for Medicare when he retired at age 65 because he hadn't earned enough credits from work. So he delayed enrollment for two years — waiting until his wife turned 62 to qualify on her work record. But when he went to sign up, he discovered he'd get late penalties for both Part A and Part B. Even though he didn't have enough work credits, he was still entitled to both Part A and Part B services at age 65 by paying premiums for them. Under the rules, he paid Part A penalties for four years but had to pay Part B penalties for the rest of his life.

Neglecting your deadline for Part D

Part D prescription drug coverage is voluntary. But it, too, comes with consequences if you enroll in a Part D drug plan later than you should. If you miss your deadline, both of the following can occur:

>> You probably won't be able to enroll in a drug plan until open enrollment, which runs from October 15 to December 7 each year, and your coverage won't begin until the following January 1.

>> You'll be penalized for every month that you were enrolled in Part A or Part B but didn't have either Part D or alternative creditable coverage after becoming eligible for Medicare at age 65 or through disability at a younger age.

This section addresses the two consequences of missing your Part D deadline in more detail. (The earlier section "Deciding Whether and When to Sign Up for Part D Drug Coverage" explains what creditable coverage means, itemizes types of drug coverage that are creditable, and indicates your deadline for Part D enrollment, according to your own circumstances.)

Being without drug coverage

Pay attention to the fact that after your personal deadline has expired, your opportunity for getting Part D drug coverage will likely come only once a year — during open enrollment in the fall — and benefits won't begin until January. (For exceptions, refer to Chapter 15.)

Being without coverage when you need it is the real cost of missing your deadline. Illness and injury can strike out of the blue, without any regard for enrollment periods. If this situation happens, and you suddenly find yourself in need of really expensive drugs when you have no coverage, the damage to your finances and/or your health may be catastrophic.

For example, Michael was diagnosed with cancer in March. The drugs his doctor said would be most effective to treat him cost more than $3,000 a month. Michael, who hadn't enrolled in Part D but assumed he could join at any time, was shocked to find that he'd have to wait until the late fall to enroll and couldn't get coverage until January 1. Without Part D, he couldn't afford the drugs his doctor had prescribed.

You may think that this scenario is an off-the-wall example: $3,000 a *month?* Sadly, many of the newest drugs used to treat the most serious health conditions cost much more — tens of thousands of dollars a month. But even drugs that are older and more reasonably priced ($300 a month, say) may still be too expensive for many people who don't have insurance.

Understanding how Part D late penalties are calculated

The other consequence of enrolling in Part D later than you should is getting penalties that are added to your Part D premiums according to how many months you've been without creditable coverage since becoming eligible for Medicare — that is, since turning 65 or starting to receive Medicare benefits due to disability at an earlier age. (The only exception, as explained earlier in this chapter, is if you've delayed enrollment in Part A or B — perhaps because you have a health savings account at work. In that situation, you're not eligible to sign up for Part D and therefore can't incur late penalties, even if your employer's drug coverage isn't creditable.)

The basis of the Part D late penalty is something called the *national average premium* (NAP). Every fall, Medicare works out the average of all the premiums that Part D plans nationwide will charge during the following year. This dollar amount becomes the NAP for that next year. If you incur the late penalty, you pay 1 percent of the NAP for every month you were without creditable coverage or Part D. This formula works out to 12 percent a year.

Here's what else you should know about Part D penalties:

>> **They're permanent.** The penalties are added to all future Part D premiums for as long as you're in the program.

>> **The amount represents 1 percent of the NAP in any particular year.** So if the NAP goes up or down from year to year, so does the penalty. For example, in 2024, the NAP increased to $34.70 from $31.50 in 2023. The penalties changed accordingly.

>> **The longer you fail to sign up for Part D when you have no other creditable drug coverage, the more the penalties will mount.** In most cases, enrollment can take place only once a year, so every extra year of delay adds a further 12 percent to the penalty.

Check out the following examples to see the math for yourself:

>> Rebecca turned 65 in March 2023. But by the time her personal enrollment period ended at the end of June, she hadn't signed up for Part D and had no other creditable drug coverage. She did enroll during open enrollment in fall 2019, and her coverage began on January 1, 2024. By then she was six months over her deadline (July through December). So her late penalty was 6 percent (1 percent times 6 months) of the NAP. In 2024, the NAP was $34.70, and 1 percent of that amount was 35 cents. So Rebecca's late penalty in 2024 was calculated at 35 cents multiplied by her six months without coverage, which came to $2.10. (Medicare rounds the penalty to the nearest 10 cents.) So Rebecca paid $2.10 a month in 2024, on top of her plan's premiums.

>> Brad was 70 years old and already in Medicare when Part D drug coverage began in 2006. Because the program was just starting, the initial enrollment period for

that year was extended into May. But Brad had some drug coverage under a Medigap policy and he opted to keep it instead of going to the trouble of grappling with the new Part D. By law, this policy could no longer be sold after Part D took effect, and over the years its premiums became ever more costly as the pool of people who had it became ever smaller. Finally, Brad decided to switch to a Part D plan. But because his Medigap policy wasn't considered creditable coverage, he had to pay late penalties for a total of eight years and seven months stretching from June 2006 to December 2014. When his Part D coverage began in January 2015, his penalty was calculated at 101 months without coverage multiplied by 33 cents (1 percent of the 2015 NAP). This penalty added an extra $33.30 a month to his Part D plan's premiums for that year, or an extra $399.60 over the whole year. In 2024, when the NAP was $34.70, Brad's penalty came to $35.35 per month, or $424.20 for the whole year.

Note: If you receive low-cost Part D drug coverage under the Extra Help program (explained in Chapter 4), you won't pay any late penalties.

Figuring out whether you can get a late penalty revoked

Depending on your situation, the answer to the question "Can I get a late penalty revoked?" may be "yes," "maybe," or "forget about it." But you have the right to challenge a penalty that you think has been unfairly imposed.

If you get hit with late penalties for Parts A or B, you'll find out about it when the Social Security Administration sends you a letter. In the case of a Part D late penalty, you'll receive a letter from the Part D plan or Medicare Advantage plan that you've signed up with. Either type of letter gives instructions on how to appeal the decision if you don't agree with it, together with deadlines for responding.

REMEMBER

The government enforces the rules strictly, and being ignorant of them isn't considered a defense. But you may have a chance if you can show that a government official made a mistake or gave you incorrect information that sent you on the wrong track.

If you think the late penalty is a mistake

Mistakes do happen. Government bureaucracies are certainly not immune to human error and computer glitches. AARP has investigated situations where Social Security imposed late penalties that turned out to be wrong, and although officials rarely admit mistakes, they do make amends. (In one case, Social Security refunded more than $14,000 to a 91-year-old widow after incorrectly deducting grossly inflated Part B premiums from her Social Security benefits for years.)

If you think you've been charged a late penalty in error, follow these steps:

1. **Check your facts.**

   Review your situation since becoming eligible for Medicare to ensure that the mistake isn't yours. You should be able to judge from the information in this chapter whether you let your enrollment deadline slip past and became liable for a late penalty.

2. **Reply in good time.**

   The letter you receive notifying you of the penalty comes with instructions on how to challenge the ruling. It also encloses a form you can use to request a *reconsideration* — an independent review of the decision. Normally, you have 60 days to complete the form and return it to the address provided.

3. **Collect your evidence.**

   Get together any documents that support your case. These items may include records showing that you had acceptable employer insurance for all or part of the time frame in question, documents indicating (for Part D purposes) when you were outside the country or in prison, immigration records, and so on. If you've lost documents showing that you had employer coverage, try to get letters from the employer or the health plan itself confirming that you had such coverage and providing dates. Make copies of these documents to submit in evidence — don't send originals.

4. **Get help if you need it.**

   Your State Health Insurance Assistance Program (SHIP) provides free, personal help from trained counselors on all Medicare issues, including late penalties. For contact information, go to Appendix A.

You need to continue paying the penalties on top of the premiums while the case is being investigated. If the decision goes against you, the penalty will stand. But if it goes in your favor, the penalty will be removed and the excess charges you've already paid will be refunded to you. If the penalty is reduced rather than waived, you'll be refunded the amounts you've overpaid. For more information on appealing decisions that you don't agree with, see Chapter 16.

If you were given wrong information

Getting slapped with a late penalty because of some regulation you've never heard of is bad enough. Getting that penalty because you acted on inaccurate or incomplete information from someone you were confident would know feels a lot worse.

I'm not talking here about family, friends, doctors, or even employers' benefits departments — none of whom can be expected to be reliable sources on Medicare's complexities. And if the misinformation came from them, you can't do anything about it anyway.

But if misleading information from a government official — whether from Social Security, Medicare, or other government agencies — caused you to miss your enrollment deadline and led to a late penalty, you may be able to get redress under a little-known process called *equitable relief*. You're allowed to apply to Social Security for equitable relief if your failure to sign up on time for Part A, B, or D was due to "error, misrepresentation, or inaction of a federal employee or any person authorized by the federal government to act in its behalf." (This group includes employees of Part D or Medicare Advantage plans.)

For example, Greg went to his local Social Security office to sign up for Medicare. The official asked if he had insurance from an employer. "I sure do," Greg replied. But the official didn't explain that Greg could only delay Part B if he or his wife were still working. So Greg was left thinking, wrongly, that his retiree benefits counted as employer insurance and that he didn't need to enroll in Part B.

For details of applying for equitable relief, see Chapter 16.

IN THIS CHAPTER

» Joining Parts A and B automatically

» Enrolling in Parts A and B within the United States or from overseas

» Refusing Part A or Part B coverage

» Making sure you're clear on when your coverage will begin

» Moving from Obamacare to original Medicare

Chapter **7**

Discovering How to Sign Up for Medicare

So you've got your personal enrollment deadline figured out and know when you should sign up to avoid nasty surprises like late penalties. In comparison, the process of actually enrolling is relatively straightforward. (Phew!)

This chapter details the actual mechanics of enrolling in Part A and Part B (original Medicare) — but not in Medicare Advantage (MA) plans or Part D. You must first be enrolled in both A and B to sign up with an MA plan, and you must have either A or B to join a stand-alone Part D prescription drug plan. Also, enrollment in an MA or Part D plan involves the more complicated process of comparing probably dozens of private plans available in your area and choosing just one. That's a whole different ballgame that is discussed in detail in Chapter 10 (Part D drug plans) and Chapter 11 (Medicare Advantage plans).

Here, the three ways of diving into the Medicare experience, according to your situation, are considered:

>> Getting signed up automatically (if you're already receiving Social Security, railroad retirement, or disability benefits)

>> Actively applying for enrollment inside the United States (if you're not yet drawing these benefits)

>> Signing up if you live outside of the United States

You'll also find out how to opt out of Part A or Part B if you have reason to want to — and why you should be very careful about doing so. In addition, this chapter discusses when your coverage will begin, depending on when you enroll. And finally, the process of transitioning from Obamacare to Medicare — a change that affects thousands of people every day — is covered.

REMEMBER

One word upfront: Enrollment and disenrollment in Medicare Parts A and B are always handled by the Social Security Administration (SSA), not by Medicare. So if you have issues about signing up or opting out and need to speak to a federal official, Social Security is the agency you need to contact.

Being Automatically Enrolled in Medicare Parts A and B

Social Security automatically signs you up for Medicare — without any action on your part — in each of the following circumstances:

>> You're coming up to your 65th birthday and you're already receiving retirement benefits from Social Security or the Railroad Retirement Board.

>> You're younger than 65, but you're about to become eligible for Medicare on the basis of disability (as I explain in Chapter 5).

>> You're older than 65 and have delayed Medicare enrollment because you have coverage from your or your spouse's active employment (as explained in Chapter 6), but you've contacted Social Security or the Railroad Retirement Board to start drawing retirement benefit payments.

Note: If you live in a foreign country, you won't be automatically signed up for Medicare even if you're already receiving Social Security or railroad benefits. If you live in Puerto Rico and have begun drawing these benefits, you'll be automatically enrolled in Part A but must apply for Part B.

In the first two situations in the preceding list, Social Security sends your Medicare ID card through the mail three months before your coverage is due to begin. In the third situation, you receive your card when Social Security has approved your retirement benefits. If you don't receive it, call Social Security at 800-772-1213 (TTY 800-325-0778 for the hard of hearing).

REMEMBER

The red-white-and-blue Medicare card is valuable. It's your passport to Medicare services, so make sure in the months before you become eligible for Medicare that you open any envelope that comes to you from the Social Security Administration. You really don't want to throw it away by accident, but tossing this important letter is easy enough — especially in the weeks before you turn 65, when you can expect to be deluged with mail from insurance companies trying to sell you some kind of private Medicare plan. (Chapter 12 has more to say about resisting sales pressure and avoiding scams.) So keep an eye out for envelopes bearing the Social Security Administration's name and official logo in the left-hand corner.

The envelope containing your Medicare card includes a letter informing you when your coverage will begin. The card itself also has printed on it the dates when you can start using Medicare services. For example, if you turn 65 on May 14, your card should arrive three months earlier, in February. The letter and the card will note that your Part A and Part B coverage begins on May 1. And that's fine if you want to use both A and B services as soon as possible. File the letter away, put your Medicare card somewhere safe, and that's it — you're done.

WARNING

But what if you want to opt out of Part A or Part B? The Social Security letter that accompanies your Medicare card describes how to decline Part B and gives you a deadline for requesting disenrollment. But whether opting out is a good idea depends on your situation — and is something you should consider very carefully. In fact, a whole section is devoted to the issues at stake in opting out of Part A or Part B later in this chapter. So be sure to read that section before taking any action.

Sign Me Up! Applying for Medicare Parts A and B

In the days when Social Security's full retirement age was 65 and most Americans retired at 65 and became eligible for Medicare at that age, it was all pretty simple. You just went down to the local Social Security office and signed up for Medicare and Social Security (or railroad) retirement benefits all at the same time. That isn't the case anymore.

Medicare sign-up for most people is still at age 65. But in recent years, full retirement age has gradually been moved back by a couple of months every year. It has now reached age 67 for anybody born from 1960 on. (Certainly, you can draw reduced benefits from age 62 onward, but you won't get the full amount due to you unless you delay collecting it until you hit 67.) Therefore, you likely won't be automatically enrolled for Medicare (as explained in the previous section) but must actively apply.

The information in the following sections is divided up according to whether you're applying for Medicare from within the United States and its territories or from outside the country if you're living abroad.

Signing up from inside the United States

The mechanics of applying from inside the United States are pretty straight-forward. But being aware of the ins and outs of the three application methods open to you — and also what you need to know if you happen to migrate to different states for parts of the year or have no fixed abode — is useful. You also need to consider how to make sure you fully understand the enrollment process if English isn't your first language. I cover all these topics in the following sections.

One . . . two . . . three ways to sign up

You have three options for enrolling in Part A and/or Part B. In most cases, you can choose any of these methods regardless of whether you're applying during your initial enrollment period (around age 65), during a special enrollment period (because you delayed enrollment beyond 65 based on health insurance from work), or during the annual general enrollment period that runs from January 1 to March 31 each year (because you didn't sign up when you should've). I discuss these enrollment periods in more detail in the later section "Knowing When Your Coverage Begins."

>> **Applying by phone:** Call Social Security's main number at 800-772-1213 (TTY 800-325-0778) and schedule an appointment for a phone interview at a convenient time for you.

>> **Applying at your local Social Security office:** Call Social Security's main number and schedule an appointment for an interview at your local Social Security office at a convenient time for you. To find the address of your local office and its hours of operation, go to the locator on Social Security's website at secure.ssa.gov/ICON/main.jsp. If you make an appointment in advance, you don't have to wait in line.

>> **Applying online:** You can apply online on Social Security's website — provided you're at least 64 years and nine months old, you don't want to apply for retirement benefits at this time, you don't yet have any Medicare coverage, and you don't live outside of the United States. Go to www.ssa.gov/medicare/sign-up, read the instructions carefully, and follow the directions.

In each case, you must provide certain information and documents to demonstrate your eligibility for Medicare. These typically include

- » Your Social Security number

- » Date of birth and original birth certificate or certified copy

- » Marital status and, if appropriate, original marriage certificate or certified copy

- » Proof of citizenship or lawful alien status if you weren't born in the United States (immigration documents, such as a green card)

- » Evidence of employer- or union-provided insurance based on your own or your spouse's active employment since turning 65 (if you delayed Part B enrollment for this reason)

- » A copy of your military service papers (DD Form 214, Certificate of Release or Discharge from Active Duty) if you served prior to 1968

- » A copy of your W-2 form and/or self-employment tax return for the previous year

WARNING

If you apply on the phone or online, you'll be asked to send in original documents (or certified copies) by mail or to drop them off at a Social Security office. If you prefer not to let these items out of your sight, you may as well enroll at your local SSA office anyway, take the documents with you, and take them home afterward. If you're a legal permanent resident, Social Security asks you not to mail in your foreign birth certificate, proof of permanent residency (green card), or any other immigration documents because they're all difficult to replace if lost. Because you need to submit these to a Social Security office, you may as well enroll there too.

WARNING

Applying online is obviously the most convenient way of signing up. Social Security officials say it should take only about ten minutes of your time. Still, in some situations, this method may not be the wisest course of action, and the old-fashioned way — actually speaking to someone — may be better:

- » If you live outside the United States, you can't enroll online. (I explain how to enroll while you're living abroad later in this chapter.)

- » If your situation is complicated, the relatively simple online application may not be able to handle it. In that case, Social Security will invite you to call in anyway to discuss it personally.

- » If you don't want to send valuable documents — such as birth and marriage certificates and immigration documents — through the mail, you should take them to a Social Security office instead, as noted earlier in this section.

- » If you're delaying Part B because you have employer-based insurance after age 65 (as explained in Chapter 6) but want to sign up for Part A during your initial enrollment period, having a personal chat with a Social Security official can help you check that you're doing the right thing according to the rules.

>> If you continue to work after 65 but your employer insurance includes a health savings account, you can no longer contribute to your account if you enroll in Medicare, as I explain in Chapter 6. So just hitting that "Submit" button online can cause you real problems.

>> If you want to ask questions — about Medicare or when the best time for you to sign up for retirement benefits is, for example — you can do so in person but not online.

Whichever sign-up method you choose, Social Security later sends you a computer printout containing the enrollment information that's been entered into your record. This hard copy gives you the opportunity to check that your info is correct — and, if it's not, to get the record changed. If you enroll online and Social Security requires more information about your situation, it'll contact you to request it.

TIP

When calling Social Security's main number, be prepared to wait for a while before getting connected to a customer service representative. Of course, you may get through in a flash. But it can take 45 minutes or more. With nowhere near the numbers of staff it needs, Social Security is faced with around 10,000 people turning 65 every day, as well as callers asking about scores of other issues besides Medicare enrollment. So be patient! Plan to read a book, tackle a puzzle, or go online while you wait. Or, when prompted, leave your phone number and wait to be called back.

If you live in different places for parts of the year

Many American retirees are sunbirds or snowbirds who migrate to cooler or warmer parts of the country for several months every year. Others spend chunks of time with family members in states far from their homes. And some are on the move all the time, with "home" being their recreational vehicles or, in a very different context, homeless shelters. In any of these situations, where do you sign up for Medicare?

REMEMBER

You're allowed to enroll in Medicare only in one place. Social Security requires this place to be your *principal residence,* which it defines as the place where you file taxes, register to vote, get your driver's license, and so on. Even if you're on the road year-round in your RV, the base you use for these activities is also the address to use for Medicare enrollment.

If you're homeless, Social Security may accept the address of a shelter or clinic, a P.O. box number, or anywhere else that you receive mail. For information, call Social Security toll-free at 800-772-1213 (TTY 800-325-0778) or contact your State Health Insurance Assistance Program (SHIP) at the toll-free phone number in Appendix A.

However, even though you must sign up for Medicare in one place, you can still receive Medicare benefits somewhere else — or indeed anywhere throughout the nation — providing you make the right decisions about the kind of coverage you choose. I discuss those decisions in detail in Chapter 9.

If English isn't your first language

Comprehending the complexities of Medicare — let alone the jargon that officials often use in trying to explain them — is hard enough even for native English speakers, but it's far more difficult if your English is less than fluent. So when signing up for Medicare, don't hesitate to ask for help to make sure you fully understand what you're told.

TIP

You have the right to ask for an interpreter when calling the Social Security Administration or visiting a local SSA office. Interpreters are available at no charge in more than 150 languages. But when calling the main SSA number listed earlier, it isn't immediately obvious how you can request interpreter services. Here's what to do when your call goes through:

1. **An automated voice tells you to press 1 for English or 2 for Spanish. If Spanish is the language you need, press 2. For any other language, press 1.**

2. **When the automated voice invites you to say what kind of service you need, say "operator."**

3. **When you're connected to a customer service representative, say "I need an interpreter in [language]."**

   This official will ask you to stay on the line while someone who speaks your language is contacted. The interpreter comes to the phone to translate what you and the official say to each other.

You can request the same service if you make an appointment to visit your local Social Security office. And of course, if you speak little English, a friend or family member can do all this work for you, if you allow that person to state your Social Security number while making the call.

Enrolling while you're living abroad

If you live outside the United States, first make sure that you've read the section in Chapter 6 that explains your options for the timing of Medicare enrollment. The choice you make — whether to sign up before your personal enrollment deadline while still abroad or leave it until you return to the United States — obviously affects the mechanics of signing up as well as your chances of getting late penalties. In the following sections, I assume you want to enroll while continuing to live abroad.

Applying if you qualify for full Medicare benefits

You're considered *fully insured* if you have enough credits from work on which you (or a spouse) paid payroll taxes, as explained in Chapter 5. In other words, you're entitled to Part A benefits without paying a premium for them.

TIP

In this situation, when living abroad, you can enroll in Medicare Part A and/or Part B by contacting the nearest American embassy or consulate in the nation where you're living. You can find contact information for them (locations, phone numbers, and email addresses) at www.socialsecurity.gov/foreign/foreign. htm. In Canada, you can contact one of the Social Security field offices listed at www.socialsecurity.gov/foreign/canada.htm.

Note: You can't enroll online on the Social Security website if you live outside the United States.

Applying if you aren't fully insured for Medicare

When you live in the United States and don't have enough work credits to qualify for premium-free Part A — as I explain in Chapter 5 — you can nonetheless get Part A services (usually hospital stays) if you pay monthly premiums. But you can't buy into the program in this way while your permanent address is in another country.

It doesn't matter whether you've maintained a U.S. address and telephone number, are on the electoral register, have family living in the States, return on regular visits, or keep regular links in any other way. Under Social Security rules, you must reside permanently within the United States or its territories to buy into Part A. Officials say a person can't establish residency in two places at the same time.

When you return permanently to the United States, you have an initial enrollment period to buy into Part A and to enroll in Part B — without incurring late penalties for either of them — regardless of how long you've lived outside the United States or how many years have passed since you turned 65. This enrollment period begins during the month of your return as a U.S. resident and expires at the end of the third month following. (For example, if you return in July, your initial enrollment period expires October 31.) Your coverage begins on the first day of the month after you enroll. But if you don't sign up within this time frame, you must wait until the next general enrollment period (January 1 to March 31), and you risk permanent late penalties.

To buy into Part A, you must also enroll in Part B. To sign up for both, call Social Security at 800-772-1213 (TTY 800-325-0778) from within the United States after your return.

Contacting Social Security from outside the United States

TIP

For questions on Medicare enrollment, you must contact the Social Security Administration. But you can't call its main toll-free phone number from overseas. However, you can get in touch with the SSA from outside the United States by mail or phone (though not email). In all cases, make sure that you provide your full name, address, phone number, and Social Security number.

>> **By mail:** Write to the Social Security Administration, Office of Earnings and International Operations, P.O. Box 17775, Baltimore, MD 21235, U.S.A.

>> **By phone:** If you're overseas, the number to call is 410-965-0160. You'll have to pay for the call because Social Security doesn't have a toll-free number that can be used from abroad. Also, you need to call during normal business hours for the U.S. eastern time zone.

Opting Out of or Disenrolling from Part A or Part B

Whether opting out of Part A or Part B is a good idea depends on your circumstances. But it's always something you should consider extremely carefully to avoid making a mistake that may cost you money and maybe coverage down the road.

When Social Security automatically enrolls you in Medicare — and this situation happens only if you receive (or are about to receive) Social Security or railroad retirement or disability benefits — it signs you up for both Part A and Part B and sends you a letter that gives you the option of declining Part B. In that case, you need to take action if you want to *opt out*. On the other hand, if you must apply for Medicare Parts A and B (because you're not receiving retirement or disability benefits), it's up to you to decide whether to *opt in*.

The following sections consider the possibilities and pitfalls for deciding not to take Part A and Part B coverage when you enroll. They also explain how you can disenroll from Part B when you already have it.

Declining Part A

Strictly speaking, you can't opt out of Part A if you're receiving Social Security retirement or disability benefits. The only way you can do so is to withdraw your application for retirement or disability benefits at this time — or, if you've already been drawing those benefits, to repay the government for all the payments you've already received.

That sounds like pretty heavy stuff, and it's already been the subject of a lawsuit (unsuccessful) against the U.S. government. But most people don't even consider declining Part A. After all, why give up a benefit that's free (no premiums) because you've already paid for it through taxes while working?

There may be one exception for opting out of Part A: If you'll continue to work when enrolled in Medicare and have from your employer health insurance with a high-deductible health plan and a health savings account (HSA) funded by pre-tax dollars. This option is only available, however, if your employer has 20 or more employees, since with fewer than 20, Medicare is the primary payer for health insurance. Under IRS rules, you can't continue to contribute to an HSA if you're enrolled in Medicare — although you can continue to use the funds in your HSA to pay for qualified medical expenses. This situation is explained in more detail in Chapter 6, together with your options if you have an HSA at work.

If you're entitled to Part A without paying premiums, you don't get hit with a late penalty if you delay enrolling in Part A. But you may incur late penalties if you can buy into Part A services by paying premiums for them but don't sign up at the right time. See Chapter 6 for details. Note that once you've signed up for Part A, you can opt out only within the following 12 months.

Opting out of Part B

You need to think twice about saying no to Part B coverage, even though you will need to pay a monthly premium. (If your income and resources are limited, you may be eligible for help paying your Medicare premiums through a state Medicare Savings Program, as explained in Chapter 4.) It's an important decision you need to make during the enrollment process — especially if you're signed up automatically — and you should be very clear on how to deal with it according to your situation.

So the following sections explain when opting out of Part B is okay — in other words, not likely to cause you any regrets (or cost you money!) in the future — and when doing so may cost you money or cause other problems. Bizarrely, the rules are different for people who have Medicare because they're 65 or older and those who have it at earlier ages on the basis of disability. So first these two groups will be looked at separately to suggest when people in each can confidently turn down Part B. Then I go into situations when refusing Part B may be risky for people in either group.

Knowing when to turn down Part B if you're 65 or older

REMEMBER

In general, when you're 65 or older, you should decline Part B only if you have group health insurance from an employer for whom you or your spouse is still actively working and that insurance is *primary* to Medicare (it pays before Medicare does), as I explain in detail in Chapter 6.

In this situation, you can delay Part B enrollment without penalty until the employment stops or the insurance ends (as explained in Chapter 6). So if you're not yet drawing Social Security (or railroad) retirement benefits, just skip signing up for Part B. Or, if you're enrolled automatically because you're receiving those benefits, you can decline Part B by following the instructions that Social Security sends you in the letter that accompanies your Medicare card and meeting the specified deadline (see the earlier section "Being Automatically Enrolled in Medicare Parts A and B" for more about this process).

Opting out ensures that you don't have to pay Part B premiums or, if you're receiving retirement benefits, have them deducted each month from your Social Security or railroad retirement check. It also ensures that you keep intact your right to buy Medigap supplemental insurance with full federal protections after you retire. Those protections prohibit insurance companies from refusing to sell you a Medigap policy and charging you higher premiums based on your health status or pre-existing medical conditions (as explained in Chapter 10) — provided that you buy it at certain specified times, notably within six months of enrolling in Part B. You forfeit that right if you sign up for Part B when you reach 65 and retire more than six months later.

Understanding when to turn down Part B if you're under 65

REMEMBER

In general, if you have Medicare based on disability, you should decline Part B only if

>> You have health insurance from an employer for whom you or your spouse actively works, and the employer has 100 or more employees.

>> You're covered as a family member on somebody else's group health plan at work, and the employer has 100 or more employees.

What does *family member* mean? It means that the employer providing this insurance regards you as eligible for health coverage based on your domestic relationship with an employee — even if you aren't formally married to that person and even if they are the same sex as you. (This situation is discussed in Chapter 6.)

Recognizing when turning down Part B at any age is risky

REMEMBER

Regardless of whether you have Medicare based on disability or age, you should definitely enroll in Part B (or not refuse it) if you have health insurance that will automatically become *secondary* to Medicare (it will pay after Medicare does) when your Medicare benefits begin. This includes the following:

>> Health insurance that you buy yourself on the open insurance market and that isn't provided by an employer

>> Health insurance from an employer with fewer than 20 employees (if you're 65 or older)

>> Health insurance from an employer with fewer than 100 employees (if you have Medicare due to disability)

>> Retiree or COBRA benefits from a former employer (your own or your spouse's)

>> Health benefits from the military's TRICARE For Life retiree program

You should enroll in Part B coverage in the preceding situations for a very good reason quite apart from the possibilities of late penalties down the road if you don't. When Medicare is considered primary coverage, it pays your medical bills first. So if you're not enrolled in Part B, you run the real risk of having your insurance plan deny any claims that Medicare could've paid — from basic ones like doctors' visits and lab tests to major ones like surgery. In other words, you may face having to pay the entire bill. Worse, if your own insurer takes a while to realize that you haven't enrolled in Part B, your plan may even ask you to pay back all the money it has spent on your medical services since you became eligible for Medicare.

This kind of thing doesn't always happen. For example, if you're a federal retiree and receiving health insurance from a plan in the Federal Employee Health Benefits (FEHB) Program, you aren't required to enroll in Part B — as explained in the section on how Medicare works with other health insurance in Chapter 8. Also, not all small employers (with fewer than 20 workers) insist that Medicare-eligible employees enroll in Medicare.

REMEMBER

The bottom line: When deciding whether to accept or decline Part B, finding out whether Medicare would be primary or secondary to any other insurance that you have is critically important.

Disenrolling from Part B

You may think that *disenrolling* means the same as opting out. And that may be so in general. But this section addresses a specific situation where you're already enrolled in Part B, but then — weeks, months, or years later — you or your spouse starts a job with health benefits. If that happens, do you really need to keep on paying those Part B premiums?

You can disenroll from Part B and stop paying premiums for it in this situation — regardless of whether it was you or your spouse who landed this new job — if it meets the same conditions described in Chapter 6. In other words, you're allowed to delay Part B without penalty if you have health insurance from current employment and the employer plan is primary to Medicare.

To disenroll from Part B, you're required to fill out a Request for Termination of Premium Hospital and/or Supplementary Medical Insurance form (CMS-1763) that you must complete either during a personal interview at a Social Security office or on the phone with a Social Security representative. For an interview, call the Social Security Administration toll-free at 800-772-1213 (TTY 800-325-0778).

Social Security insists on an interview to make sure you know the consequences of dropping out of Part B — for example, that you may have to pay a late penalty if you want to re-enroll in the program in the future. However, the penalty isn't an issue if you're leaving Part B to enroll in primary health insurance from an employer. In the event that you lose this coverage in the future, you won't incur a late penalty as long as you sign up for Part B again within eight months of the job's or the insurance's ending (whichever happens first), as explained in Chapter 6.

WARNING

What do you do about Medigap supplemental insurance if you had a policy before becoming eligible for employer health insurance? If you opt out of Part B, you also have to drop your policy, because having both Part A and Part B is a condition for Medigap insurance. Keep in mind, though, that when you later want to re-enroll in Part B, you won't get a second chance of buying Medigap with full federal protections except in limited, specific circumstances. (I explain these protections and exceptions in Chapter 10.)

Knowing When Your Coverage Begins

Identifying when your coverage begins can affect some of the decisions you make about enrolling. For example, if you know that missing your personal enrollment deadline means being able to sign up only during the general enrollment period at the beginning of the year, you may make an extra special effort to sign up on time.

Or here's a different example: Say that you delayed Part B because you worked in a job with insurance until long after you turned 65, and now that you're about to stop work, your nice employer is giving you excellent retiree health benefits for the rest of your life. (Hey, it's rare, but it can happen!) You decide to sign up for Part B just in case (because no retiree benefits are set in stone) but want to avoid paying premiums for as long as possible. So instead of signing up as soon as you retire, you leave it until the end of the eight-month special enrollment period that you're entitled to — temporarily saving hundreds of dollars in Part B premiums but avoiding a late penalty.

REMEMBER

Depending on the situation, you can sign up for Part A and Part B during any of the following time frames:

>> During your seven-month *initial enrollment period (IEP),* in which the middle (fourth) month is the one when you reach age 65 or become eligible for Medicare based on disability

>> During an eight-month *special enrollment period (SEP)* granted after you or your spouse stops working for an employer that has provided health coverage you received beyond age 65

>> During a three-month *general enrollment period (GEP)* that runs from January 1 to March 31 each year, which you use only if you miss the deadline for your IEP or SEP

Take a look at Table 7-1, which shows when your coverage will begin if you sign up in any of the preceding enrollment periods. (Note that this table doesn't apply to anyone who is automatically enrolled. Also, it applies only to Part A and Part B enrollment. Sign-up periods for Part D drug plans and Medicare Advantage plans are discussed in Chapters 10 and 11.)

TABLE 7-1   Parts A and B Coverage Start Times by Enrollment

Enrollment Situation	Coverage Begins
IEP/When You Turn 65	
During the first 3 months of your IEP	First day of the month in which you turn 65 — or, if your birthday falls on the first day of the month, the first day of the previous month
During the 4th–7th months of your IEP	First day of the following month
SEP/When Covered over 65 by Insurance from a Current Employer	
At any time while you have this coverage, provided that your IEP has expired	The first day of the month after you enroll
During your 8-month SEP after active employment or insurance ends (whichever comes first)	The first day of the month after you enroll
Outside IEP/SEP	
During the GEP	The first day of the month after you enroll

Source: Social Security Administration/Public Domain

When you sign up during the first three months of your IEP

The middle month of your IEP — the fourth of the seven — is almost always the month in which you turn 65. If you sign up for Parts A and B during any of the first three months of your IEP, your coverage begins as soon as possible — normally on the first day of the month in which you turn 65, regardless of how far into the month your birthday falls.

But if your 65th birthday happens to fall on the first day of the month, your initial enrollment period is pushed forward, so that your coverage starts on the first day of the previous month. Hardly any ordinary Medicare beneficiary has ever heard of this little-known regulation, but if you were a first-of-the-month baby, you should be aware of it. Here are a couple of examples of IEP enrollments:

>> Betsy turned 65 on April 29, so her seven-month initial enrollment period began on January 1 and ended on July 31. Because she enrolled during the first three months of her IEP (January through March), her coverage began on April 1.

>> Dan's birthday fell on September 1. Therefore, instead of his seven-month IEP running from June 1 to December 31, it actually ran from May 1 to November 30. So the first three months of his IEP were May, June, and July. If he enrolled during these three months, his coverage would begin on August 1 — a whole month ahead of his real birthday.

When you sign up during IEP months four through seven

If you don't enroll during the first three months of your IEP, your coverage will begin the month following enrollment. Previously, if you enrolled in months four to seven of your IEP, your coverage didn't begin until two to three months later, but this delay was eliminated in 2023 as a result of the Beneficiary Enrollment Notification and Eligibility Simplification Act of 2020 (BENES Act).

When you are awarded Medicare coverage retroactively

If you are under 65 and apply for Social Security disability benefits, you would normally have to wait for 24 months before becoming entitled to Medicare, as explained in Chapter 5. But consider this scenario: Social Security turns down your application for disability benefits; you appeal the decision; you win your case, and you're granted disability retroactively — maybe months or years after you first applied. What then?

In this situation, disability benefits are backdated to the time when Social Security accepts that your disability began. If that date is at least two years earlier, you are also granted immediate Medicare coverage, without having to wait any longer. If the date is less than two years previously, the wait for Medicare is adjusted accordingly. For example, if disability is backdated to 18 months earlier, the beginning of Medicare coverage is delayed for 6 months instead of two years.

What happens if you're granted Medicare coverage retroactively? This can happen if your appeal for disability benefits takes a long time to succeed. In that case, you have two options:

» You can accept Medicare coverage retroactively and use it to help pay for Medicare-covered services that you've already received and paid for out-of-pocket — but you must also pay Part B premiums back to the time when Social Security deems you were first eligible for Medicare.

» You can decline the Part B backdated coverage that you've been offered, in which case you will not have to pay Part B premiums retroactively.

After winning your appeal, Social Security sends an award letter, which informs you when your disability payments will begin and the date on which Medicare coverage starts. If you're entitled to Medicare retroactively, the letter explains how to accept or decline it.

Note that if you're awarded retroactive Medicare coverage, you cannot claim refunds for premiums that you paid to obtain other insurance while waiting for Medicare.

Transitioning from Obamacare to Medicare

Millions of people have gained health insurance through the online Marketplace that was set up under the Affordable Care Act ("Obamacare") in 2014. And thousands of them turn 65 every day. If you're in this situation, you may be wondering how and when you can transition from one system to the other — or even whether you should. This section answers typical questions consumers have on this topic.

REMEMBER

What follows is information relating to the Affordable Care Act as it stands in early 2024.

Figuring out whether you need to make the switch

Not doing something often feels much easier than taking action. However, you still need to weigh the pros and cons of switching to Medicare versus staying with the Marketplace so that the decision you make is informed and takes account of the consequences. This section addresses the questions of people in different circumstances.

"If I'm happy with the Marketplace plan I currently have, must I switch to Medicare?"

The law allows you to keep your plan if you want, but there are good reasons why you shouldn't:

>> Your Marketplace plan may not renew your coverage at the end of the year you turn 65, since you would be eligible to enroll in Medicare. That could mean a gap in coverage if you must wait until the general enrollment period in January to sign up for Medicare, with coverage starting the following month.

>> If you're eligible for premium-free Part A, you will no longer qualify for any subsidies or tax credits that reduce the cost of your Marketplace premiums — and paying the full amount is likely to cost a lot more than Medicare. If you

continue to remain in the plan, you need to go back to the Marketplace website (at www.healthcare.gov) and terminate any subsidies you get, or you run the risk of having to repay them at the end of the tax year.

>> Unless your Marketplace plan comes from an employer (a situation I describe in the next section), delaying signing up for Medicare beyond age 65 makes you liable for a gap in coverage and late penalties that would be permanently added to your Medicare premiums. (The consequences of signing up late are explained in more detail in Chapter 6.)

Insurance companies in the Marketplace are banned from knowingly selling new policies to people enrolled in any part of Medicare. However, if you're enrolled in a Marketplace plan before becoming eligible for Medicare, your plan can't reduce or terminate your coverage before the end of the calendar year unless you request it.

"My employer bought my Marketplace insurance through SHOP. If I keep working after 65, must I enroll in Medicare?"

It depends on how many employees your employer has and what the employer's insurance company requires. The Small Business Health Options Program (SHOP), which makes it possible for small businesses to buy health insurance for their employees through the Marketplace, defines a small employer as having 50 or fewer employees. But under Medicare rules, a small employer is one that has fewer than 20 employees. Therefore, the following rules apply:

>> If your employer has 20 or more employees, you have the right to continue receiving the employer insurance and to delay Medicare enrollment until you stop work, without risking any late penalties.

>> If your employer has fewer than 20 employees, you must find out whether the employer insurance is primary or secondary to Medicare. If it's primary, you don't need to sign up for Medicare at 65 and can delay enrollment until the job ends. If it's secondary, you really do need to sign up for Medicare Part A and Part B because the employer plan will pay only for medical services that it covers but Medicare doesn't — so if you don't enroll, you would essentially be left with little or no healthcare coverage. To be on the safe side, get that information in writing from your employer or its insurance provider.

For more information about how Medicare works as primary or secondary coverage in large or small businesses, see Chapter 8.

"I don't have enough work credits for premium-free Part A. Can I stay on my Marketplace plan until I've earned enough?"

Yes, you can. In this situation, you can choose to stay on your Marketplace plan or even enroll in one for the first time, instead of signing up for any part of Medicare. You're also entitled to keep any government subsidies you've been receiving to reduce your Marketplace premiums. Staying in a Marketplace plan can save you from paying quite high premiums on Part A benefits alone, although you need to compare the overall costs of each program to see which one is the least expensive for you.

WARNING

However, there is a catch. Even though you don't qualify for premium-free Part A, you're still entitled to enroll in Part B, which doesn't require any work credits — provided that you're a U.S. citizen or a permanent legal resident (green-card holder) who has lived in the United States for at least five years. And if you delay signing up for Part B beyond the end of your initial enrollment period at age 65, you'll face the same consequences for delayed coverage and permanent late penalties that are described in Chapter 6.

"I'm in Part A but missed my deadline for Part B sign-up. Can I enroll in a Marketplace plan until Part B coverage kicks in?"

The answer, unfortunately, is no. Under Medicare rules, you risk a gap in coverage and late penalties if you don't sign up for Part B when you should (as explained in detail in Chapter 6). But under Marketplace rules, anybody who has premium-free Part A alone is considered to have qualifying health coverage, which protects people from having to pay Marketplace penalties for non-coverage. The rules also insist that insurance companies can't sell a Marketplace plan to anyone who is enrolled in any part of Medicare, because that would violate the law that protects consumers from being sold insurance that would duplicate Medicare benefits.

"If I enroll in Medicare, I'll have to pay high Part B premiums due to high income. Can I stay on my cheaper Marketplace plan?"

You can, but it may actually prove more expensive in the long run. When you eventually sign up for Medicare, you will be liable for the Part B late penalties I describe in Chapter 6. For example, a delay of ten years would double your standard Part B premiums for all future years. It wouldn't increase the higher-income surcharges themselves, which range from $69.90 to $419.30 a month in 2024, depending on income level, and are added to the standard Part B premiums. Even so, overall, your already-high premiums would be made even higher by the addition of late penalties. Also, as noted earlier, Marketplace plans may choose to not renew your coverage if you are otherwise eligible for Medicare.

Knowing how and when to switch from Marketplace to Medicare

This section answers questions about the process of transitioning from a Marketplace plan to Medicare and how to get help if you need it. The process varies according to your circumstances — for example, whether you currently have an individual Marketplace plan on your own or share one with your spouse and/or other family members.

"I have a Marketplace plan on my own. How do I switch from that plan to Medicare?"

First, sign up for Medicare in one of the ways explained earlier in this chapter. If you already receive Social Security benefits, the Social Security Administration will automatically enroll you and send your Medicare identity card through the mail, specifying the date when your coverage becomes effective. Otherwise, you must actively apply for Medicare coverage by contacting the SSA. If you apply during the first three months of your seven-month initial enrollment period (IEP), coverage will begin on the first day of the fourth month.

When you know the date on which your Medicare coverage goes into effect, you can cancel your Marketplace coverage. For example, if Medicare is to begin May 1, you want your Marketplace coverage to end April 30. To make this transition, it's important to cancel your Marketplace policy at least 15 days before you want the coverage to end, and to specify that you want it terminated on the final day of the month. (Medicare coverage always begins on the first day of the month.)

If you bought your Marketplace plan through the federal website (www.healthcare.gov), you can cancel it in one of two ways:

>> **By phone:** Call the Marketplace Call Center at 800-318-2596 (TTY 855-889-4325).

>> **Online:** Log into your Marketplace account. Follow the step-by-step instructions for plan cancellation provided on the Marketplace website at www.healthcare.gov/how-to-cancel-a-marketplace-plan. Choose the heading "You're ending coverage for everyone on the application." Even if you have no one else on your plan, you count as "everyone" in this context.

If you bought your plan through the marketplace run by your state, contact the state's health program for information on how to cancel. The process has different rules in different states.

"My family is on a Marketplace plan, but I'll be eligible for Medicare soon. Can my family stay on the plan after I leave?"

Yes, you can end your own coverage under your Marketplace plan while your family members stay on it.

If you bought the plan through the federal website, at www.healthcare.gov, the cancellation process varies according to your circumstances:

>> If you are the "household contact" for your plan — meaning the person who set up the Marketplace account and who probably filled out the application for your family members as well as yourself — you can cancel your coverage only by calling the Marketplace Call Center at 800-318-2596 (TTY 855-889-4325) and designating another family member as the new household contact. This ensures that your dependents will be able to stay on the plan, according to government officials, who also warn that in this situation you should not try to cancel your own coverage online.

>> If you're the spouse of the household contact and you are the one making the transition to Medicare, your spouse can either contact the Marketplace Call Center or go online to end your participation in the Marketplace plan. Follow the step-by-step instructions provided on the Marketplace website (www.healthcare.gov/how-to-cancel-a-marketplace-plan) under the heading "You're ending coverage for just some people on the application."

If you bought the plan through a marketplace run by your state, contact the state program to find out how its cancellation process works.

"My Marketplace plan provides dental coverage. Does Medicare do so?"

Original Medicare does not include coverage for routine dental care — although some Medicare Advantage plans do.

Depending on where you live, you may be able to buy a stand-alone dental plan through the Marketplace, even though you no longer have health insurance from that source. Note that this is possible only if your state runs its own marketplace insurance exchange and the state allows dental plans to be sold separately from healthcare plans. Some states do and some don't. But if you bought your current plan through the federal Marketplace (because your state doesn't operate its own), be aware that stand-alone dental plans are not permitted.

"Can I sign up for any Medicare plans through the online Marketplace?"

No. The Medicare and Marketplace systems are entirely separate. As you've had a Marketplace plan, you'll be familiar with the process of signing up online — either through the federal website or a state website. Medicare has a similar website where you can compare the details of private plans available to you: the stand-alone Part D prescription drug plans or Medicare Advantage plans, such as HMOs and PPOs.

For step-by-step guidance on how to navigate Medicare's online plan finder program, see Chapter 10 (for Part D drug plans) or Chapter 11 (for Medicare Advantage plans).

"If I need help in cancelling my Marketplace plan or starting Medicare coverage, whom should I call?"

TIP

Depending on the kind of help you need, contact any of the following:

>> The Marketplace Call Center at 800-318-2596 (TTY 855-889-4325) for help with any Marketplace issues.

>> The Social Security Administration at 800-772-1213 (TTY 800-325-0778) for help with Medicare eligibility or enrollment issues.

>> The Centers for Medicare & Medicaid Services at 800-633-4227 (TTY 877-486-2048) for issues on Medicare coverage, Medicare Advantage plans, or Part D drug plans.

>> Your State Health Insurance Assistance Program (SHIP) for personal help, free of charge, from trained counselors on all Medicare and Medicaid issues. See Appendix A for contact information.

Chapter **8**

Understanding How Medicare Fits In with Other Health Insurance

nsurance for healthcare can come from a variety of different places as well as from Medicare. Let's count the ways: Medicaid, Medigap, a current or former employer or union, COBRA, the Federal Employees Health Benefits Program, TRICARE, Veterans Affairs, the Indian Health Service, the Federal Black Lung Benefits Program, workers' compensation, and no-fault insurance or liability insurance. Phew — that's quite a list!

So the question arises: What if you have two types of coverage — Medicare plus another? What if you have three types, four, or even more? How do your medical bills get paid? How does it all work together? This chapter explains how Medicare works in conjunction with each of the other types of insurance (except for Medicaid and Medigap, which are discussed in Chapter 4). As you may suppose, the regulations are different in each case. And whether Medicare or another insurance pays your bills first depends on the situation. So flip to the information given for any extra insurance you have to see how it fits in with Medicare and what action — if any — you need to take.

This chapter also introduces you to the concept of *coordination of benefits* — a system set up by the federal government that determines when, and in which order, Medicare or other insurance pays your bills, saving you a lot of effort.

TIP

You may also want to read the official publication "Medicare & Other Health Benefits: Your Guide to Who Pays First" at www.medicare.gov/publications/ 02179-Medicare-and-other-health-benefits-your-guide-to-who-pays- first.pdf.

Understanding Medicare's Coordination of Benefits System

Here's a nightmarish scenario to imagine: You go into the hospital for surgery. You have Medicare and two other types of insurance. You need to figure out which type pays your bill — or which type pays for different parts of the bill. And then you have to submit claims to each insurer, possibly receiving the money only after you've first paid the bills out-of-pocket.

Don't freak! You won't have to go through such an ordeal (or at least not in the vast majority of situations), thanks to Medicare's coordination of benefits system.

This system is primarily designed to ensure that Medicare doesn't use taxpayer dollars to pay claims that are covered by other insurance. In other words, it's a big cost-saving device. But the process also ensures that your medical bills are paid on time without your having to submit a whole lot of paperwork or take any other action. Okay, maybe it doesn't work perfectly every single time, and in some situations, you may need to fill out claim forms. But on the whole, the coordination of benefits system is a godsend.

REMEMBER

Here's how it works: Each type of insurance you have, Medicare included, is known as a *payer*. If you have more than one payer, Medicare's coordination of benefits rules determine which one pays first (or second or third). So when you go to a doctor or other provider, the bill is sent to the first payer — the *primary payer* — which pays what it owes. If that amount doesn't fully meet the bill, the provider sends the remainder to the next payer (the *secondary payer*) and maybe even a third. Mostly, all you do is check the statements that each of these payers sends you and, once all the statements are in, pay for anything that's not already covered.

How smoothly the system works depends on its receiving huge quantities of information. This info comes from employers, insurance companies, doctors, and other medical service providers. It should also come from you, both when you first become eligible for Medicare and also later if your coverage changes.

Helping Medicare help you: Filling out your initial enrollment questionnaire

Medicare doesn't automatically know what other health coverage (if any) you have. So about three months before you become eligible for Medicare, you receive through the mail a letter telling you how to complete the *Medicare Initial Enrollment Questionnaire.* Completing this questionnaire is very much in your interest. Your answers help Medicare make sure that payments for medical services you use are made promptly and accurately.

You can fill out the questionnaire in one of two ways:

>> Create an online account at www.medicare.gov/account/login, a personal, secure portal that allows you to access claims and other information, as explained in Chapter 13. You can complete the questionnaire on this site from three months before you become eligible for Medicare to six months after coverage begins, but outside that time frame it won't work.

>> Phone Medicare's Benefits Coordination & Recovery Center (BCRC) toll-free at 855-798-2627 (TTY 855-797-2627).

The questions may vary according to whether you qualify for Medicare because you're turning 65, have received disability benefits for 24 months, or have kidney failure (otherwise known as end-stage renal disease, or ESRD). In each case, the form is designed to help determine whether Medicare will be your primary or secondary coverage. For example, it asks whether you or your spouse is currently working for an employer that provides health insurance — and if so, for the employer's name and address. It also asks whether the employer has 20 or more employees (if you're 65 or older) or 100 or more employees (if you're under 65 with disabilities). Answering "yes" to either of these questions means your employer health plan will pay your medical bills first. Answering "no" means Medicare will pay first. (This setup is explained in more detail in the later section "Seeing How Medicare Works with an Employer's Health Insurance Plan.") Checking the "don't know" box means Medicare will contact your employer to find out.

Keeping Medicare informed if your coverage changes

REMEMBER

Over time, of course, your coverage may change. If any changes may affect the way Medicare fits in with other insurance — for example, if you stop work or otherwise lose coverage from a current employer — you should contact Medicare's Benefits Coordination & Recovery Center (BCRC) to ensure that these new circumstances are recorded in your file. (Medicare will determine whether they mean a different entity is now your primary payer.) The BCRC is also available for you to ask any questions about your coverage and how it fits in with Medicare. Call toll-free 855-798-2627 (TTY 855-797-2627). Here are some examples of coverage change:

>> When Diana filled out her Initial Enrollment Questionnaire at age 65, she was still working for a medium-sized company that had more than 20 workers. Therefore, her employer plan was primary and Medicare secondary. On her retirement a couple of years later, she accepted the retiree health benefits her employer offered her. Under Medicare rules, Medicare now became the primary payer and her retiree benefits secondary.

>> Colin's Medicare benefits began at age 57 because of his disabilities. His wife, Marlisse, worked for a large company (with more than 100 employees), and her employer health plan covered him. This plan became Colin's primary insurance, and Medicare was secondary. But a few years later, Marlisse changed her job, working for a smaller company with only 40 workers. Because Colin was under 65 and covered by insurance from an employer with fewer than 100 workers, under the rules Colin's Medicare then became his primary payer, and the employer plan became secondary.

Seeing How Medicare Works with an Employer's Health Insurance Plan

The greatest source of tension people who are about to qualify for Medicare have is how it will fit in with health insurance from current or former employers or how becoming eligible for Medicare will affect that insurance.

These are totally legitimate concerns. And in many cases, just calling the employer's human resources department or benefits administrator is enough to get questions answered promptly and correctly. But not all such administrators are fully clued in, and there are cases where the information they've told folks is plain wrong.

Chapter 6 explains how the type of employer insurance you have affects the timing of when to sign up for Medicare, especially Part B. This section covers what happens to your employer benefits as a result of that decision and what rights you have under the law.

One source of confusion — as always in Medicare — is that the rules affect people in different circumstances in different ways. So this section is divided into information about having health insurance from a current employer or from a former employer — either your own or your spouse's — in a question-and-answer format.

Working with insurance from a current employer

In this section, I assume that you're covered by health insurance from an employer for whom you or your spouse is still actively working.

Is my employer insurance primary or secondary to Medicare?

REMEMBER

Under the rules, which insurance pays first depends on how many people work for your employer:

>> Your employer health plan is usually primary if one of the following is true:

- You're 65 or older, and the employer has 20 or more workers.

- You're under 65 (with disabilities), and the employer has 100 or more workers.

>> Medicare is usually primary if one of the following is true:

- You're 65 or older, and the employer has fewer than 20 workers.

- You're under 65 (with disabilities), and the employer has fewer than 100 workers.

Note: I say "usually" because some small employers team up with other small employers to form a larger group that offers health insurance to all their employees. This arrangement may affect the "20 or more" or "100 or more" rule that determines whether Medicare is primary or secondary. If you're in doubt, ask your employer or call Medicare's Benefits Coordination & Recovery Center (toll-free 855-798-2627, or TTY 855-797-2627). Also, if you have Medicare on the basis of ESRD, see the later section "How does my ESRD-qualified Medicare work with my employer coverage?"

Do I get the same health benefits at work as I get now?

Provided that your insurance is primary to Medicare, by law the employer is subject to the following restrictions:

>> It must offer the same health insurance benefits to employees who are 65 or older as it does to younger employees.

>> It must offer covered spouses of any age (including 65 or older) the same health benefits as those offered to other employees' spouses.

>> It must offer the same health benefits to employees or their spouses who have Medicare based on disability as it does to other employees.

>> It can't require employees to drop employer benefits and enroll in Medicare.

>> It can't offer employees who are eligible for Medicare any inducements designed to persuade them to choose Medicare and drop the employer insurance — for example, offering to pay their premiums or out-of-pocket costs for Medigap supplemental insurance or Medicare Advantage plans. (See Chapters 4 and 10 for details on Medigap; Chapter 11 has details on Medicare Advantage.)

TECHNICAL STUFF

These rules are very important protections. In case you need to argue the point, the laws that established them are the Age Discrimination in Employment Act (ADEA) of 1967; the Tax Equity and Fiscal Responsibility Act (TEFRA) of 1983; the Deficit Reduction Act (DEFRA) of 1985; the Omnibus Budget Reconciliation Act (OBRA) of 1986; the Consolidated Omnibus Budget Reconciliation Act (COBRA) of 1986; and Medicare Secondary Payer rules.

If you think your employer is violating any of these rules, you can call the Employee Benefits Security Administration's Office of Enforcement, at the U.S. Department of Labor, to file a complaint. Go to www.dol.gov/agencies/ebsa/about-ebsa/about-us/regional-offices to find contact information for your regional EBSA office.

REMEMBER

The laws mentioned earlier don't give the same protections to people working for employers who have fewer than a certain number of employees (20 in the case of regulations affecting people 65 and older; 100 where younger people have Medicare because of disability). This difference doesn't mean that smaller employers can't provide the same or similar protections, only that they don't have to. It really depends on the individual employer, and you need to contact yours for details of its policy.

How else does having an employer plan affect me?

Having primary insurance from a current employer can affect you as a Medicare beneficiary in several other ways, all of which I explain in Chapter 6. You can flip to that chapter for details, but here's a quick recap:

>> You (and your spouse) can delay signing up for Part B, and therefore avoid paying Part B premiums, until the employment or health coverage comes to an end — without risking late penalties if you follow the rules.

>> You (and your spouse) can delay signing up for Part D prescription drug coverage without risking late penalties, provided that your employer drug coverage is considered *creditable* (meaning it's at least of equal value to Part D). If it's not creditable, you need to consider signing up for Part D — unless you have delayed enrolling in Parts A and B, during which time you don't qualify for Part D and can't incur late penalties.

>> If your employer coverage includes a pre-tax health savings account, you should consider delaying enrollment in Part A, as well as Part B and Part D, because under IRS rules you can't (as an employee) continue to contribute to an HSA if you're enrolled in any part of Medicare.

Can I choose to drop my employer plan and have just Medicare?

You always have the right to drop your employer insurance entirely and rely on Medicare alone. But keep in mind that you probably won't be able to get your employer coverage back if you change your mind. So before taking any action, consider Medicare's costs and benefits compared to those you have now.

Be aware that if you drop your plan, your employer can't — by law — provide any benefits that supplement your Medicare coverage. Otherwise, the employer may run the risk of prosecution and large fines for violating the law. In fact, your employer will probably ask you to sign a statement saying that your decision to make Medicare your primary insurance is voluntary.

So if you wanted supplemental coverage, you'd have to pay for Medigap insurance out of your own pocket. (See Chapters 4 and 10 for details on Medigap.) Also, if your spouse, your domestic partner, or another family member is covered by your employer plan, they would almost certainly lose coverage if you dropped out of the plan.

How does my ESRD-qualified Medicare work with my employer coverage?

When your only entitlement to Medicare is that you have ESRD, and you're also covered by an employer or union group plan (including COBRA benefits), the first 30 months on Medicare count as a coordination period. During these 30 months, your employer coverage is primary — regardless of how many people work for the employer — and Medicare is secondary.

At the end of the 30-month period, Medicare becomes your primary payer for all services that Medicare covers. Your employer plan generally pays for services that Medicare doesn't cover, although you should check with its administrator to see exactly what it covers. For example, Medicare pays only 80 percent of the cost of dialysis (as well as other Part B services), so find out whether your employer plan will pay for the remaining 20 percent.

REMEMBER

While you're in this 30-month coordination period, make sure that your doctor and any other provider know that you have both employer insurance and Medicare. Show them both your insurance ID card and your Medicare card to help ensure that your bills are paid promptly and correctly.

Do you have to enroll in Part B (and pay monthly premiums for it) if you have employer insurance? No, you can opt out if you want, or opt out just for the 30-month period. But think about it carefully and do your homework. For more information, see the official publication "Medicare Coverage of Kidney Dialysis & Kidney Transplant Services" at www.medicare.gov/Pubs/pdf/10128-Medicare-Coverage-ESRD.pdf.

Having insurance from a former employer

This section assumes that you have private health insurance from a former employer or union — either your own or your spouse's — for whom neither of you now works. This insurance may come in the form of *retiree benefits* (an employment perk still enjoyed by about one in three Medicare beneficiaries) or *COBRA insurance*, which extends employer health benefits for a limited time after the job has ended.

Are retiree/COBRA benefits primary or secondary to Medicare?

REMEMBER

Retiree and COBRA health benefits are always secondary to Medicare if you have either of them and Medicare at the same time. In this case, the size of the employer and the number of workers don't matter. For Medicare purposes, the only thing that matters is that you or your spouse no longer works for the employer that provides the benefits. They don't count as health benefits from current employment.

This information may affect your decision about when to sign up for Part B. Being covered by either retirement health benefits or COBRA beyond age 65 doesn't allow you to delay Part B enrollment without risking late penalties and maybe a temporary loss of coverage, as I explain in Chapter 6.

How do my retiree benefits work with Medicare?

Some employers require you to sign up for Medicare as a condition of continuing to be eligible for retiree health benefits — so if you don't enroll, it would be like having no coverage at all. (That's also true of the military retiree health program, TRICARE For Life, which is considered later in this chapter.) On the other hand, some employers provide retiree benefits without any regard to whether you enroll in Medicare and leave the decision entirely up to you. (That's also true of the Federal Employees Health Benefits Program, as explained later in this chapter.) Between these two extremes lies an almost limitless variety of different arrangements.

REMEMBER

Every employer's health package for retirees — if one is offered at all — is different from the next. The laws that give protections to active employees who are eligible for Medicare (as explained in the earlier section "Do I get the same health benefits at work as I get now?") don't apply to retirees. Essentially, employers can do whatever they want in regard to retirement benefits unless legally bound by cast-iron union agreements. In most cases, employers are free to

>> Choose not to offer any retiree health benefits at all

>> Change, limit, or terminate retiree health benefits at any time

>> Provide retiree health benefits in the form of a specially designed plan unique to the employer, or maybe a choice of such plans

>> Provide benefits that supplement Medicare in ways the employer chooses, such as paying Medicare's deductible and co-pays or helping pay for services that Medicare doesn't cover (for example, routine vision, hearing, and dental care)

>> Provide benefits by paying the premiums of regular plans (such as Medicare Advantage plans or Medigap policies) available to other Medicare beneficiaries

>> Require you to enroll in Medicare Part B as a condition for continuing to receive retiree benefits

>> Allow you to use retiree benefits regardless of whether you enroll in Medicare Part B, leaving that decision to you

REMEMBER

So before you retire, finding out exactly how Medicare will fit in with any health benefits you'll receive from an employer during retirement is critical. Here are some specific questions that are worth asking the employer, benefits administrator, or union rep:

>> Am I required to sign up for Medicare? If I don't enroll, how will that affect my retiree benefits?

>> Do I have a choice of plans? If so, when must I make that choice? Will I be able to change to an alternative option in the future?

>> Will my plan choices and benefits be affected by where I choose to live in retirement?

>> Is the plan specially designed for this employer's group of retirees, or is it a regular Medigap policy or Medicare Advantage plan for which the employer contributes the cost of premiums?

>> Does the plan pay any of Medicare's out-of-pocket expenses, such as premiums, deductibles, or co-pays?

>> Must I pay any deductible before the plan's benefits kick in? If the plan has a high deductible, does Medicare cover all or part of it?

>> Does the plan help pay for services that Medicare doesn't cover, such as routine vision, hearing, and dental care?

>> Does the plan provide creditable prescription drug coverage, or do I need to enroll in a Medicare Part D plan for my medications?

>> Does the plan place an annual limit on my out-of-pocket costs? If so, does the plan pay for all my care after I meet that limit in any year?

>> Does the plan set any annual or lifetime dollar limit on how much it pays for my healthcare?

>> Does the plan cover my spouse? Will they still be covered if I die?

>> Does the plan coordinate with Medicare in making payments? If not, how will my medical claims be settled?

TIP

Try to get the answers in writing. Otherwise, keep notes of the conversation with a record of when and where it took place and the name of the person you talked to. Don't be afraid to repeat a question if you don't understand the answer you're given. You have a right to a clear explanation of the rules relating to your retiree benefits — one that's not shrouded in jargon.

Can I choose to drop my retiree benefits and have just Medicare?

That's always an option. But think hard about it first. You've earned those benefits, and if you drop them you likely won't be able to get them back. The decision really depends on whether your retiree plan gives you any worthwhile coverage that truly supplements Medicare, and how much it costs.

How does COBRA work with Medicare?

If you retire or lose your job, you may be eligible for insurance under the COBRA law. This program provides exactly the same coverage you had while working. The difference is that you must pay the employer's share of your premium as well as your own, which is likely to more than double the cost. And COBRA is temporary; it lasts usually for up to 18 months after your job ends, although the laws of your state may provide longer periods, as explained in Chapter 5. COBRA also applies only to employers with 20 or more workers, although some state laws give similar protections for people working for smaller employers.

If you're eligible for COBRA, so are your spouse and any dependent children. They may also qualify for COBRA in their own right if their coverage under your work insurance ends because of your death, divorce, or separation.

REMEMBER

COBRA is mainly useful for people without any other source of health insurance. But if you are (or will soon be) signed up for Medicare, knowing how it affects you and your family can be helpful. In this situation, the key factor is when you become eligible for Medicare:

>> **Before COBRA:** If you have Medicare before becoming eligible for COBRA, you can continue to have both. Medicare will be your primary coverage. The exception is if you have Medicare because of ESRD. In that case, COBRA will be primary for the first 30 months, and Medicare will become primary only when the 30-month period ends (as explained earlier in this chapter) or when COBRA coverage ends.

>> **After COBRA:** If you become eligible for Medicare after you've signed up for COBRA, your COBRA benefits cease. COBRA coverage for your spouse (and any dependent children) may be extended up to 36 months, in some situations, because you qualified for Medicare.

If you qualify for Medicare before deciding whether to take COBRA, does having COBRA offer any advantage, especially if it will be secondary to Medicare? Maybe, if COBRA (which is the same as the insurance you had from the job you're leaving) provides really good coverage. In that case, it may kick in to cover services that

Medicare doesn't. On the other hand, COBRA is usually very expensive, and buying Medigap supplemental insurance (find details in Chapter 10) may offer a far less costly alternative.

What if I have prescription drug coverage from my retiree or COBRA plan?

It depends on whether the coverage is *creditable* — that is, considered at least as good as Part D. If it is, you don't need to enroll in a Part D plan, and when you lose your COBRA drug benefits, you'll get a special enrollment period of two months to sign up without penalty. If your retiree or COBRA drug benefits aren't creditable, you should consider getting on board with a Part D drug plan to avoid late penalties. (The details of Part D enrollment are explained in Chapters 10 and 11.)

Figuring Out How Other Federal Health Benefits Fit In with Medicare

The federal government provides health coverage to millions of people, quite apart from Medicare. Some receive benefits as active or retired employees of the federal government — from the Federal Employees Health Benefits (FEHB) Program if they're civilians, or from TRICARE if they are or were in the military. And some receive federal health benefits if they belong to certain groups — veterans of the armed forces; members of Native American tribal nations; or former coal miners who are totally disabled as a result of black lung disease. In the following sections, I consider each of these programs in turn because — how did you guess? — each interacts with Medicare in a different way.

The Federal Employees Health Benefits Program

The Federal Employees Health Benefits (FEHB) Program is the health insurance program that's available to you if you work (or used to work) in any civilian job for the federal government — from delivering the mail in Alaska to conducting medical research in Georgia to serving as president of the United States in Washington, D.C. The program offers you (and your spouse) a choice of several healthcare plans, each with a different set of benefits and costs, regardless of whether you still actively work for the feds or are retired. The following sections answer some common questions about FEHB and how it works with Medicare.

What if I become eligible for Medicare while I'm still working?

You come under the same rules as if you were working for any other large employer. (And the federal government is by far the largest employer in the United States, so concern about the number of employees isn't an issue here.) In other words, you're entitled to delay Part B enrollment beyond age 65 for as long as you or your spouse (if they are the federal employee) has FEHB coverage and is still actively working and then to get a special enrollment period to sign up without penalty when the employment ends. If for any reason you wanted Medicare as well, your FEHB plan would be primary and Medicare would be secondary. And you and your spouse would have access to the same plans and benefits as younger federal workers.

How does Medicare fit in with my plan after I retire?

After you stop working, you don't have to enroll in Part B if you don't want to, and your FEHB plan can't require you to. Your benefits under the plan you choose are the same regardless of whether you sign up for Part B. But if you do have both types of insurance, Medicare will be your primary coverage. And of course, if you want to drop your FEHB plan and rely on Medicare, that's a choice you're free to make.

TIP

Should you take Medicare? The Office of Personnel Management (OPM), which administers the FEHB Program, suggests some factors to consider:

>> Your FEHB plan may pay for some services that Medicare doesn't cover, such as annual physicals, dental and vision care, and emergency coverage outside the United States.

>> Medicare may pay for some services that your FEHB plan doesn't cover, such as some medical equipment and supplies, orthopedic or prosthetic devices, and home healthcare.

>> If you're enrolled in an FEHB fee-for-service plan, such as Blue Cross Blue Shield, GEHA, or MHBP (formerly known as the Mail Handlers Benefit Plan), and you're also signed up for Medicare Parts A and B, the two types of coverage may combine to pay almost all your medical expenses, so you won't need separate Medigap supplemental insurance. The FEHB plan may also waive its own deductibles and co-pays for services that are also covered by Part B.

>> If you're enrolled in an FEHB managed care plan, such as an HMO, it may provide all the care you need for low co-pays. But having Part B as well covers doctors and other providers who are outside the plan's provider network or service area should you need them.

>> If you have both an FEHB plan and Medicare, your benefits are coordinated so that you don't have to file claims yourself.

>> Prescription drug coverage in your FEHB plan is creditable, so you don't need Medicare Part D coverage, even if you enroll in Parts A and B, unless Part D's Extra Help program for low-income people (explained in Chapter 4) would be useful to you.

>> If you want to enroll in a Medicare Advantage plan (see Chapter 11), you're allowed to suspend your FEHB benefits — saving you the FEHB plan premium — with the guarantee of being able to re-enroll in an FEHB plan at a later date. If you're interested in this option, call your retirement office.

>> If you don't sign up for Part B but need to do so at some future date (for example, if you lost FEHB coverage or it became too expensive to maintain), you will be liable for permanent Part B late penalties.

REMEMBER

The bottom line: Look at the brochure of the FEHB plan you enroll in to see exactly how its benefits fit in with Medicare. Or call your plan.

For more detailed information on FEHBP and Medicare, see the Office of Personnel Management's guidance at www.opm.gov/healthcare-insurance/health care/medicare/medicare-vs-fehb-enrollment. You can also call OPM toll-free at 888-767-6738 (TTY 855-887-4957) or 202-606-0500 from the Washington, D.C., metropolitan area.

How does my FEHB coverage work if I have Medicare due to disability or ESRD?

If you're under age 65, entitled to Medicare because of disability, and continue FEHB coverage, your FEHB plan is primary to Medicare and covers your medical bills first.

Your FEHB plan must also cover your bills first for the first 30 months that you're entitled to Medicare on the basis of having permanent kidney failure (ESRD), regardless of whether you're employed or retired. After the first 30 months, Medicare covers your bills first, as explained in the earlier section on employer health benefits.

TRICARE and TRICARE For Life

TRICARE and *TRICARE For Life* (TFL) are the federal health insurance programs available to active-duty military personnel and their spouses (TRICARE), or military retirees age 65 or older who served at least 20 years and their spouses

(TRICARE For Life). The following sections answer some common questions about these programs and how they work with Medicare.

What if I become eligible for Medicare while I am (or my spouse is) still on active duty or I have coverage from another job?

For as long as you or your spouse is on active duty for the military after you turn 65, you're not required to enroll in Medicare Part B — although if you do, TRI-CARE will continue to be your primary insurance. Just as if you were working for any other employer (see Chapter 6), you're entitled to delay Part B and sign up for it without penalty at any time during your active military service beyond age 65, and so is your covered spouse.

WARNING

However, in this situation, you must make sure you enroll in Part B *before* the date of your retirement; otherwise, you may lose TRICARE benefits. This deadline also applies to your covered spouse if they have reached 65 by the time you retire. In other words, you need to ignore the eight-month special enrollment period you'd normally be entitled to in this situation after retirement.

What if you are working for another (non-military) employer after you turn 65, yet remain eligible for TRICARE? In this case, if the employer has 20 or more employees, you can delay Part B enrollment until you retire (as explained in Chapter 6), and your TRICARE For Life coverage will kick in as soon as you sign up for Part B. If you choose to have all three types of coverage at the same time, the current employer plan would be your primary coverage, Medicare would be secondary, and TFL would come in third place in the order of paying claims.

What if I become eligible for Medicare based on disability?

The information in the preceding section applies to you, too, in the sense that you can delay Part B for as long as you're on active duty, and so can your covered spouse if they receive Medicare based on disability.

However, if you have Medicare due to ESRD, TRICARE will be your primary coverage for your first 30 months of eligibility, and therefore you must enroll in Part B so that TRICARE can pay your bills — otherwise, you'd have no coverage at all. After 30 months, Medicare becomes primary, as explained in the earlier section "How does my ESRD-qualified Medicare work with my employer coverage?"

Sometimes, people with disabilities or ESRD become eligible for Medicare under age 65 only after winning an appeal, and then Medicare eligibility can be back-dated months or years. Be aware that in this situation, you won't be asked to pay

Part B premiums retroactively or repay TRICARE for benefits you received during that time. Just sign up for Part B as soon as you're eligible in order to keep TRI-CARE benefits going forward.

How does Medicare fit in with my TRICARE For Life benefits?

You (and your spouse) become eligible for TRICARE For Life at age 65, if you've already retired, after at least 20 years of military service with an honorable discharge. TRICARE coverage then morphs into TFL coverage provided that you enroll in Parts A and B as soon as you're eligible.

REMEMBER

Be sure to sign up for Part B a month or so before you turn 65 (or before you retire, if you're older than 65 by then). Your TRICARE benefits abruptly come to an end on the first day of the month in which you reach 65, or the first day of the month after retirement, if you aren't already enrolled in Part B.

If you miss this deadline, you'll get TFL benefits as soon as you enroll in Part B, but TFL won't pay for any medical care you've received during the lapsed period. In effect, you'll have no healthcare coverage at all during that time, unless you have coverage from elsewhere, such as from another job or the VA (Veterans Affairs). And note that the times when you can enroll in Part B and when coverage starts are determined by the Medicare rules for specific enrollment periods, as explained in Chapter 7. If you delay Part B enrollment too long, you may not be eligible for TFL again for many months.

If you're retired from the military and your spouse reaches age 65 before you do, they must transfer from TRICARE to TFL and enroll in Part B at the same time, even though you're still receiving TRICARE. (Your current TRICARE premiums will be halved as a result.) Conversely, if you reach 65 before your spouse, they will stay on TRICARE until reaching Medicare age even though you've transferred to TFL.

The TFL program provides excellent wraparound insurance, covering services and costs that Medicare doesn't. A military official once told me that TFL "is the best Medicare supplemental coverage anyone could buy — except you don't have to buy it." And he was right. Here's how Medicare works with TFL:

>> You don't pay premiums for TFL. But you must pay the Medicare Part B premiums ($174.70 a month in 2024, or more if your income is over a certain level, as Chapter 3 explains).

>> TFL pays the other out-of-pocket costs of Medicare — your deductibles and co-pays — so you get coverage at minimal cost. You don't need Medigap supplemental insurance.

>> When you use a medical service that's covered by both Medicare and TFL, Medicare pays first. The provider bills Medicare, which pays its share, and the rest of the claim is sent to TFL. TFL pays the remaining share of the bill directly to the provider. You receive a Medicare Summary Notice and a TFL Explanation of Benefits statement showing what each has paid.

>> If you use a medical service that's covered by Medicare but not by TFL (such as some chiropractic treatment), TFL won't pay Medicare's deductible or co-pay or anything else toward the bill.

>> If you use a service that's covered by TFL but not Medicare (such as healthcare outside of the United States), TFL pays at the same rate as the TRICARE Standard program, and you pay its deductibles and co-pays. If you go to a doctor who has opted out of Medicare, Medicare won't pay any of the bill, but TFL will still cover the percentage (typically 20 percent) that it would have paid if you'd been treated by an opted-in doctor.

>> If you use any services that aren't covered by either Medicare or TFL, you're responsible for the entire cost.

>> If you have yet another type of insurance (such as from a former employer), Medicare pays first, the other insurance pays second, and TFL pays in third place for any remaining costs you're responsible for.

>> TFL's prescription drug coverage is better and less expensive than Medicare Part D's, so you don't need to enroll in a Part D drug plan.

For more info about TFL, go to its website at www.tricare.mil/tfl. To check eligibility or report changes of status, call the Defense Enrollment Eligibility Reporting System (DEERS) toll-free at 800-538-9552 (TTY 1-866-363-2883).

Here are some examples of how TFL works with Medicare and other insurance:

>> When Valerie turned 65 and retired, her employer offered retiree benefits that she decided to accept. Earlier in life, she'd served for more than 20 years in the military, so she also qualified for TRICARE For Life benefits. And now she had Medicare too — giving her three different types of coverage. Because Valerie was retired from both her military and civilian work, Medicare became her primary coverage. So Medicare paid her medical bills first. Her civilian retiree benefits paid the costs for services it covered but Medicare didn't. And her TFL benefits came in last, covering her Medicare deductibles and co-pays and maybe a few services that the others didn't cover.

>> Jonas had been retired from the military for some years before turning 65. He knew he'd have to sign up for Medicare Part B to receive TFL benefits but thought it'd be okay to enroll a few days before his March 15 birthday. Under Medicare rules, this situation meant his Part B coverage didn't begin until

April 1. And under TFL rules, he should have been receiving Part B coverage by March 1. So, lacking other insurance, he had no healthcare coverage for a whole month and had to pay some medical bills out-of-pocket.

>> Miguel continued on active service until he was 68, and until then he and his wife, Julia, were covered under his TRICARE Prime insurance. Miguel made sure to sign up for Medicare Part B in October, the month before he retired, so that both his Medicare and TRICARE For Life coverage kicked in on the first day of the following month (November 1). Because Julia was still only 64 when her husband retired, she continued to be covered under TRICARE Prime. A month before her 65th birthday in February, she signed up for Part B, and her Medicare and TFL coverage both began seamlessly on February 1. Medicare became primary insurance for both husband and wife.

The Veterans Affairs health system

The VA's health system provides comprehensive medical benefits to about 9 million veterans a year in some 1,321 facilities across the nation. To receive these benefits, you must be a veteran (with a discharge that wasn't dishonorable), enroll in the system, and go to VA doctors and facilities.

REMEMBER

If you have VA coverage and are eligible for Medicare, you're not required to enroll in Part B, but you may have good reason to do so. In fact, the VA strongly recommends that all veterans with VA healthcare also enroll in Medicare Parts A and B as soon as they become eligible (unless they have group insurance from a current employer). Here's why:

>> **VA health coverage isn't set in stone and isn't the same for everyone.** The VA assigns enrollees to different priority levels according to various factors, such as income and whether they have any medical condition that derives from their military service. If federal funding drops or doesn't keep pace with costs, some vets in the lower priority levels may lose VA coverage entirely.

>> **Having both Medicare and VA benefits considerably widens your coverage.** If you need to go to a non-VA hospital or doctor, you're automatically covered under Part A or Part B — whereas with VA coverage alone, you may end up having to pay the full cost yourself, even in emergencies. This point is an important one to consider if you live some distance from the nearest VA facility — unless you qualify for non-VA care under its Community Care program, as explained further on in this section.

>> **You may be subject to penalties or fees later.** If, someday, when you're well past 65, you happen to lose VA coverage or otherwise decide that you need

Medicare and aren't already signed up for Part B (or have insurance from a current employer), you'll pay late penalties that are permanently added to your Part B premiums, as explained in Chapter 6.

Your VA prescription drug coverage is much better and less expensive than Medicare's, so you don't need to join a Part D drug plan, and you won't get hit with Part D late enrollment penalties if you lose VA drug coverage in the future. But if you have both Part D and VA drug benefits, you have the flexibility of being able to use one or the other, which allows you to

>> Get prescriptions from non-VA doctors and fill them at local retail pharmacies.

>> Obtain medications the VA doesn't cover.

>> Apply for low-cost drug coverage under Part D's Extra Help program if your income is under a certain level. (Chapter 4 has details on Extra Help.)

REMEMBER

VA health benefits aren't coordinated with Medicare, so primary or secondary coverage isn't relevant. If you're enrolled in both programs, you use your VA identity card at VA facilities and your Medicare ID card anywhere else. Similarly, if you're enrolled in a Part D drug plan, you can use that plan's card at retail pharmacies or use the VA's mail-order pharmacy system. For both medical care and drug coverage, you can't double up; you must use only one type of insurance for each service or prescription.

Some vets may qualify for treatment under the VA's Community Care program. This allows you to go to non-VA facilities and doctors in certain circumstances, such as living too far from a VA facility that can provide needed treatment. Usually prior authorization is required, and if you're approved, the VA covers your bills. In an emergency, if you need to go to a non-VA facility, the VA recommends that you inform the facility of your VA enrollment. But payment for emergency treatment depends on your specific eligibility for non-VA care, so it's important to understand the rules in advance. For more information, go to www.va.gov/communitycare/.

For more information on the VA healthcare system in general, go to www.va.gov/health.

The Indian Health Service

The *Indian Health Service* (IHS) is a federal program that provides comprehensive healthcare for roughly 2.6 million Native Americans and Alaska Natives who are members of 574 tribes across 37 states in the United States.

If you receive healthcare from an IHS, Tribal, or Urban Indian Health Program facility, you must enroll in Medicare Parts A and B if you're eligible. IHS is regarded as the *payer of last resort* under the law, meaning that if you qualify for any other health coverage — including Medicaid and private employer benefits, as well as Medicare — you must apply for and use those services. They're all primary to IHS coverage.

You don't need to sign up for Medicare Part D prescription drug coverage because the drug coverage you receive from IHS clinics and other Tribal programs is creditable. But you may want to consider enrolling in a Part D drug plan, especially if you qualify for Extra Help (described in Chapter 4). The money Medicare spends on your drugs saves precious federal dollars that support your local clinic, allowing it to provide needed care for more people in your community.

As you approach age 65, visit your local clinic or contact the benefits coordinator of your health program to talk over what you need to do to enroll in Medicare, and what signing up for Part D would mean for you and your community.

The Black Lung Program

The federal Black Lung Program provides income and medical benefits for former coal miners who became totally disabled due to black lung disease (*pneumoconiosis*) contracted while working in or near American coal mines. The program provides medical coverage for eligible former miners but not for their spouses or other family members.

When you have Black Lung coverage as well as Medicare, you should show your identity cards for both programs to doctors and other providers when you receive medical care. Or tell them that you have Black Lung coverage and give them your Social Security number. Your coverage works like this:

>> The Black Lung Program pays only for medical services related to the diagnosis and treatment of black lung disease.

>> Medicare pays first for any other covered medical services that aren't related to black lung disease.

>> Doctors and other providers should send your bills to the correct program for payment.

>> If any providers tell you that the Black Lung Program has denied payment for a claim, ask them to send your bill directly to Medicare, together with a copy of the letter from the Black Lung Program saying that it won't pay the bill.

The Black Lung Program is run by the Department of Labor. For more information about Black Lung medical benefits, call 800-638-7072. Or see the DoL's frequently asked questions on the program at www.dol.gov/owcp/dcmwc/regs/compliance/cm-6.pdf.

Mixing Medicare with Workers' Comp or No-Fault or Liability Insurance

Workers' compensation, no-fault insurance, and liability insurance are very different from each other, but they're lumped together here because they have one thing in common — claims for them can take a long time to settle, sometimes even years. If you're in this situation, Medicare has a system to tide you over and pay your medical bills before a settlement is made.

But you need to know the rules on how the system works and what Medicare expects of you if that big insurance claim eventually pays out; Medicare always counts as the secondary payer in such cases and has to recoup as much money as possible on what it's spent on your care.

What do these three types of insurance cover? Briefly, it's the following:

>> *Workers' compensation* uses special funds administered by the state to pay medical expenses and loss-of-income benefits to employees who are injured on the job or become sick as a direct result of their employment.

>> *No-fault insurance* pays medical expenses that people have as a result of an accident — regardless of whose fault it was. Claims for this type of insurance may be made on automobile, homeowners, and commercial insurance policies.

>> *Liability insurance* pays medical expenses on claims that involve *negligence* — where an action (or lack of action) results in somebody being harmed. Claims may be covered under several types of policies, such as automobile, homeowners, product liability, and malpractice insurance.

The issues involved in making claims on these types of insurance can be complex, and in most cases other people will be helping you make them (for example, your employer, union, insurance company, and/or lawyer). The following sections cover only what you need to know if you're in one of these situations and also receiving medical services from Medicare.

When you first make a claim

If you have other private insurance that's primary to Medicare (such as a plan from a current employer, as discussed earlier in this chapter), the doctor, hospital, or other provider bills that insurance company first. And you can bet that, quick as a flash, the insurer will contact you to find out whether your injury happened in a vehicle collision, on somebody else's property, and so on. These questions are designed to determine whether your health plan can make a claim under somebody else's no-fault or liability insurance. Very often, the two companies (your health plan insurer and the liability insurer) will negotiate and come to a settlement without much input from you.

Much the same happens if Medicare is your primary or only insurance. The doctor or hospital is required to ask whether your injury occurred in circumstances that could be covered under no-fault or liability insurance — and, if possible, send the bill to that insurance company rather than to Medicare. The codes that a doctor or hospital uses to bill Medicare for your treatment may also alert Medicare to investigate the circumstances.

If you were injured at work or developed some illness caused by conditions at work, you should inform your employer as soon as possible and file a claim for workers' compensation. Your employer must provide the appropriate forms that tell you how to do so. You should ask your doctor or other health providers to send your medical bills to the state workers' compensation insurance fund to get payment.

REMEMBER

As soon as you've filed a claim — whether for workers' compensation, no-fault, or liability insurance — you or your lawyer should notify Medicare's Benefits Coordination & Recovery Center that you've done so. Call the BCRC at 855-798-2627 (TTY 1-855-797-2627).

If the claim isn't settled promptly

In this situation, Medicare defines *prompt* as anything less than 120 days. So if your doctor has billed workers' compensation or somebody else's no-fault or liability insurance for the cost of your treatment and the bill has been paid within 120 days (four months), that's it; the claim has been settled.

But very often the bill isn't paid within 120 days. Workers' compensation — for reasons too complicated to go into here — can take many months or years to reach settlement. So can liability insurance if the company disputes the claim, and even no-fault insurance can drag on.

REMEMBER

In these circumstances, Medicare kicks in with a system known as *conditional payment.* It means that Medicare pays the bills for your treatment after the 120 days are up. It also means that if and when you receive a cash settlement under workers' compensation, no-fault insurance, or liability insurance, you must repay Medicare for the money it spent on your care for the specific injury or illness in question.

For example, Frank was taken to the emergency room after a truck hit the car he was driving. The hospital billed the truck driver's liability insurance, but the insurance company disputed who was at fault and refused to pay the claim immediately. When 120 days had passed, the hospital billed Medicare, which paid for Frank's care on a conditional basis. Eventually, the liability insurance made a cash settlement, and out of this amount Frank repaid Medicare for the money it had spent on his medical care as a result of the accident.

If you have a claim pending — whether for workers' compensation, no-fault insurance, or liability insurance — you can track developments on a website known as the Medicare Secondary Payer Recovery Portal (MSPRP). This site requires you to register and log in to view and upload documents electronically. It's mainly for lawyers, insurers, and others involved in the resolution of claims, but as a beneficiary, you can also access it through your personal account on Medicare's website at `www.medicare.gov/account/login`. (If you haven't already registered for an account, you can do so by following the instructions in Chapter 13.) After logging into your account, click on the MSPRP button, using the same login and password. You can also download an MSPRP User Guide from the "Reference Materials" menu option to help navigate the program.

When the claim has been settled

When an insurance award is made, Medicare has *priority right of recovery.* In other words, it has first claim on the money. You (as the injured person) or your lawyer needs to inform Medicare of the settlement as soon as possible after it has become final.

WARNING

You need to pay attention to the fact that the money due to Medicare must be repaid within 60 days of the settlement — otherwise, interest charges may be added.

If you had legal help making this claim, you should find out whether your lawyer has taken steps to contact Medicare about reimbursement and whether Medicare has issued a recovery letter specifying the amount to be repaid. If not, you should call Medicare's Benefits Coordination & Recovery Center as soon as possible, at 855-798-2627 (TTY 1-855-797-2627).

What if the claim isn't decided in your favor — with no cash settlement forthcoming? In that case, you don't have to repay Medicare for any of the conditional payments it has made for your care. Similarly, if you have to settle for a smaller amount than the medical care for your injury actually costs, Medicare claims the amount of the insurance payout but no more.

REMEMBER

Be aware that in many workers' compensation settlements, payments are awarded not just for medical expenses already incurred but also to pay for the expected costs of future medical services and prescription drugs arising from the work-related injury or illness. These funds are called Workers' Compensation Medicare Set-Aside Arrangements. You can use them only to pay for services and items related to the injury or illness that Medicare would otherwise have covered. And Medicare won't pay for any of those things until your set-aside funds have been used up. In this situation, you need to keep careful records so you can prove you spent the set-aside funds appropriately. (Medicare will, of course, cover your other medical expenses — those not related to this particular injury or illness — in the usual way.)

3

Making Smart Choices among Medicare's Many Options

Understand specific differences between original Medicare and the Medicare Advantage program and the differences between types of Medicare Advantage plans.

If you choose original Medicare, know how to compare Part D drug plans and select the one that covers your prescriptions at the lowest cost. Discover the ins and outs of Medigap policies if you decide to buy this type of supplemental insurance.

Expertly compare the details of Medicare Advantage plans offered in your area, and choose one according to your own needs and preferences.

Get help making these choices by using free services that provide personal help without sales pressure. Be aware of how to sidestep frauds and scams.

Chapter **9**

Making Sense of Medicare's Many Options

t always amuses me, in a grim kind of way, when I hear politicians talk about Medicare as a "one-size-fits-all" system. Using that tired old phrase is an instant giveaway of their total ignorance of how the program works. Just imagine if Medicare *were* a one-size-fits-all system. It would be far simpler to navigate and understand, with no need for long explanations. I sure wouldn't be taking 400-plus pages to untangle it in this book!

But, in fact, Medicare offers many different options. Of course, it's that range of choice that causes so many people to become utterly baffled and lost in the weeds, with the result that many blindly make decisions that aren't in their best interests. Nonetheless, choices do allow you to tailor your coverage to your own particular needs as long as you know how to evaluate them.

In this chapter, I explain how Medicare is broadly divided into two completely different systems for delivering your benefits — the original Medicare program and the array of private health plans known collectively as Medicare Advantage (MA). This chapter describes how choosing one or the other of these systems directly determines other options that are available to you and the decisions you must make. I then detail the differences between the two systems and among types of MA plans. Finally, I discuss a question that often perplexes people who are new to Medicare: What is the difference between Medicare Advantage plans and Medigap supplemental insurance?

Seeing the Big Picture: Your Starting Point to Navigating the Medicare Maze

When you enter a maze, you can't see the whole structure because of those high hedges hemming you in, but you hope you'll pick your way through it by trial and error. Yet if you hover over that maze in a helicopter, you can quite clearly see the entrance and the exit and the quickest way connecting the two. Okay, I'm not going to push this analogy any further, but looking at the big picture from the get-go is enormously useful in helping you navigate the Medicare maze more efficiently to where you want to be. That's what this section aims to do. Here, I explain the consequences of your system choice and compare the systems. I also describe situations when you may not have a choice and when you could be automatically enrolled in a plan without your knowledge.

Understanding the consequences of your choice of system

REMEMBER

Here's a quick summary of how each of the two systems works, very differently, in delivering Medicare benefits:

>> **Original Medicare:** This option is the original government system that has been in place since 1966; that's why it's also called *traditional Medicare.* It comprises Parts A and B, and it works on a *fee-for-service* basis. In other words, Medicare directly pays a portion of the costs of any medical service it covers to any provider that accepts Medicare patients. You, the patient, pay a percentage of the cost or, in some cases, a fixed amount for each covered service you receive. Overall, the government contributes subsidies amounting to about 75 percent toward beneficiaries' medical costs.

>> **Medicare Advantage (MA):** *Medicare Advantage* is the name used collectively for Medicare's private health plans. They deliver Medicare benefits in a different way from the original system and are run by Medicare-approved private insurance companies. Medicare pays each plan a monthly amount for each enrollee's medical care, regardless of how much healthcare a person

actually uses. You receive your medical benefits through the plan of your choice and pay the charges required by the plan. Because plans vary greatly in their costs and benefits, you need to compare them carefully to pick the one that best suits your needs.

At the outset, though, the key point to understand is this: Choosing either of these systems triggers a mini-cascade of other choices, as the following sections illustrate.

Considerations for choosing one system over the other

If you decide on original Medicare, you must consider

>> **Whether you need Part D prescription drug coverage:** If so, you must enroll in a stand-alone Part D drug plan (one that provides only drug coverage), choose your plan from among the 15 to 24 plans offered in your state, and pay a monthly premium. You don't need Part D if you have *creditable* (equivalent) drug coverage from another source; head to Chapters 6 and 8 for the lowdown.

>> **Whether you want Medigap supplemental insurance:** Medigap pays many of your out-of-pocket expenses in original Medicare. If you want it, you must choose a policy with the set of benefits that you prefer (out of a maximum of ten choices), contact insurance companies that sell that policy in your area for a price quote, and pay the monthly premium required. (I give more details on Medigap in Chapters 4 and 10.)

If you decide on Medicare Advantage, you must think about the following:

>> **Whether you need Part D prescription drug coverage:** If so, you must choose an MA plan that includes drug coverage in its benefits package. If you have creditable drug coverage from another source, such as the Veterans Affairs (VA) health system, you can choose an MA plan that offers only medical benefits with no drug coverage.

>> **Which plan to enroll in:** Where you live determines how many MA plans are available to you. A few rural areas have no MA plans at all. Some big urban areas have 30 plans or more. In 2024, the average beneficiary will have access to 43 MA plans for individual enrollment, according to the Kaiser Family Foundation, and 89 percent of all plans will include prescription drug coverage. Each plan has its own mix of costs and benefits. Comparing them isn't always an easy process. (Get an explanation for how to do this comparison in Chapter 11.) But you must choose just one, enroll in it, and pay a monthly premium (in addition to the Part B premium) if one is required.

How soon must you make this first cut? Well, when you first sign up for Medicare Parts A and B, you're automatically enrolled in the original Medicare program; you'll continue to receive your benefits from that program unless you specifically choose to switch to a Medicare Advantage private plan. Similarly, if you're already in either original Medicare or one of the MA private health plans, you remain with that coverage unless you take action to switch. In other words, you make the call.

REMEMBER

You can decide to enroll in an MA plan when you first sign up for Part B, whether that's during your initial enrollment period or a special enrollment period, if you want to. Of course, whichever system you choose, your decision isn't set in stone. Regardless of which option you pick to begin with, you're free to switch to the alternative at least once a year during an appropriate enrollment period, as I explain in Chapter 15.

An important limitation on your choice

You do face one limitation on this otherwise-open choice. What happens if you enroll in a Medicare Advantage plan and then want to return to original Medicare? Can you still buy a Medigap policy with full federal protections — that is, a guaranteed right to buy the policy of your choice, without paying higher premiums based on your current or past health issues? You have that right within six months of enrolling in Part B (as explained in Chapter 4), but in only a few other circumstances:

>> You joined an MA plan as soon as you became eligible for Medicare at 65 and you're still in the first 12 months of being in the plan.

>> You dropped a Medigap policy to join an MA plan, it's the first MA plan you've ever been in, and you've been in it for one year or less.

>> You move out of your MA plan's service area and decide to switch to original Medicare.

>> Your MA plan stops providing services in your area.

>> Medicare allows you to drop out of your MA plan after determining that the plan broke the rules or misled you.

WARNING

The first two of these situations count as a trial period. The other three describe very specific circumstances. In all other situations, if you drop out of an MA plan and switch to original Medicare, you may still be able to buy a Medigap policy, but you won't get the federal guarantees and protections (especially in regard to pre-existing medical conditions) that are described in detail in Chapter 10 — unless you live in a state that gives similar rights.

Can you suspend a Medigap policy while you are covered by Medicaid or insurance from a current employer? That may be possible in some situations, as explained more in Chapter 10.

Weighing the two systems

So how do original Medicare and Medicare Advantage stack up generally in delivering healthcare? To answer that question, I take a big-picture viewpoint in this section, highlighting a range of issues to consider: overall costs; premiums; co-pays; the long-term stability of costs, benefits, and care; choice of providers and whether care is coordinated; extra benefits; geographical service areas; and quality of care.

Thinking through these issues and applying your personal preferences makes gravitating toward one system over the other easier for you. Then, in the later section "Digging into the Details of Original Medicare versus Medicare Advantage," you can look at the details of original Medicare and the different types of Medicare Advantage plans to refine your thoughts and settle on the system that works best for you. At that point, you need to get down to the nitty-gritty of comparing individual plans, a process I explain in Chapter 10 (for stand-alone Part D plans and Medigap policies if you go with original Medicare) or Chapter 11 (for Medicare Advantage plans).

Overall costs

On the whole, MA plans offer lower out-of-pocket costs than original Medicare. Certainly, they may provide a lower-cost alternative for people who can't afford Medigap supplemental insurance. Here's how it happens:

>> *Managed care plans,* such as HMOs (health maintenance organizations) and PPOs (preferred provider organizations), keep costs relatively low by limiting access to doctors, hospitals, and other providers within their own provider networks and service areas or by charging enrollees more if they go outside them. They may also require enrollees to ask for prior authorization before covering certain kinds of treatment.

>> A change in the law in 2003 allowed Medicare to pay the private plans far more on average for enrollees' care than it pays for people enrolled in the original system. The extra payments allowed the plans to charge enrollees less and/or to offer better benefits than original Medicare.

>> MA plans must set an annual limit on their enrollees' total out-of-pocket expenses (deductibles and co-pays) — also a requirement of the Affordable Care Act. The limit is set by law, though individual plans can choose to set a lower cap. Original Medicare has no out-of-pocket limit.

However, Medicare Advantage's private plans may not be the less-expensive option for everyone. Several studies have suggested that people with greater healthcare needs may ultimately pay more for their care in MAs than if they were in original Medicare, though these reports don't reflect recent developments in the law.

Premium costs

Many people in original Medicare pay three monthly premiums — one for Part B, one for prescription drug coverage (Part D), and one for a Medigap supplemental insurance policy. In contrast, most people in Medicare Advantage plans pay at most two premiums — one for Part B and one for the plan itself, which may or may not include Part D drug coverage as well as other supplemental benefits. However, the majority of plans charge no premiums of their own at all, even if they include all those extras.

Co-pay costs

Medicare Advantage plans have traditionally charged fixed-dollar co-pays for doctor visits, which may be less expensive and more convenient than the percentage of the cost (typically 20 percent) that original Medicare charges. A flat co-pay is also more predictable: If your plan charges $20 this year to see your primary-care doctor, you know in advance that this amount will be your payment for every visit throughout the year; however, you can't be certain what 20 percent means in dollar terms when the total cost on which it's based may fluctuate. Still, recently an increasing number of Medicare Advantage plans have also begun charging percentages of costs for some services rather than flat co-pays — sometimes less than 20 percent and sometimes more.

Stays in the hospital are also charged quite differently under original Medicare and MA plans — but whether one costs more than the other depends mainly on how long your stay is, as detailed in Chapter 11.

When you're in original Medicare, you can purchase a Medigap supplemental policy that pays your hospital deductible, Part B deductible, and Part B co-pays. This setup not only makes your out-of-pocket costs more predictable but also essentially eradicates them so that you pay nothing or very little. But under Medicare rules, you can't use Medigap to cover out-of-pocket costs if you're enrolled in a Medicare Advantage plan.

Cost and benefit stability

Medicare Advantage plans can change their costs and benefits each calendar year, increasing or reducing them as they choose. Original Medicare is more stable, but it usually increases the Part A and Part B deductibles slightly each year, and the 20 percent coinsurance it charges for most Part B services also tends to rise as healthcare costs in general go up. Services that original Medicare covers (and which, by law, MA plans must cover, too) generally don't change much from year to year, although sometimes new ones are added.

Care stability

WARNING

Original Medicare is there, year after year. Medicare Advantage plans can choose annually whether to stay in Medicare or withdraw, or whether to enter or exit a particular service area. Occasionally, Medicare doesn't renew a particular plan's contract. If any such changes occur, affected enrollees are notified in advance and can switch to another private plan or to original Medicare, but this change can be a disrupting experience.

Provider choice and care coordination

The main reason people give for choosing or staying in original Medicare is that they can go to any doctor or hospital they please — or, at least, any that accepts Medicare patients, and most providers still do. (However, the shortage of primary-care doctors is having an impact on Medicare, as in other health systems, in some areas. Chapter 13 delves into this further.)

In contrast, the majority of Medicare Advantage plans — those that provide managed care through HMOs — limit the choice of providers to those in their networks and service areas. However, this arrangement may be considered a benefit rather than a restriction if care is properly coordinated.

Because your medical needs are handled and monitored by a single local system, you're more likely to be encouraged to get tests and screenings early enough to prevent serious health problems later on and less likely to be prescribed drugs that may interact badly with each other.

Original Medicare relies on the fee-for-service system and has therefore never coordinated care. Nonetheless, that may change in the future. Many studies have shown that properly coordinated care improves health outcomes — especially for people with chronic conditions such as diabetes and heart disease — and saves tons of taxpayer money, mainly because fewer patients need expensive hospital care. As a result, in some areas Medicare is now beginning to offer programs in which providers get rewarded not for the number of services they bill to Medicare but for the outcomes of their patients' care. This new approach goes by various names, including *patient-centered medical homes* and *accountable care organizations.*

Extra benefits

All MA plans must provide the same medical services as original Medicare. But they can also offer extra benefits that may be well worth having. Some plans with these extras don't charge higher premiums, but many do — often quite a lot more. Look at the coverage details of extra benefits carefully when comparing plans; some are significant, whereas others are very limited.

Geographical area

Geography is a key consideration if you travel a lot or live in another state for part of the year. Original Medicare covers you anywhere in the United States, whereas most MA plans require you to either see providers in their service area or pay more to go outside the network. However, all plans must cover emergency treatment or urgently needed care anywhere in the country. Some Medigap policies and MA plans also cover emergency care abroad.

Quality measures

Medicare has an elaborate system of testing the quality of services provided by MA plans and stand-alone Part D plans, using feedback from customers, complaints, surveys, undercover spot checks, and so on. Based on this info, Medicare gives each plan a quality rating that is posted on the Medicare plan finder website at www.medicare.gov for all to see. (I explain this system in more detail in Chapters 10 and 11.) Medicare also uses these ratings to reward the highest-quality plans with bonus payments. Quality measures aren't used to rate services in the original Medicare program, which by definition are too fragmented among thousands of providers to be tested.

Recognizing when you may not have a choice

You may not be free to make a choice — either between original Medicare and the private Medicare Advantage system or among the private plans themselves — if you have health coverage from a former employer or union. Here are some of the ways this limitation can occur:

>> Your current plan is a special one offered only to retirees of the employer or union that sponsors it.

>> Your current plan pays the premiums for a Medigap supplemental policy. This type of policy can be used only with original Medicare, not with a Medicare Advantage plan.

>> Your current plan gives you coverage under a specific Medicare Advantage plan, meaning you can't also be enrolled in the original Medicare program or any other MA plan.

Be aware that if you enroll in an alternative plan (unless it's an alternative specifically offered by your former employer or union), you may automatically lose your current coverage for you and your dependents and may not be able to get it back later if you change your mind.

REMEMBER

Some employer plans are so expensive or have such skimpy benefits that dropping them and relying wholly on Medicare may make sense. But think carefully before taking this step. Always check with your current plan's benefits administrator so that you fully know the consequences.

Also, you likely don't have a choice if you spend some months of the year in one place and the rest in another or travel around the United States most of the time. To maximize your chances of getting medical treatment anywhere, you need to enroll in original Medicare and choose a Part D drug plan that allows you to fill prescriptions at pharmacies throughout the nation.

Being on your guard against "default enrollment"

You may have heard about a little-known practice that allows insurance companies to automatically enroll new Medicare beneficiaries into Medicare Advantage plans without their explicit consent. This scenario is known as *default enrollment* or *seamless conversion.* It works like this: Before becoming eligible for Medicare, you had health insurance that was provided by an insurance company. When you become Medicare-eligible, that same company enrolls you in a Medicare Advantage plan that is one of its own insurance products. As required by law, it sends you a letter saying you will be automatically enrolled in this plan, unless you specifically opt out. While default enrollment used to affect people in a wide range of insurance plans, currently, only those enrolled in *Medicaid* managed care plans (who will soon be eligible for both Medicaid and Medicare) are subject to default enrollment.

WARNING

Default enrollment sounds very convenient. After all, it saves you from having to make a decision as to which kind of Medicare coverage you want. But experts point to several drawbacks about this practice that you should be aware of:

>> It greatly restricts your immediate coverage choices. It denies you the option of enrolling in original Medicare or in any other Medicare Advantage plan that may better suit your needs, preferences, and wallet. (Note, though, that original Medicare does not coordinate with Medicaid; people with both

Medicaid and Medicare may want to stay in a private plan that coordinates benefits from both programs.)

» It restricts your choice of doctors to those who are signed up with this particular plan.

» The auto-enrollment letter from the insurance company comes at a time (just before your 65th birthday) when typically an avalanche of mailings from companies selling Medicare plans comes surging through your mail slot. So if you toss that letter with all the rest, you'll be automatically enrolled in the plan the company chooses for you without even realizing it.

REMEMBER

The best way to avoid finding yourself in a Medicare Advantage plan you didn't choose is to open and carefully review any mail that arrives from your current or former insurance company. Mailings from other companies can be tossed, but be sure to keep and read any letters from Medicare, Social Security, or the company that's been providing your health insurance before you become eligible for Medicare. And if you do receive a default enrollment letter, remember that you have the right to opt out — or to consider your other Medicare options before deciding to stay in. You may also call your current insurance company and find out whether it uses default enrollment or seamless conversion for people newly eligible for Medicare.

Digging into the Details of Original Medicare versus Medicare Advantage

Good news: Nobody's going to ask you to take a quiz on all this information! But you do need to do some homework to make an informed decision about getting your healthcare from original Medicare or a private Medicare Advantage plan — and, if you choose the latter, about the kind of plan you prefer. The more thoroughly you understand the differences among all these choices, the more likely you'll be content with the one you pick.

TECHNICAL
STUFF

Whichever way you choose to go, one thing is certain: You're still under the big umbrella of Medicare. As a whole, more than 66 million people are enrolled in the program in 2024. Of these, 51 percent (34 million people) are in original Medicare, and 49 percent (32 million) are in a Medicare Advantage plan, according to government figures.

Figure 9-1 shows at a glance the main differences between original Medicare and the two types of MA plans that are chosen by 95 percent of people enrolled in the Medicare Advantage program: HMOs and PPOs.

Questions to Consider	Original Medicare	Medicare HMOs	Medicare PPOs
Can I get my medical care from any doctor or hospital?	Yes, anywhere in the country as long as the provider takes Medicare patients and accepts new ones.	No. You must go to in-network providers, except in an emergency or if your HMO has a point-of-service option.	Yes. PPOs have provider networks in their service areas but also allow you to go out of network for a higher co-pay.
Must I have a primary care doctor?	No.	Yes.	No.
Do I need a referral to see a specialist?	No.	Usually.	No.
Can I get more benefits if I pay a higher premium?	No. But you can buy a private Medigap policy to cover most of your out-of-pocket costs and a few extra benefits.	Some plans offer some coverage for vision, dental, hearing, and/or other benefits.	Some plans offer some coverage for vision, dental, hearing, and/or other benefits.
How do I get prescription drugs?	Only by joining a stand-alone Part D plan and paying a separate premium.	Only by joining an HMO that offers Part D drug coverage in its benefit package.	Only by joining a PPO that offers Part D drug coverage in its benefit package.
How is my share of the costs decided?	You pay standard deductibles and co-pays unless you have a Medigap policy that covers them.	You pay whatever your plan requires. Going out of network may mean paying full cost except in emergencies.	You pay what your plan requires. Going out of network means paying higher co-pays, except in emergencies.
Is there an annual limit on my total out-of-pocket costs?	No.	Yes. A maximum annual limit is set by law, but some plans have lower limits.	Yes. A maximum annual limit is set by law, but some plans have lower limits.

FIGURE 9-1: Comparing Medicare Advantage HMOs/PPOs and original Medicare.

© John Wiley & Sons, Inc.

The following sections drill down to more-detailed information on all the plan choices available to you. In each case, I explain how each type of plan works: its eligibility rules, its choice of doctors and other providers, whether extra benefits may be available (more than original Medicare covers), and how it fits in with Part D prescription drug coverage. (Excluded here are details of out-of-pocket costs, because those are covered extensively in Chapter 3.)

Opting for original Medicare

Original Medicare is the program you're in unless you opt for one of the private plans described in the next section:

- >> **Eligibility:** You must have Part A or Part B (or both), as explained in Chapter 5. To receive services, you can live anywhere in the United States or its territories.

- >> **Choice of doctors and hospitals:** You can go to any doctor, hospital, or other provider that accepts Medicare patients (and is accepting new ones) anywhere in the country. You don't need a referral from a primary-care doctor to see a specialist. (For more on finding doctors who participate in Medicare, check out Chapter 13.)

- >> **Extra benefits:** Original Medicare covers many kinds of healthcare, but by no means does it cover all the services you're likely to need, as Chapter 2 explains. For example, it doesn't cover routine hearing, vision, and dental care. Medigap supplemental insurance (explained in Chapters 4 and 10) may provide a few extra benefits, such as emergency care abroad, depending on the policy you buy.

- >> **Prescription drugs:** Original Medicare covers only drugs administered in hospitals, doctors' offices, and clinics. You need to enroll in a private, stand-alone Part D plan and pay an additional premium to get coverage for outpatient drugs you use at home.

Looking at Medicare Advantage plans

You can choose among several very different types of plans within the Medicare Advantage system. Some types, such as HMOs and PPOs, have been part of Medicare for many years. Other types of MA plans are much newer. Medicare Private Fee-for-Service plans surged for a time after 2004, and Medicare Medical Savings Accounts gained some traction too, but now both types of plan are available in relatively few areas. The following sections explain the key features of these and some other types of MA plans.

Health maintenance organizations (HMOs)

HMOs are the most popular Medicare Advantage plans, chosen by about two-thirds of people in the MA program in 2021. They offer managed care, which typically requires primary-care doctors to coordinate care and refer patients to specialists and other services. HMOs operate locally in limited geographical service areas — usually a county or even a zip code. The same HMO may offer costs and benefits different in one service area than in another right next to it. Here are the main features of HMOs:

>> **Eligibility:** You must have both Part A and Part B and live within the service area of the plan you select.

>> **Choice of doctors and hospitals:** You must be treated by doctors and hospitals within the plan's network of contracted providers in its service area, except in an emergency or if you urgently need care. You usually need a referral from your primary-care doctor to see a specialist. (If the plan offers a *point-of-service* option, however, you can go out of network for a higher co-pay.) An HMO can supply you with its list of providers to help you find out in advance whether it covers your preferred hospitals and doctors. An HMO is allowed to drop any of your doctors from its network during the plan year, but it must give you at least 60 days' notice.

>> **Extra benefits:** Some plans offer routine vision, hearing, and/or dental services, though just how good this coverage is varies greatly among plans and some offer them as separate optional packages for an additional premium. Some plans offer other extras and supplemental benefits like health-club memberships and transportation to medical appointments. But sometimes these supplemental benefits are limited only to enrollees with specific medical conditions.

>> **Prescription drugs:** Most HMOs include Part D drug coverage in their benefit packages, but not all do. If you join a plan that doesn't, you can't get drug coverage from a stand-alone Part D plan.

Preferred provider organizations (PPOs)

PPOs are plans that offer managed care with fewer restrictions than HMOs. *Regional PPOs* cover large areas — maybe several states. *Local PPOs* operate within smaller areas, such as in one or several adjacent counties. In 2021, about a third of people enrolled in MA plans chose PPOs. These plans' features include the following:

>> **Eligibility:** Like HMOs (see the preceding section), you must have Parts A and B and live within the service area of the plan you pick.

>> **Choice of doctors and hospitals:** You can go to a doctor, hospital, or other provider outside of the plan's network — but if you do, it'll cost you more in higher co-pays. You don't need a referral to see a specialist. A PPO can give you its list of network providers so you can see in advance whether your preferred doctors and hospitals accept the plan. If a PPO drops any of your doctors from its network during the plan year, it must give you at least 60 days' notice.

>> **Extra benefits:** Some plans offer vision, hearing, and/or dental services, though just how good this coverage is varies greatly among plans and some offer them as separate optional packages for an additional premium. Some plans offer other extras and supplemental benefits like health-club memberships and

transcription to medical appointments. But sometimes these supplemental benefits are limited only to enrollees with specific medical conditions.

>> **Prescription drug coverage:** Most PPOs include Part D drug coverage in their benefit packages, but not all do. If you join a plan that doesn't, you can't purchase coverage from a stand-alone Part D plan.

Private Fee-for-Service (PFFS) plans

Medicare Private Fee-for-Service (PFFS) plans don't offer managed care. They directly pay providers for each covered service, similar to the way original Medicare works. In 2021, less than 1 percent of people enrolled in the MA program chose PFFS plans. Here are their main features:

>> **Eligibility:** You must have Parts A and B and live in the service area of the plan you select (even though you aren't limited to seeing providers in that area).

>> **Choice of doctors and hospitals:** You can go to any doctor or hospital anywhere in the country if the provider accepts the plan's conditions and payment rates. You don't need a referral to see a specialist, and the plan can't require you to ask for preauthorization before covering treatment. But many providers don't accept PFFS plans. Also, providers are allowed to accept or reject the plan for each service visit — so if they accept it once, you have no guarantee they'll do so next time. To be sure of where you stand, you or the provider can ask the plan for a written decision on coverage before you receive each service.

>> **Extra benefits:** PFFS plans may offer extras like routine vision, hearing, and dental care and fitness classes or gym memberships if they choose.

>> **Prescription drug coverage:** Not all PFFS plans offer Part D drug coverage. If you join a plan that doesn't, you can enroll in a stand-alone drug plan to obtain coverage (unlike HMOs and PPOs).

TIP

For more information, see the official publication "Medicare & You" at www.medicare.gov/pubs/pdf/10050-medicare-and-you.pdf.

Special Needs Plans (SNPs)

Medicare Special Needs Plans (SNPs) are relatively new additions to the Medicare Advantage program and aren't available in all areas. They're similar in structure to HMOs and PPOs (described earlier in this chapter), but each individual SNP serves people in only one of the following specific categories:

>> People who live in institutions (such as nursing homes)

>> People who are eligible for both Medicare and Medicaid

>> People who have at least one chronic disabling condition, such as congestive heart failure, mental illness, diabetes, or HIV/AIDS

Here are the main features of SNPs:

>> **Eligibility:** You must have Parts A and B and live in the service area of your selected plan. To be accepted into an SNP, you must fall into the single category (one of the three just described) that the plan serves.

>> **Choice of doctors and hospitals:** If the SNP works like an HMO, you must go to the doctors and hospitals within the plan's provider network, except in emergencies or for urgently needed care, and you need a primary-care doctor to refer you to a specialist. If the SNP works like a PPO, you can go out of network for a higher co-pay and don't need a referral for a specialist. The plan may assign a care manager to help coordinate your healthcare needs and other services in the community.

>> **Extra benefits:** SNPs come with a built-in extra benefit in that they focus on your special circumstances or health condition and coordinate the services you need accordingly. Some plans offer vision, hearing, and/or dental services (though the extent of that coverage greatly varies among plans) and extras such as fitness classes or gym memberships.

>> **Prescription drugs:** All SNPs must offer Part D drug coverage.

TIP

For more information, see the official publication "Medicare & You" at www.medicare.gov/pubs/pdf/10050-medicare-and-you.pdf.

Medical Savings Account (MSA) plans

Medicare Medical Savings Accounts (MSAs) work very differently from other Medicare Advantage plans. Medicare gives an MSA plan a certain amount of money for each of its enrollees. The plan then deposits a portion of this money into a special health savings account for you. You draw on the money in the account to pay for medical care. If you use up the entire amount, you then pay 100 percent of your medical costs until you've reached the plan's deductible limit. (The deductible may be very high — up to $10,000 or more.) Beyond that limit, the plan pays all your costs for Medicare-covered services for the rest of the year. These are their main features:

>> **Eligibility:** You must have Parts A and B. You must live in the United States for at least 183 days of the year and have no other health coverage (like a retiree plan) that would cover the MSA deductible.

>> **Choice of doctors and hospitals:** You can go to any doctor or hospital, but the cost may be lower if you choose a provider that has a contract with the

MSA plan to treat its enrollees. If the MSA offers this option (and not all do), you can ask the plan for a list of providers.

>> **Extra benefits:** You're free to use the money in your account to pay for medical services not covered by original Medicare, but these payments don't count toward your deductible.

>> **Taxes:** MSA accounts aren't taxed as long as you use them for what the IRS calls "qualified medical expenses." Each year you must report your account withdrawals to the IRS, using Form 1040 and Form 8853, even if you aren't otherwise required to file an income tax return.

>> **Prescription drugs:** MSAs don't cover prescription drugs. You can enroll in a stand-alone Part D plan to receive drug coverage. You can use your MSA account to pay for your Part D premiums and co-pays, but these expenses don't count toward your MSA deductible.

TIP

For more information, see `www.medicare.gov/health-drug-plans/health-plans/your-coverage-options/MSA`.

Checking out three other types of Medicare health plans

The following types of plans don't fall within original Medicare or the Medicare Advantage program and aren't available in all parts of the country:

>> **Medicare Cost plans:** You can join a Medicare Cost plan even if you have only Medicare Part B. If you go to doctors and hospitals outside the plan's provider network for Medicare-covered services, original Medicare helps pay for those services. You can join a Medicare Cost plan at any time (if it accepts new members), and you can disenroll from it and return to original Medicare at any time. If the plan doesn't cover prescription drugs, you can enroll in a stand-alone Part D plan. These plans are only offered in certain limited areas.

>> **Programs of All-Inclusive Care for the Elderly (PACE):** These plans combine medical, social, and long-term care for frail people age 55 and older who are eligible for nursing home care but live in the community. I describe PACE plans in detail in Chapter 4.

>> **Medicare demonstration and pilot programs:** Medicare uses these special projects from time to time in specific parts of the country to test new ideas for improving Medicare coverage. If you want to know whether any are available in your area and how they work, call Medicare at 800-633-4227 (TTY 877-486-2048) or your State Health Insurance Assistance Program (SHIP; see Appendix A for contact information).

Discovering How Medigap Policies Differ from Medicare Advantage Plans

All those *M*'s — Medicare, Medicaid, Medicare Advantage, Medigap! No wonder so many people are confused about what each means. And a big chunk of that perplexity is related to the difference between Medigap and Medicare Advantage.

Technically, only Medigap counts as "Medicare supplemental insurance" — in fact, that's its formal name — but MA plans may offer extra benefits that can be considered to supplement Medicare.

Yes, I know: This section repeats a lot of stuff found elsewhere in this book. But I think it's important to explain the precise differences between these two forms of coverage more succinctly so that you can see at a glance how they compare (flip to Chapters 4 and 10 for full details on Medigap):

>> **Eligibility:** To be eligible for Medicare Advantage, you must be enrolled in Parts A and B and live in the service area of the plan you choose. Medigap also requires that you be enrolled in both Part A and Part B, and you must buy a policy based on where your home is, which must be within the United States or its territories.

>> **Choice of plans:** Medicare Advantage plans have expanded greatly over the past few years. In 2023, the average rural Medicare beneficiary had a choice of 27 MA plans, and urban beneficiaries had a choice of 46 plans on average. Each plan has a different mix of costs and benefits from the next.

   If you're 65 or older, in most states you have the choice of a maximum of ten Medigap policies, each with its own set of benefits that are standardized by law, making them easy to compare. In some states, additional types of policies may be available, as described in Chapter 4.

>> **Pre-existing medical conditions:** An MA plan can't refuse to accept you on the basis of any past or present medical conditions. Any MA plan must provide exactly the same coverage for people who have Medicare because of disabilities as they do for people age 65 and older.

   If you're 65 or over, a Medigap insurer can't deny you coverage or charge you higher premiums based on current health status or pre-existing conditions, provided that you buy a policy within certain time periods that give you these protections under federal law. Outside those time periods, the insurer can take current and past health problems into account, unless you live in a state that provides more leeway. If you're under 65, you're not entitled to federal guarantees, but some state laws provide similar protections.

>> **Coverage:** MA plans must cover the same Part A and Part B services and benefits that original Medicare does but can charge different co-pays and deductibles and provide some extra services.

Medigap policies mainly cover the out-of-pocket expenses of original Medicare, depending on which policy you buy. All policies extend coverage for hospital stays and (except for policy N) cover the full 20 percent co-pays charged for doctors' visits and other Part B services.

>> **Care stability:** MA plans can change their costs and benefits every calendar year, or withdraw from Medicare in some areas, and can drop individual doctors from their provider networks during the year.

The benefits in the Medigap policy that you buy are guaranteed to continue unchanged from year to year, provided that you pay the premiums. The premiums, however, usually increase over time.

>> **Geographical range:** Most MA plans (HMOs and PPOs) allow you to go only to doctors and hospitals in their own provider networks and within their local service area or, in some cases, to go outside the network for a higher co-pay. PFFS plans allow you to go to providers throughout the country, but you need to be sure that they accept these plans before you visit them for consultation or treatment. Some plans cover medical emergencies outside the United States, which original Medicare does not.

If you receive Medicare-approved services from doctors or providers anywhere in the country, Medigap covers your co-pays for that service, depending on the terms of your policy. (However, a type of policy known as *Medigap SELECT* covers only providers within a limited service area, with no coverage for any you see outside it.) Some policies cover medical emergencies outside the United States — a benefit Medicare doesn't cover.

>> **Prescription drugs:** Most MA plans provide Part D drug coverage as part of their benefit packages. By law, no new Medigap policies have provided coverage for prescription drugs since Part D began in 2006.

Chapter **10**

Choosing Wisely If You Go with Original Medicare

D eciding on original Medicare as the way to receive your medical benefits under Part A and Part B means that you may need to add Part D prescription drug coverage and may want to buy Medigap supplemental insurance to cover most of your out-of-pocket costs. But note that many people who choose original Medicare don't need Part D drug coverage or supplemental insurance. So if you have retiree benefits that provide good drug coverage, take care of services that Medicare leaves out, and/or pay for some of Medicare's deductibles and co-pays, you can skip this chapter and head to Chapter 13.

Similarly, if you've decided to get your benefits through a Medicare Advantage plan, such as a health maintenance organization (HMO) or preferred provider organization (PPO), rather than original Medicare, skip this chapter and turn to Chapter 11, where I discuss how to go about comparing plans to find the one that suits you best.

In this chapter, I assume that you want to stay in traditional Medicare and don't have any other insurance that provides extras like coverage for medications or out-of-pocket costs. And therefore, you're faced with some choices: deciding which Part D drug plan you should enroll in and, if you opt for supplemental insurance, which Medigap policy you should buy. This chapter focuses on how to choose among the many options that confront you in Part D and in Medigap. The info in this chapter is in do-it-yourself mode: It explains, step by step, how you can figure out your best options. The alternative — getting someone else to help you — is discussed in Chapter 12. (For an introduction to Medigap, flip to Chapter 4.)

Understanding the Need to Compare Part D Plans Carefully

REMEMBER

Medicare advises people who are choosing a Medicare prescription drug plan to consider the three Cs: cost, coverage, and convenience. That's perfectly true. But I say you should add three more Cs: compare, compare, compare! And even a fourth: Do it *carefully!* I can't emphasize this point enough: Comparing plans carefully is the single most important step you can take in finding the Part D plan that's best for you. It may save you unexpected hassle and will certainly save you money.

"Well, yeah," you say. "But what about the fact that I'm faced with more than 22 drug plans in my state? And they're all different!" I know that the number of plans available to you often makes choosing just one — let alone the right one — seem like a daunting prospect. But take heart; you don't have to grope your way through that multitude of plans. In the later section "Picking the Part D Plan That's Best for You," I demonstrate a quick strategy for finding a plan that focuses only on your needs.

Here, though, I explain why comparing plans properly is better than the less-than-ideal alternatives you may be considering. Then I suggest ways to get organized so that you're all ready to go when you start the actual process of comparing plans and choosing one.

Knowing what not to do

WARNING

In a famous scene in *Indiana Jones and the Last Crusade,* Indy and his enemy choose what each thinks is the Holy Grail from an array of goblets. The evil Nazi picks a gold one and instantly dies a horrible death. "He chose . . . poorly," observes the ancient knight who's been on guard duty for about 700 years. Indy picks a simple wooden cup. "You," intones the knight, "have chosen . . . wisely." Well, I guess the Part D plan that's best for you isn't the Holy Grail exactly, but you still need to choose wisely to get it. And people use so many poor ways of choosing:

- » **Picking the same plan as your spouse, best friend, neighbor, or second cousin:** These people aren't you! They don't necessarily take the same prescription drugs or want the same things out of a plan as you do.

- » **Choosing the plan with the lowest premium in your area:** Unless you don't take any drugs right now, premiums are far less important than co-pays in adding to your expenses under any plan.

- » **Agreeing to enroll in a plan that a sales agent pitches you at a shopping mall, a pharmacy, a senior center, or anywhere else:** Agents talk up the plans they're paid to sell, often without a thought to your personal needs or preferences.

- » **Picking a plan from the marketing brochures that plans send to your home:** These mailings are advertising materials designed to make a sale, again without regard to your own circumstances and needs.

- » **Deciding on the plan with the most familiar name:** It won't necessarily provide you with the deal that's best for you.

REMEMBER

Using any of these methods to choose a plan isn't much better than closing your eyes and jabbing a pin in a list because they don't account for the prescription drugs you take. Your own set of drugs — down to the exact dosage of each and how often you take them — is the most important factor in picking the plan that's right for you. It's the essential key to choosing wisely.

Defining "the best plan"

In theory, the "best" plan is the one that covers any prescription drug you may conceivably need, not just now but also in the unforeseeable future. But that's not how Part D works. No plan covers all drugs, as I explain in Chapter 2.

REMEMBER

I believe that the best plan has to be the one that covers all, or almost all, the drugs you're taking now — meaning the time when you're deciding which plan to sign up for — at the lowest out-of-pocket cost and with the fewest hoops to jump through to get those drugs. If later on you need a drug the plan you pick doesn't cover, you can ask your doctor whether an alternative drug on your plan's *formulary* (list of covered meds) would work as well for you, or you can ask the plan to cover your prescribed drug anyway through the exceptions process (as described in Chapter 14).

TIP

You can also change to another Part D plan at the end of the year during open enrollment or during the year in certain other circumstances (see Chapter 15). In fact, comparing plans annually is wise because they change their costs and benefits each year, so the plan that's best for you this year may not be as good for you next year.

Recognizing that comparing plans is worth the effort

Comparing plans carefully — in the way I suggest in the later section "Drilling down to important bits of info when comparing Part D plans" — is definitely worthwhile! Doing so tells you the following:

>> **Which two or three plans cover all your prescription drugs but cost you the least out-of-pocket over the whole year.** Identifying these choices immediately whittles down that huge list of available plans to a manageable few.

>> **Which of these plans has the best record for customer satisfaction and quality service and which, if any, has a poor record.**

>> **Which of these plans has the fewest or no restrictions for your specific drugs.** Different kinds of *restrictions* — known as prior authorization, quantity limits, or step therapy — are described in Chapter 14.

>> **Which of these plans has the most reasonable co-pay structure in case you need other meds later in the year.** *Co-pay structure* refers to the different amounts you pay in each tier of charges. For example, Plan X may charge a co-pay of $70 for all its nonpreferred brands, whereas Plan Y may charge more than $100 for drugs in its own nonpreferred brand tier.

>> **Whether you'll fall into the *doughnut hole* (also known as the coverage gap) with the set of drugs you take now.** If so, in which month of the year will that happen? And will it occur later under one plan than another? (Chapter 2 has details on the doughnut hole.)

>> **Which of these plans have network pharmacies convenient to you.**

>> **Which of these plans have a mail-order option, if you want one.**

>> **Which of these plans have arrangements with certain pharmacies (known as *preferred pharmacies*) that will save the most money on your meds.**

>> **Which of these plans will allow you to fill your prescriptions in any state if you travel or live away from home for part of the year.**

REMEMBER

This list is a whole lot of critical information. And the only really effective way of getting it is to use the online Medicare Plan Finder — or get someone else to use it for you, as I explain in Chapter 12. This tool is also the safest way of choosing a Part D plan because when *you* do the comparison, *you* stay in control. You can't fall for a sweet sales pitch or, worse, fall prey to a scam or hard sell from some unscru-pulous person who exploits your uncertainty for personal gain. (Chapter 12 also has the scoop on marketing scams and hard sells.)

Seeing how comparing plans can save big bucks

Most folks don't compare Part D plans before choosing one, so most of them are paying far more than they need to for their drugs. That's because the variation in what Part D plans charge, even for the same drug, is enormous.

Don't believe it? Take a look at Table 10-1, which compares two drugs and the variation in co-pays that were charged for a 30-day supply among all Part D plans in a given area in 2024. The first med — Procrit (for anemia) — is a brand-name drug that now has a cheaper generic alternative. The second drug is a generic copy of Lipitor (for high cholesterol), once the world's best-selling medication, which commanded high prices before facing generic competition in 2012.

TABLE 10-1 **Comparing Co-Pays for the Same Drugs among Part D Plans in 2024**

Drug, Dosage, and Frequency	Geographic Area (Number of Part D Plans)	Lowest/Highest Co-Pay for 30-Day Supply
Procrit, 4,000 ml, three times a week for one month (50-100 units per kilo)	Miami, FL (19 plans)	$47/$572.91 Difference: $525.91
Atorvastatin, 20 mg once per day	Phoenix, AZ (20 plans)	$0/$7 Difference: $7

Source: Centers for Medicare & Medicaid Services(CMS)/Public Domain

Notice the gigantic range in co-pays for one month's supply of Procrit — from $47 (after meeting the plan's $200 deductible) to $572.91. It seems too outrageous to be true. But here's what's happening: The plans that charge low-to-moderate amounts require you to pay fixed-dollar co-pays, whereas those that charge the mega bucks require you to pay a percentage of the cost of the drug.

This percentage (technically known as *coinsurance*) varies a lot among plans. In the Procrit example noted in the table, one plan was charging a 47 percent coinsurance rate on the brand-name medication. That doesn't matter so much when the full price of the drug — that is, the price the plan has negotiated with the manufacturers — is relatively low. But the full price of some drugs can be hundreds of dollars or more a month, which is why the highest-cost plan in this analysis ends up with whopping co-pays. But how would you know if you didn't compare plans head-to-head according to the drugs you take?

REMEMBER

Another lesson here: If you need expensive drugs, try to avoid Part D plans that charge percentages of the cost. However, this isn't always possible. An analysis from the Kaiser Family Foundation found that in 2024, most brand name drugs had coinsurance of between 21 percent and 46 percent, depending on what pricing tier they fall under. Individual plans often require dollar co-pays in some tiers but percentages in others. (For more information on pricing tiers, flip to Chapter 14.)

WILL YOU AVOID PART D BUYER'S REMORSE?

Not realizing how much more you'd pay for the same drug in some plans than others is one sure way of making an unfortunate choice. Here are a few examples of how comparing plans carefully can save you money — and how failing to do so can teach you a hard lesson:

- **Going by a well-known name:** Back in November 2005, a few weeks before Part D started, an old friend named Bill told me he'd signed up with a plan. I asked how he'd chosen it. Well, he'd picked an insurer whose name he knew and felt he could trust. "Fine," I said, "but let's do a comparison." It took me about 15 minutes to run the information for his six meds through the online Medicare Plan Finder; the least expensive plan — also provided by a well-known insurer — turned out to cost about $1,000 a year less than the one he'd chosen. Because Bill was still within the open enrollment period, he was able to switch plans. Every year until his death in 2010, I ran the numbers for Bill. And every year the plan that worked best for him was different from the plan he'd had the year before.

- **Choosing the same plan as your spouse:** Before he retired, Joel had health insurance from his company that covered drugs for both him and his wife, Mae. When he needed Part D, Joel left it to Mae to pick a Part D plan for both of them because she took a lot of drugs and he rarely took any, and they felt more comfortable being in the same plan. So Mae chose Plan X, which covered all her drugs for a monthly premium of $61, and signed them both up. That was fine for Mae, but Joel was actually wasting money. Because he almost never needed drugs, he'd have been better off on Plan Y, which had a premium of $15 (the lowest in their state) and would've saved him $46 a month or $552 over the course of the year.

- **Failing to research a sales pitch:** Joanne was in the mall buying gifts for her grandkids when a sales rep invited her to sit down, have a cup of coffee, and talk about Part D. Joanne already had a drug plan and wasn't thinking of changing it, but she was happy to take a load off and listen for a few minutes. Yet what the rep said about Plan X sounded like a better deal than Joanne's current plan, so she signed up on the spot. What she didn't know was that for her set of drugs (two brand names and two generics), Plan X ranked 27th highest in expense out of the 37 plans in her state. If she'd compared plans according to the drugs she took instead of listening to a sales pitch, she'd have found Plan Y. This plan had higher premiums than Plan X but charged far lower co-pays for her drugs. So over the course of the year, Joanne paid about $1,200 more under Plan X than she would've paid under Plan Y.

Getting organized with two crucial lists

The information you must have at hand before comparing Part D plans properly — whether you hop online and use the Medicare Plan Finder yourself or get someone else to do it for you — is very simple. All you need is your zip code and the following two lists:

>> An accurate list of your prescription medications

>> A list of personal preferences that may make you lean toward one plan rather than another

Creating an accurate list of your meds

Gather together all those bottles that contain the prescription drugs you're currently taking — tablets, capsules, liquid solutions, sprays, creams, or whatever form they come in. (But leave out any medications you buy over the counter without a doctor's prescription, as well as vitamins and supplements, because Part D doesn't cover these items.) Then make a list of the following characteristics, using the information provided on the labels. (Alternatively, if you use just one pharmacy, you can ask the pharmacist for a printout of all your current prescription drugs.)

>> **The exact name of each drug:** Many prescription drugs have the same name but come in different forms, with differences marked by a second word or combination of letters following the name — for example, ER (extended release), SR (sustained release), or CR (controlled release). Part D plans may price these forms very differently from each other.

>> **Dosage:** Entering the wrong dosage in a plan search may distort your cost results. Part D plans often charge the same co-pay for different strengths of the same drug — for example, 10 milligrams (mg), 20 mg, 100 mg — but not always. The full price of the drug (the price the plan pays the manufacturer) may also vary according to dosage, a situation that may affect what you pay if your plan has a deductible, if you fall into the doughnut hole, or if the plan

charges a percentage of the full price rather than a flat-dollar co-pay for your share of the cost.

>> **How often you take your drugs (frequency):** Of the three factors that can alter the results for your out-of-pocket costs during a plan search, frequency is the most important. If, by mistake, you indicate that you take a pill once a day when in fact you take it twice a day, the search results will show a cost that's half as much as you'll actually pay at the pharmacy. That's one surprise you don't want! On the flip side, if you take a drug once a week but mistakenly indicate that you take it once a day, the results will show an out-of-pocket cost seven times higher than what you'd actually pay. Neither of these situations helps you accurately compare plans.

REMEMBER

I'm not just being persnickety in saying that you should note the three items — name, dosage, and frequency — exactly as they're written on the container label. Unless you enter correct information into the Plan Finder, your search results will be distorted and you won't obtain accurate-enough information to be able to compare plans properly. These exact details are equally important if you ask someone else to help because that person is also going to use Medicare's Plan Finder to assist you. I explain how to find personal help in comparing plans in Chapter 12.

Drawing up a list of your plan preferences

Finding a plan that covers all your drugs and costs you the least out-of-pocket may be at the top of your list of priorities. But chances are high that you're going to identify several Part D plans that cover your drugs and vary by only a few dollars in the overall amount they charge. So consider some other factors that may be important to you, such as the following:

>> **Does this plan restrict any of my drugs?** Any plan may require you to ask permission before it'll cover certain drugs through restrictions known as prior authorization, quantity limits, or step therapy. (I explain these requirements, and how to deal with them, in Chapter 14.) But plans don't all restrict the same drugs, so you want to look for a plan that has the fewest restrictions on the ones you take (or, ideally, on none at all).

>> **Does this plan have a good track record?** Plans that provide quality service — answer calls without keeping callers on hold forever, respond to questions properly, pay their share of prescriptions correctly, and deal with complaints promptly — are obviously preferable. Medicare rates the plans so that you know in advance which are likely to give good service and which are best avoided.

>> **Are the pharmacies in this plan's network convenient to where I live?** Each plan has its own network of pharmacies, and going to a pharmacy outside

that network costs you a lot more (probably even full price) for your drugs. So you need to be sure that the plan you select has network pharmacies within a reasonable distance of your home. (See Chapter 13 for more on this topic.)

>> **Does this plan have preferred pharmacies in my area?** Plans designate certain pharmacies as "preferred." These pharmacies often charge substantially lower co-pays than the plans' regular in-network pharmacies.

>> **Does this plan have a mail-order option?** If you prefer to receive all or some of your prescriptions by mail order in 90-day supplies (which costs less in many plans), you need to be certain that the plan offers a mail-order service. Some plans don't.

>> **Will this plan cover my prescriptions when I'm away from home?** If you expect to travel during the year or live in another state for part of it, you need a plan that covers your prescriptions at network pharmacies throughout the United States. Some plans offer a national service, and some don't. (None cover drugs purchased abroad.)

Picking the Part D Plan That's Best for You

So how do you sort out the wheat from the chaff on all the Part D drug plans you're considering? You can find the answers in Medicare's online Plan Finder, an interactive website that allows you to plug in details of your own prescription drugs to find out which plans cover them and approximately what each plan will charge you. (You can also use the Plan Finder to compare Medicare Advantage private health plans, as I explain in Chapter 11.) In other words, this tool makes light work of an otherwise-difficult calculation by doing the math for you automatically. It also answers all those other questions that I raise in the preceding section. This section discusses the Plan Finder's reliability, takes you through the steps of using the Plan Finder, and helps you get the details of the plans in your results. (If you don't have internet access and/or need personal help to find the same info, go to Chapter 12.)

Assessing the Plan Finder's reliability

Everybody who wants impartial information about Part D plans, free of sales pressure, uses the online Plan Finder. And I mean everybody: not only people enrolled in Medicare but also doctors, pharmacists, counselors, social workers, advocates, help groups — anyone who assists a Medicare beneficiary in finding a plan. Clearly everybody depends on the Plan Finder, so asking "How reliable is it?" is a reasonable question.

The Plan Finder is a complex and sophisticated computer program. And in offering consumers a way to compare plans head-to-head to find their best deal, it has long been a pioneer in the health insurance world. But of course such comparisons are only as reliable as the pricing information fed into them — in this case, by the Part D plans themselves.

Medicare officials say they rigorously monitor the accuracy of plan prices and, when errors are detected, remove all information about that plan from the website until corrections are made. Medicare also includes pricing accuracy as one of the measures of its quality assessment system, which rates individual plans from one star (poor) to five stars (excellent). Officials say the ratings, displayed on the Plan Finder, are based on Medicare's own regular reviews and the feedback (including complaints) it receives from consumers.

TIP

Nonetheless, the Plan Finder isn't free from glitches and errors. Here are some guidelines for eliminating or minimizing your chances of choosing a plan based on misleading information:

>> **Know that late September/early October is when Medicare first posts online the new plan information for the following year.** The first two weeks of this period are when pricing errors are most likely because huge amounts of information are being uploaded into the system. If you do a plan search at this time, recheck the information after open enrollment starts on October 15.

>> **Do your due diligence before signing up.** After you've used the Plan Finder to choose the plan you like best but before you enroll in it, take the following sensible measures:

- **Double-check the accuracy of the drug information that you entered into the Plan Finder — especially dosages and frequencies.** I describe how to compile this information in the earlier section "Creating an accurate list of your meds."

- **Print out the plan's complete details for your set of drugs and keep this hard copy with your records.**

- **Call the plan to verify what you'll pay for each of your drugs.** Make sure you correctly specify the dosages and frequencies. Keep notes of this conversation; the plan likely won't confirm the details in writing.

>> **Bear in mind that the prices quoted for drugs on the Plan Finder are estimates.** The exact prices may vary according to the pharmacy you get them from and may fluctuate during the year. However, the plan's fixed charges — premiums, deductibles, and co-pay tiers — are invariably accurate on the Plan Finder; they change from year to year but can't change during the year.

>> **If you discover errors, report them to Medicare.** Your information will be investigated and fed into Medicare's quality rating system.

What do you do if you've already made a decision based on faulty info? If you discover you were misled into enrolling in a plan due to erroneous pricing information on the Plan Finder, you have the right to ask Medicare for a special enrollment period to switch to another plan, as I explain in Chapter 15. This scenario is when keeping a printout of the details you got from the Plan Finder comes in handy; you can use the documentation as evidence.

Using the Medicare Plan Finder to discover options available to you

The Medicare online Plan Finder is loaded with information and offers several different kinds of searches. But in this section, I focus only on navigating the program as quickly as possible to get you to the point when you can begin to compare stand-alone Part D drug plans.

The Plan Finder has undergone numerous updates in recent years and is more user-friendly than when it first went live in October 2005. But its architects do change things from time to time — how can computer techies ever resist tinkering? — and if they do so after this book publishes, navigating the program may not follow exactly the same steps as I indicate in this section. Still, you should be able to follow along. Medicare also offers an online tutorial video on how to move through the program. But keeping the instructions that follow next to your keyboard is easier.

Walking through a few steps

These simple steps are designed to help you navigate the Plan Finder keystroke by keystroke. Sometimes I tell you to ignore certain questions or information. These items are stuff that you don't need right now but that you can return to later when you begin to compare plans in detail, according to your circumstances and preferences. I consider those details in the later section "Drilling down to important bits of info when comparing Part D plans."

Have your prescription drug list handy and follow these steps:

1. **Go to the Plan Finder launch page on Medicare's website at** www.medicare.gov/plan-compare/#/?lang=en.

    You can choose to log in, create an account, or continue without logging in. If you do not log in, you first need to enter your zip code.

2. **Answer a few quick questions on Medicare coverage and check the options that apply to you.**

    The first question asks you to identify what type of Medicare coverage you want. In this instance, check "Medicare Drug Plan (Part D)." Then click the button that reads "Find Plans."

Then you're asked, "Do you get help with your costs from one of these programs?" Most people check "I don't get any help from any of these programs" for this question. However, if you do qualify for Extra Help (as explained in Chapter 4), you need to check the option that applies to you so that you obtain accurate information about your costs as you progress through the Plan Finder.

You then will be directed to the "Tell us your search preferences" page. Here, you're asked, "Do you want to see your drug costs when you compare plans?" By selecting "yes," you will be directed to the "Add prescription drug" page. You have an option to enter all your drugs, dosages, quantities, and frequencies or an option to "See plans without drug costs." To do a comparison, add your drug information where noted. Keep reading!

3. **Enter the name of the first drug on your list into the box provided and click on "Add Drug."**

    Choose the correct dosage, quantity, and frequency in the box that appears and then click on "Add to My Drug List."

TIP

    If you've entered a brand-name drug, another box may appear saying that a lower-cost generic is available and inviting you to select the brand or the generic. Make sure you check the brand — the one your doctor prescribed — for reasons that I explain in the later section "Lowering your drug costs." (You can make another search, using the generic, at a later time.)

4. **Repeat Step 3 until all your drugs are on the list, then click "Done Adding Drugs."**

5. **You now see a list of retail pharmacies in your area; click up to five of the options given.**

    You can also select whether you want to see drug prices using a mail order pharmacy in this step. To see more options, click "Next" or the arrow to go to the next page of the list. You can also filter the list by distance. Click on "Done" at the bottom of the page, next to the pharmacies you've selected.

    Note: From a user-friendly point of view, this required pharmacy selection is the weakest part in the Plan Finder process — for reasons I explain in the later section "Examining retail pharmacy choices" — but right now you can't progress any further without selecting at least one pharmacy. So select two, even if they're random.

6. **Next, you're directed to the results page, which identifies how many plans are available.**

    You can then search the list using a filter for ratings or insurance carriers, or simply scroll through the list. The list is automatically sorted by lowest drug and monthly premium cost. Using the drop-down menu on the right, you can also sort by lowest monthly premium cost, or lowest yearly drug deductible.

At the top of the page, you have an option for Medicare Advantage plans, but ignore it because right now you're reading this chapter in order to choose a stand-alone drug plan to use with original Medicare.

Don't click on anything else on this page, or you may limit your options.

Ta-da! What you now see is a list of ten plans, which the program has ranked as the least expensive plans for you according to the drug details you've entered and the pharmacies you've selected. If your search has turned up more than ten total Part D plans available in your state, click through to the following pages to see more of them.

7. **Pat yourself on the back for getting to the point where you can start narrowing down your options!**

Homing in on handy features of the "plan results" page

The plan results page is actually the beginning, not the end, of your search, because it shows only the broadest information for each Part D plan. But it does have some nifty features that may be immediately useful to you. (The following section lets you in on how to access the all-important details of each available plan.)

>> **Comparing three plans at the same time:** You can compare up to three plans by clicking on the "Add to compare" box. Details of these plans then appear side by side.

>> **Changing the order of the plans you see:** By default, the plans you see on this page are listed in the order of "Lowest drug and premium cost." But you can change the order by using the "Sort plans by" drop-down menu. For example, if you don't take any drugs and want a low-cost plan just to maintain coverage, select "Lowest monthly premium."

>> **Seeing whether any plans have earned the top quality rating:** As I note earlier in this chapter, Medicare rates each plan on a scale of one to five stars, which you can see after the name of each plan. You can switch to a five-star plan at any time during the year (except for one week, from December 1 through December 7) instead of waiting until open enrollment.

>> **Determining which plans to avoid:** Medicare alerts you to any plan with consistently poor quality ratings — one that has earned low ratings for three years in a row — by posting a red warning icon next to its name. If a note says the plan is "sanctioned," it means that Medicare may allow no new enrollments until the plan has rectified violations and met the required standards.

Drilling down to important bits of info when comparing Part D plans

When you click "Plan Details" below any plan on the list of results, the next page you see on-screen contains the details of your costs under that plan. It comprises a wealth of information — premium, deductible, what you'll pay in this plan over the whole year for the drugs you've entered, whether you'll fall into the doughnut hole, how the costs of your drug compare by pharmacy/mail order, whether you need to jump through any hoops to get your drugs, and so on.

Most of this information is self-evident and available pretty much at a glance. But in the following sections, I show you how to dig deeper to make the most of certain important bits of information that may not be immediately clear: how to read the charts that show your total costs each month through the year, how you may be able to lower those costs, and how to find pharmacies that give the best deal on your meds. *Note:* You may see items on the Plan Finder that require more-detailed explanations — for example, the different tier pricing systems of co-pays among plans, and navigating the doughnut hole. I consider these topics in Chapter 14 in the context of the finer points of Medicare coverage and how to get the most out of your benefits.

Finding out your month-by-month costs

Part D is weirdly constructed so that you may pay different amounts at different times of the year for the same drugs, according to the coverage phase you're in. (I explain these phases — deductible, initial coverage period, coverage gap or doughnut hole, and catastrophic coverage — in Chapter 2.) Well, the chart that appears on each plan's details page shows you at a glance how much you can expect to pay month by month throughout the year in this plan according to the information you've entered. (If you join Part D partway through the year, the chart shows the monthly payments for the rest of the year.) It's a very cool tool personalized to your own costs.

Getting this month-by-month information in any other way is difficult. If you call a plan to find out what it charges for your drug(s), the customer service rep typically tells you the co-pay charged during the initial coverage period but ignores what you'd pay during the deductible phase or the doughnut hole.

What you see in the chart is a profile of your out-of-pocket costs (premiums plus co-pays) determined by the drug information you've entered, the plan's charges, and the way the plan is structured. That's why the profile for each plan is different even though the drugs are the same. For example:

>> If the plan has no deductible and your drug costs aren't high enough to reach the doughnut hole, your payments for each month, January through December, will be the same.

>> If the plan has a deductible and your costs are high enough to reach the doughnut hole, you see a higher amount at the beginning of the year (because you're paying full price until the deductible is met), followed by lower payments (initial coverage phase) for some months, followed by higher payments (in the doughnut hole, also known as the coverage gap) for the rest of the year.

>> If you take very expensive drugs or a lot of drugs, you see a profile that is very high at the beginning of the year (because you go through the deductible, initial coverage, and doughnut hole phases very quickly, maybe even in a single month) but then dwindles to the same flat monthly payment for the rest of the year, or even $0 for some drugs once you hit the catastrophic coverage period.

Lowering your drug costs

You can dramatically reduce your costs if any of the brand-name drugs you now take has a generic version or a similar, older alternative that your doctor thinks would work as well for your medical condition. I discuss this option in Chapter 4. But here I explain how the Plan Finder can show you which alternatives are available and what they'd cost.

WARNING

When you first log onto the Plan Finder and enter the name of a brand-name drug (Step 3 in the earlier section "Walking through a few steps"), you're invited to switch to the generic version (if one exists) immediately. In my opinion, this juncture isn't the right time to make any switch because the names of the drugs you're entering are those your doctor has prescribed; it seems to me that you'd prefer to find out the prices of those drugs before looking to see whether any lower-cost alternatives exist. That way, you know how much you'd save if you switched to the alternatives. So if you've entered a brand-name drug and a notice appears informing you of a generic version, click on the button that ensures your prescribed brand name will be used in your plan search. Otherwise, the Plan Finder will automatically use the generic by default, and the results will reflect the costs for that drug and not the one your doctor prescribed.

TIP

A much better way to identify lower-cost options is to wait until you get to the details page of any Part D plan you're interested in. Below the heading "Drug coverage & costs," click on the link labeled "See if there's help to lower costs for drugs you take." This links you to Medicare's "Help with drug costs" page (www.medicare.gov/basics/costs/help/drug-costs).

Note that savings made by switching to generic or similar drugs vary from plan to plan, so if you want to compare plans for this reason, you need to repeat this process for each plan.

REMEMBER

If you find you'll save money by switching to another drug, now is the time to ask your doctor whether that drug would work well for you — and, if so, to get a new prescription for the lower-cost drug. You can then recalculate your overall costs by entering the lower-priced drug into the Plan Finder.

Examining retail pharmacy choices

When you're enrolled in a Part D plan, you must go to one of the pharmacies within its network to ensure you pay the price you expect. (Going out of the network costs a lot more, unless you do so for an unavoidable reason, as I explain in Chapter 13.)

Also, within their networks, some plans have *preferred pharmacies,* which dispense prescriptions for lower co-pays than at regular network pharmacies. For example, you may pay a $10 co-pay for your generic drug at a plan's regular network pharmacy but $5 if you go to one of its preferred pharmacies. Therefore, knowing whether the prices you're being quoted on-screen on the Plan Finder are the best you can get is very important.

The Plan Finder requires you to select one or two local retail pharmacies very early — immediately after entering the names of your drugs. As I note in the earlier section "Walking through a few steps," this requirement isn't at all user-friendly. Here's why:

>> At this stage, you can't tell which pharmacies among those presented on-screen are in which plans' networks, or even whether they're in any plan's network.

>> You also can't determine which pharmacies are preferred by which plans.

>> You must select at least one pharmacy, even if you aren't familiar with any of the options, so your selection may well be completely random and not tailored to your situation. And yet that selection will determine the out-of-pocket costs quoted for each plan.

TIP

In other words, the required system distorts the Plan Finder's results. So let me try to suggest a way around this issue:

1. **When you have your list of results (Step 7 in the earlier section "Walking through a few steps"), notice that each plan shows the monthly premium, yearly drug and premium cost, and deductible for that plan.**

   Beneath that information, you can select either the "Enroll" or "Plan Details" option, as well as a box to check to compare plans.

2. **Select "Plan Details" and scroll down until you see the heading "Drug Coverage" (about midway down the page).**

   This section displays a list of the pharmacies you selected and whether they are preferred and/or in network. You can also change pharmacies on this page to compare more. Below that are charts showing the dollar amounts for your drugs both annually and monthly in the various stages of coverage.

3. **Use the "Back to search results" link to select different plans to review, or keep going further back in the search with the "Back to drugs & pharmacies" link on the search results page to remove any pharmacies that aren't preferred ones.**

   You can continually repeat this process for any other plan that interests you; different plans use different networks and preferred pharmacies.

TIP

This workaround is a real pain, isn't it? But Medicare officials say they can't create a better system for pharmacy selection without overhauling the whole Plan Finder. Perhaps they will one day. Meanwhile, you may be looking for a quicker way of finding out which plans use preferred pharmacies in your area. You can try calling the plans; the Plan Finder provides each plan's contact information for both existing members and nonmembers. Or you can call around to the pharmacies in your area. They'll tell you which Part D plans' networks they're in and whether their status is network or preferred.

WHERE DID ALL THESE PART D PLANS COME FROM?

Strangely enough, nobody expected so many Part D plans to pop up. In fact, members of Congress were uncertain whether enough private insurers would offer enough Part D plans to provide competition, especially in rural areas. Some insurance honchos even predicted that the industry wouldn't be interested in offering any *stand-alone plans* — the kind that provide only drugs and no other healthcare — because such plans had never existed before and were regarded as unprofitable. (The CEO of one leading insurance company went so far as to call stand-alones a "harebrained idea" that just wouldn't fly. Today, his company offers these plans in almost every state.)

So when the law was written in 2003, it included a clause allowing the federal government to provide its own fallback drug plan in any area where fewer than two private plans entered the market. In other words, Congress guaranteed that at least two drug plans would be available to everyone on Medicare.

(continued)

(continued)

At least two! How quaint that seems today, with dozens of stand-alone plans (and Medicare Advantage plans that include Part D drug coverage) plying their wares in every locality. What happened? As it turned out, the insurance industry — drawn by large federal subsidies — saw Medicare prescription drug coverage as a money-making bonanza. The result was much like the California Gold Rush of the mid-1800s, with insurers scrambling to carve out their shares of a huge new market. That's how Medicare beneficiaries came to be confronted with a bewildering number of choices.

So will there always be so many plans? Some experts anticipate that over time the market will shake out, with only a few of the largest plans — those that have attracted the greatest number of enrollees — remaining in business. This scenario would reduce the choices but, with less competition, probably also increase enrollees' costs. Another potential turnaround is if Congress reduces or eliminates federal subsidies to plans, causing many of them to pull out of Part D. And yet another possibility, favored by some members of Congress and health-policy experts, is to simplify plan choices by standardizing their designs — limiting them to maybe ten different options, each provided by a number of insurers at varying costs — in the way that Medigap supplemental insurance works today.

Meanwhile, until any of those scenarios happens (or some entirely different development occurs), it's safe to say that the days of a Part D plan plethora won't be over anytime soon.

Choosing the Medigap Supplemental Policy That's Best for You

I focus on the mechanics of choosing and buying Medigap supplemental insurance in this chapter because, for many people, it's a crucial part of the process of opting to enroll in original Medicare rather than its alternative, Medicare Advantage. I assume here that you've at least reached the point of reviewing the different sets of benefits available under each of the Medigap policies. If not, flip to Chapter 4, where I explain how Medigap works and show you how to compare the policies in terms of the benefits each offers. I also provide a handy chart that shows each policy's benefits at a glance.

In the following sections, I suggest some useful tips to keep in mind as you go about the business of choosing a policy and finding an insurance company that sells it in your area. Then I explain the single most important element in buying Medigap — timing. This means ideally buying it within a specific time frame when you get full legal protections, regardless of your health or any pre-existing medical conditions. Thirdly, I zero in on an issue that may be of great concern to you if you're under age 65 — the fact that federal law does not give you the same rights and protections to buy Medigap; I show you how to find out which policies are available according to the laws of your state. Finally, I discuss some limited circumstances in which you may be able to suspend a Medigap policy without losing legal protections for a certain length of time.

Choosing a Medigap policy

Your choice of a Medigap policy depends on two things: which one provides the set of benefits that comes closest to your needs and preferences and how much you'd pay for it. The first is pretty easy to decide when you compare the benefits that each policy covers. For example, if you never intend to travel abroad, you don't need a policy that covers emergency care outside the United States. The second is trickier because what you pay for a Medigap policy depends on several factors:

>> **What type of policy you buy:** Policy A has the fewest benefits (four), whereas policy F has the most (nine). However, Medigap policy C and policy F are no longer available to people who turned 65 on or after January 1, 2020.

>> **When you buy the policy:** Buying during a time frame when you get important consumer protections (which I explain in the next section) makes a huge amount of difference in your premiums.

>> **Where you live:** Medigap premiums vary according to geographical area. On the whole, premiums are lower in areas where a lot of people are buying policies and higher where they're not.

>> **Whether the insurer gives you a discount:** Some Medigap insurers give lower rates to certain groups of people, such as women or non-smokers.

>> **How the insurer prices your policy:** Insurance companies use one of three rating methods, which can greatly affect the price of the premium:

- **Community rating:** You pay the same premium as everybody else in your area who bought the same policy from the same insurer, regardless of age, and the premium can't rise each year as you get older.

- **Issue-age rating:** Your premium is based on the age you've reached when you buy your policy, and it can't rise each year as you get older.

- **Attained-age rating:** Your premium is raised each birthday for as long as you keep the policy.

TIP

Experts say that if you intend to buy a Medigap policy, you should purchase the one with the most comprehensive set of benefits that you can afford at that time because upgrading to another a few years down the road can be more difficult and costly. (I discuss the process for switching Medigap policies in Chapter 15.)

When you've decided which policy you want, your next step is to compare policies and premiums. Medicare has an online comparison tool at `www.medicare.gov/medigap-supplemental-insurance-plans` that works like the Plan Finder for prescription drug plans. Enter your zip code, answer a few questions about your age and health status, and then select the plan letter you want to learn more about and click "View Policies." The caveat is that the Medigap policy finder only provides estimates, and you will need to contact each company for specific pricing.

You can also directly call several insurance companies that sell this policy in your area and ask for a *quote* — that is, what they'll charge you in premiums. Keep in mind that the policy provides exactly the same benefits regardless of which insurer you choose, so it's worth shopping around.

WARNING

When getting quotes, find out in particular what kind of rating method each insurer uses. (This is also noted on the Medigap policy finder tool.) But be aware that paying more at the beginning may be more economical in the long run. Community-rated and issue-age-rated policies tend to cost more than attained-age-rated policies at first. But as you get older, the latter becomes far more expensive than the other two. Understand, however, that premiums for all policies — regardless of rating method — can rise from year to year for reasons other than age, such as general inflation.

How do you find Medigap insurers? Mostly, they find you! You can expect to be hit with a torrent of marketing materials in your mailbox around the time you turn 65. But to keep the ball in your court, you may prefer to be the one initiating contact. You can find contact info for insurance companies that sell Medigap on Medicare's website (at `www.medicare.gov/medigap-supplemental-insurance-plans`) or by calling your state department of insurance. (You can find the department's number from the National Association of Insurance Commissioners' website at `www.naic.org/state_web_map.htm`.) Or you can get help in choosing a Medigap policy from a counselor at your State Health Insurance Assistance program (SHIP), free of charge and free from sales pressure. (For the phone number of your SHIP, flip to Appendix A.)

Buying a Medigap policy at the right time

REMEMBER

If you're going to get a Medigap policy, I can't emphasize enough the critical importance of buying it at the right time. For most people, that means purchasing a policy within six months of enrolling in Medicare Part B — either at age 65 or at a later date if you delay Part B because you're covered by a group health plan from your own or your spouse's employment. This advice is so crucial that I'm going to say it again: Buy Medigap within six months of getting Part B!

The reason is very simple. During that six-month time frame, federal law gives you solid guarantees and protections if you're 65 or over: Medigap insurers can't refuse to sell you a policy; they can't charge you higher premiums because of your health or pre-existing medical conditions; and they can't impose a waiting period before your policy starts. But outside of those six months (and some other windows of time that I list in Figure 10-1), they can do all three.

Your Current Enrollment	Your Situation at Age 65 or Older	Your Guaranteed Right to Buy Medigap	When You Can Buy Medigap
In (or about to be in) original Medicare	You're not working and have no other insurance or are working with employer insurance secondary to Medicare.	Any policy sold in your state.	Within six months of enrolling in Part B at age 65.
In (or about to be in) original Medicare	You're covered by a group health plan that is primary to Medicare and from an employer for whom you or your spouse is still working.	Any policy sold in your state.	Within six months of enrolling in Part B, if you wait to enroll until this employment ends.
In original Medicare	You have health insurance from a current or former employer or union (including retiree benefits and COBRA) that is secondary to Medicare, and this coverage is ending.	Medigap policy A, B, K, or L* sold in your state by any insurance company.	No later than 63 days after this coverage ends.
In original Medicare	You have a Medigap SELECT policy, but you move outside its service area.	Medigap policy A, B, K, or L sold in your state by any insurance company.	No later than 63 days after your Medigap SELECT coverage ends.
In a Medicare Advantage plan	You're moving outside the plan's service area and want to return to original Medicare.	Medigap policy A, B, K, or L sold in your state by any insurance company.	No later than 63 days after your MA plan's coverage ends.
In a Medicare Advantage plan	Your plan withdraws from your area, leaves Medicare, or goes out of business.	Medigap policy A, B, K, or L sold in your state by any insurance company.	No later than 63 days after your MA plan's coverage ends.
In a Medicare Advantage plan	You joined an MA plan at age 65, are still in the first 12 months on that plan, and want to switch to original Medicare.	Any Medigap policy sold in your state by any insurance company.	No later than 63 days after your MA plan's coverage ends.

FIGURE 10-1: The circumstances in which you can buy Medigap with full federal protections if you're 65 or over.

© John Wiley & Sons, Inc.

Your Current Enrollment	Your Situation at Age 65 or Older	Your Guaranteed Right to Buy Medigap	When You Can Buy Medigap
In a Medicare Advantage plan	You dropped a Medigap policy to join an MA plan for the first time, have been in the plan for less than 12 months, and want to switch back to original Medicare.	The same Medigap policy you had before, if it's still sold, or any A, B, K, or L policy sold in your state by any company.	No later than 63 days after your MA plan's coverage ends.
In original Medicare plus Medigap	Your Medigap insurer goes out of business, or your Medigap coverage ends through no fault of your own.	Medigap policy A, B, K, or L sold in your state by any insurance company.	No later than 63 days after your first Medigap coverage ends.
In a Medicare Advantage plan or original Medicare with Medigap	You leave an MA plan or drop a Medigap policy because the company misled you or didn't follow the rules.	Medigap policy A, B, K, or L sold in your state by any insurance company.	No later than 63 days after your coverage from this MA plan or Medigap policy ends.

*Plans C and F are no longer available to people who were new to Medicare on or after January 1, 2020. However, if you were eligible for Medicare before January 1, 2020 but not yet enrolled, you may be able to buy Plan C or Plan F.

FIGURE 10-1: Continued

"But wait a minute," I hear you say. "Surely the Affordable Care Act prohibited insurers from denying coverage or charging more on the basis of current and past health problems?" That's true for insurance policies sold through the ACA Marketplace. But, unfortunately, it doesn't apply to Medigap. So to be crystal clear on the circumstances and times in which you can buy a Medigap policy with full federal guarantees, look at Figure 10-1.

If your situation is one of those described in Figure 10-1 and you buy a Medigap policy within the specified time period, not only do you get those valuable federal protections, but the policy you buy is also guaranteed renewable every year going forward. In other words, when you're older and maybe in poorer health than you are today, your policy can't be canceled for any reason as long as you continue paying the premiums.

WARNING

All this timeline talk doesn't mean that you can't buy Medigap at other times or in other circumstances. You can, or at least you can try. But be prepared for the fact that insurers may turn down your application, charge you more on the basis of illness you've had in the past (a practice formally known as *medical underwriting*), or exclude coverage for some pre-existing conditions for several months. Because the law allows it.

Keep in mind, though, that Medigap insurance is regulated by the state you live in, and some states have passed laws that give people more rights. For example, New York and Connecticut residents can buy Medigap at any time and can't be charged higher premiums based on age or health status.

If you want to find out more about Medigap rules in your own state, or you have reason to think that an insurance company is breaking them, contact your state department of insurance. (You can find contact information in your local phone book or on the website of the National Association of Insurance Commissioners at www.naic.org/state_web_map.htm.)

TIP

For more detailed information on buying Medigap insurance, refer to the official publication "Choosing a Medigap Policy" at www.medicare.gov/publications/02110-medigap-guide-health-insurance.pdf.

Buying Medigap if you're under 65

One of the most glaring examples of discrimination in Medicare is the fact that if you're under 65 and have Medicare because of disability, you don't get the same guarantees and protections when buying Medigap that federal law gives to people who are 65 and over.

TECHNICAL STUFF

Over the years, many consumer organizations, health-policy experts, and some politicians have worked hard to end the discrimination. Some held hopes that the Affordable Care Act would do so. But so far Congress hasn't acted to change things on the federal level. This situation means that under federal law, insurance companies are free to refuse to sell you a policy or charge high premiums based on your pre-existing medical conditions — which, by definition, everybody with disabilities has.

However, 33 states have passed laws that give their residents under 65 some protections when buying Medigap: Arkansas, California, Colorado, Connecticut, Delaware, Florida, Georgia, Hawaii, Idaho, Illinois, Kansas, Kentucky, Louisiana, Maine, Maryland, Massachusetts, Michigan, Minnesota, Mississippi, Missouri, Montana, New Hampshire, New Jersey, New York, North Carolina, Oklahoma, Oregon, Pennsylvania, South Dakota, Tennessee, Texas, Vermont, and Wisconsin.

Some of these states offer protections almost identical to those given to people 65 and older under federal law. Hawaii, Louisiana, Maine, New Hampshire, and New York allow all Part B enrollees to buy Medigap, regardless of age. Others give far fewer rights. For example, in California, Massachusetts, and Vermont, you can't buy a Medigap policy if you have end-stage renal disease (ESRD). Otherwise, all these states give you the right to buy at least one type of Medigap policy. For up-to-date information on which states give rights and protections for people under 65 buying Medigap, see the official publication "Choosing a Medigap Policy" at www. medicare.gov/publications/02110-medigap-guide-health-insurance.pdf.

TIP

Even outside these states, some insurance companies may still sell Medigap policies to people under 65, so it's worth checking out. The quickest way to find out what choices you have in your state for buying a policy is to go to https://www. medicare.gov/medigap-supplemental-insurance-plans/#/ on the Medicare website and follow these steps:

1. **Enter your zip code and click on "Start."**

   The page you now see lists all Medigap policies. This list is organized like the Part D Plan Finder, with the plan, monthly premium range, deductibles, and plan details.

   Those listed as Plans C and F have a disclaimer that reads, "This plan isn't available if you turned 65 on or after January 1, 2020, and to some people under age 65."

2. **Click the box under the field for "Age" that says "Show only plans for people under 65."**

   You get an updated list of Medigap policies. Clicking on the "View policies" link on the right-hand side takes you to contact information for the insurance companies that sell the Medigap policy in your state, together with the pricing method they use. In some areas, the choice of insurers for any particular policy is very limited — maybe no more than one.

You can also find this information by calling Medicare at 800-633-4227 (TTY 877-486-2048) and asking a customer service representative to mail you a list. Or you can call your state department of insurance. (For contact information, see the website of the National Association of Insurance Commissioners at www.naic. org/state_web_map.htm.) If you need personal help choosing a Medigap policy, call your State Health Insurance Assistance Program (SHIP); for the phone number, see Appendix A.

REMEMBER

If this search turns out to be dismal news — meaning that you can't buy the Medigap policy you prefer, or maybe no policies are available to you in your state — keep in mind the light at the end of this particular tunnel. When you turn 65 and become eligible for Medicare on the basis of age rather than disability, you can buy any Medigap policy of your choice with full federal guarantees and protections. If you already have a policy by then, you'll still have the right to buy another policy, from the same or a different insurer, and your premium will most likely be reduced.

Suspending a Medigap policy

You'd think that it would make sense to be able to put a Medigap policy on hold if you become entitled to any other type of health insurance and get it back later on without losing legal protections. In fact, this may be possible under current law, but only in the following specific circumstances:

>> **You become eligible for Medicaid when you already have a Medigap policy.** In this situation, you can suspend your policy for up to 24 months, provided that you notify the insurance company within 90 days of your Medicaid coverage beginning. You do not pay Medigap premiums while the suspension continues, and when it ends, you're entitled to the same Medigap coverage that you had before. In renewing the policy, the insurer cannot apply medical underwriting (asking about your past or current health conditions) or make you wait for coverage. Your right to suspend Medigap is the same regardless of what degree of Medicaid you receive — full benefits, partial benefits under a Medicare Savings Program, or time-limited benefits under Medicaid spend-down arrangements. (I discuss these programs in Chapter 4.)

>> **You are under 65, already have a Medigap policy, and obtain health coverage through your own or your spouse's current employer.** In this situation, you can suspend the Medigap policy for an unlimited time while you have the employer coverage. When it ends, you're entitled to the same Medigap coverage (benefits and premiums) that you had before, provided that you notify the insurance company within 90 days of the employer plan's coverage ending.

>> **You are 65 or older, already have a Medigap policy, and obtain health coverage through your own or your spouse's current employer.** In this situation, you do not have a federal right to suspend your Medigap policy, but you can do so if your state allows similar suspension under its own law. To find out, contact your State Health Insurance Assistance Program (SHIP) at the phone number listed in Appendix A.

TIP

In case you need to argue with anybody about these rights for suspending Medigap policies, be aware that they are spelled out in sections 1882(q)(5)(A) and 1882(q)(6) of the Social Security Act at www.ssa.gov/OP_Home/ssact/title18/1882.htm.

REMEMBER

Note that if you suspend a Medigap policy that was issued before 2006 and it includes coverage for prescription drugs, that coverage will be absent from your policy when it is renewed after the suspension ends. Instead, you will need to enroll in a Part D drug plan if you want Medicare to cover your prescriptions, as explained earlier in this chapter.

Chapter **11**

Making Smart Choices If You Opt for Medicare Advantage

In this chapter, I assume that you're aware of the differences between original Medicare and the Medicare Advantage (MA) program and of how the various types of MA plans work. (If not, flip to the explanations in Chapters 1 and 9.) And I assume that you now want to consider the details of plans available to you to see whether you want to enroll in one. What kind of choice do you face? That depends on where you live. A few rural counties in the United States don't have any MA plans operating there — and in those places, your only choice is original Medicare. In 2024, the average Medicare beneficiary has access to 43 MA plans, double the number offered in 2018.

What's more, each plan has its own mix of costs and benefits. I won't pretend that choosing among them is necessarily easy when you're not comparing apples to apples. For example, how do you compare one plan's flat-dollar co-pay for visiting a doctor with another plan's percentage of the cost charge? Still, taking a hard look at the differences among several plans can help you make an informed decision.

In this chapter, I explain how to compare Medicare Advantage plans so you can understand differences in plan benefits and costs and make your decision — free of sales pressure. I also suggest ways to narrow your choices down to the one plan that best meets your needs and preferences and show you how to enroll. Finally, I explain options available if you change your mind.

Comparing Medicare Advantage Plans

Weeks before your 65th birthday rolls around — and every year during the open enrollment period that allows you to change Medicare coverage — your mailbox will overflow with mailings from insurance companies selling Medicare Advantage plans (and also stand-alone Part D plans and Medigap policies). My advice: Toss the lot!

WARNING

Insurance companies have a perfect right to solicit your business, at least by sending marketing materials about their own Medicare plans through the mail. (Calling by phone or showing up at the door without your invitation is illegal, as I explain in Chapter 12.) But you can't properly compare plans this way. The mailing for each plan is a general advertising pitch for that particular plan. Mailings for different plans can't provide the key details you need to make a decision based on your own needs and preferences. If you call the phone number provided for any plan, you'll be in contact with an agent whose job is to sell that plan. Again, that's perfectly legitimate, but it doesn't take into account the fact that you may be better off with a different plan than the one the agent is pitching.

There's a better way to determine how many MA plans are available to you and then to compare them. The fastest and most effective way of identifying your options among MA plans is to use the Medicare Plan Finder on Medicare's website. I describe the Plan Finder in Chapter 10 in relation to comparing stand-alone Part D prescription drug plans. But this process has an inherent pitfall that you should be aware of before you start so that you can steer clear of it.

WARNING

The Plan Finder requires you to use the identical process for finding MA plans as for stand-alone drug plans. In other words, it invites you to enter your prescription drugs and select pharmacies in the same way. The strategic flaw here is that when using the Plan Finder to figure out your best drug plan, you're comparing plans that provide *only* drugs and nothing else — which is fine. Yet when considering Medicare Advantage plans, you need to compare a whole range of medical benefits and their costs: co-pays for doctors' services, hospital stays, diagnostic tests, and many others as well as prescription drug costs. It's a different ballgame entirely.

The original architects of the Medicare Plan Finder recognized this fact and designed a different search for each type of plan. But a few years ago, they decided to "streamline" the process into a single search engine. They believe that people can easily compare plans by using the same process, regardless of whether they're looking for Part D drug plans or MA health plans. I disagree. Just think about it: Entering the names of your drugs into the search engine early in the process of finding health plans guarantees that the Plan Finder will zoom in on the plans that cost the least for your drugs while ignoring other medical benefits and costs that are just as or even more important to you. (For example, I did a search for a set of drugs among MA plans in my own zip code. The plan listed first certainly charged the least for those drugs, but it cost twice as much for doctors' visits as some of the other available plans.)

I propose a strategy that gets around this problem and is, I think, more consumer-friendly. I divide the process of finding and comparing MA plans into two different searches, which I describe in the following sections:

>> **Search 1:** This search ignores drug coverage and focuses on getting to the list of MA plans available to you as soon as possible. You can then look at the costs and benefits of their medical services and pick out a few plans that you think are worth considering.

>> **Search 2:** This step focuses on drug coverage. You enter the names of your drugs, their dosages, and how often you take them so that the Plan Finder can work its math magic and find what you'd pay for your drugs under any MA plan available to you. You then see which of the two or three MA plans you're already considering (from Search 1) offers you the best coverage-and-cost deal for your drugs.

TIP

If you don't need a Medicare Advantage plan that provides Part D drug coverage as well as medical benefits — perhaps because you already have good drug coverage from elsewhere, such as retiree benefits or the Veterans Administration — you need to consider only Search 1. You'd then be looking for an MA plan that doesn't include Part D coverage, if one is available.

Comparing plans' benefits

In this section, I walk you through Search 1 so that you can quickly see how many MA plans you can choose from and begin to compare the benefits of those plans. In the later section "Adding prescription drug coverage," I introduce Search 2. (If you don't have computer access or prefer that someone else do this search for you, turn to Chapter 12.)

Moving through the Plan Finder

All it takes to see the array of Medicare Advantage plans available in your area is a few fast steps at the keyboard. When you reach that point, you can instantly see key information about each plan, which may help you make a first cut to narrow your choices. (To dig deeper into costs and benefits, I show you how to scrutinize plan details in the following section.)

1. **Go to Medicare's website at** `www.medicare.gov` **and click on "Find health & drug plans" on the home page.**

   This will lead you to the "Find Medicare health and drug plans" site. Or you can go directly to this site to search for Part D prescription drug and Medicare Advantage plans at `www.medicare.gov/plan-compare/#/?lang=en`.

2. **To get the information you need as quickly as possible, enter your zip code and click on "Continue without logging in."**

3. **Identify the type of Medicare coverage you want in the list (select "Medicare Advantage Plan") and click on "Find Plans."**

4. **Answer the question on whether you get any help with costs, checking the options that apply to you, and then click on "Next."**

5. **When you're asked, "Do you want to see your drug costs when you compare plans?" click on "No" and then "Next."**

   You can search for drug information later, as I explain in the later section "Adding prescription drug coverage."

Congratulations! You've now arrived at the list of Medicare Advantage plans in your area. If more than ten plans are available, click the link that lets you page through them all. This results page gives broad information about each plan, some of which is immediately useful because you can use it to narrow down the number of options pretty quickly. You can do that, for example, by filtering the type of plan that interests you (health maintenance organization, preferred provider organization, and so on), the type of extra benefits available (such as vision, dental, and hearing coverage), the plan's quality rating, the insurance carrier, and whether the plan is for people with special needs, such as chronic conditions. This page gives you the ability to reduce the list to a manageable few. So you don't need to look at the details of every plan available to you — unless only a few are offered in your area anyway. But you do need to look at the details for the plans on your shortlist, as I explain in the next section.

TIP

This page even tells you which plans are best avoided. A red "Caution" notification icon identifies plans that have received low ratings from Medicare for at least three years in a row. You also have an option to view any "sanctioned" plans, meaning that Medicare can suspend new enrollment in this plan until it has fixed its violations of Medicare rules, at the bottom of each page of plan listings.

Digging for plan details

The nitty-gritty details necessary to compare plans properly include what each plan charges to visit a primary care doctor or specialist, stay in the hospital, have an X-ray, use an ambulance, and more. In other words, most of the fine-print stuff you want to know. To access those details, just click the "Plan Details" button below any plan summary.

You can choose to see the details of up to three plans side by side. To do so, click the "Add to Compare" button below each plan summary, and a line of boxes will appear at the bottom of your screen. When you've made your selections, click the "Compare" button in the bottom right corner. (You can check the details of original Medicare if you want to compare the details of that program with one or two MA plans that interest you.) When the plans appear on-screen, click the "Plan Details" button, which provides the main details of each plan.

Walking through an example

For example, look at Figure 11-1, which shows selected details of three MA plans in my own zip code. The details and costs are real, but I've changed the actual names of the plans to alphabetical trios: ABC, LMN, and XYZ. This chart isn't exactly what you'll see on your own screen. Instead, it's a compilation of key details — though by no means all the details — that I've made about three plan options that show how different they are. You can make your own shortlist of the plans in your own area that interest you, with their key details. But right now I want to show you how to *look* at these details to extract the information that may make all the difference in finally selecting the plan that's right for you.

Figure 11-1 features several important takeaways:

>> **Don't judge a plan by its premium!** You'd naturally expect a plan with a high monthly premium to give you better coverage than one that charges a low or $0 premium. But that usually isn't true in Medicare Advantage. The plans in Figure 11-1 feature premiums ranging from $0 to $20. If you compare their details, you can see that ABC scores the medium-level quality rating but charges the highest premium.

>> **Look out for deductibles.** Most plans don't charge an annual deductible for their medical benefits (though they may for their prescription drug coverage).

>> **Pay attention to hospital charges.** These amounts vary greatly among plans. Spending five days in the hospital under plan ABC would cost $1,750 (or $350/day); under plan LMN, the cost would be $1,500. (For comparison, in original Medicare in 2024, a similar hospital stay costs $1,632 — the maximum Part A deductible for a stay up to 60 days — unless you have other insurance that covers this expense.)

Services/Costs	ABC Plan (HMO)	LMN Plan (HMO)	XYZ Plan (PPO)
Monthly premium	$20	$0	$0
Annual deductible	$0	$0	$0
Annual out-of-pocket spending limit	$7,550 (in network)	$7,200 (in network)	$5,900 (in network) $8,950 (in and out of network)
Quality rating	3 stars	3.5 stars	4.5 stars
Doctor visit co-pay	$0	$10	$0
Specialist visit co-pay	$45	$0-40	$35
Emergency room visit co-pay	$100	$100	$120
Inpatient hospital care	Days 1-5: $350 Days 6-90: $0	Days 1-5: $300 Days 6-90: $0	Days 1-5: $345 Days 6-90: $0
Medical equipment	20% per item	0-20% per item	15% per item
Skilled nursing facility stay	Days 1-20: $0 Days 21-100: $203	Days 1-20: $0 Days 21-100: $203	Days 1-20: $10 Days 21-100: $203
Extra/Supplemental Benefits	--Routine hearing care --Routine dental care (additional dental services available for extra $23/month) --Routine vision care --Some transportation to medical appointments	--No hearing care --Routine dental care; limited comprehensive treatment --Routine vision care --No transportation to medical appointments	--Routine hearing care --Comprehensive dental benefits --Routine vision care --Fitness benefit --Some transportation to medical appointments

© John Wiley & Sons, Inc.

FIGURE 11-1: Comparing Medicare Advantage plans online.

>> **Check out skilled nursing facility charges.** These numbers also vary. If you needed to spend as many as 100 days in a skilled nursing facility — the full limit of coverage — plans ABC and LMN would charge $203 a day after the first 20 days; a bit less than plan XYZ (which charges $10 a day for days 1–20, and $203 for days 21–100). Under original Medicare in 2024, you would pay nothing the first 20 days and $204 a day thereafter.

>> **Look carefully at out-of-network charges in PPOs.** Being able to go to a doctor or other provider outside your plan's network, as PPOs allow, is useful. But MA plans that are PPOs often have higher out-of-pocket spending limits. Plans ABC and LMN have annual out-of-pocket maximums at $7,550 and $7,200, respectively. But plan XYZ, the PPO, has an out-of-pocket limit of $5,900 for in-network expenses, and $8,950 for expenses incurred both in and out of network.

TIP

The Medicare Plan Finder provides details of each Medicare Advantage plan's coverage. This includes fine-print information on extra services such as coverage for gym memberships and other fitness programs; routine vision, hearing, and dental services; and even telehealth and opioid treatment services.

REMEMBER

Actual coverage varies enormously among plans. Sometimes it means the plan offers one or more of these extras as an optional package for an additional monthly premium. In some plans, the coverage may be skimpier: perhaps no more than one checkup a year. Other plans may offer better deals — coverage for hearing aids and glasses or contact lenses, as well as checkups — with reasonable co-pays. But you will need to contact a plan — in advance of enrolling — to find out exactly what it's offering. Contact information for each plan is provided on the Plan Finder.

Adding prescription drug coverage

After performing Search 1 (as I explain in the earlier section "Comparing plans' benefits") to narrow down the number of Medicare Advantage plans to the few that interest you in terms of medical benefits, you're ready to embark on Search 2 to see which of these plans gives you the best deal on Part D coverage for your prescription drugs. *Note:* You don't have to perform this search if you already get creditable drug coverage from elsewhere. (*Creditable* means drug coverage that is at least as good as Part D; see Chapter 6.) And in this case, you're probably looking at Medicare Advantage plans that don't include drug coverage in their benefit packages.

REMEMBER

You may be hesitating because you don't take any medications right now. Do you even need Part D coverage? First, read what I say about that issue in Chapter 6. Then I think you should choose a Medicare Advantage plan that includes drug coverage — just in case you should suddenly need it — but select the plan primarily on the basis of its medical benefits. (MA plans don't necessarily charge higher premiums if they offer drug coverage, and some charge no premiums for either medical or drug coverage.)

Entering your drugs into the Plan Finder

To find the coverage that works best for the meds you take, you need to go to the Plan Finder on Medicare's website and again go through the Search 1 process that I list earlier in this chapter, this time clicking "Yes" in Step 5, choosing how you normally fill prescriptions and entering your drugs. In fact, it's exactly the same step-by-step progression that I explain in detail in Chapter 10, so flip to that list and work from it.

This takes you to the main list of Medicare Advantage plans available in your area. Look at the coverage for your drugs under the three or four plans that you're considering (on the basis of their medical benefits) according to the personal drug info you've entered. At this stage, you can either

>> Click on the "Plan Details" button of one of those plans, where you can view "Drug Coverage & Costs." Repeat this process for each plan.

>> Click on the "Add to compare" boxes of two or three plans you're interested in. At the bottom of the page, you will see the plans listed and an option to "Compare." This will take you to the "Comparing Medicare Advantage plans" page where you see the plans side by side. Click on the "Plan Details" button for each individual plan for coverage details.

You'll see big cost differences between the plans.

Checking out an example

Look at the example in Figure 11-2. This chart takes the same Medicare Advantage plans (which I call ABC, LMN, and XYZ) from Figure 11-1 earlier in this chapter but shows how a certain set of three common drugs stacks up under those plans. The drugs I've chosen are 70 milligrams (mg) taken four times a month of Fosamax, a brand-name drug for osteoporosis; 20 mg once daily of atorvastatin, the generic version of the anticholesterol drug Lipitor; and 50 mg once daily of levothyroxine sodium, the generic version of Synthroid, for hypothyroidism.

Drug coverage	ABC Plan (HMO)	LMN Plan (HMO)	XYZ Plan (PPO)
Covers all three drugs? (Fosamax/atorvastatin/levothyroxine)	No/yes/yes	No/yes/yes	No/no/no
Annual drug deductible?	None	None	None
Cost of three drugs over whole year (retail pharmacy)	$1,277.55 (includes full cost of Fosamax)	$1,349.10 (includes full cost of Fosamax)	$2,876.40 (includes costs of all drugs)
Cost of three drugs over whole year (mail order)	$1,273.62 (includes full cost of Fosamax)	$1,264.62 (includes full cost of Fosamax)	$2,876.40 (includes costs of all drugs)
Monthly out-of-pocket costs (premium + co-pays)	$141.95	$149.90	$319.60
Restrictions	Yes, quantity limits on atorvastatin	None (Fosamax not covered)	None (no drugs covered)

FIGURE 11-2: Comparing drug coverage in three MA plans.

© John Wiley & Sons, Inc.

As you can see, the results for each plan (all taken from the Medicare Plan Finder) are different. Taken with the same plan's medical benefits shown in Figure 11-1 earlier in this chapter, here's how (in this example) they may affect your final choice for a Medicare Advantage plan:

>> None of the three plans covers Fosamax; if you needed the brand-name medication (versus the generic version), you would either pay full price or want to search for a plan that covers it.

>> The cost of drugs is lowest in plan LMN, provided you receive them by mail order.

>> Plan XYZ, as a PPO, has a more expansive provider network and offers more comprehensive dental benefits (refer to Figure 11-1) and transportation to medical appointments.

So where does this information leave you? Which plan would you pick? The one that provides less-expensive coverage for this particular set of drugs, or the one that offers other supplemental benefits?

REMEMBER

I'd argue that this example perfectly demonstrates the trade-offs that you must expect to make when choosing a Medicare Advantage plan. I'd also argue that this analysis is a useful and even strengthening process: It sharpens your focus on competing options and reduces them to two or three possible choices. Now all you need do is get down to that final one.

Choosing the Medicare Advantage Plan That's Right for You

Getting all your information in order really helps when you're comparing Medicare Advantage plans. If you research plans by using Medicare's online comparison tool, as I explain earlier in this chapter, you can print out the details of the few that interest you. (Or you can ask someone else to perform this same search and send you the details, as I explain in Chapter 12.) After you have this information, notice how the options become tons clearer when you write down the key details alongside each other — as I do in Figures 11-1 and 11-2 earlier in this chapter. Feel free to use those tables as templates, or you can design your own.

But now you need to consider a question that isn't answered on the Plan Finder but may be the game changer in picking one plan rather than another: Which doctors and hospitals accept the plans you're considering? In the following sections,

I suggest how you may go about finding answers to that question and provide pointers for enrolling in a Medicare Advantage plan. I also show how to switch out of the plan you choose if you change your mind.

Figuring out which providers accept the plans you're considering

This point is really the $64,000 question, as they used to say on the old TV game show. If you prefer to continue seeing doctors you know, you won't want insurance they don't accept. On the other hand, if you've had difficulty finding doctors recently, you may welcome a plan that pretty much guarantees access to certain doctors even if you don't know them personally.

Most Medicare Advantage plans — HMOs and PPOs — draw up contracts with doctors and other providers within a certain geographical service area for a period of one calendar year. So being in a plan may give you access to a larger pool of doctors willing to accept you as a patient. Or it may exclude you from doctors who don't accept coverage from some specific plans or even from any plans in the Medicare Advantage program.

One way around this issue may be to choose a PPO that allows you to go to any doctor or hospital outside its provider network for a higher co-pay. But first check out how much extra you'd pay. In theory, Medicare Private Fee-for-Service plans also allow you to go to any provider, but doctors may accept this type of insurance on a visit-by-visit basis only, as explained in Chapter 9.

So how can you find out which doctors and hospitals are contracted to the plans you're considering, before signing up for one? The options are

>> Go to the "Benefits & costs" section of any plan on the Medicare Plan Finder site and click on the "View Provider Network Directory" link. This usually takes you to a page on the plan's website that has a searchable directory of providers.

>> Call each plan and ask for its provider list to be mailed to you.

>> Call the offices of the primary-care doctor, specialists, and hospitals you currently use and ask to speak to the person who handles insurance billing. Then ask whether that provider accepts the particular Medicare Advantage plans you're considering.

Of the three, the third is the least time-consuming because, even armed with a provider list, you still need to confirm that those providers accept the plan. Doing this check is really important, because you can't just take a plan's word for it that any particular doctor is in its network.

Also, be aware that Medicare Advantage plans are allowed to drop doctors from their provider lists during the plan year. If a plan does this, it must notify patients in writing at least 60 days in advance.

Enrolling in a Medicare Advantage plan

After you compare plans carefully and find out which ones work with the doctors and hospitals you want, it's time to pick a plan. Only you can make this final decision, according to your own preferences and the information you've researched on each plan. If you get stuck, talking through the options with a counselor from your State Health Insurance Assistance Program (SHIP) may help to resolve the dilemma. (See Appendix A for contact info.)

In contrast, actually enrolling in a plan is simple, with three options:

>> Click on the "Enroll" button to select the plan of your choice on the Medicare Plan Finder.

>> Call Medicare's help line at 800-633-4227 (TTY 877-486-2048).

>> Sign up with the plan directly by going to its website or calling its customer service number.

If you're new to Medicare, you can enroll in an MA plan during your initial enrollment period or, if you've delayed signing up for Part B beyond age 65, during the special enrollment period (see Chapter 6 for details). Otherwise, you can sign up or switch to a different plan during any open enrollment period (October 15 to December 7).

Taking action if you change your mind

After you enroll in a Medicare Advantage health plan, what happens if you discover you don't like it? There are two times of the year when you have the right to change to any other MA plan, or leave Medicare Advantage to return to original Medicare: the fall open enrollment period (October 15 to December 7) and the

Medicare Advantage Open Enrollment Period (January 1 to March 31). Outside those two time frames, Medicare allows you to switch only for several specific reasons. However, here are several escape clauses (I explain them in more detail in Chapter 15):

>> **If you joined an MA plan as soon as you enrolled in Medicare at age 65:** Medicare considers this first year a trial period. So you have the right to disenroll from the plan at any time within 12 months of first receiving coverage from it to switch to original Medicare and a stand-alone Part D drug plan. You also have the right to buy a Medigap policy within 63 days of your MA plan coverage's ending.

>> **If this enrollment is your first time in an MA plan and you dropped a Medigap policy to join it:** You have the right to return to original Medicare and be reinstated in Medigap at any time during your first 12 months in the plan. (Check out Chapters 4 and 10 for more on Medigap.)

>> **If you receive Extra Help:** You can change to another MA health plan, or to original Medicare and a stand-alone Part D drug plan, once during each of the first three quarters of the year. (Flip to Chapter 4 for more about Extra Help.)

>> **If you move outside your plan's service area:** You can disenroll from the plan and sign up with another, or switch to original Medicare and a stand-alone Part D drug plan in your new area when you move. In these circumstances, you also have the right to buy a Medigap policy with full federal protections if you do so no later than 63 days after coverage from your MA plan ends.

>> **If you enter or leave an institution, such as a skilled nursing facility or a long-term-care hospital:** You can change to another MA plan, or to original Medicare and a stand-alone Part D drug plan, at any time while living there or within two months of leaving.

>> **If you live in a nursing home as a long-term-care resident:** You can change to a different MA plan, or to original Medicare and a stand-alone Part D drug plan, at any time of the year.

>> **If an MA plan that has earned Medicare's top five-star quality rating is offered in your area:** You can switch to that plan at any time of year.

>> **If you joined a Medicare Cost plan:** You have the right to disenroll from it and switch to original Medicare at any time. If you received drug coverage from this plan, you can also switch to a stand-alone Part D drug plan at the same time. (I describe Medicare Cost plans in Chapter 9.)

Chapter **12**

Getting Help in Making Medicare Choices

I f you're feeling pangs of inadequacy because you just can't face all the Medicare options on your own, banish the thought. Don't feel bad if you've glanced at Chapters 10 and 11 on using the online Medicare Plan Finder and feel daunted. I hope that if you try using the Plan Finder, you'll get the hang of it. But not everybody has a computer or reliable internet access, or feels comfortable with online searches. And you know what? That's fine. You can find the same information by getting help from a live person.

The question is *which* live person? The options come down to these:

» Asking a family member or friend to do an online search for you

» Contacting your State Health Insurance Assistance Program (SHIP)

» Calling the Medicare help line

» Taking advice from other professional and volunteer sources

I discuss each of these options in this chapter. I also draw attention to the help that's available to you if English isn't your first language. I strongly advise you to use that help because understanding what you're signing up for in Medicare and how your choices affect your benefits and costs is important.

This chapter also focuses on the "help" you seriously need to avoid — the kind that comes from scam artists intent on ripping you off or from hard-sell marketers who are selling legitimate insurance products but not with your best interests in mind.

One on One: Getting Personal Help on Medicare Issues

Talking things out with someone else is often a good way of refining your ideas and making a reasoned decision, and choosing the Medicare plan that's right for you is no exception. Still, your conversation will be tons more productive if you already have some knowledge of the options you're discussing. So even if you're asking for help from the sources listed in the following sections, reading at least some of the information in Chapters 10 and 11 better equips you to understand and evaluate what they say.

TIP

Anytime you talk to someone providing professional help, keep notes of whom you talked to and when. They may become invaluable if you need to file a complaint later on.

Asking family and friends

Don't count on family or friends for reliable information on Medicare! But if you just want technical help to access and use the online Medicare Plan Finder, that's different. Even if you're not so hot with computers, I'm willing to bet that someone in your family or circle of friends is. And no matter how antsy you feel about asking for help, finding a good Medicare option is an excellent reason to do so.

TIP

Maybe you have teenage grandkids who are computer whizzes and would be thrilled if you asked them to help. Never underestimate the ability of youngsters to pick their way through a complicated database — like the Medicare Plan Finder — without turning a hair. They've grown up with this stuff and know perfectly well that they're more expert than you. Provide them with a list of your drugs, an idea of your general preferences, and the step-by-step instructions that I give in Chapter 10 (for Part D plans) or Chapter 11 (for Medicare Advantage plans). Be sure to get printouts of the results — and to give your helper a big hug (and maybe a treat!) for helping you.

Another advantage of turning to family and friends is that they may help with language if you're not fully fluent in English, are deaf and rely on American Sign

Language, or are blind. Relatives or friends may be able to translate Medicare documents (such as consumer guides or official forms) or act as interpreters if you contact other sources of help mentioned in the next few sections. However, if you feel uncomfortable about disclosing info on the drugs you take to people close to you, you may prefer to use the following resources anyway.

Contacting State Health Insurance Assistance Programs

When it comes to helping make Medicare choices or dealing with issues that the program throws up, a State Health Insurance Assistance Program (SHIP) is your best friend. You get personal, one-on-one help from counselors who've had extensive training on Medicare. You get advice that's wholly objective and devoid of sales pressure. And it's free!

So is there a SHIP in every port? Well, almost. SHIPs operate in all 50 states, the District of Columbia, Puerto Rico, Guam, and the U.S. Virgin Islands. (In some areas, they may go by other names, such as HICAP, SHIBA, or SHINE.) Nationwide, more than 12,500 trained SHIP counselors (mainly volunteers) at 2,200 local sites provide counseling and outreach to roughly 6 million people every year on a wide range of Medicare and Medicaid issues. Funding comes from the federal government, but the SHIPs are organized within each state. Some offer a large network of counselors covering virtually every county.

Here are just some of the things SHIP counselors can do:

>> Review your options and help you decide whether you want to pick original Medicare or a Medicare Advantage (MA) plan.

>> Use the Medicare Plan Finder to identify the stand-alone Part D prescription drug plan that covers all your drugs at the lowest cost and with the least hassle, if you choose original Medicare.

>> Search the Medicare Plan Finder to identify which Medicare Advantage plan in your area best meets your healthcare needs and preferences, if you choose to get your benefits through an MA plan.

>> Check out whether you qualify for the Extra Help program, which provides low-cost Part D drug coverage to people with limited incomes. (Flip to Chapter 4 for details on this program.)

>> Determine whether you qualify for Medicaid, a Medicare Savings Program, Supplemental Security Income (SSI), or any other income-based federal or state assistance programs that may lower your costs (see Chapter 4).

>> Help you understand and compare Medigap supplemental policies and long-term-care insurance policies (see Chapter 4).

>> Assist you with issues arising from having Medicare through disability.

>> Help troubleshoot problems you face with Medicare, Social Security, or the plan you're enrolled in, depending on the circumstances, and in some cases take action on your behalf.

TIP

If English isn't your first language, the SHIP program can provide interpreters or refer you to local organizations that offer counseling in your own language (including sign language), free of charge. Let the SHIP know that you need this service when you or somebody acting on your behalf calls your SHIP.

To see contact information for each SHIP, turn to Appendix A.

Calling Medicare's help line

Medicare's consumer help line takes any questions on Medicare at no charge. That includes asking a customer service representative to do a search of the online Plan Finder for the Part D or Medicare Advantage plans that best meet your needs and preferences — and then to mail printouts to you. This way, you can get details of two or three plans, all ready for you to compare and pick the one you think will give you the best service and/or deal on cost.

When you call the help line — at 800-633-4227 or TTY 877-486-2048 — you don't have to identify yourself (unless you want info mailed to you). But if you want assistance choosing a plan, the rep needs to know your zip code and some other information in order to perform an accurate search. If you don't speak English fluently and want the help of an interpreter, tell the rep immediately. You won't be charged any money for an interpreter's services.

WARNING

How helpful is the help line? Medicare uses contracted workers as customer representatives and gives them basic training, though their knowledge of Medicare isn't extensive. Feedback from customers (and others who call the number to test the quality of the service) is mixed, as you may expect. Some callers get through to a rep in a jiffy; others remain on hold for several minutes or longer, especially during open enrollment. Some are satisfied with the information they receive; others aren't.

TIP

When you talk with a rep, it helps to be as specific as possible. Use the following pointers to explain what you want:

>> Tell the rep whether you're looking for a stand-alone Part D drug plan, a Medicare Advantage plan, or a Medigap policy. (I explain the differences among these options in Chapter 9.)

>> If you need a plan that includes Part D prescription drug coverage, give the rep the following information:

- The names of the drugs you're taking, plus their dosages and how often you take them. (Keep in mind that making an accurate list of your meds is essential, as I explain in Chapter 10.)

- Whether you qualify for Extra Help.

- Whether you want a plan that offers mail-order services.

- Whether you want a plan that covers prescriptions at network pharmacies anywhere in the country.

>> If you want details of a few plans that charge the least for your drugs, ask the rep to check whether each plan

- Covers all your drugs

- Places any restrictions on your drugs (prior authorization, quantity limits, or step therapy — see Chapter 14)

- Has good quality ratings

- Has in-network or preferred pharmacies that are convenient for you

>> If you're interested in Medicare Advantage plans, ask the rep to narrow the number of plans to reflect what's important to you — such as co-pays for doctors and hospitals or extra benefits such as vision, hearing, or dental care, or gym memberships.

>> Ask the rep to mail you printouts of the three plans that best meet your needs so that you can make a final choice. If these options are Medicare Advantage plans, be sure to specify that you want printouts of the plans' *detailed* health benefits information.

REMEMBER

If the customer service rep doesn't give you all the info you request (or refuses to do so), ask to speak to a supervisor. You have a right to ask as many questions as you like. If the rep gives the impression that finding plan information for you is tedious or taking too much time, you also have the right to complain. (Chapter 16 has details of how to file a complaint.)

Seeking advice from other sources

You may well be able to get advice on picking a Medicare plan from a variety of other sources. For example, many people report that they turn to their doctors, pharmacists, and insurance agents. Others receive help at senior centers, seminars, and info sessions of many kinds. Others are turning to Medicare plan–finding businesses that have popped up on the internet.

Which of these outlets can you trust to find a plan that meets your personal needs? Essentially, when can you believe what you hear and when should you be skeptical? The following sections note some rules of thumb that may help.

Doctors and pharmacists

WARNING

Just because someone's a professional doesn't necessarily mean they know enough to be useful to you in picking a plan. Doctors and pharmacists are professionals in their own fields and may be absolutely terrific in their jobs. But unless they're able to run your particular set of drugs through the Plan Finder to search for the Part D plan that covers your drugs at the least cost, they can't really help you.

Insurance agents

Insurance agents are also professionals, and many of them are very knowledgeable about the range of Medicare's plan options. Others aren't, and some are paid high commissions to sell a particular plan — which isn't illegal or unethical but may not be in your best interests.

WARNING

If you have an independent agent who's handled other insurance for you in the past and whom you trust, you may naturally turn to them to find a Medicare plan. However, you should ask whether they're able to use the Plan Finder to search for your best bet. If not, going to someone who can may be wiser.

Seminars and information sessions

People of Medicare age are often invited to info sessions at senior centers, retirement communities, hotels, or other venues and offered help in finding Medicare plans, especially Part D plans. Some of these sessions provide excellent value — for example, the ones run by volunteers from SHIPs (discussed earlier in this chapter) or other consumer groups. These trained people, who aren't connected to insurance companies and have no financial interest in pushing any particular plans, either show you how to use the Plan Finder yourself or run your drug info through it to help you pick a plan.

WARNING

Other sessions are basically sales pitches for a single insurance company, promoting only the Medicare plans it sells. Such pitches are not unethical or illegal in themselves, but they're not focused on your needs, and because you haven't had the benefit of comparing them with other options, you can't tell whether they're the best for you.

Businesses dedicated to Medicare help

Wherever an opportunity opens up, some entrepreneur steps in to fill it. So the growing number of businesses offering to help sort out Medicare options for seniors, often for a fee, really isn't surprising. If these operations are legitimate, whether offered through the internet or by mail, they rely on the Medicare Plan Finder for their results. If using these businesses saves you effort, you may consider it money well spent — although you're basically paying for the same service as the free ones I describe earlier in this chapter.

Perhaps a number of these businesses legitimately offer a useful service. But I've found that some of them charge fees without properly disclosing the charges upfront on their websites. And some that don't charge fees to consumers are actually paid behind the scenes by insurance companies for signing people up — a practice that, again, isn't illegal but in my opinion is unethical because of its lack of transparency.

Buyer Beware! Avoiding Scams and Hard-Sell Marketing

Medicare's private insurance options are commercial marketplaces where products (Medicare Advantage plans, Part D prescription drug plans, and Medigap policies) are sold to consumers (Medicare beneficiaries). And like all other marketplaces, they attract their share of swindlers and rip-off artists whose sad aim in life is to separate unsuspecting customers from their money.

So in the following sections, I explain how to be on your guard against two quite different types of deceptive practices: the outright scam and the hard sell. In both cases, they're most likely to come from people who are very skilled in trying to convince you that they're there to help.

Steering clear of outright scams

An *outright scam* is when some thief pretends to be from Medicare, Social Security, a Medicare health or drug plan, or anything that sounds official and asks for sensitive information — such as your Social Security, credit card, or bank account number — in an attempt to steal your identity or money.

Outright scammers have nothing to do with Medicare. They're just using it as a pretext to cheat you. The scam may be relatively simple, such as trying to con you into paying for something that doesn't exist, or it may be a much more serious attempt to commit identity theft. Identity thieves hunt for key pieces of personal information, which they use to buy merchandise, apply for new credit cards in your name, or make a profit by selling it to other identity thieves. This crime also robs people of their good credit ratings — which can take years to restore. This nightmare is one you want to avoid at all costs. That's why I explain what you need to know in the following sections.

Watching out for red flags

WARNING

Scams happen unexpectedly. You answer the phone or the doorbell and find someone who sounds or looks perfectly respectable offering help. How can you tell whether to trust this person? Here are some instant warning signals:

>> **A person at your door claiming to be from Medicare or Social Security:** The real agencies never send anyone to your home on official business without an appointment.

>> **A person claiming to represent a particular Part D, Medicare Advantage, or Medigap plan:** Medicare prohibits anybody from coming to your home uninvited to sell any kind of Medicare insurance. It also prohibits plans from cold-calling you on the phone unless you request it.

>> **A person asking for an enrollment fee or an advance premium:** Neither the enrollment fee nor the advance premium exists. You never have to pay someone to enroll you in a Medicare health or drug plan, nor pay any one-time payment that supposedly takes care of your premiums for months, years, or forever. Asking for either charge is illegal.

>> **A person requesting your personal financial or identification information:** Never give out your Social Security or Medicare ID number, any details about your credit cards or bank accounts, or any other financial information, especially on the phone. Legitimate callers don't ask for this info.

Surveying some common scams targeting seniors

WARNING

Con artists dream up new and creative ideas all the time for ways to target older Americans and steal their money and/or identities. The following are some typical scams involving Medicare that seniors have reported in addition to those noted in the previous section:

>> **The loss-of-Medicare-coverage threat:** The caller claims to be a government official needing to check your Social Security or Medicare ID number and implies that if you don't provide it, you'll lose your Medicare coverage. *Remember:* The government has your number on file. You can't lose Medicare benefits by refusing to give it out.

>> **The need-a-new-card scam:** In 2018, Medicare issued new cards to all Medicare enrollees that removed all Social Security numbers from the cards.

A resurfacing scam now has criminals asking you for your Medicare ID number so they can issue you a newer version of the card with a chip. *Remember:* Medicare never calls to offer you a new card; if you lose your card, you can go online to request a new card.

>> **The free-genetic-test offer:** Criminals claiming to be genetic testing representatives tell you they're offering "free" DNA, cancer, or genetic screenings to anyone with Medicare. All they request is your Medicare card number, which is then used to steal your medical identity and falsely bill Medicare. *Remember:* You should use only a trusted doctor to request screening tests; do not share your Medicare information with unfamiliar people.

REMEMBER

You're probably not going to encounter any of these scenarios. And what if one of these situations does happen? You can hang up the phone or shut the door. Yes, you can! Don't be deceived by a friendly voice or a willingness to chat. Con artists are experts at controlling the conversation to win your confidence and keep you on the phone or get invited inside. These people don't care about you. They're criminals who see you as a potential sucker. So show them you're not.

Reporting a scam

Authorities who receive reports of scam attempts send out alerts to put consumers on their guard. So if someone tries to scam you, do everyone a favor by reporting the incident to any of these offices:

>> Your state's attorney general or insurance commissioner. Find contact information in the phone book or on your state's website. Or go to the map provided by the National Association of Insurance Commissioners at www.naic.org/state_web_map.htm and click on your state.

>> The Federal Trade Commission (FTC), the official consumer protection agency.

- Call its toll-free help line at 877-382-4357.

- Write to FTC Consumer Response Center, 600 Pennsylvania Ave. NW, Washington, DC 20580.

- File a complaint online at reportfraud.ftc.gov.

>> The Inspector General of the U.S. Department of Health and Human Services.

- Call its toll-free hot line at 800-447-8477 (TTY 800-377-4950).

- Write to DHHS, Office of the Inspector General, Attention: OIG Hotline Operations, P.O. Box 23489, Washington, DC 20026.

- File a complaint online at oig.hhs.gov/fraud/report-fraud.

- Contact the agency's Senior Medicare Patrol, which fights fraud locally. Go to smpresource.org/you-can-help/report-fraud/ and select your state.

Taking steps if you're ripped off

Suppose you fall for a scam despite your best intentions. You can probably stop a payment (or be reimbursed for merchandise a thief has purchased with your card) by informing your bank or credit card company immediately.

REMEMBER

If you give out any personal information — such as your Social Security or Medicare ID number or your credit card or bank account numbers — you should seriously assume that you may be a victim of identity theft. The following can give you excellent advice on what to do next:

>> **The Privacy Rights Clearinghouse:** This California-based nonprofit consumer organization provides assistance and information to likely or actual victims of ID theft. For fact sheets on what to do, go to privacyrights.org/consumer-guides/identity-theft-what-do-if-it-happens-you.

>> **The Federal Trade Commission:** This agency provides guidance on dealing with identity theft at consumer.ftc.gov/identity-theft-and-online-security (available in English and Spanish).

Resisting hard-sell marketing tactics

The *hard sell* is when a plan's salesperson or an independent insurance agent uses aggressive or unethical tactics — such as bait and switch — to try to push you into signing up for a plan that you don't want or that has consequences you don't understand.

The insurance companies that sell Medicare plans aren't supposed to pressure or mislead you into buying one plan versus another. And in recent years, Medicare has introduced much tougher rules to prevent such practices. So you probably won't run into them at all. Certainly you can avoid sales pressure altogether if you make your own plan choices (see Chapters 10 and 11) or get help from unbiased sources, as explained earlier in this chapter.

Your best protection against unethical tactics is being informed. It helps to know the differences between the various kinds of Medicare insurance — Part D drug plans, Medicare Advantage plans, and Medigap supplemental policies — so that you can be sure that the plan an insurance agent is talking about is the type you actually want. Several chapters in this book explain aspects of these different plans in detail; Chapter 9 brings them together.

In the following sections, I arm you with another kind of protection: knowing what people selling these plans can and can't do — in other words, which practices are okay and which are illegal. Also, I explain the importance of checking information before you sign up for a plan if you do so through a salesperson or insurance agent, and I note what to do if you feel you've been misled into joining a plan.

Knowing which marketing methods are (and aren't) allowed

Recognizing what insurance companies or their sales agents are allowed to do (and are prohibited from doing) when selling Medicare products is an excellent way of spotting whether a sales pitch is out of line and should be mistrusted. You don't have to keep all the following rules in your head, but do keep them handy for easy reference before or after meeting with salespeople or to check through before signing on the dotted line.

Medicare allows plans to

>> Send promotional materials to you through the mail, but not enrollment forms

>> Send sales reps to your home, but only with your prior permission and only to discuss the single type of coverage (for example, a Medicare Advantage plan, a stand-alone Part D drug plan, or Medigap insurance) that you specify when making the appointment

>> Give sales presentations in public places such as shopping malls or hotels

WARNING

Medicare does *not* allow plans to

>> Send salespeople to your home uninvited

>> Telephone you directly to make a sales pitch unless you invited the call or already had a relationship with the plan

>> Tell you that a home visit is required for the purpose of explaining details of the plan or for you to enroll in it

>> Ask for personal information on the phone, including your address, prescription meds, Social Security or Medicare ID number, credit card or bank account numbers, or any other financial information

>> Enroll you in a plan on the phone unless you call the plan

>> Sell you a Medigap policy if you already have one or are enrolled in a Medicare Advantage plan

>> Sell you an Obamacare health insurance plan if you're enrolled in Medicare

- » Give sales presentations or distribute enrollment forms in doctors' offices, hospitals, pharmacies, nursing homes and other long-term-care facilities, or anywhere patients go to receive healthcare-related services (except in common areas such as public lounges at such facilities)

- » Give sales presentations at educational events such as health information fairs and community meetings

- » Offer gifts, cash, meals, or any giveaways as an inducement to enroll

Medicare requires plans to

- » Explain clearly in their marketing materials and verbal sales pitches that not all doctors and hospitals accept their Medicare Advantage plans.

- » Ensure that any independent sales agents they hire are licensed by the state in which they work.

- » Guarantee that sales agents are paid the same commission for each Medicare Advantage plan the sponsor sells in any given year in order to remove any incentive for them to push one rather than another. Also, they must guarantee that agents are paid the same commission for each stand-alone Part D plan the sponsor sells. (However, agents can still be paid different commissions for selling Medicare Advantage plans than for stand-alone Part D drug plans.)

- » Train sales reps, independent insurance agents, and brokers who sell their products, and hire only those candidates who score at least 85 percent on a written test of their knowledge of the Medicare program, its rules, and the details of the plan(s) they'll sell.

- » Ensure that sales agents who meet with consumers to discuss a particular type of plan (such as Medigap insurance) can't also, at the same meeting, discuss other types of plans (such as Medicare Advantage or Part D drug plans). Instead, they must schedule a separate appointment, at least 48 hours after the first, to discuss another kind of plan (unless the 48-hour window coincides with the end of an enrollment period).

- » Call consumers who sign up for any Medicare Advantage plan to check that they understand its conditions and consequences and allow them the opportunity to withdraw from the enrollment if they want to.

- » Provide interpreter services at the plan's call center so that people with limited English can be given information in their own language.

TECHNICAL
STUFF

You may think that these rules are the inevitable and unnecessary result of government red tape. But in fact, most were introduced after a huge marketing abuse scandal that revealed the large number of Medicare beneficiaries who'd been tricked by such unethical sales practices.

Thinking and checking before you sign

REMEMBER

Taking the time to think and verify information is a strong defense against signing up for the wrong plan. Never let anyone rush you into enrolling in a plan. Ask for the agent's name and contact information. If you have any qualms, call your state's department of insurance to verify that this agent is licensed. Then consider the plan carefully. If it's a Medicare Advantage plan, check out which doctors accept it, as discussed in Chapter 11.

Taking action if you're misled into joining a plan

Medicare has some consumer protections for people who believe that they've been tricked or misled into enrolling in a Medicare Advantage or Part D plan they don't want or that they weren't given enough information about to fully understand the consequences. Here's what you can do:

>> Call the Medicare help line at 800-633-4227 (TTY 877-486-2048). Explain the circumstances and say you want a special enrollment period to disenroll from the plan and switch to another — or, if you're in a Medicare Advantage plan, to switch to original Medicare and a Part D plan if you prefer, as explained in Chapter 15.

>> If you have medical bills that the plan refuses to pay — for example, if you were treated by doctors and/or a hospital outside the Medicare Advantage plan's provider network when you thought you were still covered by original Medicare — call the Medicare help line and ask to be re-enrolled into original Medicare *retroactively* (dating back to the time you joined the plan). Medicare will then pay any outstanding bills at its usual rate, and you'll pay the usual share of the cost.

>> If calling the Medicare help line doesn't bring results, call again and ask to be put in touch with a caseworker at your regional Medicare office. Or ask the help line for the phone number of the regional office that serves your state. Then call that office to explain what happened.

>> You also have the right to file an official complaint against the plan, as explained in Chapter 16.

REMEMBER

If you do come across sales agents who use unethical tactics, you should report them to your state department of insurance. For contact information, see your phone book or go to the website of the National Association of Insurance Commissioners at `www.naic.org/state_web_map.htm`.

4

Navigating Medicare from the Inside

Find masses of practical information that you need to be aware of when you're just getting used to the way Medicare works — for example, knowing how to pay your premiums, finding doctors who accept Medicare patients and knowing what they can charge you, understanding what to do if you hit problems when first filling a Part D prescription, and much more.

Home in on some of the finer points of Medicare coverage, especially those that aren't always properly explained in the official guides. Find information designed to empower you if you find yourself in specific situations where knowing the rules is critical.

Switch to a different kind of coverage if you need or want to change from one Medicare option to another. Pick up practical pointers on the appropriate times to switch and how to go about it.

Discover information that can help you understand your right to accurate information from government officials, recognize when and how to make a complaint, and know how to navigate the several levels of appeal open to you if you challenge a decision you don't agree with.

Chapter **13**

Starting Out as a New Medicare Beneficiary

You're in. Social Security has confirmed your enrollment and sent you your Medicare ID card, which displays the date when your coverage for Part A and Part B becomes effective. (I'm assuming here that you've signed up for Part B. If you delayed Part B enrollment, for reasons I explain in Chapter 6, you don't need to know most of the stuff in this chapter right now; know that it's here for you when you do sign up.) Maybe you've also enrolled in a Part D drug plan or a Medicare Advantage plan, as explained in Chapters 10 and 11.

So what happens next? This chapter focuses on what to expect from your Medicare coverage first time out, when you're getting used to the system. I zero in on those small but all-important rectangles: the ID cards that confirm the coverage you may have for different bits of your healthcare. I explain the practical basics that you'll quickly come to take for granted but that may not be obvious at the start — knowing how to pay your Medicare premiums (as ever, the methods vary according to your circumstances), what happens if you get behind with premium payments, and how to keep track of other expenses.

I also focus on your dealings with doctors — not only the thorny issue of finding doctors who accept Medicare patients but also what you should pay physicians in different situations. I'm there with you at the pharmacy when you fill your first Part D prescriptions, all ready to answer the questions you may be indignantly shouting aloud if the process doesn't go as smoothly as it should.

Playing Your Cards Right

You may find yourself with several cards entitling you to different Medicare services. And sometimes seeing at a glance which card is which or remembering what each is used for isn't easy. It can be especially confusing if, for example, you have a Part D drug plan and a Medigap policy sold by the same insurance company, and its name appears on both cards.

So this section looks at each type of card in the Medicare pack. How do you tell them apart? How do you use them? How can you protect them? What if you lose them?

Understanding when to use each card

REMEMBER

Presenting the correct card when you show up at a doctor's office or hospital is critically important. That's not just because it proves you have health insurance. It's mainly because the card tells your provider whom to bill. For example, if you're in a Medicare Advantage HMO plan and by mistake show your regular Medicare card rather than your HMO plan membership card, the provider will bill Medicare and not the plan. Medicare will then deny your claim, and you or the provider will have a lot of hassle sorting it out. So it pays (no pun intended) to know your cards and how to use them appropriately, as the following sections explain.

Your Medicare ID card

Printed on plain white thick paper, your red, white, and blue Medicare ID carries the circular logo of the Department of Health and Human Services and has "Medicare Health Insurance" emblazoned across it. The front of the card indicates your name, your Medicare ID number, the coverage you're entitled to (Part A, Part B, or both), and the date(s) that coverage begins. The back shows the phone number of Medicare's help line and website.

Use this card to obtain medical services if you receive your health benefits through original Medicare. You may need to show other cards as well if you also have stand-alone Medicare Part D drug coverage and/or Medigap supplemental insurance (I describe these cards later in this chapter), or benefits from a retiree plan or other source that acts as a supplement to Medicare.

Your Medicaid ID card

If you're entitled to both Medicaid and Medicare services or the benefits of a Medicare Savings Program (as I describe in Chapter 4), you'll receive a Medicaid ID card from your state. Because Medicaid is run by the states, each card has a different look and color. It carries your name, gender, and Medicaid ID number, and the name of your state or its abbreviation (for example, KY for Kentucky). It may also say "Medicaid," but some states use more general phrases on the card, such as "medical benefits" or "medical assistance," or have other names for the program, such as MediCal in California and TennCare in Tennessee.

Show this card every time you use a medical service. If you're also enrolled in original Medicare, show your Medicare ID card, too (or your Medicare Advantage plan membership card if you're enrolled in one of these plans; see the next section).

Your Medicare Advantage plan membership card

This card bears your name, your Member ID number, the plan's name and its Medicare identification number, and the plan's customer service phone number. It must also say what type of Medicare Advantage (MA) plan it is: for example, health maintenance organization (HMO), preferred provider organization (PPO), or Private Fee-for-Service (PFFS) plan. The name of the insurance company that sponsors the plan may be incorporated in its name or shown separately. Of course, card designs vary among plans.

WARNING

Use this card (*not* your Medicare ID card) to get medical services according to your plan's terms and conditions. For example, if the plan restricts your choice of doctors to those within its provider network, its card won't work if you present it at a doctor's office outside that network — most likely leaving you responsible for the whole cost (except in cases of medical emergency). The exception is if you're enrolled in a Medicare Cost HMO. In this situation, you can use your Medicare card for services outside the plan's network regardless of medical urgency, as explained in Chapter 9. Otherwise, you can't use your regular Medicare ID card to obtain services when you're enrolled in a Medicare Advantage plan.

If your plan includes drug coverage, you may be able to use the same card when filling your prescriptions or be given a separate card to use at the pharmacy, depending on how your plan does things.

LAMINATING YOUR MEDICARE CARD

To laminate or not to laminate? Your Medicare card is printed on thick, nondescript paper that cries out for a touch of protective glossiness, but should you laminate it with a plastic coating? You'd be surprised at the strong opinions people hold on this topic. Some say the card should never be laminated because doing so prevents information embedded in the card from being scanned when presented at the doctor's office. Others shrug and say lamination has never caused a problem for them. So who's right?

Medicare officials say the cards are made out of a mix of paper and linen threads that give them extra strength but that no information is actually embedded in them. They say that some doctors' offices and hospitals put Medicare cards through drum scanners to take copies of them. Lamination doesn't prevent the scanners from reading cards, they add, but the process can damage the lamination.

Your stand-alone Part D prescription plan membership card

This card shows your name, your Member ID number, the plan's name, its identification number, and its customer service phone number. The card likely has wording that indicates you're entitled to Medicare prescription drug coverage. It may simply say PDP — initials that stand for prescription drug plan, the phrase Medicare uses for stand-alone plans.

Use this card to get your prescriptions filled under Part D if you receive your medical benefits from original Medicare or from a Medicare Advantage plan that doesn't cover drugs (Medicare Cost plans, some PFFS plans, and Medicare Medical Savings Accounts).

Your card works like a key. It enables the pharmacist to access the Part D computer system and determine what you should pay for your prescriptions, according to the plan you have and what level of coverage you're in — deductible, initial coverage, doughnut hole, or catastrophic coverage. (I explain these levels in more detail in Chapter 2.)

Your Medigap supplemental insurance card

This card shows your name and Medigap ID number, the name of the insurance company, its customer service phone number, and the type of Medigap policy you have, labeled with a letter of the alphabet — for example, "Medicare Supplement Plan F." (Chapter 4 explains the details of Medigap.)

Use this card to prove that you have separate insurance to help cover your co-pays for medical services when you're enrolled in original Medicare. Show it every time you receive services from a doctor, hospital, or other provider.

Replacing your cards

Cards don't just get lost or stolen; they may also become tattered and even difficult to read. Whatever the reason, you can easily get a replacement for your Medicare card by calling Medicare at 800-633-4227 (or TTY 877-486-2048) or online through your account at Medicare.gov. Your new card will take about 30 days to arrive in the mail. If you need a card sooner, you can print a copy from your online Medicare account.

If the card you need replaced comes from any of the private plans described earlier in this chapter — a Medicare Advantage plan, a stand-alone Part D plan, or a Medigap policy — you should contact the insurance company that issued it. If you lose a Medicaid card, contact your state Medicaid program. (For contact information, do a web search for "Medicaid" and the name of your state.) This range of providers is a good reason for writing down a list of any insurance plans you have, with contact information for each, and keeping it in a safe place.

Beyond the Cards: Checking Out the Extent and Limits of Your Coverage

When you enroll in original Medicare, you don't get much information about it sent to you along with your Medicare ID card. (The official handbook, "Medicare & You," is mailed out to beneficiaries each fall. You can read the current issue at any time online at www.medicare.gov/pubs/pdf/10050-Medicare-and-You.pdf.)

But if you join one of Medicare's private plans — a Medicare Advantage plan of any type, or a stand-alone Part D drug plan — you're essentially entering into a legal agreement with that plan. So sooner or later (either together with your plan membership card or separately), you'll receive a hefty information packet that should include the following documents:

>> **Evidence of coverage:** This booklet is important, so be sure to keep the information in a safe place. As required by Medicare law, it contains masses of stuff you can use for reference when you first join the plan and throughout the year. Here are some examples:

- **Phone numbers:** Call if you have any questions or problems.

- **An explanation of how the plan works and its conditions and rules:** This part lays out the plan's responsibilities in giving you coverage and the rules you must accept.

- **Details of the plan's benefits and costs:** This information spells out the plan's costs and benefits for this particular year, which may be different from those the same plan provided last year or will provide next year.

- **An explanation of your legal rights if you have a complaint against the plan or disagree with a decision it makes:** This section includes detailed instructions on how to file a complaint or make an appeal. (I cover the general process of doing both in Chapter 16.)

» **Drug coverage information:** If the plan in question is a stand-alone Part D drug plan or a Medicare Advantage plan that includes Part D drug coverage, the packet should include the following:

- **The plan's formulary:** A *formulary* is a list of all the medications the plan covers. It also shows which drugs come with restrictions such as prior authorization, quantity limits, and step therapy. (I explain these restrictions in Chapter 14.) It also says which pricing tier of co-pays each drug falls into, so you can tell what you'll pay.

- **The plan's pharmacy network:** This list shows all the pharmacies in your area that accept your plan's card. It also shows which ones are *preferred* pharmacies (where your drugs may cost less) or *specialty* pharmacies (which stock special drugs, such as those that are injected or require special handling). You can read more about pharmacy types later in this chapter.

» **Provider information:** If your plan is a Medicare managed care plan (HMO, PPO, Special Needs Plan, or Medicare Cost plan), the packet should include the following:

- **The plan's provider directory:** This item lists doctors, hospitals, and other facilities that are in the plan's network of providers and have agreed to treat its members.

- **The plan's service area:** This list indicates all the areas that your plan covers. It may be a collection of counties or zip codes or (in the case of regional PPOs) a state or group of states.

REMEMBER

Everything in your plan's info pack is critical, so keep it someplace where you can remember to find it in case you need to look up the fine print of the plan's rules sometime during the year. If any item listed here is missing (according to the type of plan it is), call the plan and ask for it.

Managing Premiums

Premiums, co-pays, deductibles — I explain how the routine costs of Medicare work in Chapter 3. But in the following sections, I focus on the basic mechanics of how you pay premiums (and what happens if you stop paying them), depending on your situation and the kind of Medicare coverage that you have.

Discovering different ways to pay Medicare premiums

You get a choice as to how to pay premiums in some situations but not in others. The methods in the first few sections relate to Part B (and maybe Part A) premiums if you're enrolled in original Medicare, followed by your choices if you're in a private Part D drug plan or Medicare Advantage plan.

TIP

A related topic that I explain in detail in Chapter 4 is worth repeating here in the context of paying premiums: If your income is under a certain level, you may qualify for

>> A Medicare Savings Program, under which your state would pay your Part B premiums (and sometimes Part A premiums if you need to pay them)

>> The Extra Help program that provides low-cost Part D prescription drug coverage, including waived or reduced drug plan premiums

Call Social Security at 800-772-1213 (TTY 800-325-0778) for information and/or to apply.

Having Part B premiums deducted from benefit checks

If you receive retirement benefits from Social Security, the Railroad Retirement Board (RRB), or the Civil Service, your Part B premiums are automatically deducted from your monthly payments before you receive them. You have no other option. The same automatic withholding occurs if you receive disability payments from Social Security or the RRB.

REMEMBER

Some people's Part B premiums are more than their retirement or disability payments. If that's your situation and you receive benefits from Social Security, your entire benefit is withheld, and you pay the balance directly to Medicare. But if your benefits come from the RRB or the Civil Service, your premium isn't deducted. Instead, Medicare sends you a bill.

Receiving a bill for Part A and Part B premiums

If you're not receiving retirement or disability payments, Medicare will send you a bill for Part B services. (That's provided that you're enrolled in Part B, of course. No enrollment means no bill!)

These bills are due quarterly in advance. But if you prefer not to pay three months' premiums at a time, you can call the Medicare help line at 800-633-4227 (TTY 877-486-2048) to request an arrangement to pay monthly. Note that this right is spelled out in section 40.7.3 of Chapter 2 of Medicare's "General Information, Eligibility, and Entitlement" manual. It says: "Premium bills are sent every three months unless the individual specifically requests a monthly bill."

If you don't qualify for premium-free Part A and need to pay premiums to receive Part A services, as I explain in Chapter 5, Medicare will also bill you for payment; however, you must make these payments monthly, not quarterly.

In both situations, you can choose to pay in one of five ways:

>> Mail a check or money order to the address printed on the bill.

>> Pay by credit card, using the bottom portion of the payment coupon sent with the bill.

>> Pay by an automatic transfer from your bank account. (You need to arrange this through your bank.)

>> Pay manually through your online account at Medicare.gov, via either bank transfer or credit card.

TIP

>> Sign up for *Medicare Easy Pay,* a system that allows premiums to be deducted from your checking or savings account each month. To arrange this free service, call Medicare at the number listed earlier or go to www.medicare. gov/basics/costs/pay-premiums/medicare-easy-pay to fill out an Authorization Agreement for Preauthorized Payments form (SF-5510).

Transitioning from direct billing to Social Security deductions

Many people these days enroll in Medicare long before they begin drawing Social Security retirement benefits. So the question arises: If you've been paying your Part B premiums directly to Medicare — which usually means quarterly in advance — how do you transition to having those premiums automatically deducted from your Social Security checks on a monthly basis? In particular, at the time of the changeover, how do you know that you won't be paying twice, by having Social Security deduct one or more premiums that you've already paid to Medicare?

For example, say that you're due to receive your first Social Security check in May, but have already paid premiums to Medicare for the months of May, June, and July. When will the automatic deductions from Social Security begin?

Many beneficiaries have asked me this question, which in turn I've sent to officials at Medicare and Social Security. But at the time of writing, there is no satisfactory answer. Social Security officials say that the agency works with Medicare to even things out and ensure that payments are not duplicated, but it may take a month or two for the adjustment to be made.

In trying to calculate what you've paid, it doesn't help that Medicare premium payments are always made in advance, whereas Social Security payments are always made one month in arrears. For example, the check you receive in May is actually your payment for April. Nor does it help that Medicare fails to provide statements showing your payment history or any means to check on what you paid when.

TIP

I suggest that in this situation, you look carefully at the Social Security amounts you receive over the period for which you've already paid premiums to Medicare. After a couple of months, if you think that you've paid twice, call Social Security at 800-772-1213 (TTY 800-325-0778) and ask for an explanation. Remember that by law you must be refunded anything you've overpaid.

Paying premiums in a Medicare drug or health plan

Part D prescription drug plans and Medicare Advantage plans vary in the options they offer for paying any premiums that the plans charge (in addition to the Part B premium). Depending on your circumstances and the rules of the plan you're enrolled in, you may be able to choose to pay these plan premiums in one of the following ways:

>> Arranging an automatic deduction from your monthly retirement or disability benefit payment (if you receive one)

>> Mailing a monthly check to the plan

>> Setting up an electronic transfer from a bank account

>> Paying by Medicare Easy Pay, a free service that automatically deducts your premiums from a checking or savings account each month, usually the 20th day of each month

>> Charging the payment to your credit card by mail, by phone, or online

When you first join a plan, you're asked to choose one of the plan's payment options. (But keep in mind that not all plans offer all the options noted here.) In most cases, you must stay with that method for the rest of the calendar year. If you need to change to another method or you have any other problems with payments, call the plan to discuss the situation.

If you join a Medicare drug or health plan, or switch to another, and choose to have the premiums deducted from your Social Security, railroad retirement, or Civil Service payments, be aware of the following situations that can arise:

>> **It may take two months or more for the deductions to begin.** This timeline means that you'll probably get a bill from the plan for those months and will need to pay the plan directly. The plan will tell you when the automatic deduction goes into effect.

>> **If you switch to a different plan, the deductions won't automatically continue.** When you join a different plan — for example, during open enrollment in the fall or if you move outside your current plan's service area — you need to make a new payment choice. If you again choose deductions from your benefits check, the delay described in the preceding bullet may happen again, and for a time the plan will send you a bill.

>> **If you have other insurance that pays part of your Part D drug plan premiums, Social Security still deducts the whole premium amount from your retirement or disability check.** Examples include insurance from an employer, union, or State Pharmacy Assistance Program (SPAP). In this situation, the plan, not Social Security, must refund the amount due to you. However, if you prefer to pay premiums to the plan directly instead of having them deducted, you'll be billed only for your share of the premium, and your other insurance will pay its share directly to the plan, too.

If you and your spouse are enrolled in the same private plan (a Part D drug plan or a Medicare Advantage plan) and choose to pay your monthly premiums by check, you may be naturally inclined to put both your payments on a single check. If you go that route, note on the check that the payment is to cover the premiums for both of you for this particular month; for example, write "April premiums for John and Mary Jones" in the memo field. Otherwise, write separate checks. These strategies help you avoid the possibility of one of you being mistakenly disenrolled for nonpayment. It's been known to happen.

Knowing what can happen when you don't pay your premiums on time

Yes, if you fail to pay your premiums, you risk losing coverage, but that can't happen instantly without warning. The following sections detail how much wiggle room you're given if you miss any payments and how you can catch up, depending on whether the problem has arisen in original Medicare or in a Part D or Medicare Advantage plan.

When you're in original Medicare

If you're billed for Part B premiums, either monthly or quarterly, here's what happens:

1. **The "First Bill" notice means either your last payment was received or it is an initial bill.**

2. **The "This Is Not a Bill" notice means that a payment will be deducted electronically through your bank account, usually on the 20th of the month, through Medicare Easy Pay.**

3. **If you don't pay the first bill, you're sent a letter marked "Second Bill," which means a payment is at least 60 days late.**

4. **If you don't pay after the second bill, you're sent a "Delinquent Bill," which means a payment is late by at least 90 days and you could lose your Medicare coverage.**

   This document provides the specific date when your Part B coverage will end if the overdue premiums aren't paid by the due date (the end of the grace period). This is your termination notice.

REMEMBER

   If you get into this situation, you should contact Social Security at 800-772-1213 (TTY 800-325-0778). If you can pay off all the premiums owed within 30 days of the termination notice, your Part B coverage will continue. Or, if you have good reason for getting behind, you may be able to set up a repayment plan.

5. **If you still don't pay, you'll receive a letter from Social Security informing you of the termination of Part B coverage.**

   It will be sent about 30 days after the end of the grace period — in other words, about four months after you received the first unpaid bill.

Note: If you pay Part B premiums directly on a monthly basis, the termination process is the same as if you pay quarterly — that is, the grace period for nonpayment is still 90 days. However, if payment is received within 30 days after termination, your coverage may be reinstated. Also, you can pay off the full amount owed at any time during that four-month period and prevent the termination process.

When you're enrolled in a Medicare drug or health plan

If you stop paying or get behind with the monthly premiums required by your Part D or Medicare Advantage plan, what happens next depends on your plan's policy. Under Medicare rules, the plan can choose to do any of the following:

>> Allow your coverage to continue (in other words, do nothing)

>> Disenroll you after giving you a grace period and notice

>> Send you a letter inviting you to contact the plan if you're having difficulty paying the premium

Your plan can't stop coverage without warning. It must first send proper notice of its intent to disenroll you and inform you of its grace period. The grace period may be one, two, or three months long, depending on the plan, and it begins on the first day of the month for which a premium has gone unpaid. (For example, if a premium is due in January, the grace period begins on February 1.) Plans also have two options on how to deal with disenrollment after a grace period ends:

>> **Single grace periods:** If one or more overdue premiums haven't been paid in full during the grace period, the plan can terminate coverage at the end of that period.

>> **Rollover grace periods:** These arrangements are more flexible options a plan can choose to provide. If more than one premium is owed but you pay off one premium during the grace period, this grace period stops and the plan sends notice of a new grace period. This process continues until either you pay off all the owed premiums in full or you fail to make any payment during a grace period, at which time the plan can disenroll you.

REMEMBER

Here are two situations in which you *can't* be disenrolled from your plan for not paying premiums, regardless of its policy:

>> **If you've asked for premiums to be paid out of your Social Security benefit payments:** The plan must work with Medicare to investigate why Social Security hasn't deducted the premiums or, if it has, why the plan hasn't received them. Whatever the reason, the plan can't disenroll you while you're considered to be in a state of *premium withhold* — that is, your premiums are being taken out of your Social Security check or you've asked for them to be deducted automatically in this way.

>> **If your full premium is paid by a State Pharmacy Assistance Program or another sponsor:** The plan must work with the SPAP or the sponsor (such as an employer or union that pays the plan's premiums for you) to receive the premiums.

REMEMBER

If these two circumstances don't apply to you but you still think you've been dropped from your plan unfairly or by mistake, call Medicare at 800-633-4227 (TTY 877-486-2048) and say you want to challenge the disenrollment. Medicare will investigate the situation. You should also call the plan and say that you want to remain enrolled. The plan must then tell you in writing that you should continue to use its services while your case is being investigated. If Medicare approves your challenge, your enrollment will be reinstated and backdated to the time you were dropped so that your coverage is unbroken. If you had to pay out-of-pocket for any services in the meantime, the plan must reimburse you.

The consequences of disenrollment

What happens if you're dropped from coverage? Can you get it back again? Yes, you can, but only at certain times. Here are the rules, depending on who cut you loose:

>> **Disenrolled from Part A and/or Part B:** You can re-enroll only during the general enrollment period, which runs from January 1 to March 31 each year. Coverage begins the month after enrollment. You may also get hit with permanent late penalties, as explained in Chapter 6.

>> **Dropped from a Part D drug plan:** You can sign up for Part D coverage again only during the fall open enrollment period, which runs from October 15 to December 7 each year. So you may go several months without coverage and incur a late penalty when you sign up again (see Chapter 6 for details). Your current plan has the right to take legal action to recover the premiums you haven't paid and/or the right not to re-enroll you until you've paid the money you owe.

>> **Cut from a Medicare Advantage plan:** Keep in mind that even if you're tossed out of your plan, you're still automatically covered for medical services under original Medicare — provided that you've kept up your regular Part B premiums. But you lose drug coverage if your MA plan included Part D services. You can enroll in a different MA plan — and pick up drug coverage again — only during the fall open enrollment (October 15 to December 7), unless you qualify for a special enrollment period, as explained in Chapter 15. Your current plan is entitled to take legal action to recover your unpaid premiums and can deny reinstatement in the same plan until you've repaid them.

Keeping Track of Your Expenses

Most people tend to be pretty slapdash about keeping records. But if you should keep one set of records safe, accessible, complete, and up-to-date, it's all the accumulated paper relating to your medical insurance. Doing so helps monitor your expenses. It also serves as protection in case you get into a dispute and need hard facts to argue your case.

In the following sections, I introduce you to the Medicare Summary Notice (MSN) — a detailed record of Part A or Part B services you've received, what they cost, and what you paid. How do you read those statements? What do they say about how much Medicare has spent on your care and how much you've paid? And what if you think they're wrong? I also share how to tidy up your medical records, including how to store them online.

Understanding Medicare Summary Notices

If you're enrolled in original Medicare, you'll receive one of these notices every three months — but only if you've had any medical services that Medicare has paid for in that period. If you want to see these notices instantly at any time, you can access them on the Medicare website, as I explain in the later section "Tracking information online."

A Medicare Summary Notice (MSN) is similar to the Explanation of Benefits statement you're familiar with if you've had health insurance in the past. It itemizes everything that's been billed to Medicare for medical services and supplies that you've received, what Medicare paid for them, and what you may still owe to the providers. The MSNs that show Part A and Part B services are different, as follows:

>> **Part A summary notice:** If you've been in a hospital, hospice, or skilled nursing facility (described in Chapter 3), this document shows how many days you've used in the benefit period, how much of the Part A deductible you've met, how much Medicare has paid, and how much you may be billed. (I explain benefit periods in Chapter 14 and the deductible in Chapter 3.) This notice also has a Part B section, which itemizes services that you received in the hospital or other facility but that are billed to Part B. Examples include doctors' services, units of blood, or maybe even a whole hospital stay if you've been placed in observation status rather than formally admitted to the hospital. (I discuss this latter situation in detail in Chapter 14.)

>> **Part B summary notice:** This statement itemizes any doctors' services, outpatient care such as screenings and lab tests, and medical equipment or supplies that you've received in the three-month period. It shows the names of the providers, how much they charged, the amount Medicare considers reasonable for each service (the "Medicare-approved" amount), how much Medicare actually paid, and how much (if anything) you still owe the providers. This notice also shows whether Medicare has denied payment for a claim and (if you have supplemental insurance, such as a Medigap policy) whether a claim has been forwarded to the other insurer for payment.

Medicare Summary Notices have been redesigned so they're much more consumer friendly than they used to be — easier to read with larger print, plainer language, better explanations, and clearer instructions on how to file an appeal. But here are some particular things worth knowing about MSNs:

>> **The MSN isn't a bill.** If it indicates that you owe money to a provider, you should wait to receive the provider's bill and pay it directly, if you haven't already done so.

>> **You should carefully compare the claim details on your MSN with the bills you receive from the providers.** Make sure that provider names, dates, billing codes, and descriptions match. That's quite easy in the case of the Part B MSN, where each service is itemized.

However, each service you receive in the hospital doesn't appear on the MSN for Part A. Medicare officials say the list is usually too long. (And if you've ever perused a hospital bill — with charges for every aspirin and even the paper that covers the operating table — you can see what they mean.) Sure, you'll receive an itemized bill from the hospital, but how can you tell whether Medicare has been billed correctly without an itemized MSN to compare it with? Medicare officials suggest that you can

- Create an online personal account at Medicare.gov (as explained in the later section "Tracking information online") and use the blue button icon to access a full itemized list of all your Part A or Part B claims.

- Call Medicare at 800-633-4227 (TTY 877-486-2048). A customer service rep can access your complete Part A claims record and tell you what you want to know or, on request, send you a printout.

>> **If you find a line item on your MSN that you don't remember receiving, first check with the provider.** If it's a mistake, ask for it to be corrected. If you see that Medicare has denied a claim you believe it should've covered, ask the provider to check the service identifier codes that were submitted to Medicare, in case the wrong one was sent.

If you suspect that a provider has filed incorrect — and potentially fraudulent — claims to Medicare, report it. The MSN encourages you to do so, even saying, "If we determine that your tip led to uncovering fraud, you may qualify for a reward." In fact, the reward may be as much as $1,000 — worth scrutinizing your MSNs for! (Which is the point. In 2021 alone, the Justice Department was able to recover over $5 billion thanks to fraud reporting.) Reporting a claim for a service or item you never received can also save you a lot of hassle. For example, if Medicare was fraudulently billed for a wheelchair in your name, later on it may deny your genuine claim for a wheelchair because, according to its records, you already have one. (For more info, see www.medicare.gov/fraud.)

WHERE HAVE ALL THE DOCTORS GONE?

It's a question heard more and more all across the United States as patients report increasing difficulty in finding a primary-care physician (PCP). No doubt about it: Over the past 20 years, the shortage of PCPs has become acute for many reasons.

I don't want to get too deeply into the weeds here, but I do want you to know something about why this drought is happening. One root cause, according to professional organizations such as the American College of Physicians, is that far fewer medical-school graduates become primary-care physicians nowadays. PCPs don't get paid as highly as specialists do, yet PCPs usually work much longer hours. In addition, PCPs' expenses as independent practitioners have ballooned because of the need to hire staff just to deal with the requirements of so many insurance companies, not to mention the increasing costs of malpractice insurance. For these same reasons, older, long-established PCPs are retiring early, further shrinking the supply.

The shortage is by no means confined to Medicare. But it's also true that, in recent years, the way Medicare paid doctors drove some out of the system and caused others to limit their caseload of Medicare patients.

>> **You have the right to file an appeal if Medicare denies a claim you believe was filed properly.** The MSN tells you how to go about it. (I also delve into appeals in Chapter 16.)

TIP

For more help in reading your MSN, you may want to check out the online MSN decoder tool devised by AARP; find it at www.aarp.org/health/medicare-qa-tool/medicare-summary-notice.

Note: If you're in a Medicare Advantage plan, you won't receive an MSN. Instead, you'll get Explanation of Benefits statements that also itemize the services and supplies you've received from the plan. If you have Part D drug coverage, your plan will send statements that show not only the drugs you've used and their costs but also how near you are to meeting the deductible (if the plan charges one) or falling into the doughnut hole, as explained in Chapter 2.

Maintaining hard-copy records you can rely on

TIP

If you hit a pothole cruising down the Medicare highway, you don't want to have to scramble for your paperwork only to find that it's missing. Here are some suggestions for keeping records in such a way that you can actually lay hands on them when you need them:

>> **Keep records for each type of health coverage you have in a separate file.** Label each folder with the name of the plan and the type of insurance.

>> **Remember that your evidence of coverage (EOC) booklet is an important document that contains details of your coverage and your legal rights.** If you have more than one plan, file each EOC and other documents in the appropriate folder for each plan. (I describe this booklet in the earlier section "Beyond the Cards: Checking Out the Extent and Limits of Your Coverage.")

>> **Track your expenses and level of coverage.** If you're in original Medicare, carefully file your MSNs in date order. If you're in a Medicare Advantage plan or a Part D drug plan, do the same with your Explanation of Benefits statements.

>> **File notes of any interaction with Medicare or your plan — including phone conversations — in the appropriate folder.** These recaps will help your case in the event that you need to file an appeal.

Tracking information online

Here are two ways to keep track of your Medicare info online and access it any time, any day of the year, depending on your type of coverage:

>> **Original Medicare:** Go to www.medicare.gov/account/login to create your own free, secure personal account, which you can use to do the following:

- Track your health claims in original Medicare.

- See the status of your Part A and Part B deductibles.

- Order a new Medicare card or a copy of a Medicare Summary Notice.

- Review which preventive tests and screenings you're entitled to.

- Keep a list of your medications.

>> **Medicare Advantage and Part D plans:** Many plans offer personal health records (PHRs) to their members for free. Some are true electronic health records, giving you access to the results of past medical tests, alerts for when future checkups are due, email contacts with your doctors, and online scheduling of appointments. Other PHRs essentially give you an online space for storing whatever medical information you want to download, such as your medications list. Call your plan or visit its website to see whether it offers a PHR.

Dealing with Doctors

Doctors, of course, are the cornerstones of your healthcare. So when you transition to Medicare, your main concern is whether your current doctors will continue to accept you as their patient and, if not, how you can find doctors who will. In this section, I consider that question and explain the rules on how much doctors can charge you for Medicare services. *Note:* This information applies only if you're enrolled in the original Medicare program. Medicare Advantage plans work differently, as explained in Chapter 9.

Finding doctors who accept Medicare patients

The great majority of primary-care doctors — 98 percent — still do participate in the Medicare program, with slightly fewer — 83 percent — saying that they are accepting new Medicare patients, according to a 2022 report from the Kaiser Family Foundation. So it's likely that your current doctor will continue to accept you as a patient when you start on Medicare. But if not, these are options to explore:

- » **Use the doctor directory on Medicare's website.** Go to www.medicare.gov and click on "Find care providers" on the home page. This links you to a page where you can enter your location (zip code or city and state) and search by name, specialty, group, body part, or condition. Or you can browse by specialty A-Z. You'll need to call the offices of the doctors shown to see whether they're accepting new Medicare patients.

- » **Contact your state medical association.** These physician groups often keep lists of doctors who are accepting new patients. Do an internet search for "[your state name] medical association."

- » **Consider using a nurse practitioner for your primary care.** Nurse practitioners (NPs) are qualified to perform many duties that physicians perform, including diagnosis and treatment, writing prescriptions, and referring patients to specialists and labs. To find licensed NPs in your area, go to the website of the American Association of Nurse Practitioners at npfinder.aanp.org.

- » **Get medical treatment from a community clinic, which is often called an** *urgent care* **or** *walk-in* **medical center.** You may have to wait a while to see a doctor, but these clinics give good care and usually accept Medicare. To find one in your area, search the internet for the clinic terms mentioned here.

Understanding what doctors can charge you

When you're enrolled in original Medicare and need to see any doctors for the first time, always ask their offices — when you call to make an appointment — whether they accept Medicare patients and, if so, whether they accept assignment. That's because their answers to these questions really affect how much you pay:

>> **Assignment:** A doctor who accepts *assignment* is agreeing to charge you no more than the amount that Medicare has approved for a particular service. (You're basically *assigning* Medicare to pay the doctor for your care.) In this situation, Medicare pays 80 percent of the approved amount, and you're responsible for the remaining 20 percent, unless you have supplemental insurance that pays your share.

>> **No assignment:** A doctor who accepts Medicare patients but *not* assignment can charge you up to 15 percent more than Medicare pays for the service you receive. You're responsible for the extra amount *(balance billing)* unless you have a Medigap policy or other insurance that covers these excess charges.

>> **Opted out:** A doctor who has *opted out* of Medicare can't bill Medicare for services you receive and isn't bound by Medicare's limitations on charges. You enter into a private contract with the doctor, agreeing to pay their bills directly and in full. You can't claim reimbursement from Medicare under this arrangement.

Figure 13-1 shows the very different amounts you can pay under each of these scenarios — in this example, $20, as much as $35, or $120 for a doctor visit. They show why determining what, if any, kind of arrangement the doctor has with Medicare in advance of being treated is a wise move. (Note that these scenarios apply only in original Medicare. If you're enrolled in a Medicare Advantage plan such as an HMO or PPO, your share of the cost is the co-pay amount that your plan charges in any particular year. I consider these options in detail in Chapter 3.)

Note: The regulations on assignment and opt-out apply not only to doctors but also to other types of Medicare providers, such as therapists and medical equipment suppliers. Whichever providers you see, finding out in advance whether they participate in Medicare is time well spent.

The following sections consider in more depth the question of how you're affected financially if you go to a doctor who's opted out of Medicare or who wants to charge a special fee for "boutique" services.

	Doctor Accepts Assignment	Doctor Doesn't Accept Assignment	Doctor Has Opted Out of Medicare
Doctor's bill	$120	$120	$120
Medicare-approved amount	$100	$100	Not applicable
Medicare pays	$80 (80% of Medicare-approved amount)	$80 (80% of Medicare-approved amount)	$0
You pay	$20 (20% of Medicare-approved amount)	$20 (20% of Medicare-approved amount) + up to $15 (15% of Medicare-approved amount)	$120
You pay in total	**$20**	**Up to $35**	**$120**

FIGURE 13-1:
Sample costs based on a doctor's Medicare acceptance.

Doctors who opt out of Medicare

WARNING

Doctors who opt out of Medicare must stay out of the program for at least two years. They offer what is known as *direct billing,* and very often they don't accept any kind of insurance. In this situation, the doctor should ask you to read and sign a document that is really a contract. In signing it, you're legally agreeing to be responsible for the whole bill, with no reimbursement from Medicare. And because Medicare doesn't cover treatment from an opted-out doctor, your Medigap insurance (if you have some) won't cover it either.

Keep in mind, though, that such a contract is with one individual doctor or doctor's practice. If you go see other doctors who do accept Medicare, their services will be covered in the usual way, and a Medigap policy, if you have one, will cover your out-of-pocket costs.

Doctors who provide concierge or boutique services

Concierge and *boutique* are fancy names for services provided by primary-care doctors who accept you as a patient (or continue to treat you) only if you agree to pay them a special fee. Patients who pay it are promised a higher level of service — for example, same-day appointments, longer visits, and more personal attention. The fee (sometimes called a *retainer* or *membership dues*) varies widely among different doctors but reportedly averages around $200 a month. Whether you think this type of arrangement is worth the money is of course a matter of personal opinion and finances. But here I want to consider concierge medicine just in relation to Medicare.

You may think that primary-care doctors who offer concierge services are just those who've opted out of Medicare. Some are in that category — they're the ones that offer the direct billing described in the preceding section.

But some doctors who offer concierge care also accept Medicare patients, as long as those patients pay the extra fees. Medicare doesn't prohibit this practice. But Medicare officials warn that such doctors aren't allowed to charge fees for any services that are already covered by Medicare, or to waive the Medicare deductibles and co-pays that normally apply. Medicare's Inspector General's office has prosecuted and fined some doctors for violating these rules.

WARNING

So before signing a contract for concierge services, look carefully at the fine print to see what is promised in return for the fee. For example, "a full physical every year" (which Medicare doesn't cover) is okay, but a "yearly overall health assessment" (if it's no more than what Medicare covers under its annual wellness benefit) isn't. This issue has many gray areas, and only a physician (not you) can run afoul of the law. But only you, over the course of a year, can decide whether you're getting your money's worth from such a contract.

Filling Prescriptions for the First Time with a Part D Plan

When you're a newbie to Part D and need your first prescription filled, I bet you're wondering, "How easily will I get my drugs under this new coverage?" Well, the process may all go perfectly smoothly. Then again, it may not, so this section anticipates the questions you may have and explains what's going on — and what you can do about any bumps you meet in the road.

When does my coverage begin?

Your Part D drug coverage doesn't start until the date it becomes *effective,* meaning the very first day you can fill a prescription under your Part D plan, even if you receive your membership card in the mail before then. In most situations, you don't have to wait long. Coverage begins on the first day of the month after you sign up with a Part D plan during your initial enrollment period or during any special enrollment period that I describe in Chapter 6.

The only variation here is if you enroll in a Part D plan during open enrollment (October 15 to December 7) — either because you failed to enroll in a plan when you should've, as explained in Chapter 6, or because you're already in a plan but want to change to another for the following year, as explained in Chapter 15. In either case, your coverage begins January 1.

But what if the time you'd normally sign up with a Part D plan happens to overlap the open enrollment period? For example, say your 65th birthday falls in December and you want drug coverage to begin December 1, along with your Part A and Part B coverage. You'd need to sign up with a plan during November — bang in the middle of open enrollment. The information you provide on the sign-up form should alert the plan to the fact that this time frame is your initial enrollment period, so your coverage should begin December 1, not January 1. But you may have to call the plan to make sure coverage will begin on the right day; open enrollment is an exceptionally busy time for the plans, and you don't want your coverage delayed in the tumult.

Which kind of pharmacy can I use?

This section explains the choices that Part D plans offer for filling prescriptions: getting your drugs at a retail pharmacy, by mail order (if your plan offers that option), at a specialty pharmacy that stocks and handles certain types of drugs, or at a long-term-care pharmacy that caters to people living in nursing homes and other institutional facilities.

Of course, you don't have to choose just one pharmacy or pharmacy type and stick with it. If you want to use mail order for some prescriptions (such as 90-day supplies of drugs you take regularly) and a retail pharmacy for prescriptions of 30 days or less, that's your call.

You can find out which in-network pharmacies your plan uses — and any that it designates as *preferred pharmacies,* where you may pay a lower co-pay for your prescriptions — on Medicare's Plan Finder (as explained in Chapters 10 and 11) or in the plan's information materials (described in the earlier section "Beyond the Cards: Checking Out the Extent and Limits of Your Coverage").

Retail pharmacies

By *retail pharmacy,* I mean a bricks-and-mortar pharmacy that you walk into (as opposed to the mail-order pharmacies that you visit only on the end of a phone or online). Part D plans use a variety of retail pharmacies: large chains, dispensing facilities in supermarkets, and small independent pharmacies.

Every Part D plan has its own *network* of retail pharmacies — those that accept the plan's card. And every plan must ensure that at least one in-network pharmacy is within a reasonable distance of enrollees' homes. What's a reasonable distance? That depends on where you live:

>> In an urban area, you're likely to have dozens of in-network retail pharmacies to choose from — many within half a mile or so, and some within walking distance.

>> In a very rural area, getting to the nearest in-network retail pharmacy may mean driving 20 miles or more. If only one pharmacy is within that sort of distance, all the Part D plans in the area are likely to include it in their networks.

Mail-order pharmacies

Most plans offer a mail-order service for filling prescriptions, though not all do. Using this option can be convenient and may save money. But when deciding about mail order, consider the following:

>> You can purchase 90-day supplies only, so mail order is best used for medicines you take regularly over a long period of time.

>> Your drugs are mailed directly to your home, which may be convenient, especially if you're homebound or live miles from the nearest retail pharmacy in your plan's network. Shipping is free.

>> Many plans (though not all) offer discounts for mail order. If so, your costs may be lower than at a retail pharmacy.

>> Because you pay for a three-month supply in advance, you pay more upfront than if you buy a 30-day supply each month. In certain circumstances, you may fall into the doughnut hole earlier as a result.

>> You have to remember to phone in your next prescription or reorder online and allow time for delivery (usually seven to ten days) to ensure you don't run out of your meds before the new ones arrive.

To find out how to use your plan's mail-order service, check out the plan's info packet, go to its website, or call its customer service number. Regardless, you'll probably need to fill out a form to request this service.

Specialty pharmacies

Certain drugs — such as some drugs used for cancer, transplant rejection, multiple sclerosis, and other treatments — must be handled extra carefully when they're being dispensed. If you take one of these types of drugs, you need to purchase it at a specialty pharmacy that's equipped to handle it. (The Food and Drug Administration allows some of these drugs to be distributed only to specialty pharmacies.)

The *specialty* label may be applied to a regular pharmacy that meets the conditions for dispensing these drugs, to a hospital pharmacy department, or to a doctor's office. Your plan's pharmacy list should indicate which specialty pharmacies are in-network.

If no in-network specialty pharmacy is in your area, you can go out of network, but call your plan first for guidance. Some Part D plans don't offer mail-order service for these kinds of drugs.

Long-term-care pharmacies

Nursing homes use special *long-term-care (LTC) pharmacies* that dispense prescriptions in special packaging — the drugs come in single, individually sealed doses rather than the usual containers. This system is for hygiene and safety reasons in a setting where nurses administer many different drugs to many patients. LTC pharmacies may be large companies that supply only nursing homes and other LTC facilities or be local retail pharmacies that can supply properly sealed medicines.

All Part D plans must include LTC pharmacies in their networks. If the ones your nursing home uses aren't in your plan's network, Medicare expects the plan to contract with those pharmacies so that you don't need to change to another plan.

REMEMBER

However, when you enter a nursing home, you (or your caregiver) should check whether its LTC pharmacy is in your Part D plan's network. If it isn't, call the plan to see whether it will cover drugs supplied by the home's LTC pharmacy. Or consider switching to another plan that does have this pharmacy in its network. Keep in mind that you have two important rights when you go into a nursing home:

>> You can switch to a different Part D plan immediately (without waiting for an open enrollment period).

>> Your current Part D plan must cover all the drugs you're taking when you first enter the nursing home for at least 90 days, even if the LTC pharmacy the home uses doesn't cover some of them. This three-month period allows you time to switch to another plan if you need to.

What happens if I go to an out-of-network pharmacy?

WARNING

Except in emergencies, you should always fill prescriptions at one of your plan's in-network pharmacies. Otherwise, you encounter the following consequences:

>> **You pay a lot more for your drugs.** In most cases, you pay the full price. Sending the receipts to your plan won't work. The plan won't pay.

>> **These payments don't count toward your out-of-pocket limit.** If you fall into the doughnut hole, your plan disregards payments for drugs bought outside its pharmacy network when calculating the expense limit that gets

you out of the coverage gap and into catastrophic coverage. Remember the donut hole closes in 2025, and your covered drug costs are capped at $2,000. (See Chapters 3 and 14 for details of this limit.)

However, situations may arise when you need to have a prescription filled outside your plan's pharmacy network. Medicare expects all Part D plans to guarantee coverage at out-of-network pharmacies in any of the following circumstances, providing that the plan covers the drugs in question and the request is reasonable:

>> If you're traveling outside your plan's service area within the United States (and maybe abroad, if your plan allows this exception for emergencies) and you run out of your meds, lose them, or become ill and need drugs for treatment

>> If you need to fill a prescription quickly outside business hours but can't find a 24/7 network pharmacy within a reasonable driving distance

>> If you need to start taking a specialty drug quickly and don't have access to in-network pharmacies that stock it

>> If you're undergoing emergency or urgent treatment in a hospital, clinic, or outpatient facility and receive Part D–covered drugs from the facility's pharmacy, which isn't in your plan's network

>> If you have to leave your home area after a local calamity that's been declared a state or federal disaster or a public health emergency

The process for claiming these exceptions is to pay full cost at the pharmacy and later send the receipts to the plan, asking for the appropriate refund. If you can't afford the full cost, call the plan and request assistance. If the plan rejects your claim, you can file a complaint and appeal the decision, as explained in Chapter 16.

Note, however, that a plan is allowed to charge you more for going out-of-network, even in these circumstances; whether it actually does depends on the plan's policy. (If you do have to pay more, though, the extra counts toward your out-of-pocket limit.) However, if you receive Extra Help (see Chapter 4), you can't be charged more than you would be at an in-network pharmacy.

How do I prove I have Part D coverage?

When a plan accepts your enrollment, your name and your information are uploaded into the pharmacy computer system. So normally, you don't have to prove anything: Just go to the pharmacy with your prescription (or have your doctor call it in), show your plan membership card, and pay whatever's due. But when you head to the pharmacy for the first time under a new Part D plan, the pharmacist needs to verify your coverage. That's likely to be a straightforward process, too. But what if you haven't yet received your card or your enrollment information isn't yet in the computer system? The following tips help avoid or minimize delays:

>> **Pick the right pharmacy.** Make sure that the pharmacy you go to is in your plan's network. You can find out which local pharmacies are in-network and which, if any, are preferred pharmacies by using the Plan Finder program on Medicare's website (as explained in Chapters 10 and 11), looking at your plan's information packet (if you've received it), or calling the plan. Or you can call ahead to a pharmacy to make sure it's in your plan's network.

>> **Have the pharmacist call the plan to confirm that you're enrolled if you haven't gotten your membership card.** You can help by providing the pharmacist with as many of the following as possible:

- The plan's name

- A letter from the plan confirming your enrollment

- A letter from the plan acknowledging your enrollment request (or a copy of your enrollment request if the plan hasn't sent acknowledgment or confirmation)

- A photo ID

>> **Bring your Extra Help documentation if you qualify because of limited income.** Your plan's membership card should be enough to confirm your eligibility for low-cost Part D drug coverage under the Extra Help program, which I explain in Chapter 4. But if you haven't yet received the card, bring one of these items with you:

- Your Extra Help confirmation letter from Social Security or Medicare, or any recent letter you've had from either agency

- A copy of your Extra Help application if you filled one out

- Your Medicaid card if you're receiving benefits from your state medical assistance program

- Any documents or recent letters confirming that you receive Supplemental Security Income (SSI) or have your Medicare premiums paid by your state

How can I ensure I get my meds?

What if your pharmacist can't confirm your plan membership, says that your plan doesn't cover one of your drugs, or indicates that you need to get permission from the plan before it will cover a drug? What if they ask you to pay more for your drugs than you think you should? Or say that your doctor isn't allowed to pre-scribe drugs for Part D? Any of these what-ifs can happen. Yet Medicare's message to people in Part D plans is plain: "Don't leave the pharmacy without your medicines." What it means by this advice is that the system has certain built-in mechanisms that ensure you get your drugs — if you know how to use these rules. I tackle them in the following sections.

If the pharmacist can't confirm your enrollment in a plan

Getting details of new enrollees into the computer system takes time — especially in early January, when many people have just switched plans. If you have no proof of coverage and the pharmacist can't verify your enrollment by calling the plan, here are your options:

WARNING

>> **Pay for your drugs (at full price), keep the receipts, and send copies to the plan.** The plan then refunds you any money that's due. However, if your enrollment is denied, the plan won't cover these bills.

Can your enrollment in a Part D plan be denied? Yes, in certain specific circumstances: Your enrollment period has expired, you don't live in the plan's service area, your eligibility for Medicare can't be confirmed in the official records, and so on. So if the pharmacist tells you the system has no record of your enrollment, you need to contact the plan to find out why.

>> **If you can't afford the prescriptions, ask the pharmacist to call Medicare's dedicated pharmacy hot line, which is used for dealing with this situation.**

If the pharmacist says the plan won't pay for one of your meds

The pharmacist will probably tell you if your plan doesn't cover a drug you've been prescribed or if the med comes with restrictions requiring the plan's consent before you can get it. (I explain these restrictions in Chapter 14.) In any event, call the plan to find out what you need to do.

TIP

If you're newly enrolled in the plan and you've already been taking this drug, you have the legal right to a 30-day supply so that your treatment isn't interrupted. Ask the pharmacist to fill the prescription under your plan's *transition* or *first-fill* policy. If they're reluctant to do so, ask them to contact your plan for approval. (This 30-day rule also applies if you've been in a Part D plan but have just switched to another.) But note that this work-around is only a temporary solution. You must take immediate steps to change to a drug your plan does cover or work with your doctor to get the restriction lifted, as explained in Chapter 14.

If the pharmacist charges you more than you think is correct

The most-common explanations for being asked to pay more than you think you should at the pharmacy are these:

- **Your plan has a deductible.** In this case, you must pay the full cost of your drugs until you've met the amount of the deductible — either at the beginning of the year or partway through the year if that's when you first join a plan. People don't always realize their plan has a deductible — especially if it didn't charge one the previous year but does now. Plans make this decision each year, as I explain in Chapter 3.

- **Your plan has changed its co-pay for your drug.** Plans can make these changes every calendar year too, as I explain in Chapter 15.

- **The pharmacy isn't in your plan's network.** In this case, as I show earlier in this chapter, you're probably required to pay full price.

- **You qualify for Extra Help, but the pharmacist can't confirm it immediately through the system.** If you have Medicaid coverage, show your card. If you're receiving Supplemental Security Income (SSI) or your state pays your Medicare premium, tell the pharmacist; in all these situations, you automatically qualify for Extra Help. If you applied for Extra Help, bring the letter from Social Security that says you qualify. Either way, you should be charged only small co-pays for your drugs, as I explain in Chapter 4.

- **You've applied for Extra Help but haven't yet heard whether you qualify.** In this situation, you have two options:

  - **Pay the plan's normal co-pays and keep your receipts.** After Social Security has confirmed your eligibility, the plan must refund you the difference between what you paid and what you would've paid under Extra Help — dating back to the time you applied for it.

  - **If you can't afford to pay the usual co-pays upfront, tell the pharmacist, who has the discretion to help you under Medicare rules.** At the very least, if you have less than a three-day supply of your meds left, the pharmacist must allow you an emergency supply. Don't be too shy or proud to ask, and — just like the Medicare honchos say — don't leave the pharmacy without your meds.

If the pharmacist says your doctor isn't an approved Medicare prescriber

In 2019, Medicare began requiring all doctors who write prescriptions to be either formally enrolled in Medicare or formally opted out — otherwise, your Part D drug plan may not provide coverage. This new rule is part of an effort to prevent fraud and illegal prescribing. I explain your rights in this situation in Chapter 14.

Chapter **14**

Getting the Inside Scoop on Using Certain Medicare Benefits

O ver the years, out of thousands of people who've sent me questions about Medicare, the folks I remember best are the ones who stumped me. They not only asked tough questions but also drew my attention to situations I never knew existed. So then, of course, I scrambled to explore those situations and obtain the answers from legal experts in government agencies, mainly Medicare and Social Security. If that experience was like pulling teeth on occasion, it most often resulted in lighting up some obscure regulations and allowed me to pass along information on these issues to a wider audience. For me, it was a form of higher education, and I'm indebted to the readers who triggered it.

Some of those answers are elsewhere in this book. In this chapter, I examine some of the other finer points of Medicare coverage that aren't always properly explained in the official guides. You may never encounter any of these issues. But if you do, I hope the information in these pages empowers you to get the most out of your coverage and avoid the occasional traps that lurk in the undergrowth of Medicare regulations.

Taking a Closer Look at Part A

I explain aspects of Part A, which primarily helps pay for different types of short-term nursing care, in several other chapters — including what it covers (Chapters 1 and 2), what it costs (Chapter 3), who is eligible (Chapter 5), and when and how to sign up (Chapters 6 and 7). This section looks more closely at Part A services. It explains how hospital benefit periods work and considers certain practices in hospitals and skilled nursing facilities (SNFs) that you may never have heard of but need to know how to deal with if you happen to run into them.

Understanding hospital benefit periods

A *hospital benefit period* is one of those pieces in the Medicare jigsaw puzzle that people find especially difficult to understand. And that's not in the least surprising. Wouldn't you think that a benefit period is simply a length of time during which Medicare will cover your care after you're admitted to the hospital? But no, it doesn't work like that.

Medicare officials explain that a benefit period begins on the day you're admitted and ends when you've been out of the hospital for 60 days in a row. If you leave the hospital on a certain date (for example, May 5) but are readmitted within 60 days of that date (say, June 23), you're still within the same benefit period. But if you go back into the hospital more than 60 days from the time you left (say, July 17), you're then in a new benefit period. The difference between the two has an impact on your costs — perhaps to the tune of hundreds of dollars.

This issue is made more complicated by the fact that any time you spend in a skilled nursing facility (where you may go for continuing care after being discharged from the hospital) also counts toward a benefit period but has different rules and out-of-pocket costs. And — wouldn't you just know — expenses in benefit periods are likely to be different depending on whether you're enrolled in original Medicare or a Medicare Advantage (MA) plan.

In the following sections, I tease apart these different strands to make more sense of benefit periods as they apply either in hospitals or in skilled nursing facilities, in the original program or an MA plan.

Hospital coverage in original Medicare

REMEMBER

Here's what you pay and what Medicare pays for hospital care in each separate benefit period:

>> **Days 1 through 60:** You're responsible for the first chunk of costs until you've met the Part A hospital deductible (a maximum $1,632 in 2024). After

that, you pay nothing further for hospital care (bed, meals, and nursing services) during the same benefit period. (However, you still need to pay Part B co-pays for doctors' services while you're in the hospital; I discuss Part B in more detail later in this chapter.)

» **Days 61 through 90:** You pay a daily co-pay ($408 in 2024), regardless of whether you've stayed more than 60 consecutive days in the hospital or have been readmitted during the same benefit period.

» **Beyond 90 days:** You're responsible for 100 percent of the costs — but you can draw on up to 60 *lifetime reserve days* for a hefty daily co-pay ($816 in 2024), as I explain in Chapter 3.

Medicare places no limit on how many benefit periods you can have. But after you've been out of the hospital for 60 days, you enter a new benefit period. So if you go back into the hospital then, you must meet a new Part A deductible (another $1,632 in 2024) before coverage kicks in again.

TIP

All Medigap policies provide extra coverage for hospital stays beyond 60 days, and several cover the whole Part A deductible. (You can see which policies cover these benefits in Chapter 4.)

Perhaps one source of confusion over benefit periods is that three of the rules involve a time frame of 60 days, yet each has a different meaning. So to be clear, here's a quick primer:

» **60 days** = the number of days you must have been out of the hospital or skilled nursing facility to qualify for a new benefit period

» **60 days** = the maximum length of time that Medicare will cover 100 percent of your care in a hospital after you've met the deductible for each benefit period

» **60 days** = the maximum number of lifetime reserve days that you can draw on to extend Medicare coverage for hospital care during one or more benefit periods

Skilled nursing care in original Medicare

The time spent in both the hospital and the SNF count toward a benefit period. And you must stay out of both for 60 days to qualify for a new benefit period.

But your share of the costs in an SNF is different from those listed in the preceding section for hospitals. In an SNF, in any one benefit period, you pay the following:

» **Days 1 through 20:** Nothing for bed, meals, and nursing care

» **Days 21 through 100:** A daily co-pay ($204 a day in 2024)

» **Beyond 100 days:** All costs

You can't use any hospital lifetime reserve days to extend Medicare coverage in an SNF beyond 100 days in any one benefit period. However, you may get more coverage if you have a Medigap policy, long-term-care insurance, Medicaid coverage, or insurance from an employer or union. If you have one of these, check with your plan to see what SNF charges are covered.

Hospital and SNF coverage in Medicare Advantage plans

Medicare Advantage plans (such as HMOs and PPOs, which I explain in Chapters 9 and 11) also use Medicare benefit periods. But their charges for hospital and skilled nursing care vary widely from plan to plan, and they may also be very different from those in original Medicare.

Typically, Medicare Advantage plans don't charge the Part A deductible for each benefit period. Most often, they charge a flat-dollar daily co-pay for the first several days (which can vary from $100 to over $500 a day) and nothing after that for the remainder of the benefit period. Also, Medicare Advantage plans may have different rules from those in the original program. If you're in one of these plans, check your coverage documents or call the plan to be sure of its rules and what a hospital or SNF stay would cost.

Taking note of the three-day rule

If you're in the original Medicare program, you must spend at least three days in the hospital as an officially admitted patient before Medicare will cover your stay in an approved SNF. This type of facility (most often a nursing home) is where you may go for further care needed after being discharged from the hospital, such as intravenous injections or physical therapy.

The three days must be consecutive. They include the day you're admitted but not the day you're discharged because one "day" counts only if you're in the hospital at midnight. Nor do they include any time you spend in the emergency room. Also — and this point is super-important — you must be an official inpatient during those three days instead of just being held in observation status, which I explain in the following section.

If you haven't met the three-day inpatient requirement, the SNF staff should tell you that Medicare won't cover your stay there. You'll be given an Advance Beneficiary Notice of Non-Coverage (ABN), which you must sign to say you understand you're responsible for all costs if you do stay. (I discuss ABNs in the later section "Receiving a notice saying that Medicare may not pay.")

However, if the SNF fails to give you this warning, and you stay for treatment in the SNF despite not having met the three-day rule, the facility can't bill Medicare — or you — for your stay.

REMEMBER

Note two important exceptions to the three-day rule:

>> It's not usually applied to people enrolled in Medicare Advantage plans.

>> It affects only coverage in a skilled nursing facility. If you're discharged from the hospital to another kind of facility for specific ongoing care, such as a rehabilitation hospital, Medicare provides coverage under different rules.

Defining observation status

When you're in the hospital — lying in a hospital bed, wearing a hospital gown, with a hospital ID bracelet on your wrist, eating hospital food, and getting nursing care — you may be forgiven for assuming that you're a formally admitted inpatient! But in reality, you may not have been admitted at all. You may have been placed in *observation status* instead. This designation means that

>> You're officially classified as an outpatient.

>> Your doctor hasn't written an order for you to be admitted as an inpatient.

>> Hospital doctors are still "observing" your condition in order to decide whether you should be admitted or discharged.

The following sections explain the effects of being in this status and what you can do to avoid big billing charges.

Understanding the consequences of being in observation status

REMEMBER

For many patients in original Medicare, the distinction between inpatient status and observation (outpatient) status is critically important — maybe even to the extent of costing several thousand dollars — for three reasons:

>> **The cost of your hospital stay as an outpatient will be paid under Part B, not Part A.** Therefore, you won't be responsible for the standard Part A hospital deductible ($1,632 in 2024). But under Part B, each service you receive requires a 20 percent co-pay. And although the amount you pay for a single service can't exceed the amount of the Part A deductible, several different services may add up to more than that. Also, if you are not enrolled in Part B, you would be responsible for the whole hospital bill out of your own pocket.

>> **Most hospitals don't allow patients to use their own prescription medicines but provide the drugs and charge full price for them on the hospital bill.** If you have Part D or other drug coverage, you must pay the hospital upfront and then see whether your drug plan will refund the cost.

>> **Medicare rules require you to stay in the hospital for three whole days as a formally admitted inpatient before Medicare will cover any continuing care you need in a skilled nursing facility.** I explain this concept in the earlier section "Taking note of the three-day rule." If you're in observation status for all or part of the three days, Medicare won't pay anything toward your stay in an SNF. (But if you're enrolled in a Medicare Advantage plan, it may not apply the three-day rule; check with the plan.)

Under Medicare regulations, hospitals are supposed to decide whether to admit or discharge patients within 24 hours and should keep them under observation for no more than 48 hours except in "rare and exceptional cases." But in recent years, hospitals have kept many patients in observation limbo for far longer periods — 72 hours is common, and even 14 days isn't unheard of. Medicare now requires all hospitals to issue notices to people who are being kept in observation to tell them that they are not admitted inpatients. These Medicare Outpatient Observation Notices (known as MOONs) should be issued to patients after they've been in observation status for at least 24 hours and within 36 hours of entering the hospital.

Protecting yourself against big bills

Here's what you can do to try to avoid the charges that may come as a result of being placed in observation status if you (or someone you're looking out for) go into the hospital:

>> **Inquire about your status each day you're in the hospital.** It can be changed (from inpatient to observation or vice versa) at any time. The MOON notice that the hospital is required to give you within 36 hours of entering the hospital should confirm your status, as explained in the preceding section. It should also provide a clinical rationale for your being kept in observation, though the stated reason may be very general — for example, "Patient's condition needs monitoring" — rather than specific to your own case. If you don't receive this notice, ask for it.

>> **Ask your own doctor whether observation status is justified.** If it isn't, ask the doctor to call the hospital to explain the medical reasons why you should be admitted as an inpatient. (Many doctors aren't aware of the financial implications of observation for Medicare patients.)

>> **Request that the hospital doctor reconsider your case or refer it to the hospital committee that decides status.**

>> **Examine other continuing care options.** If you need rehab or other kinds of continuing care after you're discharged from the hospital but discover that Medicare won't cover your stay in a skilled nursing facility because you were in observation status, ask your doctor whether you qualify for similar care at home through Medicare's home health benefit or Medicare-covered care in a rehabilitation hospital.

>> **If you go to a skilled nursing facility and have to pay for it yourself, you can try appealing Medicare's decision.** When you receive your Medicare Summary Notice (see Chapter 13), make a copy and highlight the SNF's charge. Send this copy to the address provided on the notice with a letter saying you want to appeal Medicare's decision of non-coverage, on the basis that you should've been classified as an inpatient during your hospital stay and not placed under observation. If this appeal is denied, you can go to a higher level of appeal, as I explain in Chapter 16.

Being aware of the improvement standard

Until recently, patients receiving certain kinds of care — notably skilled nursing, home health, or physical therapy — could suddenly have their Medicare coverage terminated on the basis that their medical condition wasn't "improving." Never mind that those services were often keeping these patients stable and preventing any further deterioration of their health. The administrative contractors that Medicare relies on to pay claims have often used a rule of thumb known as the *improvement standard* to determine whether Medicare should continue to pay these patients' bills. ("Administrative contractors?" you say. Don't worry; I discuss them in a bit more detail later, in the section "Zooming In on Part B.")

Jimmo v. Sebelius, a class action lawsuit brought by the Center for Medicare Advocacy and settled in 2013, made it clear that this practice — though never part of Medicare law or regulations — should no longer happen.

But just in case the improvement standard is still alive and kicking someplace and being applied to you, be aware of a statement that Medicare officials issued on the lawsuit's outcome in April 2013: "The settlement agreement is intended to clarify that when skilled services are required in order to provide care that is reasonable and necessary to prevent or slow further deterioration, *coverage cannot be denied based on the absence of potential for improvement or restoration.*" (The emphasis is mine.) If necessary, you could use Medicare's FAQ on this topic as official evidence of its policy: www.cms.gov/center/special-topic/jimmo-settlement/faqs.

TIP Self-help packets on how to deal with (and appeal) coverage decisions that appear to be based on the improvement standard are available on the center's website at www.medicareadvocacy.org/take-action/self-help-packets-for-medicare-appeals.

Fighting premature hospital discharge

Within two days of your being admitted, the hospital must give you a notice titled "Important Message from Medicare on Your Rights." The most important thing about this message is that it tells you what to do if you think the hospital is requiring you to leave before you feel ready to go home or to a nursing facility for ongoing care.

REMEMBER

If you stay in the hospital for more than two days after signing this notice, the hospital must give you another copy of the message before discharging you. It can do so as late as four hours before you're supposed to leave, which isn't a lot of time to consider what to do next if you think the hospital is discharging you too soon. However, all you need do is call your area's *Beneficiary and Family-Centered Care Quality Improvement Organization* (BFCC-QIO) — an independent review agency — and file an immediate appeal, following the instructions contained in the notice. You must contact the BFCC-QIO before noon on the first business day after you receive the discharge notice.

When you've requested this immediate review (also known as an *expedited decision* or *fast appeal*), here's what you can expect to happen:

>> **The hospital must give you a "Detailed Notice of Discharge" in writing by noon of the day after it hears from the BFCC-QIO that your appeal has begun.** This notice explains the reasons for the hospital's discharge decision. At the same time, the hospital must send to the BFCC-QIO any records that agency requests.

>> **The BFCC-QIO must make its decision one day after it receives these records.** The whole process, from filing your appeal to receiving the BFCC-QIO's expedited decision, should take no more than two days. The hospital cannot discharge you while your case is under review.

>> **You can't be charged for the cost of this continued hospital stay while the BFCC-QIO is reviewing your case, even if it finally rules against you.** However, if the decision does go against you and you stay in the hospital beyond noon of the day when you receive the decision, you'll be responsible for all costs after that time. If the BFCC-QIO rules in your favor, you can continue to stay in the hospital with appropriate Medicare coverage until a new discharge decision is made. If you disagree with the BFCC-QIO's decision, you can ask it to reconsider. It must issue a decision within three days.

For example, Helen is told she'll be discharged from the hospital on Tuesday, and she calls the BFCC-QIO on Tuesday afternoon. The hospital sends her records to the BFCC-QIO by noon Wednesday. The BFCC-QIO tells Helen and the hospital its decision on Thursday. Because she requested a BFCC-QIO review before midnight on Tuesday, she can't be held responsible for the costs of staying in the hospital for those two days (Wednesday and Thursday) while the BFCC-QIO considered her appeal.

Proceeding if the hospital makes a mistake

They're known as *never events* — hospital errors that should never happen but frequently do. They include surgeries on the wrong limb, instruments left inside the patient, transfusions with the wrong blood type, infections and blood clots developing after certain procedures, and severe bedsores. Yikes!

If any of these or other preventable errors that Medicare has listed should happen to you, the only good news is that the hospital can't charge you or Medicare for treatment during a readmission to put things right. Unbelievably, until 2008 hospitals could — and did — charge big money for rectifying their own mistakes (which is sort of like an auto repair shop accidentally damaging your car and then handing you a bill for fixing it).

But then Medicare cracked down and refused to pay up. That helped boost a growing trend among many hospitals to reduce preventable errors, which is why you're now more likely to see the surgeon signing their name on the specific body part you're about to have repaired or going through a safety checklist to make sure everything is done just right. Still, these and other sensible precautions aren't always used.

REMEMBER

So if a hospital makes a serious mistake, readmits you to correct it, and then tries to make you pay for whatever's being done, don't pay the bill. Instead, contact Medicare's QIO in your area and file a complaint. You can find contact information for the QIO by calling Medicare at 800-633-4227 (TTY 877-486-2048) or going to qioprogram.org/contact.

Knowing your rights in a skilled nursing facility

People go into SNFs at a time when they feel especially vulnerable — when they've been in the hospital and still have a ways to go before they're well enough to go home. Federal and state laws confer many rights and protections on SNF residents. These include basic rights to respect, privacy, good care, choice of visitors, and management of their own money, plus the right to freedom from discrimination of all kinds, from abuse and neglect, and from restraints — the physical and pharmaceutical kind. In fact, the SNF must give you written information of your legal rights and the facility's policies when you first enter it.

But in the following sections, I focus on a few situations where, to my knowledge, the administrators of some skilled nursing facilities have given Medicare patients incorrect information. This information will help you separate fact from fiction and arm you with knowledge of the appropriate legal authority in case you or someone close to you runs into one of these situations.

Leaving the SNF for short periods

Some members of a family in Michigan told me how badly their mother wanted to spend two days attending the wedding of her grandson, several states away from where she was recuperating from surgery in a nursing facility. Her doctor gave his blessing based on her health status and the level of support her family had arranged. But the SNF administrator told them that if she went, Medicare wouldn't cover her stay in the facility after she returned. Was this assertion true?

REMEMBER

Not true. Medicare rules allow you to go away from an SNF for brief excursions for activities you'd enjoy, providing that you're well enough to leave the facility temporarily without harming your health or recovery.

Yes, Medicare coverage does stop when a patient is considered no longer in need of the care the SNF provides. But section 30.7.3 of Chapter 8 of the *Medicare Benefit Policy Manual* specifically says, "An outside pass or short leave of absence for the purpose of attending a special religious service, holiday meal, family occasion, going on a car ride or for a trial visit home is not, by itself, evidence that the individual no longer needs to be in an SNF for the receipt of required skilled care." What's more, the regulation adds, it's "not appropriate" for an SNF to tell a patient that "leaving the facility will result in a denial of coverage."

Medicare coverage for SNF care is based on 24-hour periods that run from midnight to midnight. So if you leave the facility for a few hours but return before midnight, you're regarded as having been there all day and lose no Medicare payment or coverage.

What about overnight absences — for example, to return to your family for holiday celebrations — or for a visit of several days? Medicare doesn't pay the SNF for days when you're absent at midnight. And you're not responsible for the cost of those days either, as long as you remain eligible for SNF coverage (as explained earlier in this chapter).

WARNING

However, the SNF may charge you a *bed-hold fee* to compensate for its loss of income while keeping your bed free for your return. Not all facilities charge this fee, at least not for a 24-hour leave of absence. But be sure to find out from the SNF administrator in advance whether the bed can be kept open and whether you need to pay a daily fee to reserve it.

Of course, much depends on your physical and mental ability to tolerate a trip away and to what extent the people or place you're visiting can cope with your needs, such as for wheelchair and bathroom access. Asking your doctor's opinion is wise. Also, keep in mind that too many jaunts may be construed as evidence that you no longer need SNF care. But otherwise, Medicare regulations say there's no reason why you can't be taken outside of the facility for an occasional excursion as long as you feel up to it and have the appropriate support you need while you're away.

Moving out of SNF care (and later returning)

A North Carolina woman contacted me because she wanted to take her husband out of a SNF where he was recuperating after a spell in the hospital. She thought he'd be better off at home with help from home health-care services. But three staff members of the SNF told her that if he left, Medicare wouldn't cover the days that he'd previously spent there. Was this information true?

Absolutely not, Medicare legal experts said, describing the SNF staffers' stance as "utterly without foundation." This kind of trial visit home — regardless of whether you eventually go back to the facility — "would *never* serve to invalidate any medically necessary SNF coverage that preceded the home visit," the experts added.

What's more, leaving the SNF doesn't jeopardize future Medicare coverage if you and your doctor decide you need to return there. If you return to the same or a different SNF within 30 days, your coverage resumes and you don't need to have another qualifying three-day stay as an admitted patient in the hospital. (I explain the three-day rule earlier in this chapter.) This regulation is spelled out in Section 20.2.3 of Chapter 8 of the *Medicare Benefit Policy Manual*. Beyond 30 days, though, you'd need to spend another three days in the hospital as an admitted inpatient.

Seeing the doctor of your choice

I heard from a woman in Florida whose mother was in a skilled nursing facility and wanted to consult her own primary-care physician (PCP). The SNF staff members said flatly that if she brought in her own doctor, she'd lose Medicare coverage for her stay there. They even added the "clarification" that it would be okay to bring in a specialist, but not a PCP. Was this statement true?

Not at all, Medicare officials said. "The SNF's statement is absolutely unfounded," they told me. "In fact, it directly contradicts the requirements that every SNF must meet in order to participate in the Medicare program."

The freedom to see any doctor you choose and to have a say in the care you're receiving is laid out in the Code of Federal Regulations (see Section 483.10 (d), under "Free Choice"). This rule specifies that when you're in a skilled nursing facility or long-term-care nursing home, you have the legal right to

>> Choose a personal attending physician

>> Be fully informed in advance about your care and treatment and of any changes that may affect your well-being

>> Participate in planning your care and treatment, or any changes in it, unless you're judged to be incompetent or otherwise incapacitated under the laws of your state

Filing a claim even if you're told Medicare won't pay

Each of the situations I describe in the preceding sections came about because skilled nursing facility staff wrongly told residents that Medicare wouldn't cover their care if they did this, that, or the other. What if you're told the same, but in a different situation, and are unsure whether they're right?

If the facility staffers believe that Medicare may not cover your stay or any particular service that you want during your stay, they're supposed to give you an Advance Beneficiary Notice of Non-Coverage. (I explain a lot more about your options when faced with this notice in the later section "Receiving a notice saying that Medicare may not pay.") But be aware that if an SNF tells you that an aspect of your care isn't covered, this statement doesn't represent an official coverage decision by the Medicare program. And be warned: If you just take the SNF's word for it, you're giving away your right to appeal.

You can insist that the SNF file a claim for Medicare coverage on your behalf with Medicare's contractor in your area — a practice known as *demand billing.* The contractor must then issue an official decision as to whether the care in question is covered. If the claim is denied, you're free to appeal the decision. (See Chapter 16 for more on the appeals process.)

If this service turns out not to be covered but you've already received it, you have to pay the SNF for it out-of-pocket. Know, however, that while you wait for the contractor's decision relating to Part A coverage (such as your stay in the facility), the SNF can't ask for payment.

Zooming In on Part B

Part B covers so many different aspects of medical care that I can't possibly get into the details of them all here (Chapter 2 provides an overview). But this section looks at some broad concerns you may have about coverage: how to find out, in advance, whether Medicare will help pay for a treatment or item you need (and what it may cost); how to maximize your chances for coverage; your rights to second opinions; and a couple of unusual situations where you may need to make a claim directly to Medicare yourself. *Note:* All these sections apply if you're in original Medicare. If you're enrolled in a Medicare Advantage plan, contact the plan for information.

Checking on whether Medicare will cover your treatment

How easily can you find out — in advance — whether Medicare will help pay for a specific medical service you need? Because Medicare is a federal program, most people assume that coverage is an either/or situation — that a particular service or item either is covered or isn't and that both situations apply equally to all Medicare beneficiaries nationwide. But that scenario isn't necessarily so. Sometimes coverage depends on where you live.

In fact, Medicare has two coverage categories:

>> *National coverage determinations* (NCDs) are decisions on which services and items Medicare will cover, and under what conditions, for all beneficiaries anywhere in the United States who need them.

>> *Local coverage determinations* (LCDs) are made by regional *Medicare Administrative Contractors* (MACs), which are companies that Medicare hires to process claims for Parts A and B. They can choose (at their discretion) to provide coverage for services not covered under NCDs. The LCDs affect Medicare beneficiaries living within the contractor's area of jurisdiction, which typically includes several states.

TECHNICAL
STUFF

In both cases, the process of deciding which services are "reasonable and necessary" — the measure required by law for Medicare coverage — must be based on scientific evidence; the opinions of medical organizations, physicians, and other providers; and comments from the general public.

You can check whether Medicare covers a service, test, or item you need in the following ways:

>> **Call Medicare (at 800-633-4227 or TTY 877-486-2048) and ask.** Medicare's customer service reps are equipped with lists of services and items that Medicare covers. If you ask about something that isn't on their lists, Medicare officials suggest that you ask the provider's office to tell you the appropriate Medicare billing code(s) for the service(s) you need and that you then call Medicare back, quote the code(s), and ask the rep to find out whether it's covered.

>> **Ask the surgeons or other specialists who will be treating you whether Medicare covers the procedure.** If they don't already know, their billing office should be able to find out by contacting the local MAC or using the Medicare Coverage Database.

WARNING

>> **Go to a Medicare website that provides coverage information and type in or select the service, test, or item that you're interested in.** I'm speaking primarily of the site www.medicare.gov/coverage. This site isn't especially informative or user-friendly, and it doesn't include LCDs that apply only to certain regions of the country, but it may be able to tell you what you need to know. You can try a more sophisticated search by using the Medicare Coverage Database (at www.cms.gov/medicare-coverage-database/), which contains all NCDs and LCDs and is updated weekly. But be warned that this site is mainly for bureaucrats and healthcare professionals and is difficult for consumers to navigate.

Receiving a notice saying that Medicare may not pay

You're more likely to get prior warning if there's a likelihood that Medicare won't cover the service you need. Any provider — a physician, hospital, lab, skilled nursing facility, home health agency, medical equipment supplier, ambulance company, and so on — can give you an Advance Beneficiary Notice of Non-Coverage (ABN) if it thinks Medicare won't pay. The following sections describe what you find on an ABN and a specific situation in which you'll almost certainly receive one: when you call an ambulance.

REMEMBER

A provider isn't required to issue an ABN for any service or item that Medicare definitely doesn't cover (such as hearing aids or routine foot care) but may do so voluntarily as a professional courtesy.

The options on an ABN

An ABN asks you to sign it after checking one of three options:

» You want the service or item in question and you want the bill sent to Medicare. You understand that if Medicare won't cover it, you're responsible for the cost; however, you have the right to appeal the decision (as described in Chapter 16).

» You want the service or item but you don't want the bill sent to Medicare. You agree to pay the full cost, and you understand that you can't make an appeal.

» You don't want the service or item. You won't have to pay for it, and you understand that you can't appeal to see whether Medicare would pay.

WARNING

Consumer advocates generally advise choosing the first option, partly because it allows you to keep your right to an appeal, but mostly because the ABN itself isn't a decision; after reviewing your request, Medicare may agree to coverage after all. Still, you encounter an element of rolling the dice here, because if Medicare denies the claim, you must pay the whole bill yourself. To help you make an informed decision, the estimated cost of the service must be shown on the ABN.

If you check option one, the provider has the right to ask you to pay upfront for the service in question and the right to keep your money if Medicare denies the claim. (In this regard, Part B claims are treated differently from claims under Part A. As I explain in the earlier section "Knowing your rights in a skilled nursing facility," you can't be asked to pay for a Part A service while your claim is being considered.) But if Medicare agrees to coverage — either initially or on appeal — the provider must refund your money, minus any applicable co-pay or deductible, within 30 days of the decision.

WARNING

The first option is certainly the one to check if you have secondary insurance (such as employer benefits) that pays for services that Medicare doesn't cover and you need proof of a Medicare denial to trigger that coverage. But if your secondary insurance is a Medigap policy (see Chapter 4), be aware that it won't pay your costs for a Part B service that Medicare doesn't cover.

A word about ambulance services

WARNING

One situation in which you're very likely to be given an ABN is if you call an ambulance. Just dialing 911 doesn't automatically mean Medicare will pay. In fact, the conditions you must meet to get coverage are strict. In general, Medicare covers ambulance services only if you're taken to the nearest facility that can provide the care you need (in addition to meeting the other conditions for coverage) *and* at least one of the following is true:

>> You're having a medical emergency and your health is at serious risk — for example, you're unconscious, in shock, bleeding or in severe pain, or need skilled care during the journey.

>> Transportation by any other means would endanger your health. In non-emergency situations, you can meet this criterion only if a doctor has made a written order saying that an ambulance is medically necessary.

>> You require urgent care and rapid transportation that can't be provided on the ground (because you're in a remote location or stalled in heavy traffic) and need to be taken by air ambulance or helicopter.

Medicare even has rules on what ambulance means: An *ambulance* must contain a stretcher and other life-saving equipment and have people onboard specially trained to provide first aid. Therefore, wheelchair vans don't meet Medicare's definition and aren't covered.

If you meet the conditions for coverage, Medicare will pay for the ambulance service under Part B, so you'll be responsible for 20 percent of the cost (unless Medigap or other supplemental insurance pays your share).

If the ambulance staffers think you don't meet the conditions, they'll give you an ABN with the same options explained in the preceding section. The ambulance service can ask you to pay the bill upfront — before it transports you — on the basis that the money will be refunded if Medicare decides it will pay.

TIP

For more details, see "Medicare Coverage of Ambulance Services" at www.medicare.gov/Pubs/pdf/11021-Medicare-Coverage-of-Ambulance-Services.pdf.

Determining whether you can find out a service's cost in advance

Reasonably enough, you may be very concerned to know how much you're likely to pay out-of-pocket for a particular treatment or procedure, especially an expensive one like major surgery. Yet obtaining an answer in advance of receiving the bill can be difficult.

REMEMBER

This ambiguity isn't just a Medicare thing. It can happen regardless of the insurance you have because charges vary enormously — sometimes by thousands of dollars — from hospital to hospital or from doctor to doctor for exactly the same treatment or procedure.

Yet the way Medicare pays claims for Part B generates another level of uncertainty because — at least in the original program — it pays doctors and other providers 80 percent of the "Medicare-approved" amount, leaving your share as 20 percent. But what does this division mean in terms of cold cash? Twenty percent of what? You have no way of knowing because Medicare pays providers according to geographical variations in local medical costs. Medicare does have a *Procedure Price Lookup* tool online at `www.medicare.gov/procedure-price-lookup/` but be warned that this tool only displays national averages for costs of outpatient procedures covered under Part B.

REMEMBER

So what can you do? Your best bet is to ask the surgeon or other specialist who will be treating you whether Medicare covers the procedure and what it will cost you. Or call the billing office of the hospital where you'll have it done. Keep in mind that if you're having surgery, you may not be quoted a precise amount because nobody can predict exactly what may happen when you're on the operating table. Note, too, that other specialists (such as an anesthetist), if needed, will charge separately from the surgeon.

Maximizing your chances for coverage

REMEMBER

Sometimes Medicare covers a service in general but still won't cover it in your particular case. No, that's not because Medicare is singling you out! It's because Medicare coverage invariably comes with certain conditions. If you're enrolled in a Medicare Advantage plan, those conditions are spelled out in your evidence of coverage documents (see Chapter 13 for more about these documents). But original Medicare doesn't provide such documents. So knowing what the conditions are in that program, and acting on them, can save you a lot of disappointment, frustration, and perhaps even money — as follows:

>> **Seeing the right doctor:** When you go to any doctors for the first time, always ask whether they participate in Medicare and, if so, whether they accept *assignment* — which means they agree to take the Medicare-approved amount for a service as full payment. This answer makes a big difference to your costs and maybe your coverage, as I explain in more detail in Chapter 13. For example, the wide range of preventive tests that Medicare provides for free (as described in Chapter 2) are free only if you get them from a doctor or provider who accepts assignment.

>> **Selecting a provider approved by Medicare:** If you need coverage for skilled nursing or rehab care, home health services, dialysis treatment, or medical equipment and supplies, you must get them from providers that Medicare has approved — otherwise, Medicare won't help pay for them. You can find lists of approved providers (known as contract suppliers) by going to Medicare's website at `www.medicare.gov`. Or you can call Medicare at 800-633-4227 (TTY 877-486-2048) and ask for a mailed list.

>> **Waiting for the correct interval between services:** Medicare limits the frequency of coverage for certain routine (non-urgent) tests — especially preventive screenings that it offers free of charge. For example, you get one mammogram every 12 months to check for breast cancer and one cardiovascular screening every five years to detect for risks of heart attack and stroke. (See Chapter 2 for a full list of covered tests.)

>> **Being specific about the service you want:** You may be charged for a service Medicare doesn't cover just because the doctor or other provider misunderstands what you want. For example, Medicare offers a free annual checkup called a *wellness visit.* This appointment is mainly a chat about your health with a doctor or nurse practitioner who also checks your vital signs (such as weight and blood pressure) and may refer you for other tests. But it *isn't* the kind of comprehensive exam that most patients and doctors call a *physical.* So if you ask for a physical instead of a wellness visit, Medicare won't cover it and you'll pay full price.

>> **Meeting other requirements:** You may need to meet other conditions before Medicare will cover a service. For example, to qualify for home healthcare, you must be homebound and your doctor must attest that you need this type of care. To get some kinds of medical equipment, your doctor has to sign and submit a certificate of medical necessity. These and other conditions for coverage are explained more fully in Chapter 2.

Recognizing your right to second opinions

When you're facing non-emergency surgery or some other serious procedure or treatment, you may naturally be concerned about making the right decision. So keep in mind that Medicare will cover a consultation with another doctor if you want a second opinion — and maybe even a third opinion.

Of course, if you need surgery in an emergency — when your health or life depends on fast medical action — you don't want to hang about for a second opinion. But for elective surgery or another major but non-urgent procedure, you can afford to take a little time to weigh your treatment options.

REMEMBER

If you're enrolled in original Medicare, you can ask your primary-care doctor to recommend an appropriate but different specialist for a second opinion, or you can go directly to another specialist of your choice. (Chapter 13 gives guidance on finding a physician.) If the first and second opinions don't agree, Medicare will cover one more opinion from a third doctor. In each case, you pay 20 percent of the Medicare-approved cost under Part B, provided you see a doctor who accepts assignment (which is also explained in Chapter 13) or unless you have supplemental insurance such as Medigap. Deciding to have the first, second, or third doctor actually perform the procedure — or not to have it at all — is entirely your choice.

You have the same rights if you're in a Medicare Advantage plan. But many plans (especially HMOs) require a primary-care physician to make the referral to a second (or third) physician within the plan's provider network. Your co-pays would also be different.

Filing a claim directly to Medicare

Most likely, you'll never need to contact Medicare directly to pay for a service you've had. The doctor or other provider sends Medicare a bill, Medicare pays its share, and you pay yours. And in most cases, if your share is covered by any secondary insurance such as Medigap or employer benefits, that claim is automatically sent to the other payer under Medicare's coordination of benefits system (which I discuss in Chapter 8). But, if you're enrolled in original Medicare, you may need to file a claim directly in one of two circumstances.

If the doctor fails to file a claim

This situation is extremely unusual. All doctors (or any other healthcare providers, such as hospitals, labs, or medical equipment suppliers) who participate in the original Medicare program are required by law to file claims with Medicare. (Keep in mind, though, that providers who opt out of Medicare can't bill Medicare for your treatment and neither can you, as I explain in more detail in Chapter 13. Also, if you're in a Medicare Advantage plan, your doctors and other providers must send their bills to your plan.)

If for some reason a provider won't or can't bill Medicare, you can file a claim yourself. All claims (whether from the provider or from you) must be submitted within 12 months of the date when you received the service; otherwise, Medicare won't pay. So regularly check your Medicare Summary Notices (explained in Chapter 13) to make sure that all your doctors' visits, tests, and treatments are noted on it, proving that all claims were submitted correctly and in good time. If not, press the provider to file the claim.

If that doesn't work, you need to send a claim directly to Medicare. Use form CMS-1490S, which comes with instructions on how to fill it out and where to send it. You can obtain the form by calling the Medicare help line at 800-633-4227 (TTY 877-486-2048) or by downloading it in both Spanish and English from www.cms.gov/Medicare/CMS-Forms/CMS-Forms/CMS-Forms-Items/CMS012949. You'll need to attach an itemized bill for the service you received.

If you need Medicare to deny a claim

Wanting Medicare to refuse payment sounds odd. But if you have secondary insurance (for example, retiree benefits), that plan may require you to obtain an official denial from Medicare (the primary payer) in some situations before it will pay for the service or treatment you've received.

If you receive a formal Medicare denial after being given an Advance Beneficiary Notice of Non-Coverage (described in the earlier section "Receiving a notice saying that Medicare may not pay"), you should send a copy of the denial letter to your secondary insurer. Otherwise, you should use form CMS-1490S, as I explain in the previous section. In this case, you're essentially submitting a claim to Medicare and requesting reimbursement for the medical service in question. When Medicare rejects the claim, you can send its notice of denial to your secondary insurer.

Delving into Part D

Part D is insurance for outpatient prescription drugs — in other words, medications you take yourself rather than those administered in a hospital or doctor's office. I explain how the program works and how to find the drug plan that's best for you in other chapters. In this section, I discuss some of the fine-print issues of Medicare's prescription drug program: what to do if your Part D plan denies coverage for your drugs or restricts access to them; why you pay different co-pays for different drugs; how to navigate rules for the doughnut hole; how to get the shingles shot; and how to take advantage of a free benefit designed to help you minimize the potentially bad effects of using a number of drugs regularly.

REMEMBER

All the information in this section applies equally to the Part D coverage you receive through a stand-alone drug plan or a Medicare Advantage plan.

Understanding how a plan may restrict your drug coverage

No Part D plans cover all drugs, as I explain in Chapter 2. If your plan doesn't cover one or more of your meds, you may be able to find ways around that. More bewildering, perhaps, is standing in the pharmacy and being told that you must ask your plan's permission before it will cover a drug that you know is on the plan's *formulary* (list of covered medications). What's going on here? Well, you've come up against the Part D practice of *restrictions.* The following sections describe different restrictions, how you can avoid them, how to request an exception with the help of your doctor, and how to obtain a prescription from the right doctor.

Defining prior authorization, quantity limits, and step therapy

Medicare allows Part D plans to use prior authorization, quantity limits, and step therapy (bureaucratically known as *utilization management tools*) as ways to hold down costs. But to people who have to face any of these restrictions, they're total hassles — hoops to jump through before the plan will cover the drugs their doctors have prescribed. Here's what each means:

>> **Prior authorization:** A plan may apply this restriction because the medication is a powerful one that may pose safety concerns when used inappropriately or for too long. Your doctor must argue that you need the drug as a matter of medical necessity in order to get this restriction lifted. Or it may be that your drug is sometimes also covered under Part B, and the plan needs to find out the circumstances from your doctor to decide whether Part B or Part D should cover it.

>> **Quantity limits:** This phrase doesn't mean that the plan will cover your meds for a certain time and then stop. It means that your doctor has prescribed a dosage or quantity that's higher than the plan considers normal to treat your condition. For example, if the doctor prescribes a pill to be taken twice a day, and the normal quantity is once a day, the plan won't cover the drug unless your doctor shows that the higher quantity is necessary to treat you effectively.

>> **Step therapy:** Your plan requires you to try other similar but lower-cost drugs before it will consider covering the more expensive one your doctor has prescribed. To avoid this restriction, your doctor must show that you've already tried lower-cost drugs that didn't work as well for your medical condition as the prescribed drug.

As you can see, some of these restrictions address safety concerns, so you may suppose that all plans restrict the same drug according to some blanket Medicare regulation. But no — each plan gets to decide which of its formulary drugs it will apply one or more restrictions to. It sounds absurdly hit or miss, but this practice may actually give you more options to sidestep the hoops and get the drugs you need.

TIP

You may be able to avoid problems of drug restrictions or non-coverage by

>> **Trying another drug:** Maybe you *can* use a different drug that is on your plan's formulary that will treat your condition just as well and probably cost you far less. This possibility is worth asking your doctor about. (See Chapter 4 for an explanation of how generic and older drugs may slash your drug expenses.)

>> **Trying another plan:** Because Part D plans vary a great deal as to which drugs they saddle with restrictions or don't cover at all, you always have the option to switch to another plan during open enrollment (as I explain in Chapter 15) and choose one that doesn't affect your drug in this way.

Requesting an exception with your doctor's help

I assume here that for some reason you can't switch to another drug or another Part D plan right now. But you can ask your current plan to waive its rules and cover the medication your doctor prescribed. Medicare law provides a process for doing this. It's called *requesting an exception* to the plan's policy or, more formally, *requesting a coverage determination.*

You or someone acting on your behalf can file an exception request. But to have any chance of succeeding, you need your doctor's help. In fact, without their supporting statement, the plan may not even consider your request — or at least, not in a timely manner. Here's how the process works:

>> Your prescribing doctor is likely to be very familiar with filing Part D exception requests and can do it on your behalf without your having to do it separately. Other health professionals who are qualified to write prescriptions — such as nurse practitioners and physician assistants — are also legally allowed to file. They can call your plan and make the request verbally or get the plan's own form to fill out. They (or you) can also download a form from www.cms.gov. **Note:** The Parts C and D Enrollee Grievance, Organization/Coverage Determinations, and Appeals Guidance is updated frequently to reflect regulatory changes; the most recent update was in August 2022. The latest information can be downloaded from the web at www.cms.gov/Medicare/Appeals-and-Grievances/MedPrescriptDrugApplGriev.

>> Under Medicare rules, your plan must respond within 72 hours of receiving the doctor's statement. (That's 72 hours by the clock, not 72 business hours.) If waiting that long would endanger your health or life, the doctor can ask for an *expedited exception,* which the plan must reply to within 24 hours (again, by the clock).

>> In most cases, exceptions granted are valid until the end of the calendar year. But in the case of some prior authorization restrictions, the plan may require another request more frequently, in which case you and your doctor must go through the whole process again and may even have to do so several times during the year.

>> If your request is denied, you can pursue the matter further by asking for a *reconsideration* — asking the plan to reconsider its decision — and, if necessary, taking the dispute to higher levels of appeal (as I explain in Chapter 16). You can also take these actions if your plan doesn't respond to your request within the required time frames.

Obtaining a prescription from the right doctor

Medicare now requires Part D plans to reject claims for prescriptions written by doctors and dentists who have neither formally enrolled in Medicare nor formally opted out of the program. This rule is intended to exclude practitioners whose medical licenses have been suspended or who have other black marks against them in an effort to combat the illegal prescribing of some medications.

In practice, the rule applies to only a small number of doctors and dentists. But if you find yourself in this situation, you should know that Medicare requires pharmacists to provide a three-month provisional supply of the Part D–covered drug specified in the prescription. The three-month grace period allows the prescribing doctor time to enroll in or opt out of Medicare, or allows you time to change your prescriber.

Grappling with the tier system of co-pays

Few things make Part D enrollees more furious than when their plans suddenly increase the co-pays for their drugs. "I can't believe this," one reader wrote, early one January. "Last month, I paid $5 for one of my drugs. This month they're charging me $45 for the same thing — and it's a generic, for heaven's sake!" I agree with him: It's unconscionable. But note the timing. The co-pay went up ninefold from December to January, and the beginning of each calendar year is when plans can change any of their charges. In this case, the plan simply moved this man's drug from one pricing tier to another. The following sections provide details on pricing tiers in Part D.

What are pricing tiers?

Pricing tiers are categories in which Part D plans place different types of drugs, charging different co-pays for each tier — which is why some of your drugs may cost a lot more than others:

- » **Tier one:** Tier one has the lowest co-pay because it covers the plan's *preferred* generic drugs — the least expensive in its formulary.

- » **Tier two:** This tier has what's considered a medium co-pay because it covers preferred, brand-name prescription drugs. (Brand names are drugs that have no cheaper generic equivalents.)

- » **Tier three:** This tier has a still higher co-pay because it covers the plan's *non-preferred* brand-name drugs (the drugs the plan prefers you not to use, either because they're expensive or perhaps because the plan hasn't managed to negotiate adequate discounts for them with the manufacturers).

>> **Specialty tier:** This tier comprises very expensive or specialty drugs, such as anti-rejection drugs used after organ transplant surgery and drugs used to treat certain cancers. Because these are usually the most expensive drugs, Medicare limits the co-pays plans can charge for them — to no more than 25 percent of the cost of the drugs in plans that charge an annual deductible, and no more than 33 percent in plans that do not charge a deductible. Even so, these percentages can mean hefty dollar outlays.

Some plans slice and dice their drugs into even more tiers — six is not unknown. Then again, a few plans have only one tier, charging the same cost percentage (typically 25 percent) for all the drugs they cover.

TIP

The Inflation Reduction Act of 2022 capped the cost of a one-month supply of each Part D-covered insulin at $35, and you don't have to pay a deductible. If you get a 60- or 90-day supply of insulin, your costs can't be more than $35 for each month's supply of each covered insulin.

REMEMBER

Note that Part D plans use pricing tiers only during the initial coverage period — after you've met your annual deductible (if the plan charges one) and before you hit the doughnut hole (if your drug costs run that high), as explained in Chapter 2.

How can you find out your plan's pricing tiers?

Each plan that provides Part D prescription drugs has its own system of pricing tiers. That's why different plans often charge widely varying co-pays, even for the same drug. (For examples, flip to Chapter 10.) You can check out which tiers a Part D plan places your own drugs in, and what it charges for each prescription in each tier, in the following ways:

>> Go to the plan's website and find its formulary, which shows each drug the plan covers, together with the pricing tier in which each has been placed for the current year. Somewhere on this formulary is a key that provides the co-pay (a dollar amount) or coinsurance (percentage of cost) for each tier.

>> Call the plan and ask for the pricing tier and co-pay for each of your drugs. Keep in mind that plans often switch drugs to different tiers from one year to another, so if you call in November or December, ask what the tiers and co-pays will be in January, too.

>> Use the Plan Finder program on Medicare's website at www.medicare.gov/find-ma-plan. Follow the instructions (or use the step-by-step guide provided in Chapter 10) until you reach the details page of the plan you're enrolled in or considering. Scroll down that page to the "Drug coverage &

costs" heading. Immediately below you will see the names of your drugs and all the tiers and co-pays used by that plan. Scroll through the menu named "Tier Drug Cost for" and choose whether you buy your drugs at a standard or preferred retail pharmacy or mail order, and whether you order a one- or three-month supply.

What if your drug is suddenly switched to a higher price tier?

REMEMBER

Part D plans often jump a drug from a lower tier to a higher tier because it's a way to offset the cost of keeping premiums relatively low. This change most often occurs at the beginning of the calendar year, when plans can change any of their costs and benefits. But if it happens partway through the year when you're already taking the drug, be aware that you have the right to

>> Continue paying the lower-cost co-pay for the rest of the year. Your plan may automatically continue to charge you the lower co-pay. If not, call the plan and ask for it to be lowered or file for a coverage determination as explained in the earlier section "Requesting an exception with your doctor's help."

>> File a request for a *formulary tier exception* to have your drug moved to a lower-cost tier. You can do so only if your prescribed brand-name drug is in a higher tier than other drugs on your plan's formulary that are used to treat the same condition, and only with a supporting statement from your doctor saying that this drug is the only one that works effectively for you. Also, you can't ask for a drug in the most expensive tier to be moved to a lower tier, and you can't ask for a brand-name drug to be placed in a low, all-generic tier.

Otherwise, the only remedy you have against your drug being placed in a much costlier price tier is to switch to another Part D plan before the new year begins. (That's why I make such a big deal in Chapter 15 about the virtues of comparing plans during open enrollment.)

Navigating the doughnut hole

The *doughnut hole* — properly called the *coverage gap* — has undoubtedly been the best-known facet of the Part D program, and also the most hated. Before 2011, people who fell into it had to pay 100 percent of the cost of their drugs out-of-pocket. The doughnut hole has been narrowing each year since the Affordable Care Act (ACA) was passed in 2010 and will close at the end of 2024. In 2024, beneficiaries pay only 25 percent of the cost of all their prescriptions while they are in the gap. You remain in the doughnut hole coverage gap until you have paid $8,000 in out-of-pocket costs, which then places you in the catastrophic coverage phase. During this phase, you pay nothing for your Part D–covered prescription drugs for the rest of the year. (The gap is technically Phase 3 of Part D coverage; check out Chapter 2 for details on all the phases.)

REMEMBER

Here's what you need to know about the doughnut hole under the Affordable Care Act:

>> All Part D enrollees are eligible for the discounts on drugs if they fall into the gap — with the exception of those receiving Extra Help (discussed in Chapter 4), which already provides year-round coverage without a doughnut hole.

>> You don't need to apply for the discounts or fill out any paperwork. They're deducted from your bill at the pharmacy (retail or mail order).

>> The brand-name discounts provided by the drug manufacturers don't prolong the time you spend in the gap. Their value counts toward the out-of-pocket limit that gets you out of the gap, even though you don't actually pay them. However, anything that the government pays toward your drugs in the gap — either brand names or generics — doesn't count toward the limit. (But keep in mind that while in the gap, you must buy your drugs through your Part D plan to have them count toward the limit.)

>> Under the law, drug manufacturers must provide the doughnut hole discounts on all their brand-name drugs as a condition for their being covered under Part D. So in the unlikely event that your drug is made by a company that declines to participate, you won't be able to get it from a Part D plan anyway.

>> The gap discounts also apply to drugs that your plan doesn't normally cover but has agreed to cover in response to your doctor's request for an exception to its rules (a process explained earlier in this chapter).

>> If your Part D plan already gives some coverage for your drugs in the gap, your plan's coverage is applied first and the discounts are applied to the remaining amount.

>> A small dispensing fee (of maybe $2 to $5) is added to your prescription cost at the pharmacy. You must pay this fee, which isn't included in the discounts.

REMEMBER

Beginning in 2025, the doughnut hole will officially close. That's because the Inflation Reduction Act imposed a maximum out-of-pocket spending cap of $2,000 for all Medicare Part D beneficiaries. This will eliminate the coverage gap, and it's estimated will lead to $7.4 billion in reduced spending on out-of-pocket drug costs.

Using Part D to get the shingles vaccine

Most common vaccines are covered under Part B. In other words, you get them in a doctor's office, the doctor bills Medicare, and — in the case of flu, COVID-19, pneumonia, and hepatitis B shots — Medicare picks up the full tab. But shots for shingles aren't free, and they're covered only through Part D.

This quirk means that to get Medicare coverage for the shingles vaccine, you must be enrolled in a Part D plan (a stand-alone drug plan or a Medicare Advantage health plan that covers drugs), get the shot through the plan, and pay whatever share of the cost your plan requires.

Under Medicare rules, all Part D plans must cover this vaccine. But you do need to watch out for some pitfalls in terms of paying for the shingles shot, depending on where you receive it:

» If you're vaccinated at a pharmacy, make sure that location is in your plan's pharmacy network. Otherwise, the shot will cost you more than the plan's normal co-pay — maybe even full price. (Pharmacists in every state can be licensed to give vaccinations.)

» If you get the shot in a doctor's office, make sure the doctor can bill your Part D plan directly through its computer billing process or can work through a pharmacy in your plan's network that can also bill the plan directly. Otherwise, you must pay the whole bill upfront and then claim reimbursement from your plan.

REMEMBER

Bottom line: If you want the shingles vaccine, call your plan in advance to find out which pharmacies and doctors in your area you should use to receive the shot at the plan's regular co-pay.

Taking advantage of free Medication Therapy Management benefits

Do you really need all those drugs? I pose this question in Chapter 4, mainly in relation to reducing your medical costs but also in terms of your health. Medications have powerful effects on the body, and not always in ways that are good for you. If you take many drugs for different conditions and they interact badly together, you may even wind up with more symptoms . . . that you then have to take yet another med for. So experts on the wise use of drugs always recommend having your pharmaceutical intake reviewed from time to time by a doctor or pharmacist.

If you're enrolled in a Part D plan, you may qualify to have this analysis done free of charge under its Medication Therapy Management (MTM) service. That's a mouthful of a name, but it's a very worthwhile benefit that you should seriously consider accepting if it's offered to you (which is the only way you can get it; you can't just sign up because you want it).

All Part D plans (both stand-alone plans and Medicare Advantage HMOs and PPOs that provide prescription drugs) must provide MTM services. But your plan will invite you to participate only if you meet certain conditions:

>> You take at least two to eight different Part D–covered drugs — your plan specifies the exact minimum number.

>> You have at least two or three specified chronic conditions (such as diabetes, heart failure, bone disease, breathing problems, and so on).

>> The total cost of your drugs (what you pay plus what your plan pays) exceeds a specified annual amount ($5,330 in 2024).

Your plan's MTM must put you (or your appointed representative, such as a caregiver) in contact personally with a clinical pharmacist who conducts a comprehensive review of all your meds (including nonprescription drugs, supplements, and vitamins) at least once a year. The MTM may also work with you to develop a medication action plan to improve your health.

The MTM can't make changes in your drug regimen; only your doctor can do that. But the MTM may contact your doctor for information and also share recommendations about the meds you take. You should also be given a detailed list of all your medications; keep it handy to share with your current or new doctor or the emergency room staff in a hospital so that they know exactly what you're taking.

IN THIS CHAPTER

» **Changing coverage during standard enrollment periods**

» **Switching plans at any time of the year in certain circumstances**

» **Separating from a plan because you or it wants out**

» **Figuring out whether to switch to another plan next year**

» **Moving to a different Medigap supplemental insurance policy**

Chapter **15**

Changing Your Medicare and Medigap Coverage

After you've done the hard work of choosing your Medicare coverage the first time around, changing to another plan is probably the last thing on your mind — especially if you need to select a stand-alone Part D drug plan or a Medicare Advantage (MA) plan from many options. But you're still better off knowing when you can switch to another type of coverage if you want or need to, when you can drop out of a plan (yeah, Medicare has rules for that, too), and whether you should compare plans all over again at the end of the year to see whether you'd get a better deal with a different one.

REMEMBER

Broadly, you can switch coverage within the following time frames, depending on what you have now and your reasons for switching:

» **October 15 to December 7 each year:** This period is *open enrollment,* when any participants can change their coverage for the following year.

» **January 1 to March 31 each year:** This time slot is formally known as the *Medicare Advantage open enrollment period* because it allows you to switch MA plans, or drop out of an MA plan and switch to original Medicare. You can do so regardless of how long or short a time you've been in the plan.

>> **Special enrollment periods:** These are allowed at any time of year, but only in specific circumstances. They come with various time limits.

In this chapter, I consider these options in detail. I also explain the circumstances in which you can drop out of a plan — or it can drop you. I cover that big end-of-year question: Stay with the coverage you have or switch to something else? And finally, I go outside Medicare and discuss the ins and outs of changing Medigap supplemental policies.

Switching Coverage during Open Enrollment

Most people who want to change their coverage for the following year do so within two standard time frames: the open enrollment period and the Medicare Advantage open enrollment period. The following sections explain exactly the types of coverage you can change during these specific terms. If you need to make a change at any other time of the year, flip to the later section "Taking Advantage of Special Enrollment Periods."

The open enrollment period

Some people may ask a question like this: "I turn 65 in June, but open enrollment won't begin until October. What can I do for healthcare if I can't sign up for Medicare until then?" So let me be very clear: Open enrollment is *only* for people already enrolled in Medicare. When you're new to the program, you get an enrollment period all your own according to your personal circumstances, as I explain in detail in Chapter 6.

Open enrollment is actually the one big time each year when all enrollees can play musical chairs with their Medicare coverage. It occurs over an eight-week period that starts October 15 and ends December 7. During this annual window, you're free to make any of the following changes:

>> Switch from original Medicare to a Medicare Advantage plan

>> Go from a Medicare Advantage plan to original Medicare

>> Change from one stand-alone Part D drug plan to another

>> Transfer from one Medicare Advantage plan to another

>> Move from a Medicare Advantage plan that doesn't offer drug coverage to a plan that does, and vice versa

>> Drop your Medicare drug coverage entirely

You can also use open enrollment to sign up for Part D coverage (either in a stand-alone Part D drug plan or a Medicare Advantage plan) for the first time if you didn't sign up when you were supposed to. (I discuss Part D deadlines for enrolling without incurring penalties in Chapter 6.)

Open enrollment gives you the chance to compare the Part D and Medicare Advantage plans that will be offered for the coming calendar year. Details of these plans are posted on the Medicare Plan Finder website starting on October 1. (I explain using the Plan Finder to compare plans in Chapters 10 and 11.) Although open enrollment finishes at midnight on December 7, coverage in your existing plan continues until midnight on December 31.

TIP

If you switch plans during open enrollment, your coverage in the new plan begins January 1. You don't need to inform Medicare or your existing plan of the change; enrolling in a new plan automatically cancels the old one. If you're moving from a Medicare Advantage plan to original Medicare, however, or if you're opting out of Medicare drug coverage completely, you will need to inform your current plan to cancel its coverage.

If you want to stay with the plan you already have, you don't need to do anything. Your current enrollment continues into next year. However, the plan's coverage and costs may change from year to year, as I explain in the later section "Reading your Annual Notice of Change to understand plan alterations."

The Medicare Advantage open enrollment period

REMEMBER

A few years ago, there was a specific six-week period between January 1 and February 14 that allowed you to disenroll from Medicare Advantage and return to original Medicare. This was replaced by a longer Medicare Advantage open enroll-ment period (January 1 to March 31) that lets people enrolled in MA plans switch or drop their plan. Here are key points to note:

>> You can use this period to disenroll from any Medicare Advantage plan and return to original Medicare regardless of whether you've been in it for a few days or several years. Similarly, you can switch MA plans, even if you selected

a new one during the fall open enrollment period with coverage beginning January 1.

>> Your new coverage will begin the first day of the month following enrollment (for example, if you make the change in January, it will be effective February 1).

>> If you're leaving an MA plan for original Medicare, you can also use this period to sign up with a stand-alone Part D drug plan. If you wait and decide to sign up for Part D coverage later on, you may face a penalty for late enrollment.

>> You may buy a Medigap policy during this period, but you don't have the right to buy it with federal guarantees and protections unless this period happens to coincide with a time frame when you do have those rights or unless your state law gives additional protection. (See Chapters 4 and 10 for more info on these guarantees.)

Taking Advantage of Special Enrollment Periods

Some people need to switch coverage — especially Medicare Advantage or Part D drug plans — outside of the annual open enrollment period discussed earlier in this chapter. So Medicare allows *special enrollment periods* (SEPs) in certain circumstances. You can use them at any time of the year, but most have specific time limits. You have to switch plans within the allotted time; otherwise, you lose your chance and must wait until the next open enrollment period to change plans. In some situations, this lag can leave you without coverage for months and expose you to late penalties.

In the following sections, I describe a number of circumstances in which you can obtain an SEP to change plans. I also explain how to ensure that your records and prescriptions are transferred safely when you switch plans. But I don't include SEPs granted for circumstances that are covered in other chapters. Flip to the appropriate chapter if you're in the following situations:

>> Receiving Extra Help (see Chapter 4)

>> Enrolling in Part B late because you were able to delay signing up after age 65 until you or your spouse stopped work (see Chapter 6)

>> Enrolling in Part D after returning from living abroad or being in prison (see Chapter 6)

Recognizing when you can use SEPs to change plans

Special enrollment periods cover a wide range of circumstances. The ones listed in the following sections are mostly those you can use to switch Medicare Advantage or Part D plans, but some also affect original Medicare coverage and Medigap supplemental policies. The word *plan* applies equally to a stand-alone Part D drug plan or a Medicare Advantage plan unless otherwise indicated.

REMEMBER

You don't literally have to go somewhere or do something to get an SEP. In most cases, you don't even need to apply. Just enroll in a new plan of your choice. It's that plan's responsibility to confirm whether you qualify for an SEP. But you do need to apply if you want an SEP because you believe your plan violated your contract or misled you into enrolling. In these situations, call Medicare at 800-633-4227 (TTY 877-486-2048 if you're hard of hearing), explain the situation, and say you want to apply for an SEP to change to another plan. Medicare will investigate and decide whether to allow it.

TIP

You may be eligible for other SEPs not described in the following sections. For a more complete list, see the Medicare publication "Understanding Medicare Advantage & Prescription Drug Plan Enrollment Periods" at `https://www.medicare.gov/publications/11219-Understanding-Medicare-Advantage-Medicare-Drug-Plan-Enrollment-Periods.pdf`.

You move permanently outside your plan's service area

The time frame of your SEP for switching to another plan depends on when (and whether) you notify your current plan of the move:

>> If you tell your plan in advance, your SEP begins the month before your move and ends two months after the month of your move.

>> If you tell your plan after your move, your SEP begins on the date you notify the plan and lasts for two months.

>> If you don't notify your plan of the move, your plan will disenroll you after six months. You then get an SEP that lasts two months.

In all these cases, after switching to another plan, you can choose when your new coverage begins — either on the first day of the month after enrolling in the new plan or up to three months afterward.

Even if the company that sponsors your old plan offers the same or other plans in your new home area, you have the right to switch to a different one if new plans are available to you there. But know that if you're in a stand-alone Part D drug plan, it serves your entire state; if you move to a new home within the same state, your coverage will continue, and you won't be entitled to change to a different plan until open enrollment rolls around again.

Of course, when you move out of the service area of your Medicare Advantage plan, you have the right to return to original Medicare coverage instead of enrolling in another plan if you want to. In that case, you also have the right to buy a Medigap policy with full federal guarantees and protections (if you're 65 or over), as explained in Chapters 4 and 10.

You move into or leave a nursing home or other long-term-care facility

You have an absolute right to change plans if you want to when you enter or leave a nursing home — whether it's a skilled nursing facility for short-term care after leaving the hospital or a residential home for long-term care — and at any time during your stay there. That's because the prescription drugs you need may change quite a bit at these times. Also, you need a plan that has in its network the long-term pharmacy that the residence uses, as explained in Chapter 13.

This right to switch plans applies if you're in any Medicare- or Medicaid-certified *institutional facility* — an umbrella term that sounds grim but actually comprises nursing homes, other skilled nursing facilities, rehabilitation hospitals or units, long-term-care hospitals, psychiatric hospitals or units, or intermediate-care facilities for people with mental disabilities.

During your time in any of these facilities and for up to two months after you leave, you have the right to

>> Change from your existing Medicare Advantage plan to another

>> Go from your existing stand-alone Part D drug plan to another

>> Switch from a Medicare Advantage plan to original Medicare and enroll in a stand-alone Part D drug plan

>> Shift from original Medicare to a Medicare Advantage plan

>> Enroll for the first time in a Part D drug plan or a Medicare Advantage plan that offers prescription drug coverage

If you want to switch plans, you don't have to apply for this SEP or disenroll from your current plan. Just enroll in the new plan, explaining the situation.

You're in a Medicare Advantage plan and want to change to original Medicare

This SEP is available only if you meet both of the following conditions:

» You joined this plan during your initial enrollment period when you first became eligible for Medicare at age 65.

» This is your first year in the same plan.

If these two conditions apply to you, you have the right to switch to original Medicare (and a stand-alone drug plan if you need it) at any time within 12 months from the time your coverage in this plan began. (The 12 months count as a trial period for "trying out" an MA plan.) You also have a guaranteed right to buy Medigap supplemental insurance, but you must apply for it no later than 63 days after your coverage in the MA plan ends.

You dropped a Medigap policy to enroll in a Medicare Advantage plan for the first time

This SEP gives you a one-time guaranteed right to buy another Medigap supplemental policy and switch back to original Medicare if both of the following are true:

» You've been enrolled in the MA plan for less than a year.

» The MA plan is the first Medicare health plan you've ever been enrolled in. (You can't obtain this SEP if you were enrolled in one before, even if it was years ago and the program was then called Medicare+Choice rather than its later name, Medicare Advantage.)

If these two conditions apply to you, you have the right to be reinstated in the same Medigap policy you had before joining the MA plan (or, if it's no longer sold, a policy from another insurer) at any time during your 12-month trial period in the plan. You can use this SEP to disenroll from the plan and re-enroll in original Medicare. You can also use it to enroll in a stand-alone drug plan; this coverage begins the first day of the month after you enroll. You can apply for the Medigap policy up to 60 days before, and no later than 63 days after, your MA plan coverage ends.

You want to switch to a high-quality five-star plan

If a Medicare Advantage or Part D drug plan that's offered in your area earns Medicare's highest five-star quality rating, you can switch to that plan at any time of the year (except for one week, December 1 through 7) without waiting for open enrollment. Coverage in your existing plan is canceled, and your new coverage starts on the first day of the month after you enroll in the five-star plan. To see which, if any, plans in your area have won five stars, use Medicare's online Plan Finder (as explained in Chapters 10 and 11) or call Medicare's help line at 800-633-4227 (TTY 877-486-2048).

Your plan withdraws service from your area, doesn't renew its contract with Medicare, or closes down

An SEP is given in each case, but the allowed periods for switching to another plan vary according to the situation. Medicare, your plan, or both will send you a letter that explains the circumstances, tells you how long your coverage will continue, identifies other plans in your area that are available to you, and specifies when you can switch to another plan.

You lose drug coverage from an employer or union, COBRA, or retiree benefits

This SEP allows you to enroll in a Medicare Advantage or Part D drug plan within two months of losing or dropping *creditable* drug coverage (equivalent to or better than Medicare's) provided by a current or former employer or union. (I provide more detail on creditable coverage in Chapter 6.)

You lose Medicaid or Medicare Savings Program eligibility

This SEP allows three months for you to change Medicare Advantage or Part D drug plans, from the date you're no longer eligible or the date you're notified you'll lose Medicaid or MSP benefits, whichever is later. (I explain these assistance programs in Chapter 4.) For all the time you qualify for these programs, however, you have the right to change to a different plan once during each of the first three quarters of the year.

A plan violates its contract with you

This SEP allows you to disenroll from your plan if it has broken its contract in some way — for example, it failed to provide promised benefits in a timely manner or in keeping with Medicare's quality requirements. You must apply to Medicare for this kind of SEP. If Medicare determines that a violation has occurred, the SEP begins when Medicare notifies you. You can then disenroll from the plan and enroll in another or (if you're in a Medicare Advantage plan) switch to original Medicare. The SEP lasts for 90 days after you disenroll from the plan. Your new coverage starts the first day of the month after you enroll.

You were misled into joining a Medicare Advantage plan

This SEP allows you to switch out of a plan that you joined based on erroneous, misleading, or incomplete information of the kind covered in Chapter 12. You must apply to Medicare for this SEP, and your case will be investigated. If Medicare decides your claim is valid, you can join another MA plan or switch to original Medicare and join a stand-alone Part D drug plan. (In this case, you also get a guaranteed right to buy a Medigap supplemental policy within 63 days of the plan coverage ending.)

A federal employee made a mistake when processing your enrollment or disenrollment in a plan

This SEP allows you to join or switch out of a Part D drug plan after an error has been made. It begins the month Medicare approves the SEP and continues for two more months.

Making sure your records and prescriptions are transferred

When you use an SEP to change plans sometime during the year, the record of your Part D prescription drug usage and payments to date (from the beginning of the year) should be automatically transferred from your old plan to your new one. This shift is very important because your records show

>> The total cost of the drugs you've used since the beginning of the year, which determines your coverage level

>> Your total out-of-pocket expenses since the beginning of the year, which count toward the limit that ends the doughnut hole (if you fall into it; see Chapter 2 for an explanation of the doughnut hole)

>> How much of the deductible you've paid (if the plan has a deductible)

How the deductible is transferred is especially worth keeping an eye on. It depends on whether the old and new plans have deductibles and on the costs of the drugs you've used since the beginning of the year:

>> **If your old plan had a deductible and you've already met it, you can't be asked to pay a deductible for this year under your new plan.** For example, Plan X has a deductible of $400, and your total drug costs so far this year have come to $460, so you've met your deductible and started receiving coverage. When you join Plan Y, which also has a deductible of $400, you don't pay this amount but instead receive coverage at once.

>> **If your old plan had no deductible but your new one does, you must meet this deductible this year before receiving coverage.** For example, Plan X has no deductible, and you've received coverage for $250 worth of drugs so far this year. But Plan Y has a deductible of $290. So you must pay a balance of $40 ($290 minus $250) for your drugs in Plan Y before coverage begins.

>> **If your old plan had a deductible that you didn't meet, what you pay this year depends on whether the new plan has a deductible.** For example, Plan X has a deductible of $310, but your total drug costs so far this year have come to $100. Plan Y has a lower deductible of $200. Because you haven't met your deductible in Plan X, you must pay the $100 difference in Plan Y ($200 minus $100). But if Plan Y has no deductible, you pay no more and your coverage starts immediately.

Keep in mind that, in all these situations, "total drug costs" means what you've paid *and* what your plan has paid for your drugs.

REMEMBER

Medicare requires the old plan to transfer your payment record to the new plan within seven days of when your coverage ends. Still, checking is wise. Compare the first Explanation of Benefits (EOB) statement from your new plan with the last EOB from your old plan to ensure your record has been transferred and correctly reflects the phase of coverage you're in. If you think the info hasn't been migrated correctly, call the plan or call Medicare and file a complaint, as explained in Chapter 16.

What if you change to a new plan but still have refill prescriptions that haven't been dispensed? Can they be transferred to the new plan? Or must you get a new prescription?

>> **If you use a mail-order service:** Any unused refills can be transferred to your new plan only if your current mail-order pharmacy serves both plans. Call its customer service number to find out.

>> **If you use a retail pharmacy:** You can use the same prescription only if the pharmacy is in the network of the new plan as well as the old one.

Dropping a Plan (or Being Dropped)

Most people are allowed to voluntarily leave a Medicare Advantage or Part D drug plan only during the open enrollment period, the Medicare Advantage open enrollment period, or some of the special enrollment periods described earlier in this chapter. Usually, this situation happens when you switch from one kind of coverage to another. But in some circumstances, you may need to cut ties with a plan without joining another. And in a few situations, your plan can cut ties with you. The following sections consider both scenarios.

Leaving a plan on your own

You can get a special enrollment period to drop out of a Medicare Advantage or Part D drug plan without joining another in the following circumstances:

>> **You get health benefits from a new job.** As I explain in Chapter 7, you can opt out of Part B after being enrolled in it if your situation changes and you begin getting health coverage under your own or your spouse's new job. You can also ditch your Part D drug coverage in these circumstances. Here's what to do:

- **Find out whether your new drug coverage is creditable.** If it's not creditable, you need to ask whether keeping your present Part D drug plan can disqualify you from the employer's health plan.

- **Call or write to your current plan, explain the situation, and ask to be disenrolled.** You need to coordinate the date when your Part D coverage ends with the date when your new coverage begins.

>> **You become eligible for TRICARE or VA drug coverage.** You can get an SEP to drop out of your current plan if you start qualifying for military or veterans' benefits under the TRICARE or Veterans Affairs programs. I describe benefits under these programs in Chapter 8.

>> **You move out of the United States.** From your plan's point of view, going to live abroad just means that you're moving out of its service area. But in this case, you won't be joining a new plan because you can't get Part D drug coverage (or any kind of Medicare benefits) abroad. In this situation, call the plan and disenroll. If and when you return to live permanently in the United States, you can apply for another two-month SEP to enroll in a plan that provides Part D drug coverage, as explained in Chapter 6.

>> **You decide you just want out of your plan.** You don't get a special enrollment period for this purpose. If you're in a Medicare Advantage or Part D plan, you're expected to wait until the open enrollment period (with the option, if you're in an MA plan, of instead using the MA open enrollment period between January and March). But if you get an SEP to disenroll from a

plan at other times of the year — for example, if you're moving out of its service area — you aren't obligated to sign up for another plan. Similarly, you don't have to sign up for another plan if you come to the end of the year and decide not to re-enroll. (In the latter case, you need to request disenrollment; otherwise, your enrollment automatically continues the following year.) And of course, you don't have to re-enroll if you stop paying premiums and get dropped by your plan (as explained in the next section).

WARNING

If you leave a plan that provides drug coverage and don't enroll in another, Medicare will probably send you a warning letter about risking late penalties if you decide to re-enroll in the future. But beyond the threat of late penalties, if you won't be covered by any of the types of coverage described in the preceding list, what you really need to think about are the consequences of being without drug coverage for even a few months. You may want to take a look at Chapter 6, where I discuss this issue.

Getting the boot from your plan

A plan *must* disenroll you (it has no choice) in any of these situations:

» **You move permanently out of its service area.** If you don't let the plan know you've moved, it will eventually find out from Medicare or from returned mail. The plan must try to confirm that the move is permanent, but if it can't contact you within six months or it receives no response, it must then disenroll you. (However, if it confirms that your move is only temporary, it must continue your coverage.)

» **You're imprisoned.** Because you lose Medicare coverage when incarcerated, the plan must disenroll you after confirming the situation from public records. (But when you're released, you have the right to a two-month SEP to sign up with a plan again.)

» **You lose your eligibility for Medicare.** This scenario is unusual but can happen in these specific circumstances:

   • If your eligibility for Medicare is based on disability but your condition improves and your disability payments end, your Medicare coverage will also eventually be terminated. (Chapter 5 has details on disability-based eligibility.)

   • If you pay premiums for Part A (as explained in Chapter 5), you must also be enrolled in Part B. If you stop paying either Part A or Part B premiums (or notify Social Security that you no longer want this coverage), your eligibility for Medicare (and Part D) ends.

» **You've misrepresented other coverage you have.** If the plan receives evidence that you intentionally withheld or falsified information about drug coverage you have from an employer — in other words, that you're double-dipping — it must disenroll you when it has Medicare's permission. Your coverage stops on the first day of the month after you're notified that you're being dropped from the plan.

>> **You're required to pay a higher-income surcharge for Part D and you fail to pay it to Medicare.** But the plan can't terminate your coverage until Medicare instructs the plan to do so.

>> **You die.** Of course, at this point, you don't exactly have to worry about Medicare. But here's some info for the benefit of family members: They can inform your Medicare Advantage or Part D drug plan, but it won't act until it's received an official death notification from the Social Security Administration via Medicare. Disenrollment takes effect on the last day of the month after the death. The plan must refund any premiums paid beyond that date.

A plan can drop you at its discretion in these circumstances:

>> **You don't pay your premiums in a timely manner.** Because disenrollment for stopping or being late paying premiums varies according to plans' individual policies, I cover this possibility in more detail in Chapter 13.

>> **You "engage in disruptive behavior."** Medicare doesn't define exactly what this phrase means, except to describe it as behavior that "substantially impairs" the plan's ability to provide services to you or any of its other members. The plan can't drop you for this reason without first trying to solve the problem, submitting thorough documentation to Medicare, and receiving Medicare's go-ahead to disenroll you. The plan must also notify you of your right to appeal the decision. Depending on the circumstances, Medicare may also grant an SEP for you to switch to another plan without loss of coverage.

>> **You allow someone else to use your plan card to obtain services or prescription drugs, or the information on your enrollment form was fraudulent.** The plan can terminate your coverage the first day of the month after it notifies you of disenrollment. The plan must inform Medicare, which will investigate the allegation of fraud.

Deciding Whether to Stay or Switch to Another Plan for Next Year

November is a busy month as the United States prepares the pumpkin pies and gets ready for other holidays beyond the bustle of Thanksgiving. As if you didn't have enough to do, November is also the key time when another pressing question arises: Should you stay with your current Medicare Advantage or Part D drug plan next year or jump to another?

November comes bang in the middle of open enrollment from October 15 to December 7, which allows everybody in Medicare the opportunity to change coverage for the following year. But most people don't even consider it. Well, I'm going to push against that trend — not to persuade you to switch, but to recommend that you look carefully at the changes your plan will make in its costs and benefits for next year and compare them with what other plans are offering. Why do I want you to go to this trouble? Because the plan that works best for you this year won't necessarily be your best deal next year.

If you decide not to change plans, you don't have to do anything; you'll simply be re-enrolled automatically in your current plan for next year. But arriving at that decision after you've considered the alternatives — not just because doing nothing seems to be the easiest option — is in your interests. In the following sections, I explain how your Medicare Advantage or Part D drug plan can change and how you'll know about those changes, why it's worth shopping around to see what other plans are offering next year, and what factors to bear in mind if you're thinking of making a switch.

Reading your Annual Notice of Change to understand plan alterations

I wish I had a dollar for every time I've heard from an outraged Medicare beneficiary — always in January — saying something like "I paid $16 a month for my drug last month, and now my plan's charging me $75. Why?" The fact is that almost every plan makes some changes for the new year, so the costs and benefits in place on December 31 may well be dramatically different on January 1. Here are changes that may or may not occur:

>> The plan may not be there next year. Plans sometimes withdraw from certain service areas or don't renew their contracts with Medicare. Some occasionally go out of business or are terminated by Medicare.

>> The insurance company that sponsors the plan may not offer this particular plan next year.

>> The plan may alter its benefit design next year.

>> The plan may change its charges for premiums, deductibles, and co-pays or switch drugs to different tiers so the co-pays change.

>> The plan may alter its *formulary* (the list of drugs it covers) by dropping some drugs or adding others.

>> The plan may change the restrictions it places on some drugs (prior authorizations, quantity limits, or step therapy, as noted in Chapter 14) by lifting them from some meds and imposing them on others.

How do you know whether any of these changes will affect you? In the case of the first possibility — that your plan won't exist next year — the plan (or maybe Medicare) will notify you in good time. In that case, you have to enroll in another plan to continue coverage. For other changes, the plan must send you details in a document called the *Annual Notice of Change* (ANOC). It's arguably the most important mailing you'll receive from your plan each year, and you should definitely read it. (See the nearby sidebar to find out what happened to someone who didn't read it and someone who was glad he did.)

TIP

The plan must ensure that you get your ANOC no later than September 30 so that you can compare its cost and benefit details for next year with those of other plans. These details are posted on Medicare's Plan Finder website from October 1 onward, in preparation for the open enrollment period. If you haven't received your ANOC by the first week of October, call your plan and ask for it. (Flip to Chapters 10 and 11 for details on using the Plan Finder.)

BEWARE OF IGNORING YOUR ANNUAL NOTICE OF CHANGE

Reading the Annual Notice of Change (ANOC) your plan sends is really important! Here are examples of what happened to someone who didn't and someone who did:

- Suzie stayed in the same Part D drug plan from one year to the next. The following summer, she emailed me, very steamed: "I chose this plan because it gave me extra coverage in the doughnut hole," she wrote. "Now I'm in it, and the plan won't pay. I feel tricked." When I explained that her plan's benefit design had changed on January 1 — no longer giving any gap coverage — and the ANOC she'd received the previous fall warned her of the changes, Suzie fessed up that she hadn't read it. "I won't make that mistake again," she said.

- Thomas began flipping through his ANOC without much interest, but then did a double-take when he saw that his premium would be raised by $15 a month the following year. That made him look more closely at the whole document. He found the co-pays for two of his brand-name drugs would also go up, from $42 to $95 a month. So Thomas used Medicare's online Plan Finder to see what he'd pay out-of-pocket if he enrolled in other Part D drug plans in the coming year. Then he switched to the one he felt would give him the best deal.

Comparing plans (yes, all over again!)

REMEMBER

I can hear the groans. No, no, not again! Of course, you can choose whether to go to the trouble of comparing Medicare Advantage or Part D drug plans this year and every year. But in my opinion — and all consumer advocates agree on this point — shopping around is well worth it. Here's why:

>> Your plan isn't the only one that may change its costs and benefits; so will all the others. A plan you decided against last year may offer a better deal next year — for example, a reduced premium, no deductible, lower co-pays or fewer restrictions for your drugs, or (in MA plans) lower costs for medical services or more covered benefits.

>> Your health condition may have changed during the past year, so now your needs may be for a different set of drugs or medical treatments. That, too, alters the equation of which plan offers the best deal next year.

>> If you don't take any drugs and have therefore opted for the Part D plan with the lowest premium (as suggested in Chapter 10), another plan may have the lowest premium next year.

>> If you compare plans and decide to stay with the one you have now, you'll have the reassurance of *knowing* that it's still the best one for you.

TIP

I'll throw in another reason why comparing plans every year is worthwhile if you use the online Medicare Plan Finder: The more often you do it, the easier it gets. After you have the routine down, you may need only a few minutes to decide that your current plan is still the one for you or that another is better.

Convinced? If so, turn to Chapter 10 for a step-by-step guide to comparing Part D drug plans online, to Chapter 11 for comparing Medicare Advantage plans online, or to Chapter 12 for other ways of getting the same information.

Looking at extra factors influencing your decision

If you're reading this section, I'm assuming that you've compared plan offerings for next year and are considering one or two alternatives to your current plan. Chapters 10 and 11 offer several suggestions for making a final choice among a shortlist of options, and all those tips apply here, too. But when you're deciding whether to switch plans rather than choosing one for the first time, you need to consider points outlined in the following sections.

Carrying over exceptions from your current plan

Did your current plan grant you an exception by covering a drug that isn't on its formulary or waive a restriction on any of your drugs because your doctor convinced the plan it was necessary for your health? If so, you need to find out whether your plan will allow these same exceptions to carry over into next year. Some plans do, but others may require you to apply for them again in the new year. The plan's information materials should state its policy on this point. If they don't, call the plan and ask for the details in writing.

Of course, if your plan allows your exceptions to be carried over, that will save you hassle and be a big factor in deciding to stay with this plan next year. If it doesn't, you have nothing to lose by changing to another plan. But in considering other plans, be sure to check out their restrictions. They may be imposed on the same drugs or on different ones you take.

Switching to a Medicare Advantage plan

If you're thinking of making a switch from original Medicare (and maybe a Part D drug plan) to a Medicare Advantage plan, you need to compare its medical costs and benefits as well as its drug coverage (see Chapter 11).

What about your Medigap supplemental insurance policy if you have one? When you drop Medigap insurance to join a Medicare Advantage plan for the first time, your first 12 months in the plan count as a trial period. During this time frame, as I explain earlier in this chapter, you have the right to a special enrollment period to switch back to original Medicare and buy a Medigap policy with the same company on the same terms you had before. Otherwise, you may still be able to buy a new policy, but it won't come with the same federal guarantees and protections that I explain in Chapter 4, so it will likely cost more than your previous one.

Here is an example: Erica turned 65 in 2020, enrolled in original Medicare, and bought a Medigap policy. But in 2022, she joined a Medicare Advantage plan and gave up her Medigap insurance. After several months, she decided this switch was a mistake. Because she'd been in the plan less than a year — and because it was the only MA plan she'd ever been enrolled in — she was able to go back to original Medicare immediately and get back the Medigap policy she'd had before.

Changing to Another Medigap Policy

Medigap — the private supplemental insurance you can buy to cover many of your out-of-pocket costs in original Medicare — has a number of moving parts that I consider at various points throughout this book. Broadly, I explain the basics of this type of insurance in Chapter 4, note how Medigap differs from Medicare Advantage in Chapter 9, and describe how to choose a policy and the best times to buy one in Chapter 10. Here, I'm assuming you already have a Medigap policy but are wondering whether you can or should switch to another and what you should know to avoid making a costly mistake.

Consumer advocates normally advise people who are about to buy Medigap for the first time to choose the best policy they can afford, just to save the hassle that upgrading to a better policy later on may involve. Still, as the years pass, you may have good reasons for wanting to change, including the following:

>> You're paying for benefits you don't really need.

>> You now need a policy with more benefits.

>> You're not happy with the insurance company that issues your policy.

>> You think another policy or another company may cost you less.

REMEMBER

In this section, I explain the mechanics of switching from one Medigap policy to another, the possible consequences of doing so, and one consumer protection that's worth considering. But first, I want to address a few misconceptions that sometimes lead people to believe they'll lose Medigap coverage if they don't take some kind of action each year. To clarify:

>> **Medigap insurance has no annual open enrollment periods of the kind that exist for Medicare drug and health plans, which I describe earlier in this chapter.** The six-month time frame after you sign up for Part B — when you can buy Medigap with full federal protections — is sometimes referred to as "Medigap open enrollment," but it's actually a one-time opportunity to buy a policy with no fear of being turned down.

>> **After you buy a Medigap policy, you have a guaranteed right for it to be renewed every year with no action on your part.** Of course, that's provided that you told the truth on your application and continue to pay the premiums.

>> **Your Medigap insurance is good all over the country when you go to doctors and other providers who accept Medicare payment.** So you need not buy a new Medigap policy if you move. (The exception is if you have a type of policy known as Medicare SELECT, which limits you to seeing providers within a local service area. But if you move away, you can buy another Medigap policy in your new home area.)

Knowing the consequences of switching Medigap policies

Be aware that federal law doesn't give you an absolute right to switch from one Medigap policy to another. Nor do you get the same full federal guarantees that probably protected you when you bought Medigap the first time around (as I explain in Chapter 10). This caveat doesn't mean that changing your policy is impossible. But the viability and ease of switching may depend on where you live (because some states have more consumer-friendly requirements than the feds or other states on this issue) and whether you can persuade your own or another Medigap insurer to sell you a different policy.

REMEMBER

Before starting on the process, be aware that under federal law the insurer

>> **Can't** exclude pre-existing medical conditions from your new coverage or require waiting periods before coverage kicks in, provided that your current policy has been in effect for six months or longer

>> **Can** temporarily deny coverage for any benefits in the new policy that aren't included in your current one — but for no more than six months after the new policy takes effect

>> **Can** require you to pay higher premiums based on your current age and state of health

>> **Can** refuse to sell you a new policy

But some states provide more protections by offering more frequent periods when you can switch plans without your current health status or pre-existing medical conditions being taken into account. For example, California and Oregon allow you to switch your current Medigap policy for another with the same or fewer benefits, or to change to a different insurer, during a 30-day window following your birthday each year. In Maine, you can switch to a policy with the same or lesser benefits at any time of the year. In Missouri, you have a 60-day period around the anniversary of when you bought your Medigap policy to buy the same policy from a different insurer. To see Medigap rules in your own state, call your state department of insurance or visit its website. (You can find contact information at www.naic.org/state_web_map.htm.)

Exploring a change of Medigap coverage

You can use the details on Medicare's website (see Chapter 4) to compare sets of benefits in different Medigap policies and find contact information for the insurers that sell them in your area. Then do the following:

1. **Decide which policy you prefer from the available standardized policies (labeled A, B, D, G, K, L, M, and N) available to you.**

2. **Call the insurance company that provides your current policy and explain that you want to switch to another.**

   You'll probably be asked to fill out an application form and answer questions about your health.

3. **If that company turns you down or you prefer to go to another insurer, make a list of others in your area that sell Medigap.**

4. **Check to see which rating system each insurer uses.**

   If your current policy has an *attained age rating* — meaning the premium goes up every birthday — note the names of those that use community rating or issue-age rating. Policies that use these systems cost less over time, as explained in Chapter 10.

5. **Call those insurers to see whether they'd sell you the policy of your choice and, if so, ask them to quote you a price for your premium.**

6. **Consider the pros and cons of switching to a new policy or sticking with the one you already have.**

Exercising your right to a 30-day free look

TIP

When you apply for a new Medigap policy, you have to agree to cancel your old one. However, federal law allows you to delay this cancellation for the first 30 days after your new policy becomes effective. This *free look* counts as a trial period that serves as a useful consumer protection. You can use it to make sure that you're comfortable with the new policy; if you have second thoughts, you can cancel the new policy and keep your old one. Still, you have to pay premiums for both policies during that month.

Chapter **16**

Knowing Your Rights

S ooner or later you may have some kind of issue over your Medicare coverage. Note that I'm saying *may*, not *will*. But just in case it happens, keep in mind that you have every right to challenge a decision you don't agree with — whether it's made by Medicare, Social Security, a Medicare Advantage plan, or a Part D drug plan — or to file a complaint about the kind of care you receive. You can try to resolve a variety of problems through different procedures, from making a simple request to pursuing a full-blown appeal. In this chapter, I walk you through those procedures and suggest ways to seek free professional help in making appeals. But first, I consider a very basic right that isn't always addressed: your right to accurate information.

Understanding Your Right to Accurate Information

A major reason for writing this book is my deep concern about how often people receive information about Medicare that's just plain wrong. If it comes from family, friends, doctors, insurance agents, employers' benefits administrators, and so on — well, it's not their fault because none of them can be regarded as reliable sources on Medicare's complexities. But sometimes the inaccurate information comes from Social Security and Medicare officials themselves, whose job is to help Medicare beneficiaries understand the law and navigate its maze of regulations.

I hear about some new incident almost every week — and surely that's just the tiniest tip of the iceberg.

As I know for sure, many officials go out of their way to be helpful, and very often the information they provide is reliable. What's more, I can't blame them for not being able to keep in their heads the whole multitude of rules and regulations; there are just too many of them. However, I do fault officials who, convinced that they *do* know it all, don't bother to check the rules. That's what the POMS manual — the Program Operations Manual System, Social Security's "bible" of guiding instructions — is there for. Medicare officials also have a whole raft of references in their manual system, with regulations on every aspect of coverage, payment, coordination of benefits, and many more topics. That's why, in this book, I sometimes quote the reference for the appropriate official instruction or regulation — especially a fairly new one — so that, if necessary, you can arm yourself with that authority to convince an official who seems not to know of it. The following sections describe strategies that can help you in the quest for accurate information.

Knowing whom to call

For historical reasons, the administration of Medicare is divided between two federal agencies: the Social Security Administration (SSA) and the Centers for Medicare & Medicaid Services (CMS). So putting your questions to the appropriate officials may be half the battle. The following sections note which agency to contact about Medicare issues in different circumstances.

Social Security Administration

Contact the SSA (800-772-1213 or TTY 800-325-0778) or go to its website (www. ssa.gov) about

>> Eligibility for Medicare

>> Medicare enrollment and disenrollment

>> Applying for low-cost drug coverage under the Extra Help program

>> Paying higher-income premiums and requesting waivers

>> Paying Part B late penalties

>> Reporting a change of address or a death

>> All questions about Social Security retirement and survivor benefits, disability benefits (SSDI), and Supplemental Security Income (SSI)

Centers for Medicare & Medicaid Services

Contact the CMS through the Medicare help line (800-633-4227 or TTY 877-486-2048) or go to its website (www.medicare.gov) about

>> Medicare coverage for medical services and supplies

>> Choosing a Medicare Advantage plan or Part D drug plan

>> Choosing Medicare supplemental insurance (Medigap)

>> Billing and payment questions

>> Obtaining a replacement Medicare card

>> Finding doctors who accept Medicare patients in your area

>> Finding a Medicare-approved medical equipment supplier in your area

>> Comparing the quality of hospitals, nursing homes, and home health agencies in your area

>> Appealing a payment or coverage decision you don't agree with

>> Reporting fraud

Seeking a second opinion

The call lines for both Social Security and Medicare are staffed by customer service representatives who have a certain amount of training but aren't equipped to answer every question that comes in. If they don't know the answer, they should consult a supervisor, but they don't always do so. And sometimes they confidently provide an answer that isn't actually accurate.

REMEMBER

If you have doubts about an answer, sometimes the simplest solution is to hang up and call again. You'll get a different person and maybe a different answer. In that case, ask to speak to a supervisor yourself and, if necessary, ask them to look up the specific regulation related to your query. Always note the date and time of your call, the name of the person you talk to, and the citation for the regulation in question (if you're told it).

Another way of seeking a second opinion on whether the information you receive is for real or not is to call your State Health Insurance Assistance Program (SHIP), which has trained counselors to personally answer questions on Medicare at no charge. You can find contact information for each SHIP in Appendix A.

Asking for an Investigation

In some circumstances, you may not need to go through a formal appeals process (which I describe later in this chapter). If you think that a mistake has been made, you may be able to have the incident looked into and possibly resolved without further ado. This section explains several ways of doing so depending on the situation.

Requesting equitable relief

Equitable relief is an obscure concept that few people have ever heard of. It allows Social Security to investigate cases and reverse decisions if it finds they were caused by a federal employee's making a mistake, giving faulty information, or failing to give correct information and may result in situations that cost beneficiaries money, especially from

>> Missing the appropriate deadline for Part B enrollment

>> Being hit with Part B late penalties

Federal employees include any official from Social Security or Medicare or anybody acting on these agencies' behalf, such as a customer service representative or an employee of a Part D plan or a Medicare Advantage plan.

According to the official instruction on this process (POMS HI 00805.170, "Conditions for Equitable Relief"), you may also qualify for relief "if the evidence shows" that you were misinformed by somebody else (such as your employer or insurance company) who in turn had been misinformed by an employee or agent of the federal government. If Social Security investigates and finds evidence that you received faulty information, it can reverse its original decision, allowing you immediate enrollment or reinstatement in Part B and waiving any late penalties.

WARNING

Be aware, though, that the evidence has to be pretty convincing. Social Security says it doesn't even consider opening an investigation unless you can provide the name of the official who misinformed you, plus the place and date when the conversation took place. (This situation is where keeping notes about every interaction you have with federal officials pays off.) Therefore, equitable relief is awarded quite rarely. Some people have obtained it only after asking their members of Congress to intervene. But other people have been successful on their own, so it's well worth a try.

To apply for equitable relief, write a letter to your local Social Security office (call SSA's main number, 800-772-1213, or the TTY number, 800-325-0778, for the address), being as specific as possible about the details. The Medicare Rights Center offers guidance on applying and a specimen letter at www.medicarerights. org/PartB-Enrollment-Toolkit/Equitable-Relief.pdf. Or call 800-333-4114 for a copy.

Contacting an ombudsman

An *ombudsman* is a person appointed to investigate and resolve complaints in a particular situation. Two types are especially useful for people in Medicare:

» **The Medicare Beneficiary Ombudsman's office:** This office receives and looks into complaints, helps resolve them, and, if it identifies any trends behind them, makes recommendations for changes of policy. You can't normally contact this office directly, but you can ask for complaints to be sent there by calling the Medicare help line (800-633-4227 or TTY 877-486-2048) or going through your State Health Insurance Assistance Program (for SHIP contact info, see Appendix A).

» **Long-term-care ombudsmen:** These folks are appointed to look after the interests of people in nursing homes and other long-term-care (LTC) facilities, act as their advocates, and troubleshoot problems on their behalf. Each state, the District of Columbia, Puerto Rico, and Guam have LTC ombudsmen. For contact info, go to theconsumervoice.org/get_help or call your local Agency on Aging (see the state pages of your local phone book).

Reaching out regarding quality of service

If you have an issue with the quality of a medical service you receive under Medicare — from a doctor, a hospital, or any other health provider — you have the right to contact your *Beneficiary and Family Centered Care Quality Improvement Organization* (BFCC-QIO) directly and file a complaint. The BFCC-QIO is an independent review panel of doctors and other healthcare experts who are trained to monitor the care that Medicare beneficiaries receive. It also hands down decisions in cases where coverage is terminated. (For example, you'd call the BFCC-QIO if you think the hospital is discharging you too soon, as explained in Chapter 14.) Medicare contracts with BFCC-QIOs in every state, plus the District of Columbia, Puerto Rico, and the U.S. Virgin Islands. For the address and phone number of your BFCC-QIO, call the Medicare help line at 800-633-4227 or TTY 877-486-2048 or visit qioprogram.org/locate-your-bfcc-qio.

Getting ahold of your plan

If you're enrolled in a Medicare Advantage plan or a Part D prescription drug plan, very often the simplest and quickest way of dealing with a concern is to call the plan, using the customer service number on your membership card.

But be aware that the plan may categorize your complaint as an inquiry, a grievance, or a coverage determination, depending on what you complain about:

>> **One of the plan's policies in general terms:** In this case, the plan can treat your complaint as an inquiry and respond with a simple explanation of the policy. It need not do anything more.

>> **How a policy affects you personally:** In this case, the plan must treat your complaint as a grievance or (if it concerns coverage or payment) as a coverage determination and take appropriate action.

Filing a grievance

A *grievance* covers many types of complaints that you can bring against your Medicare Advantage or Part D drug plan — but *not* those that have anything to do with coverage or payment. Instead, it can focus on any aspect of a plan's service or quality of care that requires some action from the plan to resolve. Situations when you may want to file a grievance include

>> **Poor or unsatisfactory customer service:** Plan representatives leave you on hold for ages or disconnect your call, don't respond to your questions satisfactorily, give wrong or inadequate answers, or are rude.

>> **Misleading information:** You choose a plan on the basis of information that turns out, after enrollment, to be untrue.

>> **Absence of important notifications:** The plan doesn't send you notices required by law — such as its Annual Notice of Change (see Chapter 15) — or you find the wording of its messages difficult to understand.

>> **Problems at the pharmacy:** A pharmacy in your plan's network gives you the wrong meds or makes other mistakes in dispensing your drugs.

>> **Poor quality of care for medical services:** You can't easily get appointments or have to wait too long for them. You have a problem with your care from doctors, nurses, hospitals, or other providers in the plan's network — including rude behavior and facility cleanliness.

>> **Tardy responses or decisions:** The plan fails to respond to your request for a coverage determination or an appeal, or it doesn't give you its decision within the required time frame.

To file a grievance, you can call or write to the plan about your complaint. Look at the informational materials your plan sent you when you enrolled. These documents give the appropriate phone numbers and address for filing a grievance, as well as instructions for how to go about it. You can also find this info on your plan's website.

You must file the complaint within 60 days of the incident that prompted it. (You can request an extension for a good reason, such as illness or a family crisis. Send your plan an explanation in writing, even if the 60-day deadline has passed.) The plan must respond to your complaint within 30 days of receiving it, or up to 14 days more if the plan needs longer to investigate.

REMEMBER

If the plan decides that no action is needed — in other words, it doesn't think your complaint is justified — you can't appeal any further. (An exception is if it's a quality-of-care issue. In that case, you have the right to take it up with your BFCC-QIO, as explained earlier in the section "Reaching out regarding quality of service.") Alternatively, if the plan decides your complaint should be handled as a coverage determination (which I explain later in this chapter), it must tell you how to go about doing that.

Taking Steps toward an Appeal

A Medicare appeal is a formal process that can begin only after certain steps have been taken:

>> If your issue involves the original Medicare program or a Medicare Advantage plan, you must first receive a formal denial of coverage or payment.

>> If the issue is about Part D drug coverage — whether it's provided through a stand-alone drug plan or a Medicare Advantage plan — you first need to request a coverage determination; if the plan turns you down, you can then proceed to an appeal.

In this section, I explain how either of these triggers works, depending on the kind of challenge you want to make. I also suggest a plan of attack that will help your case if you decide to continue with an appeal.

Obtaining a formal denial

If you're in the original Medicare program, you may obtain a denial of coverage for a medical service or piece of equipment in one of two ways:

>> **Checking your Medicare Summary Notice (MSN):** This document is the statement that Medicare sends you every three months as a record of the services you've received during that time. (I explain MSNs, and how to access them more frequently, in Chapter 13.) If you see a service or an item that Medicare has denied payment for, this denial means the determination has already been made. To appeal that decision, you must file within 120 days, following the detailed instructions on the notice.

>> **Checking the first option on an Advance Beneficiary Notice of Non-Coverage (ABN):** You may be given this notice by any providers (doctors, hospitals, skilled nursing facilities, medical equipment suppliers, and so on) if they believe that Medicare won't cover the service or item you've asked for. (I explain ABNs in detail in Chapter 14.) By checking the first option on that notice, you're essentially asking for a determination on whether Medicare will pay.

In either case, the determination is made by the administrative contractor that Medicare uses in your region to decide claims. If you want to challenge a denial, you can proceed to Level 1 of the appeals process, which I describe later in this chapter.

If you're in a Medicare Advantage plan (which I describe in Chapters 9 and 11), the process is different. These plans don't use Medicare Summary Notices. Instead, they send regular Explanation of Benefits notices to itemize the medical services their members have received. Nor do they issue ABNs, because they must explain their coverage policies in the evidence of coverage documents they send to enrollees each year.

Nonetheless, if you think your plan should provide, pay for, or continue to pay for a service or an item, you have the right to request it. The plan must respond within 14 days or, if your doctor says a faster decision is needed for the sake of your health, within 72 hours. If the plan turns down your request, the notice it sends you counts as a denial of coverage that you can challenge through the appeals process. The notice explains how to appeal the decision.

Requesting a coverage determination

A *coverage determination* always relates to coverage or payment issues in the Part D prescription drug program. And you have the right to appeal (described later in this chapter) if the decision goes against you.

Whether you're getting drug coverage from a stand-alone Part D drug plan or a Medicare Advantage plan that provides medications as well as medical care, you can request coverage determinations in two distinct situations:

>> **Asking for your meds to be covered:** You have the right to ask your plan to take the following actions (see Chapter 14 for details on them), but be sure to always do so with your doctor's help:

- **Cover a drug not on its *formulary* (list of covered drugs):** You're requesting an *exception* to the plan's general policy on the basis that you need this drug for sound medical reasons.

- **Waive a restriction:** You want the plan to set aside a restriction — such as prior authorization, quantity limits, or step therapy — it has placed on one or more of your drugs.

- **Cover an excluded drug:** In most cases, plans have the right to refuse to cover any drugs that Medicare excludes from Part D. But sometimes Medicare pays for these meds if they're prescribed for a specific medical condition that Medicare accepts. (For more info, flip to Chapter 2.)

- **Charge you a lower co-pay:** If your doctor thinks that a nonpreferred, brand-name drug on your plan's formulary is the only one that works effectively for you, you can ask for it to be covered at the plan's preferred-tier charge.

>> **Asking for certain costs to be paid:** You can also ask your plan for a coverage determination in matters related to your pocketbook, as well as to your health. You don't need your doctor's support in the following situations:

- **You think the plan is charging you at a higher tier level than it should.** Sometimes a plan moves a drug into a higher tier of charges. If this happens when you're already taking the drug, the plan should charge you the lower-tier co-pay for the rest of the calendar year.

- **You want to be reimbursed for going to an out-of-network pharmacy.** You've gone out-of-network for a good reason (as outlined in Chapter 13), but the plan won't reimburse the extra charges you've paid. Send copies of the pharmacy receipts when making this determination request.

- **You want the plan to reimburse you for the cost of drugs you've already paid for.** This scenario may crop up in a number of situations when you may pay out-of-pocket for a time, such as if confirmation for your enrollment or eligibility for Extra Help (discussed in Chapter 4) is delayed.

- **You believe the plan isn't charging you appropriately for the phase of coverage you're in.** For example, you think you're being charged doughnut-hole rates when you're not in the coverage gap. (I detail the phases of coverage in Chapter 2.)

If you're filing for a determination about any payment-related issues, you can call the plan and file on the phone or (preferably) write a letter or use a form that the plan provides for this purpose. The advantage of using a form is that it tells you what information is required. But if you call or write a letter instead, be sure to use the correct terminology. Say, "I want to request a coverage determination because. . . ." The plan should respond within 24 hours.

Having a game plan in mind before you move ahead with an appeal

If you have received a coverage or payment denial from Medicare or your plan, have decided to challenge it, and are now on the brink of working through the appeals process, I want to suggest a general game plan to make the tasks ahead a bit easier:

>> **Gather any documents that support your case.** These items may include statements from your doctor, pharmacy receipts for drugs you think your plan should cover, and so on, depending on the situation.

>> **Put your problem in writing.** You may try to get an issue resolved just by calling Medicare or your plan. But if possible, put it in writing and keep a copy so that you have a record. Be sure to date all communications.

>> **Keep all paperwork.** Retain copies of all correspondence relating to your request, complaint, or appeal, including receipts and tracking numbers of anything sent by registered mail. This strategy establishes a paper trail you can use as evidence.

>> **Make notes of conversations.** Keep track of all the people you talk to at Social Security, Medicare, or your plan. Write down their names and phone numbers; the dates, times, and places where you spoke to them; and the gist of what was said. Having records of your conversations gives you evidence that may prove valuable later on.

>> **Try to use the right terminology.** Consumer advocates who help people with appeals find that sometimes decisions are delayed or derailed just because the consumer doesn't talk (or write) the same jargon that officials or plan administrators use. In this chapter, I tell you the correct terms for different situations so they're handy when you need them.

>> **Stick to the deadlines.** At every level of appeal, you have a certain time frame (usually 60 days) to file for a review of the previous decision that went against you. If it looks like you'll miss a deadline for good reason, such as sickness or a family crisis, you can ask for an extension.

» **Don't give up!** If you think you're right, don't be put off by a "no" decision or feel intimidated by grand-sounding titles at higher levels of appeal. The title "administrative law judge" may sound formidable, but ALJs more often decide in favor of consumers than officials or plans. If you have a reasonable case, you may well win it.

» **Get help if you need it.** You can designate anyone of your choice to help you or act on your behalf in pursuing a complaint or an appeal. At higher levels of appeal or in tricky situations, however, it's best to seek help from people who are experienced in dealing with appeals on behalf of consumers, such as the advocates I suggest in the later section "Getting help in making an appeal."

Filing a Formal Appeal

The appeals process begins when Medicare provides a formal denial of coverage, or when your Medicare Advantage or Part D plan turns down your request for a coverage determination or fails to give you a decision within the required time frame. In this section, I guide you through the five levels of appeal, show you what to expect, and suggest where you can go for help if you need it.

TIP

For more information on the appeals process, see the official publication "Medicare Appeals" at www.medicare.gov/Pubs/pdf/11525-Medicare-Appeals.pdf.

Walking through the five levels of appeal

You have up to five opportunities to argue your case through the appeals process. Just because all these levels exist doesn't mean you necessarily have to go the full distance, though. At each level, you have a chance of winning. If you don't win, the denial triggers the opportunity to take your case to the next level if you want to do so.

Just what those levels are and who presides over them depends on whether you're challenging a decision concerning your coverage in original Medicare, a Medicare Advantage plan, or a Part D drug plan. As you can see from Table 16-1, the first level has a different review panel for each type of coverage, whereas in Level 2, Medicare Advantage plans and Part D plans share the same panel. For Levels 3, 4, and 5, all three programs use just one type of judgment per level.

The following sections provide more details on what happens at each appeal level. *Note:* In each case, if you receive a denial, you'll also receive a full set of instructions on how to go about taking your case to the next level.

TABLE 16-1

The Five Levels of Appealing a Medicare Decision

Level of Appeal	Who Reviews Your Case
1	Original Medicare: Medicare Administrative Contractor
	Medicare Advantage: Your MA plan
	Part D: Your Part D plan
2	Original Medicare: Qualified Independent Contractor
	MA and Part D: Independent Review Entity
3	Administrative law judge or Office of Medicare Hearings and Appeals (OMHA) adjudicator
4	Medicare Appeals Council ("the Council")
5	Federal district court

Source: U.S. Department of Health and Human Services/Public Domain

Level 1: Redetermination by Medicare or your plan

Redetermination, the first level of appeal, gives you the opportunity to challenge a denial of coverage or of an initial coverage determination request if you don't agree with the decision. You're asking the Medicare contractor (in the case of original Medicare) or your plan (in the case of Medicare Advantage or Part D) to reconsider its first decision. In effect, you're signaling your intent not to take no for an answer.

You (or anyone acting on your behalf) must make this appeal within a certain time frame of the denial determination, according to which program or plan you're challenging: 120 days (original Medicare) or 60 days (Medicare Advantage or Part D plan). If you have good reason for delay (such as sickness), you can ask for more time. Make sure you have supporting paperwork to back up your appeal. If you have documents (such as a doctor's statement) you used in the original coverage determination request or new evidence that wasn't submitted before, be sure to send in all this information now.

TIP

Form CMS-20027 ("Medicare Redetermination Request Form") provides a useful template for making this Level 1 request in the original Medicare program. You can download, fill out, and print the form from the web at www.cms.gov/Medicare/CMS-Forms/CMS-Forms/downloads/CMS20027.pdf.

How long you have to wait for a reconsideration decision again depends on which program or plan you're challenging:

>> **Original Medicare:** Within 60 days, but if you submit new information after your original request, the decision can be delayed for a further 14 days.

>> **Medicare Advantage plan:** Within 30 days for a standard request, within 72 hours if you submit an expedited request that needs a fast turnaround because delay could jeopardize your life or health, or within 60 days if your request involves a payment issue.

>> **Part D plan:** Within 7 days for a standard request (or 14 days for a payment request), or within 72 hours for an expedited request.

If you disagree with the decision made in Level 1, you can take your appeal to the next level. In original Medicare, you must do this within 180 days of receiving the Medicare Administrative Contractor's reconsideration decision. In a Medicare Advantage plan, your case is automatically referred to the second level of appeal if the Level 1 decision goes against you. In a Part D plan, you can request a Level 2 reconsideration within 60 days of the date of the plan's decision.

Level 2: Reconsideration by an independent panel

In Level 2, you leave behind the organizations that decided against you (or didn't decide at all) in the first round of appeal, and your claim is investigated by an independent panel with no connection to the Medicare contractor or your plan. This panel is either the Qualified Independent Contractor (QIC) if the issue concerns original Medicare services or the Independent Review Entity (IRE) in the case of a Medicare Advantage or Part D drug plan.

By requesting a *reconsideration*, you're asking one of these panels to re-evaluate the outcome of your Level 1 appeal by taking a fresh look at your claim. The panel considers Medicare regulations, information in your case file (submitted by your plan or a hospital, for example), and any information that you provide. You have the right to ask the QIC or IRE for a copy of every document in your case file, though you may be charged a copying fee. If English isn't your first language, you're entitled to ask that the QIC or IRE send letters to you in the language you understand best.

The process is somewhat different depending on the circumstances:

>> If you're appealing a service in original Medicare, the QIC should send you a written response about 60 days after receiving your request for a reconsideration. If you disagree with its decision, you have 60 days to request a hearing with an administrative law judge (Level 3). But if you don't receive a timely decision, you can ask the QIC to move your case directly to Level 3.

>> If a Medicare Advantage plan decides against you in Level 1, it must automatically send your case to the IRE. You'll receive a letter from the plan telling you

the specific reason for the denial. If you want to send further information to the IRE, you should do so quickly. The IRE must receive your letter within 10 days of the date of the denial from your plan. The IRE should send its decision within 30 days for a standard request (or 60 days if the issue involves payment), or within 72 hours if you've asked for an expedited (fast) decision on the basis that delay would put your life or health at risk. If you disagree with the decision, you have 60 days to request a hearing at Level 3 of the appeals process.

>> If your Part D drug plan decides against you in Level 1, it should send you not only a denial but also a form that you can use to request a reconsideration (Level 2). If you don't receive this form, call your plan and ask for one. Send your request to the IRE at the address or other contact information included on the form. After reviewing your case, the panel must make a decision within 7 days (14 days for payment request) or within 72 hours if you request an expedited response. If you disagree with the IRE's decision, you have up to 60 days to request a hearing at Level 3.

Level 3: Hearing with an administrative law judge

An *administrative law judge* (ALJ) is a lawyer authorized to conduct hearings on disputes between a government agency and anyone affected by the agency's actions.

REMEMBER

The ALJ level introduces a new requirement that doesn't exist at lower levels of appeal. This requirement is the *amount in dispute* (sometimes called the *amount in controversy*) — a specified dollar minimum that represents the cost to you of having your appeal denied. In 2024, this amount is $180, but it goes up slightly every few years. If your likely cost is less than this amount, you can't appeal to an ALJ. But if you file more than one claim, you may be able to combine them to meet the minimum amount.

You or your representative must request an ALJ hearing within 60 days of receiving the Level 2 denial. Make this request on the form sent to you with the denial and send it to the given address with supporting documents or statements that you want considered. You can ask for a translator or interpreter in your own language (including sign language) if you need to.

TIP

At the ALJ level of appeal, your best bet may be to get professional help from one of the sources listed later in this chapter. Someone who's experienced in such appeals can guide you through the process and may act on your behalf in making the appeal in some circumstances.

You can ask the ALJ to conduct a hearing just on the written evidence, without your taking part, but it's usually best to participate. In that case, the hearing is held on the telephone, via video conference, or (more rarely) in person in a hearing room before the judge. Somebody representing the other side (Medicare or your plan) is also likely to participate. You and other witnesses are asked questions under oath, but ALJ hearings are more informal than a civil court case. Judges are usually understanding and easy to talk to, and they often rule in the beneficiary's favor.

ALJ decisions are usually made within 90 days, but some cases are settled more quickly and some take longer. If the decision goes against you, you have the right to appeal to the Medicare Appeals Council within 60 days.

Level 4: Review by the Medicare Appeals Council

TIP

The Medicare Appeals Council (MAC) is a section of the U.S. Department of Health and Human Services. If you want to take your case to this stage — the fourth level of appeal — I recommend that you have an advocate or lawyer with experience of the process to represent you. The MAC review often focuses on a question of law (such as whether the ALJ interpreted Medicare law correctly), a question of fairness (such as whether the ALJ considered all the evidence), a question of fact (such as whether the evidence supports the decision), or a question of policy (such as when there's a dispute about how Medicare interprets the law). Most people are way out of their depth here without an advocate helping their case.

At this level of appeal, the MAC decides a case simply by reviewing the written evidence. No hearing is required, and the amount in dispute doesn't matter. If the MAC denies your request for a review or rules against you, you can file for a federal court hearing.

Level 5: Hearing in federal court

REMEMBER

If you go to this final stage of appeal, which typically involves issues of law, you really want to be represented by a licensed attorney. (See the next section for information on legal help.) At this level, the amount in dispute is again a factor, but the minimum dollar claim is much higher than at the ALJ level: $1,840 in 2024. To request this review, you must file within 60 days of the MAC's decision, following the instructions given in the MAC's denial letter, and a federal court judge reviews your case. If the case goes to court, the judge determines whether the decision of the MAC (in reversing or modifying the ALJ's ruling or allowing it to stand) is supported by substantial evidence.

Getting help in making an appeal

Anyone can help you file an appeal — a relative, friend, doctor, consumer advocate, lawyer, or whoever. If you want any of these people to *represent* you — that is, prepare and present arguments — that person must fill out a form as instructed in any denial letter you receive.

TIP

If you don't happen to have any Medicare lawyers in the family tree, free legal help from professionals who are experienced in Medicare appeals is available from the following sources:

>> **The Medicare Rights Center (MRC):** This national, not-for-profit consumer service offers free counseling. Call its hot line toll-free at 800-333-4114; visit www.medicareinteractive.org, a free online resource with hundreds of answers to Medicare questions; or go to www.medicarerights.org.

>> **The Center for Medicare Advocacy (CMA):** A national, not-for-profit advocacy group, the CMA litigates class-action lawsuits on behalf of Medicare beneficiaries from time to time. It offers free self-help packets containing detailed guidance on some types of Medicare appeals at www.medicareadvocacy.org/take-action/self-help-packets-for-medicare-appeals.

>> **California Health Advocates (CHA):** This nonprofit consumer watchdog organization serves the needs of California's Medicare and Medicaid beneficiaries. For resources to help make appeals, go to the CHA website at www.cahealthadvocates.org/appeals.

>> **Medicare Advocacy Project (MAP):** A program run by Greater Boston Legal Services, MAP operates through legal-aid offices throughout Massachusetts. MAP advocates help low-income Medicare beneficiaries obtain the services to which they're entitled. Call 800-323-3205 or go to www.gbls.org/our-work/elder-health-disability/elder-health-disability-community-partnerships.

>> **State Health Insurance Assistance Programs (SHIPs):** All states have SHIPs that give free help and counseling to people with Medicare. If your state program doesn't directly provide legal help with Medicare appeals, it can put you in contact with local services that can. To find your SHIP's phone number, head to Appendix A.

Other resources for finding a licensed lawyer to represent you include

>> The National Academy of Elder Law Attorneys (www.naela.org)

>> The American Bar Association's lawyer referral directory (www.americanbar.org/directories/lawyer-referral-directory.html)

>> The Legal Services Corporation (www.lsc.gov)

>> LawHelp from ProBono Net (www.lawhelp.org/find-help)

5

The Part of Tens

Check out the most frequent mistakes made when navigating the complex Medicare system — and how to avoid them. Avoiding the most-common mistakes in Medicare can make a world of difference to your costs and sense of satisfaction with the program.

Discover strategies for staying healthy, happy, and, above all, independent for as long as possible in the years after 65. Research shows that many diseases and injuries can be staved off or avoided altogether in very simple ways that cost little or nothing.

Chapter **17**

Top Ten Medicare Mistakes

M edicare is uncharted territory for most of the 10,000 people who come into the program each day. It's not a minefield, exactly, but lurking in the undergrowth are pitfalls and traps that can be costly unless people take care to dodge them.

Avoiding the most common mistakes in Medicare can make a world of difference to your costs and sense of satisfaction with the program. I've heard from people who are forced to go without coverage for many months or to pay higher premiums for the rest of their lives — just because they didn't know the rules about enrollment.

Right now, no government agency — Medicare, Social Security, or any other — is required to provide information on Medicare enrollment for people who are about to turn 65. Consequently, most have no clear idea of their options, and many make wrong decisions, which can cost them dearly. Hopefully, this situation will change one day.

TECHNICAL
STUFF

Legislation has been introduced in Congress that would mandate a notice to be sent to prospective enrollees a few months before their 65th birthday. The notice would explain when and how people should enroll, according to their situation, and provide a number to call with questions. This legislation, known as the BENES

Act 2.0, goes a long way toward helping people avoid enrollment pitfalls and provides additional protections that I discuss in Chapter 6. While Congress passed a bill in late 2020 (the first BENES Act) that helped eliminate lengthy waiting periods for coverage in Medicare, as of this writing, Congress has not passed this second iteration of the legislation.

This chapter condenses warnings about the top ten mistakes in Medicare into a handy checklist that I hope you can use to ensure that you avoid them.

Thinking You Must Reach Full Retirement Age before Signing Up

For many years after Medicare began, most people enrolled in the program and started drawing Social Security retirement benefits at the same time: when they turned 65. But things have changed.

REMEMBER

Social Security's full retirement age is now 67. But if you want to avoid late penalties, you need to sign up for Medicare at age 65, unless you have health coverage from your own job or from your spouse's current place of employment. You don't need to wait until you are collecting Social Security benefits to enroll in Medicare.

Assuming You Don't Qualify If You Haven't Worked Long Enough

Earning at least 40 credits by paying payroll taxes at work — about 10 years' work — means just one thing: It ensures that you won't have to pay premiums for Part A benefits (which mainly cover stays in the hospital) after you join Medicare. But you don't need any work credits to qualify for Part B (which covers doctors' services, outpatient care, and medical equipment) and for Part D (prescription drug coverage). You can get Part B and Part D benefits just by paying the required monthly premiums, provided that you're 65 or older and a U.S. citizen or a legal resident who's lived in the United States for at least five years.

You may also qualify for Part A benefits on your spouse's work record, or you can pay premiums for them, as I explain in detail in Chapter 5. But if you don't have 40 credits when you reach 65 and wait to sign up for Part B until you've earned them, you may have to wait several months for coverage and end up paying permanent late penalties.

Failing to Enroll in Part B When You Should

Signing up at the time that's right for you is critical. If you don't, you risk two consequences:

>> **Delayed coverage:** You can sign up only during a general enrollment period (GEP), which runs from January 1 to March 31 each year — with coverage beginning the month after you enroll.

>> **Late penalties:** An extra 10 percent for each full 12-month period that you delayed enrollment is added to your monthly Part B premiums for all future years.

The exception here is if you have health coverage beyond age 65 from an employer for which you (or your spouse) actively work and the employer has 20 or more workers. In that situation, you can delay Part B enrollment without penalty until the job ends, as I explain in detail in Chapter 6.

Otherwise, you need to sign up during your seven-month initial enrollment period, in which the fourth month is usually the month in which you turn 65 — also described in Chapter 6.

Believing You Don't Need Part B If You Have Retiree or COBRA Coverage

Part B is optional, so you are not obliged to enroll. But you should be aware that retiree benefits and COBRA coverage, though provided by a former employer, do not count as "active" employment and therefore do not protect you from delayed coverage and late penalties (see the preceding section) if you want to sign up for Part B at some future date:

>> **Retiree benefits:** Carefully check with your retiree plan to see how it fits in with Medicare. In most such plans, Medicare automatically becomes primary coverage, and the plan pays only for a few services that Medicare doesn't cover. In that case, if you fail to sign up for Part B when you're required to, you'll essentially have no coverage.

>> **COBRA coverage:** This allows you to continue on your former employer's healthcare plan after your job ends, usually for about 18 months, while paying its full premiums. In this situation, to avoid late penalties, you need to sign up for Part B before the end of your initial enrollment period at age 65, or (if your job ended after that period) no later than eight months after you stopped work.

See Chapter 6 for more information on this topic.

Not Signing Up for Part D Because You Don't Use Prescription Drugs

Why pay Part D premiums if you need no medicines? Because you don't have a crystal ball and can't be sure that you won't get some unforeseen illness or suffer a serious injury that takes expensive drugs to treat. (Some cancer drugs cost thousands of dollars a month.)

Part D, like all insurance, provides coverage when you need it but doesn't allow you to wait to sign up until the need becomes urgent. And if you delay enrollment, you risk having late penalties permanently added to your Part D premiums — unless you have "creditable" drug coverage from elsewhere (such as retiree benefits) that Medicare considers at least as good as Part D.

But the more serious consequence of not enrolling is going without coverage. If you don't sign up with a Part D plan when you're first eligible — and don't have creditable drug coverage from another source — you must wait until the next open enrollment period. This runs from October 15 to December 7 each year, with coverage beginning January 1. One solution to this conundrum: Pick the plan with the lowest premium, so you get coverage at the least cost.

See Chapter 6 for more on enrollment.

Picking a Part D Drug Plan for the Wrong Reasons

The "wrong" reasons include choosing a plan on the basis of its premium, or because it has a familiar name, or because that was the plan your spouse or best friend chose.

The best way to pick a plan is according to the specific prescription drugs you take. That's because Part D plans do not cover all drugs and they charge widely differing co-pays, even for the very same drug. Co-pays, much more than the premiums, determine how much you will spend out-of-pocket in any plan.

You can compare coverage and costs for your own drugs among the different Part D plans available to you by using the Plan Finder on Medicare's website — as I explain step by step in Chapters 10 and 11 — or by getting help from one of the sources listed in Chapter 12.

Misunderstanding Enrollment Periods

You may have read about "open enrollment" and gotten the idea that this is the only time you can sign up for Medicare. Not true! In Medicare, open enrollment (October 15 to December 7 each year) is *only* for people who are already in the program and want to change their coverage for the following year.

If you're joining Medicare for the first time, you get your very own enrollment period. This may be your seven-month initial enrollment period (around the time you turn 65) or a special enrollment period if you have health coverage from an employer for which you or your spouse actively work, or some other time frame depending on your situation — for example, if you qualify for Medicare due to disability, live outside the United States, or are a legal immigrant. Enrollment periods for all these circumstances are explained in detail in Chapter 6.

WARNING

If you miss your personal deadline because you're waiting for open enrollment, you risk delayed coverage and permanent late penalties.

Being Too Late to Buy Medigap with Full Protections

Medigap supplemental insurance is extra coverage that you can choose to buy privately to cover some or most of your out-of-pocket expenses in original Medicare, such as deductibles and co-pays. But to get the full federal protections, you need to buy it at the right time and you must be 65 or older. If you buy a Medigap policy within six months of enrolling in Part B or in a few other specific circumstances, Medigap insurers can't deny you coverage or charge higher premiums based on your current health or pre-existing medical conditions. Outside those time frames, they can do both — unless you live in one of the few states that provide additional protections.

The six-month window that you're allowed after enrolling in Part B is a one-time opportunity. So if you sign up for Part B when you turn 65 but continue to have employer insurance from your own or your spouse's current employment beyond the six-month deadline, you will fail to qualify for federal protections if you want to buy a Medigap policy when you (or your spouse) stop work.

However, if you enrolled in Part B under age 65 because of disabilities, you get another opportunity for federal protections if you buy a Medigap policy during the six months following your 65th birthday.

For full details about buying Medigap, see Chapters 4 and 10.

Failing to Read Your Annual Notice of Change

This important document comes in the mail each September if you're enrolled in a Medicare Advantage plan (HMO or PPO) or a Part D prescription drug plan. It specifies what changes the plan will make in its costs and coverage for the following year. For example: The plan may increase or reduce its premiums, or place your drugs in a pricing tier that charges higher co-pays for your drugs than what you pay now.

Carefully reading this notice provides you with the information you need to compare your current plan with others that will be available to you next year. You can make this comparison during open enrollment, which runs from October 15 to December 7, following the step-by-step guide I provide in Chapter 10 (for Part D drug plans) or Chapter 11 (for Medicare Advantage plans). If you find a plan that gives you a better deal, you can switch to another for the following year, a process I discuss in Chapter 15.

In contrast, failing to read this notice can result in nasty shocks on January 1 if you stay with a plan that hikes its charges in the new year.

Not Realizing You May Qualify for Help to Lower Your Costs

Medicare comes with many expenses — premiums, deductibles, co-pays — that many people find hard to pay. So if your income is limited, be sure to check out three programs that can reduce those costs if you qualify:

>> **Medicaid** is a state-run program that provides virtually free health insurance for people with very low incomes. If you qualify, Medicare will be your primary insurance and Medicaid will be secondary, paying your out-of-pocket expenses in Medicare and covering some services that Medicare doesn't provide.

>> **Medicare Savings Programs** are run by the state and pay Part B premiums and sometimes other expenses for people with incomes under the limits set by the state.

>> **Extra Help** is a federal program that provides low-cost or reduced Part D prescription drug coverage for people with incomes and savings below a certain level.

I describe these programs in detail in Chapter 4.

TIP

To see whether you qualify for any of these programs, contact your State Health Insurance Assistance Program (SHIP), which provides free counseling on Medicare and Medicaid issues. To find the toll-free phone number of your SHIP, turn to Appendix A.

Chapter **18**

Ten Ways to Stay Healthier beyond Age 65

Nobody really feels "old" at 65 anymore, and many can expect to live for another 20 years or so after that, with an ever-growing number of Americans (an estimated 101,000 in 2024, according to the U.S. Census Bureau) getting to see 100 candles on their cakes. The prospect of increased longevity is great, as long as you stay healthy enough to enjoy it.

Looking after your health as much as you can isn't just a matter of feeling good. It also helps preserve your independence so that you have a chance of living for many more years on your own terms in your own home. This chapter considers ten ways to achieve these goals.

Taking Action to Avoid Falls

Making sure not to fall is about the best thing you can do to keep your independence and prevent costly medical treatments. Falls among older adults led to 3 million visits to the emergency room and 36,000 deaths in 2020, according to the National Safety Council. Yet experts say that many of these tumbles can be avoided in very simple ways, as follows:

>> Wear sensible shoes that fit properly and don't slip.

>> Clip your toenails (or have them clipped) regularly.

>> Have your vision checked regularly and keep your eyeglasses clean.

>> Remove loose rugs or use adhesive tape to make them nonslip.

>> Use nonslip mats in the tub or shower.

>> Keep packaged or canned foods and kitchen utensils within easy reach.

>> Repair worn carpeting or floorboards.

>> Keep walkways and stairs well-lit and clear of objects you may fall over.

>> Paint the lowest step a different color, or line the edge with colored tape.

>> Practice exercises designed to improve balance and muscle strength.

You may also consider installing some basic safety equipment in your home, even if you don't quite need it yet, such as

>> Grab bars in the bathroom

>> Handrails on staircases or steps where none exist

>> A seat with nonslip leg tips in the shower stall so that you can safely sit to take a shower, using a handheld showerhead

>> New electric lights to illuminate dark areas, and switches at both the top and bottom of stairs

TIP

Original Medicare doesn't cover these costs (see Chapter 2), though some Medicare Advantage plans may cover some home safety devices through their supplemental benefits. If you need to have work done but have a low income, contact Rebuilding Together, which provides volunteers to make repairs and modifications or install safety measures free of charge. Call 800-473-4229 or go to rebuildingtogether.org for local information. Or contact the Eldercare Locator for other local resources; call 800-677-1116 or go to eldercare.acl.gov/Public/ Index.aspx. See also the AARP HomeFit Guide (at aarp.org/homefit) for ideas on making your home safe and fit for your changing needs as you get older.

Exercising Regularly

Regular exercise has extraordinary benefits. Apart from slimming you down, it can reduce high blood pressure and high cholesterol and lower the risk of diabetes, heart disease, stroke, and breathing problems. For many people, it can do a better job than the prescription drugs designed to treat these same conditions — without the costs or unwelcome side effects. Another benefit of exercise is that it gives you a lot more energy and better sleep. And it strengthens your bones, tones your muscles, and improves your balance — in other words, greatly reduces your risk of falling (see the preceding section).

REMEMBER

I'm not saying that you should be doing a heavy workout at the gym every day — which for most older people isn't wise anyway without a doctor's agreement — or spending a fortune on home exercise equipment. Any of the following alternatives is just as effective:

>> **Walking:** About 2,400 years ago, the great Greek physician Hippocrates said, "Walking is man's best medicine." And modern research confirms that he was absolutely right. Start with a short distance but work up to a couple of miles or more several times a week.

>> **Swimming:** Swimming provides excellent exercise, especially for people with arthritis and other joint problems who have a harder time walking.

>> **Practicing gentle exercise:** Disciplines such as yoga and tai chi reduce stress, anxiety, and depression, and build muscle tone and energy.

>> **Pursuing active hobbies:** Get creative with other activities: dancing, bicycling, gardening, shooting hoops, bowling, taking up archery, you name it — anything to keep moving.

TIP

For more information on the benefits of exercise and how to do it safely, see the guidance provided by the federal Centers for Disease Control and Prevention (CDC) at https://www.cdc.gov/physical-activity-basics/benefits.

Quitting Smoking

Tobacco use is the leading cause of preventable illness — heart disease, stroke, cancer, lung disease, and cataracts of the eye — and is responsible for an estimated one-fifth of deaths in the United States each year.

REMEMBER

When you've smoked tobacco for 30, 40, or 50 years and you're now in your 60s or 70s, the classic defense against quitting is "It won't do any good after all this time. It's too late for me." But that isn't true. Studies show that the risk of heart attack declines 50 percent within one year of quitting, and within five years the risk of cancer begins to approach that of a person who's never smoked, according to the Center for Tobacco Research and Intervention at the University of Wisconsin. And the Society for Vascular Surgery claims that within only 48 hours of quitting, blood pressure and pulse rate drop, nerve endings in the lungs start to regrow, the ability to smell and taste improves, and carbon monoxide in the blood returns to normal levels. The largest study to date, reported by the National Cancer Institute in 2016, found that people who quit smoking in their 60s had a 23 percent lower risk of death from all causes than those who didn't stop. The basic message: "It's never too late to quit."

Nicotine is said to be more addictive than heroin, so quitting cold turkey is a tough call for long-term smokers, and most can't rely on willpower alone. But various devices can help the process — nicotine patches and gum, electronic cigarettes that deliver a small shot of nicotine in water vapor but without the toxic chemicals ingested by smoking tobacco, and anti-smoking drugs.

TIP

Counseling is said to be effective, too — especially when combined with medications — so know that Medicare covers up to eight anti-smoking sessions in any 12-month period free of charge for people who want to quit. Talk to your doctor or call Medicare (800-633-4227 or TTY 877-486-2048) for details.

Eating Healthfully

More and more, medical science is finding solid evidence for the old idea that you are what you eat. Food has an enormous impact on health, for good and for bad. Researchers investigating longevity in certain places around the world where people typically enjoy very long lives usually find that the subjects' meals are small but rich in fruit, vegetables, fish, whole grains, and nuts. Yes — the exact opposite of an American fast-food diet, with its emphasis on red meat, saturated fat, processed foods, sugar, and super-sized everything.

Being very overweight has long been seen as a risk factor for early death and serious diseases, but in 2013, the American Medical Association designated obesity as a disease in its own right. The hope is that more doctors will suggest treatment (such as counseling sessions available for free in Medicare — see Chapter 2) to help the one-third of adult Americans who are obese.

To eat healthfully and lose weight, you don't have to give up everything you like or keep rigidly to some lettuce-leaf diet that you're bound to break after a while. Just pay attention to what you're putting in your mouth every day and eat less of it. Avoid food that's heavy on calories but low in nutritional value, such as fried foods, processed meats, white bread, and white rice. Look more closely at food labels, because some marked "low-fat" are actually loaded with salt or sugar, which can also cause serious health problems.

TIP

The National Institute on Aging's website (www.nia.nih.gov/health/healthy-eating-nutrition-and-diet) has excellent information for older people on eating wisely and well, including links to several sources of food assistance for people with limited incomes.

Cutting Out Soft Drinks and Extra Sugar

Dangerously high levels of sugar and high fructose corn syrup in sodas and other soft drinks cause obesity, diabetes, heart disease, tooth decay, gout, and many other health problems, according to a multitude of medical studies. Just one 20-ounce soda contains the equivalent of 15 teaspoons of sugar, according to the Center for Science in the Public Interest — far more than the daily maximums recommended by the American Heart Association of 6 teaspoons for women and 9 for men.

Reducing your intake of soft drinks — or better still, eliminating them altogether — is one of the easiest ways to lose weight and get healthier. Also try to avoid some salad dressings and processed foods that contain more sugar than you may think. Good news, though: Dark chocolate may be good for you! Providing that it contains at least 70 percent cacao, dark chocolate has been shown to lower blood pressure and may help combat heart disease by preventing the hardening of veins and arteries.

Keeping an Eye on Prescription Drugs

Over two-thirds of Americans age 60 and older take at least one prescription drug, and roughly a third take at least five, according to the CDC. Often these meds do a great job keeping people healthy and functioning. But the sobering fact is that serious side effects from medications send more than 1.3 million Americans to the emergency room each year.

Not all bad effects of drugs cause dramatic results and trips to the emergency room, but for that reason they can be harder to recognize. For example, they may affect your balance or vision (making falls more likely), disturb sleep, and cause depression and memory loss. Medication experts say that if you experience such symptoms, doctors should regard the drugs you take as the prime suspects in detecting their causes. That's partly because new drugs are rarely tested on older people or people who have several medical conditions.

REMEMBER

Don't stop taking your meds, but do try to be vigilant about noticing side effects, and, as I explain in Chapters 4 and 14, consider having your drugs regularly checked out to see whether you still need to take them all.

Continuing to Work or Stay Active

An increasing number of Americans stay employed beyond age 65, but the jury is still out on whether people who continue to work function better than those who retire. Many studies suggest that those who work are more agile mentally and have better memories, but it's unclear whether this observation is a chicken-or-egg conundrum: Does working cause those benefits, or do people who already have them tend to continue working longer?

Whatever science comes up with, however, staying active — whether working for money or doing things in retirement that interest you — helps generate feelings of contentment, self-confidence, and joy in life, which sounds like a good working blueprint for staying healthy, too.

Staying Connected and Engaged

Time and again, research shows that older people who routinely connect with other people — families, friends, and folks in the community — remain physically and mentally agile far longer than those who become isolated. Studies have even found that joining choirs and singing groups can strengthen seniors' immune systems, reduce stress and depression, and just make them feel better. Similar results are found among people who volunteer in the community and regularly interact with grandchildren or other youngsters.

Seniors today have unprecedented opportunities to stay connected with others — even if they live thousands of miles away — and to engage in what's going on in the world. So put your computer, laptop, tablet, or phone to good use: Reach out via your favorite social media and download those apps!

Keeping Your Brain in Shape

Momentarily forgetting your keys, your glasses, your neighbor's name, and the reason you just came into this room — that kind of short-term memory loss is a normal part of aging and doesn't mean you're getting Alzheimer's. But you may be wondering whether you can do anything to avoid or stave off this and other dreaded mental diseases that are associated with getting older.

REMEMBER

Nobody yet knows exactly what causes Alzheimer's and similar dementias or how to cure them or avoid them. Certainly, mental exercises like solving crosswords, Sudoku, and other puzzles may well help keep your brain in working order, and anyway, they're fun. But really, most of the topics discussed earlier in this chapter — in particular, exercise, healthy eating, staying active, and socializing — all contribute a lot more to brain health.

TIP

Opportunities for putting your brain to work are boundless: taking classes in your community, learning a new language or a new skill, using the internet to follow the news and download free lectures, investigating your family history, volunteering your skills to a good cause, and many more.

Addressing Tough Choices before They're Necessary

When should you quit driving, move in with family members or into assisted living or long-term care, make a living will, and appoint someone as your power of attorney? These are all difficult issues for anyone to confront, but experts say discussing them sooner rather than later with family members or close friends is best. Some issues, such as quitting driving at the right time or deciding to stop living alone, may play a direct role in preserving your life and health. Others, such as making a living will, can bring peace of mind.

REMEMBER

Having a game plan that you've worked out when you're still relatively fit makes necessary decisions easier for you and your caregivers later on. That way, you can be more confident that your wishes will be carried out even if there comes a time when you can no longer make decisions. You can find loads of information on these issues in the caregiving section of AARP's website at `aarp.org/caregiving` and in AARP's book *The Other Talk: A Guide to Talking with Your Adult Children About the Rest of Your Life* at `aarp.org/OtherTalk`. Sally Hurme's book *Checklist for My Family: A Guide to My History, Financial Plans, and Final Wishes* (`aarp.org/formy family`) is an invaluable guide to compiling in one place the critical information that your family needs to know should something happen to you.

Appendixes

Appendix **A**

Sources of Help and Information

Often, the help you're looking for to deal with Medicare issues is only a toll-free phone number or a website away. In this appendix, I provide contact information for government help lines and online resources, independent organizations that offer direct help or ways to save money, advocacy organizations that work on behalf of people on Medicare, and sources you can look to for updated Medicare information. Throughout, I note special help provided for people whose first language is something other than English.

Government Help Lines and Websites

The go-to sources for help provided by federal and state governments are the Centers for Medicare & Medicaid Services (CMS), the Social Security Administration (SSA), the State Health Insurance Assistance Programs (SHIPs), and the Eldercare Locator.

The Centers for Medicare & Medicaid Services

CMS is the federal agency that runs Medicare (under the umbrella of the U.S. Department of Health and Human Services) and oversees Medicaid in partnership with the states. It provides updated information and direct help to consumers in English and Spanish in the following ways:

>> The *Medicare & You* handbook goes out to everyone on Medicare every September (or read it online at www.medicare.gov/pubs/pdf/10050-Medicare-and-You.pdf). This basic overview of Medicare services includes brief details of the Medicare Advantage health plans and the stand-alone Part D drug plans that will be available in your area for the following year.

>> Medicare's toll-free help line at 800-633-4227 (or TTY 877-486-2048) is available 24/7. The folks on the other end of the line can answer your questions and give you help on many Medicare issues. If neither English nor Spanish is your first language, you can ask for an interpreter; more than 150 languages are available.

>> Medicare's website at www.medicare.gov offers a huge amount of information. Go to this site to learn what's covered, find providers, and compare Part D plans, Medicare Advantage plans, hospitals, and nursing homes. You can also shop and compare health and drug plans using the Medicare Plan Finder at www.medicare.gov/plan-compare.

>> If you need someone to contact Medicare on your behalf, you can fill out the "Medicare Authorization to Disclose Personal Health Information" form. Visit www.medicare.gov/basics/forms-publications-mailings/forms/other, or call 800-633-4227 (TTY 877-486-2048).

The Social Security Administration

The Social Security Administration, or SSA, is the federal agency that administers not only Social Security benefits but also certain aspects of the Medicare program. Call the SSA toll-free at 800-772-1213 (TTY 800-325-0778) or check out its website at www.ssa.gov for information on getting Social Security disability and retirement benefits, enrolling in Medicare Part A and/or Part B, understanding the higher-income Part B and Part D premium surcharges, and applying for Part D's Extra Help program.

Note: You can read the SSA website in Arabic, Armenian, Chinese, Farsi, French, Greek, Haitian Creole, Italian, Korean, Polish, Portuguese, Russian, Somali, Spanish, Tagalog, Ukrainian, and Vietnamese, as well as English and American Sign Language. To choose a language, click on the "Other Languages" button at the bottom of the home page. You can also ask for an interpreter in any language when you call the help line or when you arrange to visit a local Social Security office.

State Health Insurance Assistance Programs

SHIPs (State Health Insurance Assistance Programs) are valuable resources for anyone who needs help with Medicare (and sometimes Medicaid) issues. They provide personal help from trained counselors free of charge when you're trying to find a Part D drug plan or Medicare Advantage plan that meets your needs, apply for Medicare Savings Programs or Extra Help, make an appeal, or resolve a variety of other problems. If English isn't your first language, they can provide interpreters or refer you to local organizations that offer counseling in your own language.

SHIPs, which are funded by the federal and state governments, are available in every state, the District of Columbia, Guam, Puerto Rico, and the U.S. Virgin Islands. The programs can have different names in some states (for example, HICAP in California and SHINE in Florida). The following list includes every program, its name, the state agency that runs it, the telephone number, and the web address. *Note:* If the phone number you call isn't working, call the Eldercare Locator at 800-677-1116 or go to www.shiphelp.org for an updated number. (Find out more about the Eldercare Locator in the next section.)

In this section, I try to provide the specific web address you'll need, but there may be changes. So if what you need isn't on the URL listed here, search for "SHIP" or the name of the program listed, or dig around on the subpages.

Alabama: SHIP, Department of Senior Services, Montgomery, AL; phone 800-243-5463; website alabamaageline.gov/ship/

Alaska: SHIP, Department of Health, Anchorage, AK; phone 800-478-6065 (TTY 800-770-8973); website www.medicare.alaska.gov/

Arizona: SHIP, Department of Economic Security, Phoenix, AZ; phone 800-432-4040; website des.az.gov/medicare-assistance

Arkansas: SHIIP, State Insurance Department, Little Rock, AR; phone 800-224-6330; website www.shiipar.com/

California: Health Insurance Counseling and Advocacy Program (HICAP), Department of Aging, Sacramento, CA; phone 800-434-0222; website www.aging.ca.gov/hicap

Colorado: SHIP, Division of Insurance, Denver, CO; phone 888-696-7213; website doi.colorado.gov/insurance-products/health-insurance/senior-health-care-medicare

Connecticut: Connecticut's program for Health insurance assistance, Outreach, Information and referral, Counseling, and Eligibility Screening (CHOICES); State Department of Aging and Disability Services, Hartford, CT; phone 800-994-9422 (TTY 860-247-0775); website portal.ct.gov/ADS-CHOICES

Delaware: Delaware Medical Assistance Bureau, Insurance Department, Dover, DE; phone 800-336-9500; website insurance.delaware.gov/divisions/dmab

District of Columbia: DC SHIP, Department of Aging and Community Living, Washington, DC; phone 202-727-8370; website dacl.dc.gov/service/health-insurance-counseling

Florida: Serving Health Insurance Needs of Elders (SHINE), Department of Elder Affairs, Tallahassee, FL; phone 800-963-5337 (TTY 800-955-8770); website www.floridashine.org

Georgia: Georgia SHIP, Department of Human Services, Atlanta, GA; phone 866-552-4464; website aging.georgia.gov/georgia-ship

Guam: Guam Medicare Assistance Program (MAP), Department of Public Health and Social Services, Mangilao, Guam; phone 671-735-7415; website dphss.guam.gov/division-of-senior-citizens-2

Hawaii: SHIP, Executive Office on Aging, Honolulu, HI; phone 808-586-7299 (TTY 866-810-4379) or neighboring islands 888-875-9229; website www.hawaiiship.org

Idaho: Senior Health Insurance Benefits Advisors (SHIBA), Department of Insurance, Boise, ID; phone 800-247-4422; website doi.idaho.gov/SHIBA/

Illinois: SHIP, Department on Aging, Springfield, IL; phone 800-252-8966 (TTY 888-206-1327); website ilaging.illinois.gov/ship.html

Indiana: SHIP, Department of Insurance, Indianapolis, IN; phone 800-452-4800 (TTY 866-846-0139); website www.in.gov/ship

Iowa: SHIIP, Iowa Insurance Division, Des Moines, IA; phone 800-351-4664 (TTY 800-735-2942); website shiip.iowa.gov/

Kansas: Senior Health Insurance Counseling for Kansas (SHICK), Department for Aging and Disability Services, Topeka, KS; phone 800-860-5260; website kdads.ks.gov/kdads-commissions/aging-services/medicare-programs/shick

Kentucky: SHIP, Kentucky Cabinet for Health and Family Services, Frankfort, KY; phone 877-293-7447; website chfs.ky.gov/agencies/dail/Pages/ship.aspx

Louisiana: SHIIP, Department of Insurance, Baton Rouge, LA; phone 800-259-5300; website www.ldi.la.gov/consumers/senior-health-shiip

Maine: SHIP, Department of Health and Human Services, Augusta, ME; phone 800-262-2232 (TTY 711); website www.maine.gov/dhhs/oads/get-support/older-adults-disabilities/older-adult-services/ship-medicare-assistance

Maryland: SHIP, Department of Aging, Baltimore, MD; phone 800-243-3425; website aging.maryland.gov/Pages/state-health-insurance-program.aspx

Massachusetts: Serving the Health Insurance Needs of Everyone (SHINE), Executive Office of Elder Affairs, Boston, MA; phone 800-243-4636 (TTY 800-439-2370); website www.mass.gov/health-insurance-counseling

Michigan: Medicare/Medicaid Assistance Program (MMAP), Lansing, MI; phone 800-803-7174; website www.mmapinc.org

Minnesota: Senior LinkAge Line, Minnesota Board on Aging, St. Paul, MN; phone 800-333-2433; website mn.gov/senior-linkage-line/

Mississippi: SHIP, Division of Aging and Adult Services, Jackson, MS; phone 844-822-4622; website www.mdhs.ms.gov/aging/finding-services-for-older-adults/

Missouri: MO SHIP, Department of Commerce & Insurance, Columbia, MO; phone 800-390-3330; website www.missouriship.org/

Montana: SHIP, Office on Aging, Helena, MT; phone 800-551-3191; website https://dphhs.mt.gov/sltc/aging/ship

Nebraska: SHIP, Department of Insurance, Lincoln, NE; phone 800-234-7119; website doi.nebraska.gov/consumer/senior-health

Nevada: Nevada Medicare Assistance Program (MAP), Aging and Disability Services Division, Carson City, NV; phone 800-307-4444; website www.nevadacareconnection.org/care-options/types-of-services/medicare-assistance-program-map/

New Hampshire: SHIP — ServiceLink, Department of Health & Human Services, Concord, NH; phone 866-634-9412; website www.dhhs.nh.gov/programs-services/adult-aging-care/servicelink

New Jersey: SHIP, Department of Human Services, Trenton, NJ; phone 800-792-8820; website nj.gov/humanservices/doas/services/q-z/ship/

New Mexico: SHIP, Aging and Long-Term Services Department, Santa Fe, NM; phone 800-432-2080 (TTY 505-476-4937); website aging.nm.gov/consumer-elder-rights/aging-disability-resource-center-adrc/ship

New York: Health Insurance Information, Counseling and Assistance Program (HIICAP), Office for the Aging, Albany, NY; phone 800-701-0501; website aging.ny.gov/health-insurance-information-counseling-and-assistance-programs

North Carolina: SHIIP, Department of Insurance, Raleigh, NC; phone 855-408-1212; website www.ncdoi.gov/consumers/medicare-and-seniors-health-insurance-information-program-shiip

North Dakota: SHIP, State Health Insurance Assistance Program, Insurance Department, Bismarck, ND; phone 888-575-6611 (TTY 800-366-6888); website www.insurance.nd.gov/consumers/medicare

Ohio: Ohio Senior Health Insurance Information Program (OSHIIP), Department of Insurance, Columbus, OH; phone 800-686-1578 (TTY 614-644-3745); website insurance.ohio.gov/about-us/divisions/oshiip

Oklahoma: SHIP, Insurance Department, Oklahoma City, OK; phone 800-763-2828; website www.oid.ok.gov/consumers/information-for-seniors/

Oregon: Senior Health Insurance Benefits Assistance (SHIBA), Department of Human Services, Salem, OR; phone 800-722-4134; website shiba.oregon.gov/Pages/index.aspx

Pennsylvania: Pennsylvania Medicare Education and Decision Insight (PA MEDI), Department of Aging, Harrisburg, PA; phone 800-783-7067; website www.aging.pa.gov/aging-services/medicare-counseling/Pages/default.aspx

Puerto Rico: SHIP, Office for Elderly Affairs, San Juan, PR; phone 877-725-4300 (TTY 787-919-7291); website agencias.pr.gov/agencias/oppea/educacion/Pages/ship.aspx

Rhode Island: SHIP, Office of Healthy Aging, Cranston, RI; phone 888-884-8721 (TTY 401-462-0740); website oha.ri.gov/Medicare

South Carolina: SHIP, Department on Aging, Columbia, SC; phone 800-868-9095; website aging.sc.gov/programs-initiatives/medicare-and-medicare-fraud

South Dakota: Senior Health Information and Insurance Education (SHIINE), Department of Social Services, Sioux Falls, SD; phone 800-536-8197; website shiine.net/

Tennessee: SHIP, Commission on Aging & Disability, Nashville, TN; phone 877-801-0044; website www.tn.gov/aging/our-programs/state-health-insurance-assistance-program--ship-.html

Texas: Health Information, Counseling, and Advocacy Program (HICAP), Department of Health and Human Services, Austin, TX; phone 800-252-9240 (TTY 800-735-2989); website www.hhs.texas.gov/services/health/medicare

Utah: SHIP, Department of Health & Human Services, Salt Lake City, UT; phone 800-541-7735; website daas.utah.gov/seniors/

Vermont: SHIP, Disabilities, Aging and Independent Living Department; phone 800-642-5119; website asd.vermont.gov/services/ship

Virgin Islands: VI SHIP, Lt. Governor's Office Christiansted, VI; phone 340-773-6449 (St. Croix) or 340-774-2991 (St. Thomas/St. John); website https://ltg.gov.vi/departments/vi-ship-medicare/

Virginia: Virginia Insurance Counseling and Assistance Program (VICAP), Division for the Aging, Richmond, VA; phone 800-552-3402; website www.vda.virginia.gov/vicap.htm

Washington: Statewide Health Insurance Benefits Advisors (SHIBA), Office of the Insurance Commissioner, Olympia, WA; phone 800-562-6900 (TTY 360-586-0241); website www.insurance.wa.gov/statewide-health-insurance-benefits-advisors-shiba

West Virginia: WV SHIP, Bureau of Senior Services, Charleston, WV; phone 877-987-4463; website www.wvship.org

Wisconsin: SHIP, Department of Health Services, Madison, WI; phone 800-242-1060 (TTY 711); website www.dhs.wisconsin.gov/benefit-specialists/medicare-counseling.htm

Wyoming: SHIP, Wyoming Senior Citizens, Inc., Riverton, WY; phone 800-856-4398; website www.wyomingseniors.com/services/wyoming-state-health-insurance-information-program

The Eldercare Locator

The *Eldercare Locator* is a free public service run by the U.S. Administration for Community Living. It acts as a national service for older Americans and caregivers to find help and resources in their own communities. It can connect you to local agencies and organizations that provide many different kinds of services and assistance programs, typically those that help people continue to function at home or in their communities as they age.

To contact the Eldercare Locator, call 800-677-1116 (toll-free) Monday through Friday, 8 a.m. to 9 p.m. Eastern Time. The Language Line can handle 150 languages. You can also access it online at `eldercare.acl.gov`; this site has links to many other sites with information on community resources.

Independent Sources of Direct Help

The following nonprofit organizations are very similar to the SHIPs I list earlier in offering free direct help to consumers on Medicare issues, but the groups here are national and sometimes provide more specialized services. They also act as advocates on behalf of Medicare beneficiaries in Congress and state legislatures.

The Medicare Rights Center

The Medicare Rights Center (MRC) is an independent, New York–based organization that provides information and free counseling on Medicare issues for beneficiaries throughout the country. It also acts as a consumer watchdog and advocate for improving Medicare benefits.

>> **National Helpline:** Call 800-333-4114 (toll-free), Monday through Friday between 9 a.m. and 3 p.m. Eastern Time to talk to a counselor about Medicare options, rights and protections, billing problems and payment denials, complaints, and appeals.

>> **Medicare Interactive:** To consult this free online primer that provides detailed answers to almost any question about Medicare, go to `www.medicareinteractive.org`.

>> **Online information:** For consumer guides and news on developments in Medicare, plus the option of getting free newsletters by email, go to `www.medicarerights.org`.

The National Alliance for Hispanic Health

The National Alliance for Hispanic Health (NAHH) promotes the health and well-being of Hispanics through community programs that reach more than 15 million throughout the country. It provides written information and free counseling services in English and Spanish on health programs for consumers of all ages, including direct help on Part D drug coverage. Based in Washington, D.C., NAHH is also a leader in advocacy and research for Hispanic health.

>> **The National Hispanic Family Health Helpline (Su Familia):** Call 866-783-2645 toll-free, Monday through Friday from 9 a.m. to 6 p.m. Eastern Time, for free one-on-one counseling on any health issues. A popular part of this service is personal help with Part D, including finding a drug plan and applying for Extra Help.

>> **Online information:** The NAHH website at www.healthyamericas.org has a wealth of health information and publications in English and Spanish. Click on the "Info for You" tab on the home page and then select "Resources" on the drop-down menu.

The National Asian Pacific Center on Aging

The National Asian Pacific Center on Aging (NAPCA) promotes the health and well-being of senior Asian Americans and Pacific Islanders throughout the United States through advocacy, education, and direct help.

The NAPCA website at www.napca.org has info on healthcare and long-term care, employment, education, and many other issues. A resource helpline is available in English, Cantonese, Japanese, Korean, Mandarin, Spanish, Tagalog, and Vietnamese between 8:30 a.m. and 5 p.m. Pacific Time. Call 800-336-2722 or visit www.napca.org/helpline for direct lines in other languages.

Resources for Saving Money

The following resources can help you save money through various public and private programs for people with limited incomes. (Chapter 4 also includes methods for reducing your out-of-pocket expenses in Medicare.)

>> **BenefitsCheckUp:** This website (www.benefitscheckup.org) is a service of the National Council on Aging that allows you to find national, regional, state, and local programs that provide benefits you may qualify for without realizing

it — or perhaps never knew existed. It asks about your zip code, age, health status, family circumstances, and income. You don't give your name, address, or any other identifying information. You can choose to search for benefits that will help pay for prescriptions and/or for other benefits to reduce your living expenses, such as assistance for food, utilities, transportation, housing, and employment training. If you don't have internet access, you can call the Benefits Helpline at 800-794-6559 Monday to Friday 8 a.m. to 7 p.m. Eastern Time to screen for resources in your community.

» **The Health Resources and Services Administration:** This federal agency, a division of the U.S. Department of Health and Social Services, provides a website (`findahealthcenter.hrsa.gov`) that allows you to locate clinics in your locality for free or low-cost healthcare and medications.

» **The National Council on Aging:** This nonprofit organization sponsors many programs designed to help older Americans stay healthy and independent, find jobs and community service opportunities, and connect with benefits and resources. It provides consumer information and hosts interactive tools at its website at `www.ncoa.org`.

» **RxAssist:** The RxAssist Patient Assistance Program Center provides a comprehensive online directory of drug companies that provide free or low-cost medications. Visit `www.rxassist.org/patients` to search by drug or manufacturer name.

Consumer Information and Advocacy Organizations

The following nonprofit organizations are leading sources of information on Medicare and act as advocates, on behalf of Medicare beneficiaries, within Congress and state legislatures. They want to hear about people's firsthand experiences with Medicare, and they welcome volunteers to help their efforts.

» **AARP:** AARP uses the power of its membership (more than 37 million members in 2024) to promote the interests of people age 50 and older. These interests include improving Medicare, preserving Social Security, and promoting legislation to achieve health insurance access for all Americans. A nonpartisan organization with headquarters in Washington, D.C., AARP has offices in every state (plus the District of Columbia, Puerto Rico, and the U.S. Virgin Islands), and advocates in Congress and all state legislatures. Through the

AARP Foundation, attorneys litigate court cases of special importance to older Americans.

- **Phone:** 888-687-2277 (TTY 877-434-7598), Monday through Friday from 8 a.m. to 8 p.m. Eastern Time. **Spanish language phone:** 877-342-2277. **Calls from overseas:** +1-202-434-3525.

- **Website:** www.aarp.org

- **Medicare Resource Center:** www.aarp.org/health/medicare-insurance

- **Information in Spanish:** www.aarp.org/espanol

>> **The Center for Medicare Advocacy:** This group promotes the interests of people on Medicare nationally and is staffed by policy experts, attorneys, researchers, and information specialists. Based in Connecticut with an office in Washington, D.C., the nonpartisan center advocates to improve Medicare services and other healthcare rights, litigates court cases, and publishes policy documents and consumer information. It invites consumers to send in questions and responds to about 10,000 telephone and email inquiries each year.

- **Phone:** 860-456-7790 (Connecticut); 202-293-5760 (Washington).

- **Website (with email link):** medicareadvocacy.org. *Note:* You can read this site in Spanish by clicking the "Se habla Español" link on the home page.

>> **Families USA:** This grassroots, nonpartisan organization advocates for high-quality, comprehensive, and affordable healthcare for all Americans from the consumer perspective. Based in Washington, D.C., it serves as a consumer watchdog on government actions related to health coverage. It also watch-dogs the pharmaceutical industry.

- **Phone:** 202-628-3030

- **Website:** www.familiesusa.org

>> **California Health Advocates (CHA):** This group is the leading consumer watchdog organization for Californians on Medicare. Based in Sacramento with another office in Irvine, CHA conducts public policy research and community outreach, promotes recommendations for improving Medicare services and rights at the federal and state level, and provides up-to-date consumer information on its website, including the free newsletter "California Medicare News."

- **Phone:** 916-465-8104 (Sacramento)

- **Website:** www.cahealthadvocates.org

Sources for Updates on Medicare

Although the bulk of information in this book is likely to remain current, new regulations and some new Medicare services are brought out from time to time. Also, payment requirements (for example, Part B premiums), Part D coverage levels, and Extra Help out-of-pocket expenses are changed annually. You can find ongoing updates from these sources:

» **Medicare Interactive:** This free, searchable, comprehensive consumer guide at www.medicareinteractive.org is developed and regularly updated by the Medicare Rights Center. Head to the earlier section "The Medicare Rights Center" for more information.

» **The Center for Medicare Advocacy:** This group (listed in the preceding section) provides news and updates on Medicare in weekly alerts at www.medicareadvocacy.org/articles/weekly-update-archive.

» **The Henry J. Kaiser Family Foundation:** This nonprofit group provides information and analysis on healthcare issues. For news and updates on Medicare, check out kff.org/medicare.

» **AARP Medicare Resource Center:** You can find online news, consumer guides, articles, and discussion boards about Medicare and Medicaid at www.aarp.org/health/medicare-insurance, and about other forms of health insurance (such as updates on the Affordable Care Act) at www.aarp.org/health/health-insurance.

Appendix **B**

Glossary

administrative law judge (ALJ): A person who presides over level three of Medicare or Social Security *appeal* hearings.

Advance Beneficiary Notice of Non-Coverage (ABN): A written warning that doctors and other *providers* must give you if they think Medicare may not cover the service or treatment you're about to receive.

Annual Notice of Change (ANOC): A notice that *Part D* and *Medicare Advantage plans* must send to their enrollees each September specifying changes in costs and benefits that will be made to their plans for the following year.

appeal: A formal request to reverse a decision (made by Social Security or Medicare) that you don't agree with.

assignment: Doctors or other *providers* who accept Medicare patients on assignment can't charge more than the Medicare-approved amount.

Beneficiary and Family-Centered Care Quality Improvement Organization (BFCC-QIO): A contracted company that Medicare uses to monitor care and assess denials of care or complaints made by patients against hospitals, *skilled nursing facilities,* and home health agencies.

benefit period: In *original Medicare,* a benefit period begins when you're admitted to a hospital and ends when you have stayed out of the hospital or a *skilled nursing facility* for 60 days.

brand-name prescription drug: A drug for which its manufacturer still has patent protection and exclusive rights to sell, often for a high price.

catastrophic drug coverage: *Part D* drug coverage that kicks in after you've spent a certain amount out-of-pocket on drugs since the beginning of the year; you owe no cost-sharing until the next calendar year.

COBRA insurance: A temporary extension of employer coverage (usually for 18 months) after employment has ended where you pay your own share of the *premiums* plus your former employer's share.

coinsurance: A percentage of the cost that you pay as your share of a medical service or item that Medicare covers.

coordination of benefits: A system that ensures your medical bills are sent to the correct insurer automatically if you have more than one insurance plan.

co-payment/co-pay: A specific dollar amount that you pay as your share of the cost toward a medical service or item that Medicare covers.

coverage determination: A decision on whether Medicare (or a *Part D* drug plan or a *Medicare Advantage plan*) will cover a particular service, procedure, prescription drug, or medically needed item.

coverage gap: A gap (also known as the *doughnut hole*) that occurs when the full cost of your prescription drugs since the beginning of the year exceeds a certain dollar amount. The gap continues until your drug expenses reach a point that triggers *catastrophic drug coverage*. The coverage gap will go away entirely beginning in 2025.

creditable prescription drug coverage: Coverage from another source (such as employer benefits) that is considered at least equal in value to *Part D*.

custodial care: Services that help you perform everyday tasks such as dressing, bathing, eating, and going to the bathroom.

deductible: The amount you may be required to pay out-of-pocket for medical services before coverage begins.

doughnut hole: See ***coverage gap.***

dual eligible: A person entitled to both Medicare and *Medicaid* benefits.

durable medical equipment: Items ordered by a doctor for medical reasons, such as wheelchairs, walkers, hospital beds for use at home, and many more.

evidence of coverage: A document that your *Medicare Advantage plan* or *Part D* drug plan must send you when you join or renew your enrollment explaining the plan's costs and benefits and your rights and responsibilities.

exception: A waiver from your *Part D* drug plan's rules that you can request, with your doctor's help, if the plan doesn't cover the drug you need or places *restrictions* on it.

Extra Help program: Special low-cost *Part D* drug coverage you can get if your income is under a certain level.

formulary: The list of prescription drugs that a *Part D* drug plan covers.

fully insured: Your status when you or your spouse has paid enough payroll taxes at work to qualify for Social Security (or Railroad Retirement Board) retirement or disability benefits and for *premium-free Part A*.

general enrollment period (GEP): The time from January 1 to March 31 each year when you can sign up for Medicare if you failed to meet your original enrollment deadline. Coverage begins the month following enrollment.

generic prescription drug: A copy of a *brand-name prescription drug* that has the same clinical effect but usually costs much less.

group health plans: Health insurance provided by employers, unions, and some other groups (such as professional associations).

guaranteed issue rights: Your right to buy *Medigap* at certain times, during which insurance companies can't deny coverage or charge higher *premiums* based on health status or pre-existing medical conditions. Also your right to have a Medigap policy renewed every year as long as you pay the premiums.

higher-income premiums: Surcharges you're required to pay on top of Part B and Part D *premiums* if your modified adjusted gross income (MAGI), as reported on your most recent income tax return, is above a certain level.

home health services: Medicare-covered medical and social services you can receive at home if you're housebound and meet certain other conditions, usually free of charge.

hospice care: Care provided in the last months of life, designed not to treat a terminal illness but to provide as much comfort as possible in the time left.

individual insurance: Health insurance bought on the open market. So-named to distinguish it from employers' *group health plans.*

initial coverage period: A phase of *Part D* drug coverage that comes after you've paid the annual *deductible* (if your plan charges one). During this period, you pay whatever *co-payment* your plan charges for your drug(s).

initial enrollment period (IEP): A seven-month period to sign up for Medicare around the time you turn 65 or become eligible through disability.

in-network: In *Part D:* retail pharmacies that accept your Part D plan's card. In *Medicare Advantage plans:* doctors and other *providers* who have contracts to provide services under your plan.

late penalties: Surcharges that are permanently added to *Part B* and/or *Part D* monthly *premiums* if you fail to meet your enrollment deadlines.

lifetime reserve days: In *original Medicare,* a total of 60 days (during the rest of your life) that you can draw on to get Medicare coverage for a hospital stay beyond 90 days in any one *benefit period.*

Medicaid: A health insurance safety-net program for people whose incomes are under a certain level, according to the rules of their state. People who receive both Medicare and Medicaid are known as *dual eligibles.*

medical underwriting: A practice used by insurance companies to deny or limit coverage on the basis of health status or pre-existing medical conditions.

Medicare Advantage plans: Private insurance plans (typically HMOs or PPOs) that provide Medicare's *Part A* and *Part B* benefits in different ways from the *original Medicare* program. Also known as *Part C*. Most plans also include *Part D* prescription drug coverage.

Medicare Savings Programs: State programs that pay the Part B *premiums,* and maybe other expenses, of people with incomes under a certain level.

Medicare Summary Notice (MSN): A quarterly statement that shows the medical services you've received — including the amount billed by *providers,* what Medicare paid, and what balance, if any, you must pay.

Medigap or Medigap supplemental insurance: Private insurance that you can choose to buy separately to cover many out-of-pocket costs of *original Medicare.*

open enrollment period (OEP): An annual period (October 15 to December 7) when you can change your Medicare coverage for the following year. A separate *Medicare Advantage* OEP runs from January 1 to March 31 each year that allows people to switch MA plans or return to *original Medicare.*

original Medicare: The Medicare program as originally devised in 1965, covering *Part A* (hospital and skilled nursing care) and *Part B* (doctors' services, outpatient care, and *durable medical equipment*) — but not *Part D* (prescription drug coverage), which began in 2006. The program is also known as "fee-for-service" Medicare, to distinguish it from *Medicare Advantage plans* (such as HMOs and PPOs) that offer an alternative way to receive Medicare benefits.

out-of-pocket limit: A dollar amount representing the most you can spend out-of-pocket (on *deductibles* and *co-payments*) during a calendar year.

outpatient hospital care: Services you receive in a hospital without being formally admitted. These are paid for under *Part B,* not *Part A.*

Part A: Medicare coverage for stays in a hospital or *skilled nursing facility, home health services,* and *hospice care.*

Part B: Medicare coverage for doctors' services (including doctors in the hospital), screenings, lab tests and other outpatient services, *preventive care,* and medical equipment or supplies.

Part C: Another name for the program that offers *Medicare Advantage plans* as an alternative to the *original Medicare* program.

Part D: Medicare coverage for outpatient *prescription drugs,* available through *stand-alone Part D drug plans* or *Medicare Advantage plans* that include drug coverage in their benefit packages.

Plan Finder: A complex and sophisticated computer tool that allows users to shop and compare *Medicare Advantage plans* and *Part D* plans head-to-head to find the best deal.

premium: An amount you pay each month for medical coverage.

premium-free Part A: Coverage you receive for *Part A* services without paying *premiums* because you (or your spouse) already paid for them through payroll taxes at work.

prescription drug: A medication requiring a doctor's prescription — in other words, not a medicine you can buy over the counter at a pharmacy or store.

preventive care: Medical tests and screenings used to detect indications of diseases that may be delayed or cured if treated early enough. Many of these tests are free (no *co-payment* or *deductible*) in Medicare.

primary-care physician (PCP): A doctor such as an internist or a family practitioner who takes care of your immediate medical needs. In Medicare HMOs, you're required to get a referral from a PCP to see a specialist.

primary insurance: The insurance that pays your bills first if you have two or more types of health coverage.

prior authorization: See *restrictions.*

provider: Anybody who provides you with a medical service or item — a doctor, nurse, hospital, medical equipment supplier, and so on.

quality ratings: An evaluation in the form of stars (ranging from one star for "poor" to five stars for "excellent") that Medicare gives to *Medicare Advantage plans* and *Part D* plans to indicate how good they are according to consumer feedback and other measures.

quantity limits: See *restrictions.*

restrictions: Practices that *Part D* plans use to control costs for specific medications. *Prior authorization* means asking your plan's permission before it will cover your drug. *Quantity limits* means that the plan places limits on the dosage or quantities it will cover. *Step therapy* means the plan wants you to try another (usually cheaper) drug before it will cover the one prescribed. You have the right to ask the plan (with your doctor's support) for an *exception* to waive any of these rules and cover your prescribed drug.

secondary insurance: The insurance that pays bills not covered under your *primary insurance* if you have two or more types of health coverage.

service area: The area in which you must live to receive benefits from a *Medicare Advantage plan* or a *stand-alone Part D drug plan.*

skilled nursing facility: A place (usually a nursing home) where you may need to go for continuing care — typically physical therapy or to finish a course of intravenous drugs — after being discharged from the hospital.

Social Security benefits: They provide income in retirement (SSRI) or income due to disability (SSDI), if you meet the eligibility conditions and have enough *work credits.*

special enrollment periods: Times when you're allowed to enroll in *Part B* or *Part D* outside of the annual enrollment periods in specific circumstances.

Special Needs Plans: Types of *Medicare Advantage plans* specifically for people who live in institutions, receive both Medicare and *Medicaid,* or have at least one chronic or disabling condition.

stand-alone Part D drug plans: Private plans that Medicare has approved to offer drug coverage for people in the *traditional Medicare* program.

step therapy: See *restrictions.*

Supplemental Security Income (SSI): A Social Security program that provides income for elderly or disabled people who don't have enough *work credits* to qualify for retirement (SSRI) or disability (SSDI) benefits, or whose benefits and other income are less than SSI.

tier pricing: An insurance practice that most *Part D* plans use to charge different *co-payments* for different types of prescription drugs. Co-pays for drugs placed in lower tiers (usually *generic prescription drugs*) are typically the lowest, whereas those in higher tiers (usually *brand-name prescription drugs*) are much higher.

work credits: Credits (also called "quarters of coverage") that you earn while paying Social Security and Medicare payroll taxes while working. To qualify for *premium-free Part A,* you or your spouse (or in some circumstances, your divorced or deceased spouse) must have earned at least 40 credits, usually amounting to ten years of work.

Index

drugs. *See* prescription drugs

dual eligibles, 70–71

durable medical equipment, 28

E

eating healthfully, 370–371

Eldercare Locator, 384

eligibility

  Federal Employees Health Benefits (FEHB) Program, 179

  health maintenance organizations (HMOs), 205

  Medicaid, losing, 328

  Medical Savings Account (MSA) plans, 207

  Medicare Savings Program, losing, 328

  Medigap, 209

  preferred provider organizations (PPOs), 205

  Private Fee-for-Service (PFFS) plans, 206

  Special Needs Plans (SNPs), 207

employer plans, 171–174

  benefits of, 172

  creditable drug coverage, 331

  disenrolling, 331

  effects of health insurance plan, 173

  end-stage renal disease (ESRD) and, 180–182

  former, 174–178

  Medigap insurance, 172

  small businesses, 171

  special enrollment period (SEP), 118

  switching to, 173, 331

employment with health benefits, 106

end-of-life care counseling, coverage for, 28

end-stage renal disease (ESRD), 169

  employer coverage, 174, 180–182

  Medicare coverage, 104–105

enrollment, 145–166

  automatic, 146–147

  disenrolling after, 157–158

  if in domestic partnership, 127

  if incarcerated, 128

  if legal permanent resident, 123–124

  if living in multiple places, 150–151

  if living outside US, 124–126, 151–153

  if working overseas, 125–126

  during initial enrollment period (IEP), 159–160

  misunderstanding enrollment periods, 363

  opting out of plans, 153–158

    claim denials when, 156–157

    if over 65, 155

    if under 65, 155–156

    Part A, 154

    Part B, 154–157

  in Part D insurance plan drug coverage, 123–128

  in Plan B, 361

  in premium-free Part A insurance plan, 126

  retroactive coverage, 160–161

  special enrollment period (SEP), 329

  in US, 148–151

equitable relief, 143, 344–345

ESRD. *See* end-stage renal disease (ESRD)

evidence of coverage (EOC) booklet, 269, 281

exercise, 369

expenses, tracking, 277–281. *See also* out-of-pocket expenses

  Medicare Summary Notices (MSNs) and, 278–280

  online, 281

  using hard-copy records, 280–281

Explanation of Benefits statements

  maintaining records with, 281

  Medicare Advantage and, 280

Extra Help program, 75–86

  after a year, 83–84

  after applying, 82

  appealing Social Security, 82

  applying for, 77–84

  choosing drug plan, 84–86

  duration of, 82–83

  enrollment process for medication in, 84

  for filling out applications, 80–81

  foreign languages, 78

  Medicare Advantage and, 248

  Part D insurance plan and, 290

  qualifying for, 76–77

  surcharges, 292

F

G

H

prescription drugs, 285–292. *See also* prescription
drug coverage

annual phases, 30–32

benefits, 15–16

costs of, cutting, 88–91

creditable, 243

dosage of, 217–218

drug manufacturer patient assistance
programs, 90

in Extra Help program, 84

formularies, 32–34

free samples of, 91

frequency of, 217–218

full price, 291

higher charges for, 291–292

if doctor isn't prescribed to Medicare, 292

if pharmacist can't confirm enrollment, 291

if plan won't pay for, 291

losing coverage for, 328

lowering costs, 90–91, 225–226

manufacturer patient assistance programs, 91

obtaining abroad, 91

older brand-name, 89–90

in out-of-network pharmacy,
288–289

out-of-pocket expenses, 288

Part D prescription drug plan, 289–290

from pharmacies, 286–288

  long-term-care, 288

  mail-order, 287

  out-of-network, 288–289

  retail, 286–287

  specialty, 287–288

plans for Extra Help program, 84–86

proof of coverage, 290–292

restriction of, 218

reviewing, 88–89

side effects, 371–372

switching plans, 90

uncovered, 34

preventable errors in hospitals, 301

preventive care, 21–24

pricing tiers

of co-payments, 315–316

when switching plans, 317

primary insurance

defined, 117

if 65 or older, 155

primary payer, 168

primary-care physician (PCP)

finding, 280

in skilled nursing facility, 303–304

principal residence, 150

printed application form, 79

prior authorization restriction, 34

priority right of recovery, 189

Privacy Rights Clearinghouse, 258

Private Fee-for-Service (PFFS) plans, 206, 267

procedures cost, determining, 308–309

Program Operations Manual System, 342

Programs of All-Inclusive Care for the Elderly
(PACE), 208

defined, 70

out-of-pocket expenses, 73–74

proof of coverage

for Part D insurance plan, 290

for prescription drugs, 290–292

provider directory, 270

psychiatric care in hospitals, 42

PT (physical therapy), 25, 42

Q

Qualified Disabled and Working Individuals
(QDWI), 72

Qualified Medicare Beneficiary (QMB), 72

qualifying for Medicare, 95–109

Qualifying Individual (QI), 72

R

Railroad Retirement, 60

disabilities, 104

initial enrollment period (IEP) and, 114

premiums deducted, 271

About the Author

Patricia Barry is a recognized expert on Medicare. As a senior editor of the *AARP Bulletin* — the newspaper that serves AARP's 37 million members — and other AARP media, she wrote extensively about the program from the consumer's point of view for 18 years before leaving the organization in 2017. For nine years she personally answered more than 14,000 questions sent by Medicare beneficiaries across the nation to her *Ask Ms. Medicare* column on AARP's website. The knowledge and insights gained from those questions form the foundation of *Medicare For Dummies.*

After her first assignment on the Medicare beat in 1999 — going to a White House press conference to hear President Bill Clinton propose adding a prescription drug benefit to Medicare — Patricia reported the bitter political battles in Washington that finally led to President George W. Bush's signing the Part D drug benefit into law in 2003. Thereafter, she wrote numerous articles and guides to explain to consumers how to navigate the unique complexities of the Part D program. This experience culminated in *Medicare Prescription Drug Coverage For Dummies* (Wiley), published in 2008.

As the first members of the baby-boom generation turned 65 in 2011, forming the beginning of a tsunami of 78 million people who will join Medicare by 2030, Patricia wrote the "Medicare Starter Kit" — a concise guide written especially for boomers — that was published as a pullout supplement in the *AARP Bulletin* and on AARP's website. She also wrote a similar supplement, "A User's Guide to Health Care Reform," which explained how the Affordable Care Act (often called Obamacare) would affect consumers.

In her long journalism career in Europe and America, Patricia has written thousands of newspaper and magazine articles and six previous books. A native of Great Britain, she's lived since 1985 in Maryland, where she and her husband raised three internationally minded children. She is, of course, a Medicare beneficiary herself.

Author's Acknowledgments

Many thanks go first to the experts at two key federal agencies, the Centers for Medicare & Medicaid Services and the Social Security Administration, who helped AARP through the labyrinth of regulations that govern Medicare eligibility, enrollment, and coverage and patiently answered hundreds of questions thrown at them. We are also indebted to the pioneering work of experts at the consumer help organizations who daily assist Medicare beneficiaries in their dealings with the program: the Medicare Rights Center, the Center for Medicare Advocacy, California Health Advocates, and the State Health Insurance Assistance Programs.

We are especially grateful for the advice and generously shared expertise of many former and current staff at AARP over the years: in particular, Joyce Dubow, Gerry Smolka, Lee Rucker, Ed Dale, John Rother, David Gross, Mike Schuster, Andrew Scholnick, Leigh Purvis, and Harriet Komisar. Many thanks, too, to Gabrielle Redford, former executive editor of health coverage for AARP publications, and to the director of AARP's books division, Jodi Lipson. Much appreciation to Brandy Bauer, Xavier Vaughn, and Marisa Vigilante who helped to update this 5th edition.

Sincere thanks to the development editor on this book, Linda Brandon, and copy editor Christy Pingleton, who have the vigilant eyes and ruthless red pens that all first-class editors share. They, together with project manager Michelle Hacker and acquisitions editor Tracy Boggier, all at John Wiley & Sons, Inc., have been a pleasure to work with. Also thanks to the Medicare Rights Center for its expert critique while providing a technical review during the book's draft stages.

Publisher's Acknowledgments

Senior Acquisitions Editor: Tracy Boggier
Project Manager: Michelle Hacker
Development Editor: Linda Brandon
Copy Editor: Christine Pingleton
Technical Editor: Ellen O'Brien
Proofreader: Debbye Butler

Production Editor: Tamilmani Varadharaj
Cover Image: © FatCamera/Getty Images

Printed and bound by CPI Group (UK) Ltd, Croydon, CR0 4YY

09/08/2024

14538818-0001